THE LAW OF DERIVATIVES

To Cherry, Freddie and Anna

THE LAW OF DERIVATIVES

BY

SIMON JAMES
Partner, Clifford Chance

LLP

LONDON HONG KONG
1999

LLP Reference Publishing
69–77 Paul Street
London EC2A 4LQ
Great Britain

EAST ASIA
LLP Asia
Sixth Floor, Hollywood Centre
233 Hollywood Road
Hong Kong

British Library Cataloguing in Publication Data
A catalogue record for this book is
available from the British Library

ISBN 1 85978 642 1

Computerset in 10/12 Sabon by
Mendip Communications Ltd
Frome, Somerset
Printed in Great Britain by
Martins Printing Group

PREFACE

The law of derivatives is not, from the legal point of view, a coherent topic. Legal analysis and study is traditionally divided into contract, tort, equity and trusts, corporate law and so on. The range of legal issues which could arise in relation to derivatives, and to any other kind of financial instrument, covers all these traditional areas and more besides.

The aim of this book is not to provide comprehensive coverage of all areas of law which might be relevant to derivatives. Even if it were within my capabilities and the tolerance of my family, which has already been strained beyond reasonable limits, the resulting work would be mammoth. This book focuses on specific topics likely to be of concern to lawyers faced with derivatives transactions. For example, since *Hazell* v. *Hammersmith*, my first introduction to derivatives, the capacity to enter into derivatives transactions has been of fundamental concern. Similarly, it seems that no claim by a counterparty outside the financial services industry is complete without a misrepresentation claim, perhaps allied to a claim for breach of fiduciary duty. The dominance of ISDA's Master Agreement makes consideration of its meaning and impact of considerable importance in most derivatives transactions. I am grateful to ISDA for permission to reproduce their Master Agreement in the Appendix to this book.

Derivatives are commonly used to protect against risk or to take on risk. Those risks are generally economic—the movement of interest rates, commodity prices, etc. But legal issues also pose risks for a derivatives transaction. Does a counterparty have the capacity to enter into the transaction? Are the terms of the transaction clear? The range of legal issues which could arise is very wide. These issues pose risks because predicting the outcome of a legal dispute is often no more black and white than making an economic forecast. For example, changes in UK interest rates are the result of deliberations by the nine members of the Monetary Policy Committee of the Bank of England. There is inevitable speculation before its meetings as to what it will do, and after its meetings sometimes surprise as to what it has done. The ultimate decision on legal issues which come before the English courts can also rest on the deliberations of up to nine people: at first instance, one judge; on appeal, three more judges; and, possibly, on further appeal, five judges. Before a decision is made, there is similar speculation as to what a judge will do, and the outcome can be equally surprising.

On some legal issues, it is possible to be pretty certain what the outcome will be; on other issues, it is more difficult. But in all cases the best that can be given is an assessment of the likely outcome—the risk involved. As a result of this inevitable uncertainty, I have not in general tried to lay down what the law is—unless it is very clear, this gives a false sense of certainty—but rather to point out where the risks lie.

I have attempted to state the law as I understand it, undoubtedly wrongly in parts, as at 1 April 1999. The law in this area is, in general, moving fast, but the most major legal changes in the offing concern regulation. In July 1998, the Government published draft legislation to replace the Financial Services Act 1986. There was then a period of consultation, including a report by a committee of both Houses of Parliament which was critical of aspects of the proposals, following which the Government published revised draft legislation in June 1999. As at the time of writing, the Government appears intent upon pushing this revised draft legislation through Parliament quickly.

Even aside from the proposed legislative changes, in June 1999 the Financial Services Authority published new versions of the Grey Paper and *The London Code of Conduct* through which the wholesale financial markets are regulated (see pages 146–149). The papers retain the same sort of exhortation, guidance and warnings as their predecessors, though with the heavier hand of the Financial Services Authority becoming apparent. Two features in particular are perhaps worthy of mention, both arising from *Larussa-Chigi* v. *CS First Boston*. First, the wording in the previous standard form letter to end-users in the wholesale financial markets has been changed to avoid the terms of the Code being introduced as a term of the contract between counterparties (see page 149). Second, there is more emphasis on the possible need of end-users for advice, the desirability of making it clear whether advice is being given and the regulatory framework within which it should be given.

SIMON JAMES
200 Aldersgate Street
London EC1

CONTENTS

* Published with the kind permission of the International Swaps and Derivatives Association, Inc.

TABLE OF CASES

TABLE OF LEGISLATION

CHAPTER 1

DERIVATIVES

1.1 INTRODUCTION

In early seventeenth-century Holland, particularly 1634 to 1637, tulipomania took hold. Demand for tulips massively exceeded supply and prices soared. Inevitably a futures market emerged, and tulip bulbs were bought and sold whilst still in the ground. The bulbs were traded by people with no intention of taking delivery, and bulbs could be involved in lengthy contractual chains. In February 1637, buyers evaporated and the bubble burst. Litigation followed which took a number of years to resolve.[1]

Derivatives, therefore, are not new.[2] Tulip futures might have been a very early example of derivatives trading, but the Chicago Board of Trade was founded as long ago as 1848, and introduced standardised contracts around 1865. The scale, use and range of available derivatives has, however, expanded enormously since the beginning of the 1980s. ISDA has estimated that the total value of outstanding off-exchange interest rate swaps alone was $682.8 billion in the second half of 1987 but had reached $22,291 billion ten years later. The reasons for this expansion are doubtless myriad but probably include the breakdown of the system of fixed exchange rates established after the Second World War and the greater volatility of interest rates caused by inflation, both of which created more uncertainty. Derivatives met the need to reduce exposure to these risks, but once the genie was out of the bottle, their nature and application has been limited only by imagination.

The public focus has tended recently to be on cases where participants in the derivatives market have lost large amounts of money as a result of their activities—from the burghers of the Netherlands to Orange County, Procter & Gamble, Gibsons Greetings, Barings and others. It is unquestionably easy to lose money on derivatives, and those who do so probably wonder why they entered the market at all. The market would not, however, survive if these examples were typical of experience in the derivatives markets. People enter transactions

1. See *The Tulip* by Anna Pavord, chapter IV.

2. Khang, *Barings Bankruptcy and Financial Derivatives*, p 31, says that the first recorded futures trading took place in Osaka in 1679, and that the first futures market, the Dojima Rice Trading Board, was established in that city in 1730.

in the derivatives markets for a variety of reasons but, in very broad terms, the market consists of those seeking to hedge the underlying risk, those trading in derivatives and those who speculate with a view to profit. Those seeking to hedge risk might, for example, wish to borrow in six months' time and be concerned that interest rates will by then have risen, raising the cost of doing so. Various strategies, including the use of swaps and/or options, could be used to hedge against this risk and lock in interest rates at or near the present level. Those trading are largely banks who buy and sell derivatives with a view to profiting from the activity, whether by taking a view as to future movements, by buying and selling derivatives with a spread between the two prices or by seeking arbitrage opportunities. Speculators enter the market with a view to profiting from price movements. Speculators have the advantage of providing liquidity to the market, making it easier for others to find counterparties for the transactions they wish to enter into.

Though participants in the derivatives market can be divided in this, and other, ways, the differences may not be as profound as any division might suggest. Speculation tends to have a bad name, but it is possible to view anyone in the market as a speculator. For example, if a producer will have a commodity to sell in six months' time and wishes to lock in the price now through a futures contract, that amounts to speculation that the price will fall—if there were no risk of the price falling, there would be no reason to enter the futures market because the commodity producer would be no worse off, and could be better off if the price rose, by not doing so. If the price does rise, the producer has lost the gain he would have made as a result of that rise. This is, however, called hedging rather than speculation because of the interest in the underlying commodity. The producer might, however, change his view in the course of the six months before the commodity is available. If so, he might reverse the earlier hedge at a profit or loss, so becoming exposed again to market movements. This puts him back into the position he was in before entering the market, and could be called hedging, removing the hedge or speculating that prices will rise. The reality is probably that anyone entering into a derivatives transaction is doing so in order to make money or to avoid losing it, though some do it for its own sake and others as an adjunct to another business, usually in relation to an underlying variable.

1.2 WHAT ARE DERIVATIVES?

1.2.1 Derivatives generally

A derivatives transaction is, according to the Group of Thirty,[3]

"a bilateral contract or payments exchange whose value derives, as its name implies, from

3. Global Derivatives Study Group of the Group of Thirty, *Derivatives: Practices and Principles* (1993), p 28.

the value of an underlying asset or underlying rate or index. Today, derivatives transactions cover a broad range of 'underlyings'—exchange rates, commodities, equities and other indices."

A vital aspect of a derivatives contract is that it is primarily a financial contract. For example, a contract for the delivery of a commodity in the future at a price determined now would not be generally referred to as a derivatives contract if the parties intended that physical delivery should actually take place. Forward and futures contracts are, however, usually included in any definition of derivatives where the expectation is that physical delivery will not take place, whether that is because physical delivery is not possible, because the contract is to be settled by the payment of a single lump sum or because of another reason. Further, the derivatives market is now such that the value of the underlying asset might derive from its derivatives, rather than vice versa.

One regulator, the SFA, defines derivatives in its rules as "options, futures and contracts for differences",[4] addressing the type of contract rather than its nature. It further defines each of these three parts by reference to paragraphs 7–9 in Schedule 1 to the Financial Services Act 1986, which in turn defines the instruments caught by financial regulation in England. This approach does not, however, necessarily catch all transactions that would now be called derivatives. For example, a fundamental technique in developing derivatives is to strip out one aspect of a broader transaction and trade in that alone; so, for example, a commodity forward strips out the risk of price movement, and allows trading in that without the other aspects of a physical commodity transaction, such as delivery and quality risk. This has been applied to, for example, credit risk to create credit derivatives, and will doubtless be applied elsewhere.

What follows is a brief thumbnail sketch of the general types of derivatives transactions, but the use to which derivatives and derivative techniques are put is limited only by the imagination of those developing them.[5]

1.2.2 Forwards and futures

Forward and futures contracts are agreements to buy and sell in the future on terms agreed now. So, for example, an agreement to buy a quantity of copper in six months' time at a price fixed now would be a forward or futures contract. What makes it a derivatives contract is the expectation (and possibly a

4. Paragraph 9–1 of the SFA's rules. The definition in IMRO's rules is the same. Options, futures and contracts for differences are defined by reference to paragraphs 7–9 of Schedule 1 to the FSA.

5. There are numerous books and other papers of varying degrees of mathematical complexity on derivatives: they include, for example, *Mastering Derivatives Markets* by Francesca Taylor (1996), and *Financial Derivatives* by Keith Redhead (1997), neither of which is particularly complex mathematically. *Derivatives: Practices and Principles* (1993), pp 28ff, by the Global Derivatives Study Group of the Group of Thirty, also gives a useful overview. The descriptions that follow are far from comprehensive, and are only intended to give an outline as a basis for the discussion of the legal issues which follows.

contractual term to the effect) that physical delivery of the commodity will not actually take place but that the contract will be concluded by payment of a sum of money, the difference between the contract price and the market price at the relevant time. Forwards and futures are in general for periods of up to about three years, though they can be for longer.

Forward and futures contracts can be entered into with regard to any commodity, but also with regard to intangible matters such as currencies, interest rates, and stock indices. For example, a very common type of contract is a forward rate agreement (an FRA), an agreement to apply a fixed rate of interest on a notional principal sum for a specific period in the future (for example, an agreement to pay interest at 7 per cent for a period starting six months in the future and ending 12 months in the future[6]). The contract would be settled at the start of the interest period by the payment of a sum representing the difference between the actual interest rate for that period and the fixed rate (though since interest is normally paid at the end of an interest period, the payments are discounted to take into account early payment[7]).

The reason for entering into a forward or futures contract could be pure speculation, but it could be to hedge an underlying risk. For example, an investor might anticipate the receipt of funds in the future but be concerned that the particular stock he has in mind to buy might have risen by the time the funds are due. In that case, the investor could buy a futures contract in the relevant stock, i.e. the right to buy the stock at the futures market price.[8] If the price is above that level at the relevant time, the buyer would receive a payment equal to the difference, but if below he would have to pay the difference. If the investor was interested in a basket of stocks, he could buy a futures contract based on, say, the level of the FT-SE 100 share index rather than an individual share.[9]

1.2.2.1 *The difference between forwards and futures*

Futures are bought and sold on an exchange, whereas forwards are purely bilateral contracts arranged between the parties. The result of dealing on an exchange is that although parties will agree a contract directly, often in a pit where face to face dealing takes place,[10] the contract will be accepted by a clearing house (in the case of, for example, LIFFE, the London Clearing House,

6. A contract of this start date and duration would normally be referred to as 6s–12s.

7. See clause D4 of the FRABBA terms. The payment at the start of the interest period has no economic effect but shortens the period of credit risk. FRABBA terms, produced by the British Bankers Association in 1985 to standardise the market, were at one time usually used to govern FRAs, but ISDA Master Agreements are now also commonly used.

8. See below for an outline of how forwards and futures are priced.

9. The investor may need to take into account the beta, the amount a particular stock price moves in line with the stock prices generally. So, for example, a beta of 1.2 means that for a given movement in stocks generally, the particular stock will move 20 per cent more. Hedging the beta of a stock or group of stocks leaves the non-systematic risk, the risk associated with the particular stock rather than with market movements generally.

10. Though dealing in this form is increasingly being replaced by electronic dealing methods.

which is independent of LIFFE and owned by major banks). The clearing house will then be interposed between the two parties, becoming the buyer to the seller, and the seller to the buyer.

By being interposed as a party to all contracts, the clearing house takes the credit risk on the parties, relieving each party of the need to investigate each other's credit standing and enabling them to rely on the high credit standing of the clearing house. In return for this, the parties must make margin payments. These are usually an initial margin payment, commonly seen as the maximum amount that the relevant contract price could move in a day, and daily variation margin payments. Initial margin is security for performance of the contract, and can commonly be deposited in cash or certain securities. Variation margin payments are of the difference between the contract price and the market price each day, and can be made either by the clearing house to the party or vice versa depending on the direction of the movement in the prices. By taking margin payments, the clearing house hopes to insulate itself against default by the counterparties.

Only members of the relevant exchange contract with the clearing house. If someone wishes to deal in futures and is not a member of an exchange, he must deal through a broker who is a member of the exchange. The broker will act as principal as against the non-member, requiring margin payments, and will generally hedge its position by entering into a back to back transaction on the exchange. The non-member does in these circumstances take credit risk on the broker, and vice versa. Where off-exchange transactions are concerned, the parties each take credit risk on the other, and do not in general make margin payments.[11] They are free to agree whatever terms they wish, but these might, for example, include the provision of security for the obligations of one of the parties.

Further differences between forwards and futures are that futures are carried out in contracts of fixed terms (e.g. dates, amounts and minimum price movements[12]) whereas off-exchange contracts can be on whatever terms the parties agree. Futures exchanges will in general only offer contracts in which there is high liquidity, which often leads to low bid–offer spreads. As a result of this, it is usually easy to close out a contract by entering an equal and opposite contract. Closing out a forward contract depends on the willingness of the other party to do so; if the other party will not agree, it is necessary to find another party which is prepared to enter into an equal and opposite contract, but this entails taking credit risk on that party as well as on the party to the original transaction. There are also procedural differences—for example, interest rate futures prices are quoted not in terms of a percentage interest rate but as a price, the relevant annualised interest rate subtracted from 100.

11. Though, for example, ISDA's Credit Support Annex and Deed both provide, in effect, for margin.

12. Minimum price movements are called ticks. For a LIFFE three month euro-dollar contract, the contract amount is $1,000,000 (and multiples of that sum) and the tick is 0.01 per cent (or $25).

1.2.2.2 Forwards' and futures' prices

The prices of forwards and futures are not a prediction of what the price will be at the relevant date in the future but are calculated on a "cash and carry" basis. The price is principally the spot price plus the cost of carry (i.e. storage costs, if relevant, and interest foregone minus the yield on the asset in question), though other factors such as commissions, spreads, and credit risks might be taken into account.[13] If prices were calculated on any other basis, an arbitrageur could make a guaranteed profit. For example, if a commodity futures price was above this level, a profit could be made by buying spot and selling futures or forwards; if prices were below this level, a guaranteed profit could be made by selling spot and buying futures.[14] For interest rates, if it were possible to borrow for three months at 8 per cent, lend for six months at 9 per cent, and buy a futures contract starting three months in the future and lasting three months also at 9 per cent, it would guarantee a profit of 1 per cent for the first three months with no risk over the second three months. The futures price is essentially the price which prevents this kind of guaranteed profit and, as such, is implied by the yield curve.[15]

1.2.3 Swaps

Futures or forward contracts invariably entail only one payment in settlement of the liabilities involved[16] whereas swaps entail a series of payments, and can be seen as a number of forward contracts stretching over time. For example, an FRA involves fixing the interest rate for one period in the future, whereas an interest rate swap involves fixing an interest rate for a number of interest periods, and can therefore entail a series of payments depending on the actual rate for the relevant period. Swaps are always off-exchange transactions.[17]

1.2.3.1 Interest rate swaps

A classic interest rate swap allows two parties to benefit from their different credit statuses. For example, suppose that one company, X, can borrow on a floating rate basis at six-month LIBOR plus 0.75 per cent and at a fixed rate of 8 per cent for five years, and another company, Y, which has a higher credit rating, can borrow at a floating rate of LIBOR plus 0.5 per cent and a five-year fixed rate of 7.25 per cent. If X wants to borrow at a fixed rate and Y at a floating rate, they could just do so at the rates available to them directly. If, however, X borrows at

13. There will be differences between the price of forwards and of futures based on, for example, the requirement to make margin payments on futures.

14. Prices are sometimes at this level—backwardation—for reasons of, for example, supply and demand as has happened in the copper market.

15. I.e. the graph showing fixed interest rates against maturities.

16. This treats margin payments as security rather than a discharge of the liabilities.

17. The London Clearing House has, however, announced plans to launch a swaps clearing operation.

its floating rate of LIBOR plus 0.5 per cent and Y borrows at its fixed rate of 7.25 per cent, they could enter a swap under which Y paid X LIBOR plus 0.25 per cent and X paid Y a fixed rate of 7.25 per cent, in both cases calculated by reference to the notional principal they want to borrow, and both be better off as follows:

	X	Y
Borrowing	(LIBOR + 0.75%)	(7.25%)
Swap receipt	LIBOR + 0.25%	7.25%
Swap payment	(7.25%)	(LIBOR + 0.25%)
Net cost	(7.75%)	(LIBOR + 0.25%)

Taking into account the swap, X and Y can therefore both borrow at a net rate of 0.25 per cent less than each could otherwise have done by taking advantage of Y's comparative advantage in the fixed rate market. In reality, this advantage would be reduced because there would be at least one bank standing between X and Y taking the credit risk on each of them in return for a margin of, say, 0.1 per cent (10 basis points). When swaps were first developing in the early 1980s banks would only enter into interest rate swaps if they could find counterparties willing to enter into the two matching transactions, leaving the bank only with credit risk but no interest rate risk. However, more sophisticated hedging techniques have meant that banks are prepared to offer prices for swaps even if there is no matching transaction immediately available.

Interest rate swaps are commonly done on a fixed versus floating rate basis but they can be done by reference to different floating rates (basis swaps). Nor does the notional principal have to remain constant; swaps can be done, for example, on an amortising basis, where the notional principal decreases, or on an accreting basis, where the notional principal increases. They can also start at a date in the future rather than on entering into the transaction. Interest rate swaps do not usually involve the payment of premiums on entry, but if a swap is done at off the market rate a premium will be payable representing broadly the net present value of the difference between the market rate and the rate on the swap in question.[18]

1.2.3.2 Currency swaps

In interest rate swaps there is no exchange of principal, but in currency swaps principal is commonly exchanged at the end and also at the outset. For example, if a borrower with easy access to the UK capital markets wished to fund a US investment, it could borrow in sterling and exchange it for dollars. It would then have a sterling liability but dollar income from its investment, and would

18. See, for example, *Westdeutsche Landesbank* v. *Islington* [1996] AC 669.

therefore be exposed to currency risk. Alternatively, it could borrow in dollars but, being less well known in the US capital markets, it might have to pay a higher margin than when borrowing in sterling. A third possibility is to borrow in sterling and enter into a currency swap, ideally with a borrower with the opposite profile in the relevant markets but more usually with a bank. The borrower would, say, issue sterling bonds, and then pass the proceeds to the bank in return for dollars. Over the life of the bond issue, the issuer would pay the bank dollar interest at a specified rate calculated on a notional principal equal to the dollar sum received, and bank would pay the issuer sterling interest to meet the payments due on the bond. At the maturity of the bond and swap, the principal sums would again be exchanged.

In some currency swaps, the principal is only exchanged at the end but, whether exchanged at beginning and end or just the end, a currency swap entails more credit risk than, say, an interest rate swap because the principal involved is not notional (purists might therefore argue that it is not a true derivative, though in the market it is invariably treated as such).

The interest rates paid in the two currencies might both be fixed (e.g. fixed sterling against fixed dollar rates), probably the traditional approach. They can, however, be fixed against floating (e.g. fixed sterling against floating dollar), called a cross currency swap, or floating against floating, a cross currency basis swap.

1.2.3.3 Equity swaps

Like interest rate swaps, equity swaps involve no exchange of principal. There is an exchange of cash flows, at least one of which is determined by reference to the performance of a particular stock or, more usually, stock index. This might include dividend payments or might just be changes in the price or the index. The other side of the swap might also be calculated by reference to a different stock or index, but it could be by reference to an interest rate. So, for example, an investor might feel over-exposed in the short term to the stock market and wish to move into cash. This could be done by simply realising some of his investments, and placing the proceeds on deposit. This involves transaction costs and may have tax consequences, perhaps doubled up if the investor anticipates moving back into equities in the foreseeable future. If the investor's portfolio mirrors the FT-SE index, an alternative would be to enter into a swap under which the investor pays the percentage increase in the index in return for receiving, say, six-month LIBOR. Every six months, the change in the index would be measured and netted off against the sum due on LIBOR (though if the index fell, the investor would generally receive both LIBOR and the decrease in the index).

Alternatively, an investor may wish to move exposure from, say, the UK stock market to the US stock market but not incur the dealing costs of selling investments and buying new ones. In these circumstances, the investor could seek to swap the change in the FT-SE index against the change in the equivalent US index.

1.2.3.4 Commodity swaps

Commodity swaps follow the same pattern as other swaps, namely a series of payments, in this case at least one of which is based on the price of a commodity. For example, a long-term user of oil (e.g. an airline) could enter into a swap in which it paid a fixed price for a notional quantity of a specified oil whilst receiving the spot price of the relevant time. This would hedge the airline to some extent against fluctuations in the price of oil. Interest rate, currency and commodity swaps are usually based on the relevant price on a specific day, but it is common for commodity, particularly oil, swaps to be based on an average value of the commodity over a period of time. This removes the effect of days on which the price might show abnormal swings, and more effectively hedges purchases made over that period.

1.2.4 Options

An option is the right, but not the obligation, to do a certain thing, usually to buy or to sell an asset. Options can be entered into in respect of any of the transactions discussed above (it is even possible to have an option on an option), and many options are traded on exchanges. So, for example, if someone anticipates that he might want a certain quantity of a particular currency in the future and wishes to protect against depreciation, he could enter into a forward or futures contract. That, however, obliges him to buy the currency whether or not he does in fact turn out to need it—it also loses him any appreciation there might be in the intervening period. An option would give him the right to buy the currency but no obligation to do so. As a result, if he had no need for the currency, he need not exercise the option,[19] and he could also refrain from doing so if rates had in any event moved in his favour.

In return for the extra flexibility an option gives, and unlike futures and forward contracts, it is necessary to pay the person who sells (writes) the option a premium in return for taking the risk associated with it. Options will be put or call options (the right to sell or buy respectively[20]). Options will also commonly

19. If, however, the acquirer of the option could make a profit by exercising the option even if he did not need the currency, he would of course do so. For example, if the spot price was above the option price, he could exercise the option, and immediately sell the currency making a profit. More commonly, the option might be cash settled, giving him the difference between the spot and option prices without any need for further foreign exchange transactions.

20. In, for example, an interest rate swap option, the right is to enter into a swap (though it may be cash settled at a price calculated to represent the sum that would be charged in the market place to enter a swap on those terms, the rate being off-market) which involves paying and receiving a particular rate. In this case, a put is a right to pay the fixed rate and a call is the right to receive the fixed rate.

be American or European,[21] a European option being exercisable only on the option expiry date while an American option is exercisable at any time before the expiry date. The sum due on exercise of a European or American option is calculated by reference to the spot rate on the exercise date; on an Asian option, however, the sum due on exercise option is calculated by reference to the average spot price over the life of the option.

In addition to transactions which are obviously options, there are also other transactions which have the same economic effect. These include caps and floors. A cap is a transaction under which if the index (e.g. interest rate, commodity price or whatever) exceeds a specified rate on the relevant day, the seller will pay the difference between the cap rate and the actual rate on a notional principal amount. This protects the buyer of the cap against movements above that level over the period of the cap—a cap, like a swap, can extend over a number of periods. A floor is the reverse of a cap in that if the relevant index drops below the specified level, the seller of the cap will pay the difference between the specified rate and the actual rate. This protects, for example, an investor against downward movements in his investments.[22] Although not described as an option, a cap, for example, is an option to fix the relevant price at the cap level with automatic exercise of the option if it is in the buyer's interest to do so (i.e. if price rises above the cap level).

There may also be options embedded in other transactions. For example, warrants, the right to acquire shares at a fixed price, and convertible bonds contain options which can be traded.

1.2.4.1 The price of options

In broad terms, an option has an intrinsic value and a time value. The intrinsic value is the option price less the current price, whereas the time value is the additional element over the intrinsic representing the chance that the price will move further in the future. The time value decreases the closer the option comes to its expiry date—there is less opportunity for the price to move. The time value is also at its highest when the option is at the money, i.e. when the option price and the actual price are the same. If an option price is heavily in the money, there is a risk of losing the intrinsic value; and if an option price is heavily out of the money, the chance of it becoming profitable is less because it has further to move. When an option is at the money, there is no intrinsic value to be lost, and a small movement can bring profit.

Pricing options is a topic of very considerable mathematical complexity, which has been the subject of much academic study, particularly since 1973 when Fischer Black and Myron Scholes published an equation for calculating

21. This is purely a matter of terminology; American options are traded in Europe, and European options in America.

22. A collar is the purchase of a cap and the sale of a floor, usually done in order to reduce the premium payable on the cap.

the price for a European option.[23] In 1997, Scholes was awarded the Nobel prize for economics for his work on this (Black had died before then). The Black–Scholes equation is not the only method of pricing options,[24] and it is not guaranteed to produce the "right" price, but it remains probably the most popular method.

Black–Scholes relies on the following as the determinants of an option price: the price of the underlying; the option exercise price; the risk free interest rate (e.g. on gilts); the time to expiry of the option; the return on the underlying; and the volatility of the price movement of the underlying. Of these, the most important is perhaps volatility as the link between volatility and the option price is linear. Volatility is a measure of the expected variability of the price of an instrument over time[25]; the higher the variability over time the greater the risk involved and therefore the higher the price. The relevant figure is the volatility over the period of the option, which Black–Scholes assumes is constant but which is in any event unknown since it lies in the future. Historic volatility might be a guide, but not necessarily an accurate one, and the price of an option always has an implied volatility, the figure for volatility which gives the price actually charged.

It is common to trade in volatility. This can be done by, for example, straddles and strangles. A straddle is the sale of identical put and call options, the seller taking the view that volatility will increase. If it does so, the value of the options will increase and can therefore be sold at a profit. A strangle is like a straddle, except that the strike prices of the options are not the same.

The factors which influence the price of an option give rise to "greeks", the effect a change in each of the factors has on the value of the option. Delta is the effect a change in the price of the underlying instrument has on the value of the option. Delta hedging is hedging this risk, through, for example, the futures market in the underlying whilst leaving untouched the other risks arising from the option, such as volatility and interest rates. The delta of an option is not, however, constant. When an option is at the money, the delta equals 0.5, but if an option is deeply out of the money the delta is zero because a movement in the price of the underlying will have no effect on the value of the option. Correspondingly, if the option is deeply in the money, the delta is 1. The effect of a change in the price of the underlying on the delta is the gamma, which can in

23. The equation involves partial differentiation (a form of calculus), and is far too complicated to set out here (even if the author understood it).

24. For example, there is a "binomial" method which involves repeated calculations for which a computer is required.

25. Volatility is generally calculated historically by reference to the natural logarithm of two successive periods (e.g. if the price in the first period is 100 and the price in the second is 110, the value is the natural logarithm of 1.1). Volatility is the standard deviation of all these figures over the relevant period. A standard deviation measures the dispersion of a collection of statistics, and is calculated as the square root of the variance, where the variance is the sum of the squares of the distances from the arithmetic mean.

turn be hedged.[26] In turn, the vega[27] (or kappa or lambda) is the effect of time on volatility, theta is the effect of time on the option price, and rho is the effect of a change in the risk free investment rate on an option price. Each of these can be hedged individually, leaving the other risks arising from an option.

1.2.5 Complex derivatives

Derivatives need not be simple transactions such as entering into one swap or the purchase of one call option, but can take more complex forms tailored to individual needs. So, for example, in *Bankers Trust* v. *Dharmala*[28] there were two derivatives transactions involved. The first transaction was for a period of two years and involved a notional principal of $50 million. It had two elements. In the first element, Dharmala paid interest at six-month US dollar LIBOR whilst Bankers Trust paid at the same rate plus 1.25 per cent. Bankers Trust was therefore paying Dharmala $1.25 million over the life of the swap as, effectively, a premium for the second part. In the second part, Dharmala paid interest at a fixed rate of 5 per cent, while Bankers Trust paid interest at 5 per cent multiplied by N divided by 183, where N was the number of days in a six-month period when LIBOR was less than 4.125 per cent. As a result, if, for example, LIBOR was more than 4.125 per cent on every day of the period, N would equal zero and Dharmala would therefore pay 5 per cent but receive nothing on the second part of the transaction, leaving a net loss over both elements of the transaction of 3.75 per cent. For Dharmala to break even, N had to be more than 137.

The second transaction was also for a two-year period and on a notional principal of $50 million. In slightly simplified form, it again involved Bankers Trust paying a premium, this time of 3.75 per cent, the difference between LIBOR plus 1.25 per cent paid by Bankers Trust and LIBOR less 2.5 per cent paid by Dharmala. Dharmala also paid a "spread" which was zero if LIBOR did not exceed 5.25 per cent on any day in the first year; if LIBOR did so at any time in that period, the spread for each of the two years of the transaction was to be the LIBOR rate at the end of the year divided by 4.5 per cent, from which one would then be subtracted (i.e. spread = (LIBOR/4.5 per cent) – 1). So, for example, if LIBOR did exceed 5.25 per cent in the first year and at the end of that year was 5 per cent, the spread would equal 0.111 or 11.1 per cent. The net loss to Dharmala would therefore be some $3.8 million in that year alone. For Dharmala to break even if LIBOR did exceed 5.25 per cent in the year, LIBOR at the end of the year had to be below 4.675 per cent, but if the rate exceeded that level the losses would increase rapidly because the division of LIBOR by 4.5 per cent produced not a percentage but a decimal, or 100 times value of a

26. Whilst deltas can be hedged in the underlying, non-option, markets, gamma (and vega—see below) can only be hedged with other options, which in turn have their own deltas and gammas.

27. Not in fact a Greek letter at all.

28. Unreported, 29 November 1995. Another example of complex derivatives transactions is given in *Procter & Gamble* v. *Bankers Trust* [1997] 6 Bank LR 330, 333–334.

percentage. As a result, if LIBOR was 5 per cent, the loss would be $3.8 million as mentioned above; if LIBOR was 5.5 per cent, losses for that year would be $9.36 million; and if LIBOR was 6 per cent, losses would be $14.92 million.

These derivatives are examples of transactions beyond, for example, plain forwards or swaps. Derivatives can be structured in many different ways to meet the needs of users. The elements, in this case, can be broken down into a premium and option structure but derivatives can be put together in ever more complex forms according to the demand for them.

1.2.6 Credit derivatives

Credit derivatives represent the application of a derivatives technique to a different area. Credit risk is a fundamental aspect of finance (and other business too), being the risk that someone will fail to pay a debt or other monetary obligation.[29] The risk can be reduced or transferred by various steps such as obtaining security or a guarantee or, of more recent innovation, securitisation. Credit derivatives allow the credit risk from a transaction to be detached in various forms from the rest of the underlying transaction. The risk can then be traded in the same way as other derivatives are or transferred to those who wish to take the particular risk in question.

Credit derivatives tend to be one of three basic types: total return swaps, credit default swaps, or credit spread options. The exact form of any particular credit derivative can be, and often is, tailor-made for the needs of the particular parties in question.

Total return swaps are the synthetic equivalent of buying the underlying asset. In a total return swap, one party typically agrees to pay the total return on an asset such as a bond, which it may or may not own, in return for receiving payment by reference to, say, a fixed or floating interest rate on the same notional principal as the asset in question. The return on the asset could include not just the periodic interest or equivalent payments but also any increase in the market value of the asset; correspondingly, if the market value declines, the other party might be required to pay whatever is necessary to compensate for the decline. Total return swaps can be done in respect of, say, a two-year period of a five-year bond, and in respect of a basket of assets rather than a single one.

Credit default swaps are approximately equivalent to letters of credit. They isolate the risk of one or more events happening whilst leaving other risks, such as interest fluctuations. One party receives periodic payments from the other in return for agreeing to make a payment to the other on the happening of a specific

29. Even if an obligation starts as an obligation to do something rather than pay a sum of money, the failure to perform is then in most cases converted into an obligation to pay damages, money, to compensate for the failure to perform. In many respects, a contractual obligation gives the right to perform or to pay damages in lieu of performance (see, for example, *Co-operative Insurance* v. *Argyll Stores* [1997] 2 WLR 898 and *Photo Productions Limited* v. *Securicor Transport Limited* [1980] 1 All ER 556, 579).

credit event or events. This event is typically insolvency related, whether formal insolvency proceedings or something short of that such as debt rescheduling. The event could, however, be less severe, like a down-grading by a rating agency.[30] The sum payable on the happening of the event is a sum to cover the loss the event has caused holders of the asset in question, usually the asset price less the market value of the asset at a relevant time. It is possible, however, for the contract to provide for the asset to be transferred rather than a deduction being made for its market value, the equivalent of an option exercisable on, or a forward contract triggered by, the happening of the reference event.

Credit spread options are usually traded by reference to bonds whose price can be measured as a spread over something else, such as US Treasury bills or gilts. The spread in effect represents the risk rating given by the market to the asset in question over the risk on the other instrument, typically something considered near risk free. In return for a payment, one party is given the right to sell the asset in question to the other at a specified price if the spread goes above a certain level. These options can be put or call options: the essence of a put option is that one party is entitled to dispose of an asset if it becomes riskier, as measured by the spread, than he is prepared to accept; on a call, one party is able to acquire an asset if its spread, and therefore its return, increases to a level at which he feels happy with the risk.

Related to credit derivatives are credit linked notes. On a credit linked note, a highly rated entity (thereby limiting the credit risk on the entity), often a special-purpose vehicle set up for the transaction, sells notes to others the return on which is linked to the return on another security or basket of securities, which the entity need not actually own. The effect is to give credit protection to the owner on the securities in question.

1.2.7 Other derivatives

Other derivatives have been developed and will continue to be developed based on the basic pattern of isolating one particular risk from a transaction or business, and seeking protection against that risk. For example, the weather can affect many businesses, such as electricity-producing wind farms. Weather derivatives can help to protect against the absence of wind over a particular period.[31] Other forms of derivatives will emerge.

30. It is obviously important to make the credit event as clear as possible. Some standard forms use phrases such as a restructuring, the terms of which are, from an economic, credit or risk perspective, less favourable. This inevitably begs questions as to how to compare the economic, credit or risk of two sets of terms, and when any differences are material.

31. Insurance companies have, of course, over a long period written insurance policies in respect of, for example, the risk of rain affecting an outdoor event.

1.3 LEGAL RISK AND DERIVATIVES

Derivatives are commonly used to remove risk, or at least to change one risk for another which the user considers more acceptable. The risks discussed in this context are largely economic risks, such as the risk that commodity prices or interest rates will rise or fall, or the risk that a debtor may not be able to honour its obligations. In law, this risk avoidance is undertaken by means of a contract, and its success depends upon the enforceability and the terms of the contract. If the contract is not enforceable as a matter of law, or if it does not achieve what was intended in the manner intended, then the underlying risk may remain, or the cost in terms of time, money and uncertainty may remove all or much of the benefit the contract was intended to provide.

The nature of a derivatives contract is discussed in the next chapter but, in general terms, the entry into a derivatives contract necessarily entails taking on a legal risk, namely the risk that the contract will not achieve from the legal perspective what it was intended to achieve, or will only do so with undue delay or at undue cost.[32] Legal risks include: the contract being wholly unenforceable[33]; the contract being enforceable but the manner in which the business was conducted infringing relevant regulations and leading to investigations or penalties; the contract being ambiguous and therefore requiring extended court action to determine its effect; the contract not including terms which were necessary to fully protect one party's rights; and the handling of an issue that has arisen in a manner which adversely affects the rights of the party. In entering into a derivatives contract, legal risk will usually be an unwelcome additional risk on top of the underlying risks the parties are seeking to address.

Most parties will therefore wish to minimise the legal risk attaching to a transaction for fear that they might be the ones who have to enforce the contract. It is, however, impossible to avoid it completely. Even the best drafted contract or statute must use words, and words inevitably engender some uncertainty.[34] Further, laws and interpretations of laws change, sometimes unexpectedly.

Any questions which arise will ultimately be legal ones for the courts, and the courts will take a decision based on the facts of a particular case rather than in a legal vacuum. Though courts commonly state their judgments in terms of the dispassionate application of abstract legal principles to the facts of the case, facts

32. This definition of legal risk is derived from one given by Trust and Harris, 1997 BJIBFL, p 291. In *Derivatives: Practices and Principles*, the Global Derivatives Study Group of the Group of Thirty describes legal risk as "the risk of loss because a contract cannot be enforced. This includes risks arising from insufficient documentation, insufficient capacity or authority of a counterparty (ultra vires), uncertain legality and unenforceability in bankruptcy or insolvency" (p 51).

33. As occurred with swaps entered into with local authorities: *Hazell* v. *Hammersmith* [1992] 2 AC 1.

34. Indeed, the courts can create uncertainty even when there is none that is obvious from the language. For example, in *Charter Reinsurance* v. *Fagan* [1997] AC 313 the House of Lords was faced with the words "the sum actually paid by the reinsured in settlement of losses ...". They decided that "actually paid" did not mean actually paid at all but only liability to pay.

are frequently allowed to influence the legal principles in order to achieve a judicially desired outcome. Facts are, therefore, often decisive in the legal process.[35] This is most obviously so where the judge has a discretion, but even outside this area those who practise in the courts often seek to make points which go to the "merits" of their clients' case, even though they might be of no obvious relevance to the legal issues, in the hope that their client will be seen as being in the right and that the judge will be induced to manipulate or apply the law to achieve the outcome that party wants.

The nature of the legal process is such that for each action before the courts there is one "right" answer. With the benefit of hindsight, this can sometimes seem inevitable, but that will seldom seem to be so whilst the case progresses through the courts. Facts can be determinative, but even if a judge has decided that, in his view on the evidence before him, certain events have occurred, it does not necessarily mean that those events actually occurred—the evidence may be incomplete or the judge may simply have got it wrong. Legal principles are also often fluid. As a result, it can often be far from clear what the outcome of a case will be before the decision is actually made—if it were otherwise, there would be far less litigation than is the case.

1.3.1 Categories of legal risk

Legal risk can be categorised in a variety of ways. Categorisation is useful for the purposes of discussion, but the underlying risks are never as discrete as categorisation tends to suggest. Inevitably one risk is related to another in a continuous manner. Nevertheless for discussion purposes, the legal risks relating to derivatives can be divided into product risk, counterparty risk, transaction risk and handling risk. These risks are discussed in greater detail later in this book.

1.3.1.1 Product risk

Product risk comprises those risks which arise from the nature of the transaction regardless of the counterparty concerned. This includes, for example, the risk that a credit derivative will be recharacterised as an insurance contract with possible criminal liability for those not authorised to carry on insurance business under sections 2 and 14 of the Insurance Companies Act 1982. It also includes the risk that a derivatives contract might be treated as a gaming contract and, as a result, be unenforceable by the parties. These risks are inherent in the nature of the particular transaction. Often they can be limited by the drafting of the

35. The common law process involves trying to decide the law according to cases rather than deciding cases according to the law. This very often leaves a judge with the option of deciding a case on its facts and distinguishing other cases or principles by reference to the facts.

relevant contract,[36] but the risk will remain that a creative court might intervene in order to strike down a transaction in a particular case, which may then have far-reaching implications for other transactions.

1.3.1.2 Counterparty risk

Counterparty risk arises from the particular counterparty. The principal legal risk is that the counterparty does not have the legal ability to enter into the transaction in question. This will arise, so far as English companies are concerned, from the constitution of the company, but on top of that there could be regulatory or wider legal issues. For example, insurance companies are prohibited from carrying out business other than in connection with or for the purposes of their insurance business[37]; it is therefore necessary to form a view as to whether a particular derivative is being entered into for the purposes of a particular insurance company's insurance business and, if not, what the consequences might be for the transaction.

These issues could arise not merely at the outset of a relationship with a counterparty but also in relation to each transaction. A counterparty might have the capacity to enter into one or two transactions, but that does not necessarily mean that it has the capacity to run a derivatives book, something which may be apparent from the volume of transactions the counterparty is entering into.

Even if the counterparty does not have the capacity to enter into a transaction, that does not mean that the transaction will be unenforceable. For example, section 35 of the Companies Act 1985 provides counterparties with some protection in this eventuality. A further question with regard to companies incorporated under the Companies Acts is, therefore, the extent to which checks should be made on the capacity of the company. There are risks in whatever course is taken, but a perfectly rational decision could be taken not to carry out any checks.

In addition to issues of capacity, there are also questions of whether the counterparty has validly entered into the contract in question. In most cases this will concern whether the person purporting to act on behalf of the counterparty has authority to bind the counterparty, whether the authority is actual or apparent. There may also, however, be regulatory issues specific to a particular counterparty or, more likely, type of counterparty, either in relation to the method of dealing with the counterparty or the information or warnings that must be given to the counterparty.

36. So, for example, before the passing of section 63 of the Financial Services Act 1986, commodity derivative contracts often included provision for physical delivery in order to reduce the risk of the contract being characterised as a gaming contract even though none of the parties ever expected delivery to occur. Since the passing of section 63, the need to provide for delivery has gone in many cases (see below) allowing the development of, for example, non-deliverable forwards.

37. Section 16(1) of the Insurance Companies Act 1982.

1.3.1.3 Transaction risk

Transaction risk is the largest category of risk. It covers the actions taken in entering into the transaction and the documentation, if any, used to do so. In negotiating and entering into the transaction, issues may arise as to compliance with regulatory requirements or with general legal requirements. For example, a misrepresentation made in the course of negotiations may give the counterparty a right to damages or to rescind the contract; and the breach of a regulatory requirement might lead to an inability to enforce a transaction or to an investigation and possible fine. The contract may include terms which are intended to exclude liability or limit the consequences of any misrepresentation. The effectiveness of these terms to do so is another category of legal risk.

The consummation of a transaction leads to risk as well. A transaction might be concluded on the telephone without any documentation being incorporated or signed. The absence of detailed terms itself creates risk because a party might not have the remedies that a well drafted contract would provide. This might be the right to terminate a contract immediately in the event of breach, or the right to recover compound interest in the event of late payment. Most derivatives are now documented by reference to market standard terms, which should reduce the risk in this area because they can easily be incorporated in a contract even if the terms are subsequently varied by agreement to meet the particular needs of both parties. But even where standard terms are used, a schedule needs to be filled in with the terms of the particular transaction. If it is, say, a structured or leveraged transaction dependent upon a formula, a vital matter is to check that the formula is correctly and clearly expressed, and the standard terms are adapted properly to meet the needs of the transaction.

Documentation is usually only tested when something goes wrong. In these circumstances, the "boilerplate" parts of the contract may be of vital importance. Can notices be served on the counterparty at a convenient location and by a convenient means in order to terminate the contract? Can payment by the counterparty be enforced in an appropriate judicial or other forum? Failure in these areas might not actually prevent enforcement, but they might delay it or make it more expensive at a vital time.

1.3.1.4 Handling risk

Finally, when something does appear to have gone wrong, the dispute, regulatory investigation or whatever consequences flow from it must be handled in order to ensure that the minimum damage results from it. This includes taking an opportunity to settle a dispute if that is the appropriate course of action, but it also includes ensuring that documents which comment on the case in an adverse way, whether or not justified, are not brought into existence without protection from the need to disclose them to anyone else who might be able to take advantage of them, whether in regulatory or court proceedings. It also includes ensuring that evidence is not destroyed, and that the story is obtained in sufficient detail at an early stage in order to assess the consequences for the institution and the strategy to be employed.

1.3.2 Dealing with legal risk

Identifying areas where legal risk can arise is important in order to enable a conscious decision to be taken as to how to minimise the risk and as to the level of residual risk that is acceptable. Product risk is something that must be assessed when an institution decides to deal in a particular product and whenever the product is varied. A new product will require new consideration as to the risks it entails, inevitably on a less routine basis than other areas of risk.

Decisions taken to try to minimise product risk are likely to flow into counterparty and transaction risk. Counterparty risk must be assessed at the outset of a relationship with a counterparty (for example, does it have the capacity to enter into the product in question? has it provided acceptable authority for those acting on its behalf?), but it is also relevant to each transaction. If a counterparty only has the capacity to enter into derivatives in relation to its other, mainstream, business, is the derivative capable of being used for that purpose? Is the transaction such as to lead to a suspicion of misconduct?

Transaction risk must also, from its nature, be assessed with regard to each transaction. If the transaction has been entered into as a result of a telephone conversation between two financial institutions which already have in place a master agreement governing their relationships, the risk may be at its minimum. In most cases, no representations will be made by one party to another but, even if a representation has been made, it is unlikely to be reasonable for the other party to rely upon it. But for other counterparties, the risk may be higher. Has any representation been made? Is there any evidence of it (tapes, e-mails, etc)? If a representation has been made, have clauses been included in the documentation to exclude any liability for it and, if so, are the clauses effective? This kind of risk is very hard to assess because it will be very fact specific.

As far as documentation is concerned, even financial institutions become insolvent and it is then that it matters most that documentation is in place which gives appropriate protection, for example the right to terminate the contract at once. Even if events are less severe than insolvency, simple issues like checking that confirmations of a transaction sent and received match can limit risk, because if there is a dispute as to the terms, it is likely to be cheaper to sort it out if it is identified early because the market is less likely to have moved against one party in a few days than a few months, with the result that an issue will be less expensive to solve.

Handling risk will hopefully only arise in a limited number of cases, but handling risk is likely to raise a similar range of issues in each case, even if the judgement as to what to do in each case may well differ depending upon the particular facts. The need to ensure that new documents are covered so far as practicable by privilege in order to avoid compulsory disclosure is likely to apply in all cases, as is, for example, the need to consider whether, and, if so, when and how, to keep the regulators informed.

Identifying the risks is essential. Having done so, checklists, particularly the "intelligent" checklists that technology now allows,[38] can be of value in reducing legal risk. Not only can they remind those concerned what the issues are, but they can also explain where the pitfalls lie and their completion ensures that responsibility is taken for issues as they arise. Equally, the mere fact that a closed question[39] can be asked (e.g. does the counterparty have the corporate capacity to enter into the transaction?), does not mean that the question does not raise difficult questions. The answer may in various cases be "probably" or even "perhaps, but the consequences of being wrong are acceptable". Judgement will be called for, but the purpose of a checklist is to ensure that a responsible person exercises judgement, even if he or she is on occasion wrong, rather than that the issues are ignored.

38. See Susskind, *The Future of Law*.
39. I.e. one demanding the answer "yes" or "no".

CHAPTER 2

THE NATURE OF A DERIVATIVES CONTRACT

2.1 INTRODUCTION

A derivatives transaction takes effect in law as a contract.[1] English law has very few requirements of form as far as contracts are concerned,[2] and these do not in the main affect derivatives transactions. A contract can be made orally, and many are arranged on the telephone, as long as the basic requirements of offer, acceptance, consideration, and intention to create legal relations are met. When a contract is made orally, there is no need for it to be confirmed in writing, although it is obviously sensible for this to be done (though tapes of conversations are admissible in evidence to prove what was agreed[3]). Subsequent negotiations over, for example, the form of a confirmation can lead to a written agreement which amends, supplements, or replaces the oral agreement; but even if there is disagreement as to, for example, amendments to the terms of an ISDA Master Agreement such that no Master Agreement or confirmation is ever signed, that will not affect the existence of the contract made over the telephone.

In general, one contract is, as a matter of law, the same as the next regardless of subject matter. There are, however, three particular issues with regard to derivatives transactions which this chapter will address. The first is whether a derivatives contract is a gaming or wagering contract, and the second is whether credit derivatives are insurance contracts. The third is whether derivatives contracts are subject to any obligations of confidentiality. The first two issues arise from statutory provisions which, in the case of gaming contracts, render them unenforceable, and, in the case of insurance contracts, in general make it a criminal offence for anyone other than an authorised insurance company to carry on insurance business. These issues will be considered in turn.

1. For a detailed treatment of the law of contract, see, for example, *Chitty on Contracts* (27th edn).

2. For example, a contract for the sale or disposition of an interest in land must be in writing (section 2 of the Law of Property (Miscellaneous Provisions) Act 1989), as must a guarantee (section 4 of the Statute of Frauds 1677).

3. See p 177 below.

2.2 GAMING AND WAGERING

Section 18 of the Gaming Act 1845 provides that:

"... All contracts or agreements, whether by parole or in writing, by way of gaming or wagering, shall be null and void; and ... no suit shall be brought or maintained in any court of law and equity for recovering any sum of money or valuable thing alleged to be won upon a wager, or which shall have been deposited in the hands of any person or to abide the event on which any wager shall have been made ..."

As a result, if a contract is one of gaming or wagering, it is void, and therefore unenforceable (subject to the effect of section 63 of the Financial Services Act 1986). The courts held, however, that if an agent paid a gaming debt for his principal, the agent could still recover the sum from his principal since that only involved the agent enforcing his right of indemnity, and not the gaming contract.[4] To avoid this, the Gaming Act 1892 was enacted. Section 1 of this Act provides that:

"Any promise, express or implied, to pay any person a sum of money paid by him under or in respect of any contract or agreement rendered null and void by the Gaming Act 1845 or to pay any sum of money by way of commission, fee, reward, or otherwise in respect of any such contract, or of any services in relation thereto or in connection therewith, shall be null and void, and no action shall be brought or maintained to recover any such sum of money."

The greatest difficulty with both these statutes is that they do not define what a gaming or a wagering contract is. This has, therefore, been left to the courts to work out, something they have struggled with. There is no doubt that betting on a horse race is gaming and wagering whether or not the gambler has an interest in the horse, but ambiguity surrounds the circumstances which turn a financial transaction into wagering. It is now fortunate that, in most cases, section 63 of the Financial Services Act 1986 renders it unnecessary to consider whether a transaction is a wagering transaction.

2.2.1 The nature of gaming and wagering

The "classic"[5] definition of gaming and wagering was given in *Carlill* v. *The Carbolic Smoke Ball Company*[6] where Hawkins J said:

"It is not easy to define with precision what amounts to a wagering contract, nor the narrow line of demarcation which separates a wagering contract from an ordinary

4. For example, *Read* v. *Anderson* (1884) 13 QBD 779.

5. See, for example, *Tote Investors Ltd* v. *Smoker* [1968] 1 QB 509, 516; *City Index Limited* v. *Leslie* [1992] 1 QB 98, 111, and *Morgan Grenfell* v. *Welwyn Hatfield* [1995] 1 All ER 1, 6. Before the adoption of this definition, a definition frequently quoted (e.g. *Forget* v. *Ostigny* [1895] AC 318, 326 and *Richards* v. *Stark* [1911] 1 KB 296, 302) was given by Cotton LJ in *Thacker* v. *Hardy* (1878) 4 QBD 685, 695: "The essence of gaming and wagering is that one party is to win and the other is to lose upon a future event, which at the time of the contract is of an uncertain nature ..."

6. [1892] 2 QB 484, 490–491. The case was upheld on appeal, but the Court of Appeal considered the suggestion that the contract in question was a gaming contract was "not worth serious attention", and therefore did not go into the issue: [1893] 1 QB 256, 261.

contract; but, according to my view, a wagering contract is one by which two persons, professing to hold opposite views touching the issue of a future uncertain event, mutually agree that, dependent upon the determination of that event, one shall win from the other, that other shall pay or hand over to him, a sum of money or other stake; neither of the contracting parties having any other interest in that contract than the sum or stake he will so win or lose, there being no real consideration for the making of such contract by either of the parties. It is essential to a wagering contract that each party may under it either win or lose, whether he will win or lose being dependent on the issue of the event, and, therefore, remaining uncertain until that issue is known. If either of the parties may win but cannot lose, or may lose but cannot win, it is not a wagering contract."

This should not, however, be treated as if it were a statutory definition,[7] nor is it even correct in one particular aspect. Hawkins J states that the transaction must concern a future uncertain event. The event can, however, be in the past, and therefore certain, but one on which the parties differ.[8] The definition does, however, bring out two essential features: first, the requirement that both parties must be able to win or lose; and, secondly, the more intangible requirement that neither party must have any other interest in the contract.

2.2.1.1 Mutuality

Both parties must be able to win or to lose a wagering transaction; if only one can win or lose, it is not a wagering transaction and therefore does not fall foul of section 18 of the Gaming Act 1845.[9] *Tote Investors Ltd* v. *Smoker*[10] illustrates this principle. In that case, the Court of Appeal rejected the argument that betting on the Tote was gaming or wagering within the meaning of the 1845 Act. This was because the Tote worked by collecting money from all backers of horses running in a particular race, and, after expenses, distributing that money to the winners. The Tote could not, therefore, either win or lose, and, as a result, contracts with the Tote were not gaming or wagering within the judicial definition, even though they would be considered betting by most ordinary people.

The requirement of mutuality has a potentially important implication for derivatives transactions. In the light of this requirement, it is arguable that no one exchange transaction is wagering. In exchange traded derivatives, the parties enter into the transaction between themselves, but it is then adopted by the exchange, and a clearing house becomes the counterparty of each original party. The clearing house neither intends to nor does make a profit from

7. *Tote Investors Ltd* v. *Smoker* [1968] 1 QB 509, 516, 518.

8. In *Rourke* v. *Short* (1856) 5 E & B 904, the bet concerned the price of an earlier lot of rags. The parties decided that if the price was, as one party contended, at a certain level, the price of the current lot would be 6s (above what either party contended the earlier price had been), but if it was what the other party contended, the price of the current lot would be 3s (below what either party contended the earlier price to have been). This was held to be a wager.

9. See, for example, *Marten* v. *Gibbon* (1875) 33 LT 561, *Thacker* v. *Hardy* (1878) 4 QBD 685 and *Earl of Ellesmere* v. *Wallace* [1929] 2 Ch 1.

10. [1968] 1 QB 509. The Court of Appeal in this case comprised Lord Denning MR, Lord Wilberforce and Lord Pearson.

movements in interest rates or whatever underlies the transaction, and insulates itself from credit risk by taking margin. On this basis, the transaction should not be considered wagering because the clearing house cannot lose on the transaction. There is, however, no authority dealing with financial transactions to support this line of argument.[11]

2.2.1.2 *Other interests in the transaction*

The aspect of gaming transactions with which the courts have had most difficulty is defining what is a sufficient interest in a transaction, outside the possibility of speculative gain, to render a transaction enforceable. It is hard to discern any real consistency in the cases, but there is a recent tendency for courts to take a more flexible approach and to incline more to uphold financial transactions than was the case at one time. The difficulties faced by the courts in this area are easy to see—it is not obvious what separates financial transactions which involve wagering within the mischief of the Gaming Acts from those which do not. For example, the purchase of shares with a view to their sale at the top of an anticipated price rise is just as much speculation as buying a forward with a provision that only the difference between the market and the forward price be paid; the latter runs, however, a very real risk of being considered a wagering transaction[12] whereas the former does not.

At one time the difference between wagering and enforceable financial transactions tended to be measured by whether or not there was a delivery obligation—if there was a delivery obligation, the contract was treated as a genuine commercial transaction, if not as a contract for differences and wagering.[13] It is still the case that a contract with a genuine delivery obligation will not be a wager.[14] A delivery obligation is easy to identify in the case of, say, commodities or currencies, but harder in the case of interest rate transactions. What delivery can there be on an interest rate swap? Interest rates are the price of borrowing and lending, and delivery would therefore presumably comprise taking or giving a loan. That would, however, remove many of the advantages of a swap transaction, besides significantly increasing the credit risk involved.

The requirement of delivery led, however, to the inclusion in contracts of a delivery obligation or option even though neither party anticipated that delivery would in fact take place. This begged the question of whether it was enough for there to be a delivery obligation, even though no one expected it to be fulfilled. In *Universal Stock Exchange* v. *Strachan*, the House of Lords considered the

11. In *Richards* v. *Stark* [1911] 1 KB 296, the depositor would either gain from the upward movement of shares or would get his stake back. Channel J nevertheless held that the risk of loss of interest that could otherwise have been earned on a deposit was enough to render the transaction wagering.

12. As in, for example, *Re Gieve* [1899] 1 QB 794.

13. For example, *Re Gieve* [1899] 1 QB 794, 798 and *Forget* v. *Ostigny* [1895] AC 318, 323. See also *City Index* v. *Leslie* [1992] 1 QB 98, 112.

14. For example, *Ironmonger* v. *Dyne* (1928) 44 TLR 497, 499.

question in these circumstances to be whether there was a "secret understanding" between the parties that there should never be delivery—as long as the delivery obligation could be enforced, the contract escaped the Gaming Acts.[15]

The more recent approach has been to consider whether the transaction in question was a "real transaction",[16] or was "entered into for a commercial purpose",[17] these being treated as the antithesis of wagering. But how is it to be determined whether a contract is a real transaction or a wagering one? The only answer at the moment is that the judiciary have been unable to define what it is that makes a transaction wagering, but presumably feel that they can recognise a wagering contract when they see one. It might come down to the ability to identify a purpose in entering into, or a benefit from, the transaction beyond purely the profit that the transaction might bring. So, for example, if a swap hedges an underlying loan, that would not be wagering because of the benefit outside the scope of the transaction.

The most recent case on this topic concerning derivatives is *Morgan Grenfell* v. *Welwyn Hatfield District Council.*[18] Welwyn had entered into two interest rate swaps: one with Islington Council; and the other a back to back transaction with Morgan Grenfell. Payments, after the initial one from Morgan Grenfell (the swap was at an off market rate), in substance passed from Islington through Welwyn (which deducted a turn) to Morgan Grenfell. Islington argued that the transaction between itself and Welwyn was a wagering transaction. Hobhouse J rejected this. He considered that:

> "Provisions for the payment of differences are commonplace in certain types of commercial or financial contract. The mere fact that there is a provision for the payment of differences does not mean that the contract must be a wagering contract. It merely raises the possibility or justifies an inference. If the other features of the relevant transaction show or confirm that it is a wagering contract, then it is unenforceable and void. If on the other hand the other features of the contract do not confirm that its character was gaming or wagering, then the contract, notwithstanding that it provides for the payment of differences, is fully effective and enforceable.
>
> . . . In the context of interest rate swap contracts entered into by parties or institutions involved in the capital market and the making or receiving of loans, the normal inference will be that the contracts are not gaming or wagering but are commercial or financial transactions to which the law will, in the absence of some other consideration, give full recognition and effect."[19]

15. [1896] AC 166. In *Garnac Grain* v. *Faure* [1966] 1 QB 650, 674, Sellers LJ said that even where "the parties do not expect to complete the transaction [by delivery] but to trade on differences in the hope that the result will be a profit, but if there is an obligation to fulfil the contract according to its tenor if circumstances require it, then the contract is enforceable" (see also p 802 and *Libyan Arab Foreign Bank* v. *Bankers Trust Co* [1989] QB 728, 764). In *The Filipinas I* [1973] 1 Lloyd's Rep 349, 357, Kerr J referred to "it being in effect agreed between [the parties] that neither party should be entitled to call for performance, then the contract will be unenforceable as being a gaming transaction". In *Morgan Grenfell* v. *Welwyn Hatfield District Council* [1995] 1 All ER 1, 7, Hobhouse J referred to the overt transaction as being a "sham".
16. *Universal Stock Exchange* v. *Strachan* [1896] AC 166, 171, 173.
17. *City Index* v. *Leslie* [1992] 1 QB 98, 112.
18. [1995] 1 All ER 1.
19. [1995] 1 All ER 1, 10.

In this case, Hobhouse J decided that Islington's motive in entering into the contract had been to raise money and not that of wagering. Welwyn had not entered into any speculation. It was insulated from speculative gain because, whatever the movement in interest rates, its profit would be the same. It took a negligible credit risk, and was looking to make a non-speculative profit. Welwyn was therefore also not entering into the contract for a wagering purpose (though it would have been enough if only one of the parties had not intended to enter into a wagering transaction). The general approach taken by Hobhouse J is welcome, but he, like judges before him, does not offer any real guidance as to what the features of a contract are that make it a wagering transaction.

2.2.1.3 Loans for wagering transactions

If a loan or credit facility is extended to a counterparty to enable it to enter into derivatives transactions which do constitute wagers, the question, subject to the effect of section 63 of the Financial Services Act 1986, is whether the loan is recoverable. This depends upon the purpose of the facility. If money is lent to enable wagering transactions to be undertaken, then it is unclear whether the money is recoverable or not.[20] If money is lent to pay wagering debts, it is irrecoverable if either paid directly to the wagering creditor[21] or if there is a contractual term that it will be used to pay wagering creditors.[22]

As a result, in so far as it is possible to see any logic in these distinctions,[23] a facility given to a customer to trade in wagering derivatives with the same financial institution may be irrecoverable. A loan which can be used for that purpose, but which need not be, will however be recoverable, but a loan which is disbursed directly to the creditor will not be recoverable.

2.2.2 Section 63 of the Financial Services Act 1986

Section 63 of the Financial Services Act 1986 provides that:

> "(1) No contract to which this section applies shall be void or unenforceable by reason of—
>
> (a) section 18 of the Gaming Act 1845, section 1 of the Gaming Act 1892 . . .

20. In *Carlton Hall Club* v. *Laurence* [1929] 2 KB 153, the Divisional Court held that a loan for the purpose of gaming was irrecoverable by virtue of the Gaming Acts 1710 and 1835, which make void securities given for the repayment of money knowingly lent for the purpose of gaming or betting. It is questionable whether derivatives could be gaming or betting, as opposed to wagering (though in *Tote Investors* v. *Smoker* [1968] 1 QB 509, 516 Lord Denning MR commented that "gaming" in the 1845 Act added nothing to wagering, but that does not mean that the reverse is also true), but in any event in *CHT* v. *Ward* [1965] 2 QB 63, 85–86 the Court of Appeal doubted the correctness of *Carlton Hall*.

21. *CHT* v. *Ward* [1965] 2 QB 63.

22. *MacDonald* v. *Green* [1951] 1 KB 594.

23. *Cheshire, Fifoot and Furmston on Contract* (27th edn) describe the law in this area as "confused and illogical" (p 348).

(2) This section applies to any contract entered into by either party by way of business and the making or performance of which by either party constitutes an activity which falls within paragraph 12 of Schedule 1 to this Act or would do so apart from Parts III and IV of that Schedule."

As a result, in order to obtain the benefit of this section, there must be a contract, at least one of the parties must enter into it by way of business, and the performance by at least one of the parties must fall within paragraph 12 of Schedule 1 to the Act.

As to business, in most cases this will be obvious. In any event, in *Morgan Grenfell* v. *Welwyn Hatfield*, Hobhouse J took a wide view of what business meant. He decided that it should not be given a technical construction but rather one which conforms to what in ordinary parlance would be described as a business transaction, as opposed to something personal or casual. As a result, he concluded that a transaction between two local authorities was one of business because they were dealing in the capital markets almost every day and were raising or placing large sums of money in a manner which would be regarded by the ordinary person as business.[24]

Paragraph 12 of Schedule 1 to the Financial Services Act 1986 merely states: "Buying, selling, subscribing for, underwriting investments or offering or agreeing to do so, either as principal or as an agent." To take advantage of section 63, one of the parties to the contract must be engaging in one of these activities. "Buying" and "selling" include any acquisition or disposal for valuable consideration, and "offering" includes an invitation to treat.[25] The most important aspect is, however, the definition of investments in the Act. This is set out in Part I of Schedule 1 to the Act,[26] and, in effect, defines the scope of the Act. The Act regulates the investment business, and that comprises transactions in the investments set out in Part I of Schedule 1.[27]

From the point of view of derivatives, the most important paragraphs in Part I of Schedule 1 to the Financial Services Act 1986 are paragraphs 7 to 9.[28] Paragraph 7 covers options to acquire or dispose of any currency or of gold, palladium, platinum, or silver, and an investment falling within any other

24. [1995] 1 All ER 1, 13.

25. Paragraphs 28(2)(c) and (d) of Schedule 1 to the Financial Services Act 1986.

26. Section 1 of the Financial Services Act 1986.

27. Section 3 of the Financial Services Act 1986 provides that no person may carry on investment business in the UK unless authorised or exempt under the Act. Section 1(2) and Part II of Schedule 1 (which includes paragraph 12) defines carrying on investment business which in turn depends upon the definition of investments in Part I (and section 1(1)).

28. The scope of the Financial Services Act 1986 is discussed further in Chapter 6 below. One general problem is that the Act sets out its scope by reference to transactions known at the time it was written. Derivatives transactions are constantly evolving and new ones being invented. It is not, therefore, necessarily easy to fit complex transactions into the Act's framework, but in most cases the courts are likely to strain to keep what are plainly financial transactions within the regulatory scope of the Act.

paragraph of Part I of Schedule 1.[29] The other paragraphs of Part I include bonds, shares, loan stock, UK public debt, and governmental debt.

Paragraph 8 of Schedule 1 covers rights under a contract for the sale of a commodity or property of any other description under which delivery is to be made at a future date and at a price agreed upon when the contract is made. This covers futures contracts, but the notes to the paragraph[30] state that it only applies to contracts made for investment and not commercial purposes. A contract is for investment purposes if traded on an exchange, expressed to be so, or on terms equivalent to an exchange traded contract,[31] and an absence of any intention to deliver is an indication that a contract is for investment purposes. This meets the prime difficulty faced with the gaming legislation because the position is now that if there is an intention or obligation to deliver, the contract would not be a gaming contract anyway; but if there is not, it is entered into for investment purposes and is therefore protected by section 63.

Paragraph 9 of Schedule 1 provides that an investment includes:

> "Rights under a contract for differences or under any other contract the purpose or pretended purpose of which is to secure a profit or avoid a loss by reference to fluctuations in the value or price of property[32] of any description or in an index or other factor designated for that purpose in the contract."

The meaning of this paragraph arose in *City Index* v. *Leslie*,[33] a case which concerned spread betting on the Dow Jones index and Treasury bonds. The Court of Appeal decided that these transactions were protected by section 63, and, in doing so, the Court of Appeal took the view that: first, to "secure" a profit in this context meant to "obtain" a profit—it was not necessary for there to be a pre-existing profit which the party was seeking to protect; and, secondly, the words "purpose or pretended purpose" referred back both to a "contract for differences" and to "any other contract".

The Court of Appeal was, however, less sure what a contract for differences actually is. Lord Donaldson MR regarded it as "pairs of contracts, one for the notional sale and one for the notional purchase of a particular quantity of the commodity, the intention of both parties being that no property in the commodity shall pass, but that the contracts will be fulfilled by paying sums of money based upon price differences at different times".[34] Lord Donaldson therefore appeared to require there to be two transactions rather than just one settled by the payment of a difference—he may have been considering transactions like those which take place on exchanges rather than over the

29. Paragraph 7(d) also covers options on options.

30. The notes are a very unusual feature of English statutory drafting, and provide clarification and explanation of the paragraphs (see *City Index* v. *Leslie* [1992] 1 QB 98, 105).

31. This is meant to catch contracts entered into with exchange members on exchange terms.

32. For these purposes, property includes any currency: paragraph 28(1)(a) of Schedule 1 to the Financial Services Act 1986.

33. [1992] 1 QB 98.

34. [1992] 1 QB 98, 106 (see also p 107). Lord Donaldson MR relied on *Universal Stock Exchange* v. *Strachan* [1896] AC 166.

counter. As a result, he took the view that the transactions in that case were not contracts for differences, but were "any other contracts" within the meaning of paragraph 9. Leggatt LJ took the more realistic view that "a contract for differences is a contract intended by both parties to end in the payment of differences".[35] He therefore regarded the transactions in that case as being contracts for differences. McCowan LJ inclined to the view that "contract for differences" was "more a term of opprobrium than a term of art",[36] and referred to a transaction which was a sham because it was set up as sale and purchase in order to seek to avoid the effect of the Gaming Act 1845. He did not express a view as to whether the transactions he had to consider were contracts for differences or other contracts, but considered that the case came down to the question of whether the contracts had as their purpose either the making of a profit or the avoidance of a loss, and concluded that they had.

In practice, the Court of Appeal's uncertainty as to the nature of a contract for differences may not be important. Paragraph 9 of Schedule 1 to the Financial Services Act 1986 covers a large range of transactions which result in cash settlement. The requirement is that the purpose of the contract is to secure (or obtain) a profit or avoid a loss[37] by reference to fluctuations in the value or price of property of any description or in an index or other factor. This covers swaps, cash settled options, and cash settled futures. Indeed, it could cover most derivatives. In *Morgan Stanley UK Group* v. *Puglisi*,[38] Longmore J considered that a "Principal Exchange Rate Linked Security" was a contract for differences. The security in question was a US dollar denominated bond the redemption sum on which, though payable in dollars, depended on the movement of two or more other currencies against each other. Longmore J considered it to be a contract for differences because payment was to be made by reference to different exchange rates, exchange rates being "other factors" for the purposes of paragraph 9 of Schedule 1.[39]

The reality is, therefore, that in most cases, a derivatives contract, even if considered a wagering contract, would not be unenforceable because the effect of section 63 of the Financial Services Act 1986 is likely to prevent that result. This has led to the development of, for example, non-deliverable forwards where there is no pretence that there can be delivery of the, say, currency

35. [1992] 1 QB 98, 111.
36. [1992] 1 QB 98, 110.
37. Why else would at least one of the parties enter into a contract?
38. Unreported, 29 January 1998.
39. In *Larussa-Chigi* v. *CS First Boston Limited* (unreported, 18 December 1997), Thomas J took the view that a foreign exchange contract where no physical delivery was contemplated was also a contract for differences. Thomas J considered that because delivery was not contemplated, the transaction could not fall within paragraph 8 of Schedule 1 to the Financial Services Act 1986. He decided that if delivery had been intended, the contracts would not have been within paragraph 8 because delivery was to take place within seven days of contract, and the notes to paragraph 8 deemed a contract for delivery within seven days to be a commercial contract outside the scope of the Financial Services Act 1986. Prior to this judgment, there had been doubt as to whether short-term foreign exchange dealing fell within the scope of the Act.

involved and a contractual recognition that there will be settlement by payment of differences only.

2.3 CREDIT DERIVATIVES AND INSURANCE

A difficulty often raised in relation to credit derivatives is whether entering into them constitutes insurance business.[40] If it does, doing so is a criminal offence unless authorised by the Secretary of State, unless done by a branch of an insurance company incorporated under the law of another member state of the European Union, unless done by a member of Lloyd's, or unless the activities fall within certain other limited exceptions.[41]

For these purposes, insurance business is set out in Schedules 1 and 2 of the Insurance Companies Act 1982, and includes the following:

Credit—"Effecting and carrying out contracts of insurance against risks of loss to the persons insured arising from the insolvency of debtors of theirs or from failure (otherwise than through insolvency) of debtors of theirs to pay their debts when due."[42]

Suretyship—"Effecting and carrying out— . . . (b) contracts for fidelity bonds, performance bonds, administration bonds, bail bonds or customs bonds or similar contracts of guarantee."[43]

Whether credit derivatives could fall within either of these categories of insurance business is considered below, but it is first necessary to consider the exception for those carrying on a banking business.

2.3.1 Banking business

Section 2(4) of the Insurance Companies Act 1982 provides that it is not a criminal offence for someone other than an authorised insurance company to carry on the two classes of insurance business identified above—credit and suretyship—together with three other categories ("miscellaneous financial loss", "legal expenses", and "assistance"[44]) if that business is carried on "solely in the course of carrying on, and for the purposes of, banking business". Unfortunately "banking business" is not defined in the Insurance Companies Act 1982.[45] This creates inevitable uncertainty as to what the nature of banking

40. There may also be some residual doubt about some other forms of derivatives, but the risk on credit derivatives is undoubtedly higher than on other transactions.

41. Sections 2 and 14 of the Insurance Companies Act 1982 (see p 32 below).

42. Class 14 of General Business in Schedule 2 to the Insurance Companies Act 1982.

43. Class 15 of General Business in Schedule 2 to the Insurance Companies Act 1982.

44. Classes 16 to 18 of General Business in Schedule 2 to the Insurance Companies Act 1982.

45. The absence of any definition of banking is not unique to the Insurance Companies Act 1982: see, for example, section 2 of the Criminal Justice Act 1987 (powers of the Serious Fraud Office to require information from, amongst others, banks), and even the Bankers Books Evidence Act 1879 has no definition.

business is for the purposes of the Act, and what the link between it and credit derivatives must be in order to take advantage of this exception.

Banking business is now many layered, but has traditionally been seen as based upon the acceptance of deposits and the keeping of accounts for customers[46]—the acceptance of deposits is the activity regulated under the Banking Act 1987. It seems probable that the business of banking would in general terms still be considered as accepting deposits and lending the money deposited to others. If, as seems likely, this means accepting deposits from the public, as opposed to on the wholesale markets, this does have the result of excluding most merchant and investment banks.[47]

There are also some suggestions that a reputation of being a bank is enough to make an institution a bank,[48] but this does not fit easily with section 2(4) of the Insurance Companies Act 1982. The section requires the carrying on of a banking business, not merely the reputation of doing so.

In these circumstances, the safe approach is to treat only an institution a significant part of whose business involves taking deposits as carrying on a banking business (it cannot be all business otherwise section 2(4) would be meaningless). Other institutions are taking a significant risk if they rely solely on this as the justification for escaping the consequences of section 2(1). It may be that the courts could be persuaded to take an expansive view of what a banking business now is, but that would be out of keeping with the more traditional approach.

In any event, the fact that an institution is carrying on a banking business within the meaning of the Insurance Companies Act 1982 is only the beginning of the enquiry. It is not enough for an institution entering into credit derivatives to be carrying on a banking business—the credit derivatives must, according to section 2(4) of the Insurance Companies Act 1982, be entered into "solely in the course of carrying on, and for the purposes of, banking business". If a credit derivatives transaction is offered to a banking client as part of a wider relationship which centres on traditional banking or to traditional banking customers, then that might fall within the statutory definition, but a transaction with a wholesale counterparty with whom there is no traditional banking relationship seems to fall outside the requirements.[49]

The only safe conclusion is, therefore, that the banking exception in section

46. See, for example, *United Dominions Trust* v. *Kirkwood* [1966] 2 QB 431, a case on the Money Lenders Act 1900, another statute which referred to the "business of banking" without defining what it was. In this case, the honouring and collection of cheques was also mentioned as characteristic of banking business, but it seems likely that banking business has moved on since then. On this topic, see, for example, *Modern Banking Law* (2nd edn) by Ellinger and Lomnicka, pp 73–102, and *Principles of Banking Law* by Cranston, pp 4–10.

47. Whilst commercial banks invariably have "bank" in their title, merchant banks do not necessarily.

48. *United Dominions Trust* v. *Kirkwood* [1966] 2 QB 431, 454.

49. At least unless the transaction can be said to be related to (e.g. to hedge) a transaction with a traditional banking customer, though that might still be too remote as being incidental to the incidental: see p 59 below.

2(4) of the Insurance Companies Act 1982 is unlikely to be of assistance in any but a limited number of cases. A classic wholesale market derivatives transaction is unlikely to fall within the banking exception.

2.3.2 Insurance business

Classes 14 and 15 in Schedule 2 to the Insurance Companies Act 1982 have been quoted above.[50] The issue is whether credit derivatives fall within either of those categories: if so, then entering into them (at least on a regular basis) constitutes insurance business; if not, then the Insurance Companies Act 1982 has no application. For this purpose, credit derivatives cannot be treated as if they formed one single category. Each derivatives contract has to be considered on its own terms. For present purposes it is, however, necessary to deal in generic types; on this basis, a credit default swap is probably the category which is closest in effect to insurance in that, in return for a series of payments, one party agrees to make a payment to the other on the happening of an event, usually insolvency or insolvency related, the payment being, potentially at least,[51] to compensate for loss suffered as a result of the event.

2.3.2.1 Insurance contracts

Class 14 in Schedule 2 to the Insurance Companies Act 1982 applies to "contracts of insurance" against the risk of loss to the person insured arising from a debtor's insolvency. This raises the question of whether a credit default swap is a contract of insurance[52]; if not, it cannot fall within this class of insurance business. What constitutes a contract of insurance is not defined by the Act. In *Prudential Insurance Co* v. *Inland Revenue Commissioners*, Channel J defined insurance as:

"It must be a contract whereby for some consideration, usually but not necessarily for periodical payments called premiums, you secure to yourself some benefit, usually but not necessarily the payment of a sum of money, upon the happening of some event. Then the next thing that is necessary is that the event should be one that involves some amount of uncertainty. There must either be uncertainty whether the event will ever happen or not, or if the event is one which is certain to happen at some time there must be uncertainty as to the time at which it will happen. The remaining essential is that . . . the insurance must be against something. A contract which would otherwise be a mere wager may become an insurance by reason of the assured having an interest in the subject matter—that is to say, the uncertain event which is necessary to make the contract amount to an insurance must be an event which is prima facie adverse to the interest of the

50. See p 30.
51. The buyer of a credit derivative need not, of course, have any credit exposure to the reference entity.
52. It seems unlikely that the words "of insurance" could be treated merely as excess verbiage.

assured. The insurance is to provide for the payment of a sum on money to meet a loss or detriment which will or may be suffered upon the happening of the event."[53]

This emphasises the requirement that insurance be against something, the risk of loss arising from insolvency. Credit default swaps are not necessarily against any risk of loss. One party may have an interest in the instrument in question, but there is in general no requirement that this is the case (any requirement there might be will increase the risk of a credit default swap being considered as insurance). Even if one party does have an interest in the underlying instrument, there is nothing to stop that party selling the instrument at an opportune moment whilst keeping the swap.

As the quote above makes clear, it is the interest in the underlying subject matter which turns a contract into insurance, but by providing that there is no requirement of any interest in the subject matter the parties can recognise the contract as a mere wager. Before the passing of section 63 of the Financial Services Act 1986, this might have rendered the transaction unenforceable, but since the entry into force of this section, being a wager is no longer the disadvantage it once was. The effect of section 63 is that a credit default swap can be a wager but still be enforceable.

Although a credit derivative may have the same effect as an insurance contract, there is no reason why parties should not arrange their affairs so that the contract in question is not an insurance contract. There are inevitably more ways than one to achieve a desired result,[54] and it is not illegal to enter into a contract which can provide the same economic outcome as an insurance contract but for the parties to seek to ensure that the contract is not treated at law as an insurance contract.[55] It is a question of construing the contract as a whole to determine its true effect. In this the label applied by the parties is of relevance, but is not decisive.[56] If the parties state that they do not intend the contract to be one of insurance, then there is no reason why the courts should construe the contract as insurance. There is, for example, no reason to require that the legal consequences flowing from insurance (for example, the obligation of good faith, and the insurer's right of subrogation) should apply if the parties do not intend them to. A contract should therefore state clearly that it is not a contract of insurance.

53. [1904] KB 658, 663. See also, for example, *Re Sentinel Securities plc* [1996] 1 WLR 316 and *Fuji Finance* v. *Aetna* [1996] 3 WLR 871.

54. See, for example, *Chow Yoong Hong* v. *Choong Fah Rubber Manufactory* [1962] AC 209, 216.

55. This assumes that the contract is not a sham. For "a document to be a 'sham'... all the parties thereto must have a common intention that the acts or documents are not to create the legal rights and obligations which they give the appearance of creating" or "the parties really made some other and different contract between them and agreed that the ostensible contract should not give rise to legally enforceable rights": Diplock LJ in, respectively, *Snooks* v. *London and West Riding Investments* [1967] 2 QB 786, 802 and *Garnac Grain* v. *HMF Faure & Fairclough* [1966] 1 QB 650, 683.

56. *Welsh Development Agency* v. *Export Finance Co* [1992] BCLC 270, 280–281 and 302.

2.3.2.2 *Other types of "insurance business"*

Although within the statutory definition of insurance business, class 15 of Schedule 2 to the Insurance Companies Act 1982 does not refer to insurance contracts. The analysis above does not therefore apply to this class. The class concerns "contracts for fidelity bonds, performance bonds, administration bonds, bail bonds or customs bonds or similar contracts of guarantee". A credit default swap is not within one of the named categories of bonds, so the issue is whether it is a "similar contract of guarantee". A difficulty with this is that all the other instruments expressly mentioned are not contracts of guarantee within the legal definition of a guarantee, i.e. a contract by which one person agrees to answer for the liability of another to a third person.[57] As a result, "similar contract of guarantee" could mean: contracts of guarantee within the legal definition which have the same effect as the instruments mentioned; or contracts which, like those mentioned, have the same effect as a guarantee even if different legal characteristics. If the former interpretation is correct, then credit derivatives fall outside this class because they are not guarantees within the legal definition.

If, as is more likely on the wording, the latter interpretation is correct, then credit derivatives could arguably fall within the wording "other similar contracts of guarantee". It is necessary to consider whether the particular credit derivative transaction is sufficiently similar to those listed in class 15. Those listed are usually given at the request and expense of the party whose default triggers payment,[58] and require one party to pay a sum on the default, or alleged default, of another in the performance of an underlying obligation. A credit default swap is unlikely to be given at the request of the party likely to be in default, and is not necessarily linked to any underlying transaction. It is therefore arguable that a credit default swap will not in general fall within class 15, but there is a risk that it could do so. The closer the terms of the instrument come to, for example, a performance bond, the greater the risk of falling within this category. If the event which triggers payment under the credit default option is non-payment on an underlying instrument, there is a greater risk that the swap would be treated as insurance business than if the event were, say, the downgrading of bonds by a rating agency. Nevertheless, on balance, credit default options are unlikely to fall within this class of insurance business.

There is, nevertheless, some residual risk that carrying on a credit derivatives business constitutes insurance business within the meaning of class 15 of Schedule 2 to the Insurance Companies Act 1982. In terms of the wholesale markets, a credit derivatives transaction does not fall within the mischief the

57. *Chitty on Contracts*, p 1305. As to guarantees generally see, for example, *Chitty on Contracts* (27th edn), ch 42 and Andrews & Millett, *The Law of Guarantees* (2nd edn). The type of contract mentioned in class 15 can, however, turn into a guarantee without careful drafting: see *Trafalgar House* v. *General Surety* [1996] 1 AC 199 regarding performance bonds.

58. Though, for example, "blind" confirmations of letters of credit are far from unknown.

Insurance Companies Act 1982 is intended to address—it is more akin to reinsurance than to insurance as such—but the wording of the statute is arguably sufficiently wide to encompass credit derivatives. To mitigate the risk, it is prudent to state expressly that a contract is neither one of insurance nor one of guarantee.

2.4 DERIVATIVES AND CONFIDENTIALITY

Derivatives contracts very rarely state expressly whether the fact of having entered into the contract or the terms of the contract are to be subject to any obligation of confidentiality. As a result, if there is any obligation of confidentiality, it can only be from an implied term in the contract.[59] Whether or in what circumstances an obligation of confidentiality would be implied is unclear—it has never been considered by the courts—but it is potentially important. For example, if there is an obligation of confidentiality, then revealing that there has been a breach of a derivatives contract could be a breach of that obligation leading potentially to liability in damages.

Terms are, in general, implied into contracts only when it is necessary to give business efficacy to a contract or where it is obvious from the factual matrix surrounding the contract that such a term was implicit. An implied term must also be clear.[60] A term will not be implied merely because it is reasonable, only if it is necessary.[61] The issue is as to the extent to which an obligation of confidentiality is either necessary or implicit in the case of a derivatives contract.[62]

59. There could, in theory, be an equitable obligation of confidence, but this seems unlikely to add anything to a contractual obligation; and if there is no contractual obligation, it is difficult in the circumstances of a derivatives contract to impose an equitable obligation. If, however, one party to a derivatives transaction discloses its existence or terms to someone other than its counterparty, there could be an equitable obligation of confidence (as to which see, for example, Toulson & Phipps, *Confidentiality*).

60. The wording in the first two sentences of this paragraph is taken from *Coca-Cola Financial Corporation* v. *Finsat International Ltd* [1996] 3 WLR 849, 854. For more detail, see *Chitty on Contracts* (27th edn), ch 13. Terms can also be implied as a matter of law where the terms implied have become standardised over time, as is probably now the case with the obligation of confidentiality imposed on those performing the traditional functions of a banker (*Christofi* v. *Barclays Bank plc* [1998] 1 WLR 1245, 1251). In *Ali Shipping Corporation* v. *Shipyard Trogir* [1998] 1 Lloyd's Rep 643, 651, Potter LJ considered that an implied term of confidentiality "ought properly be regarded as attaching as a matter of law" to an arbitration clause.

61. See, for example, *Hamlyn & Co* v. *Wood & Co* [1891] 2 QB 488, 491; *Liverpool City Council* v. *Irwin* [1977] AC 239, 266; and *The Super Servant Two* [1990] 1 Lloyd's Rep 1, 6.

62. Section 9(a) of ISDA's Master Agreement contains an entire agreement clause—"This Agreement constitutes the entire agreement and understanding of the parties with respect to its subject matter and supersedes all oral communications and prior writings with respect thereto." This is probably not enough to exclude any terms which might otherwise be implied. An implied term is part of the agreement rather than an oral communication or prior writing.

2.4.1 Bankers and confidentiality

The starting point, and often the finishing point, of any consideration of a banker's obligation of confidentiality to its customers is *Tournier* v. *National Provincial and Union Bank of England*.[63] Tournier was overdrawn at the bank and had failed to honour arrangements to pay off his overdraft over time. The bank, when acting for another customer, saw a cheque passing through its hands drawn in Tournier's favour. It telephoned the collecting bank and discovered that Tournier had endorsed the cheque in favour of a bookmaker. In the course of a conversation with Tournier's employers, the bank told them of Tournier's indebtedness to it and of the cheque endorsed to the bookmaker. In the light of this information, Tournier's employers refused to renew his contract when it expired. Tournier sued the bank for slander and breach of an implied contractual obligation of confidentiality. By majority,[64] he succeeded in this latter claim.

The Court of Appeal accepted that a term could only be implied into a contract if it was necessary,[65] but felt that it was necessary in this case. There was no real analysis as to why it was necessary. The only explanation was offered by Bankes LJ:

"The privilege of non-disclosure to which a client or a customer is entitled may vary according to the exact nature of the relationship between the client or the customer and the person on whom the duty rests. It need not be the same in the case of the counsel, the solicitor, the doctor, and the banker, though the underlying principle may be the same. The case of the banker and his customer appears to me to be one in which the confidential relationship between the parties is very marked. The credit of the customer depends very largely upon the strict observance of that confidence."[66]

It has also been suggested that the confidential relationship arises from the fact that a contract between a bank and its customers embodies elements of agency or of a contract of highly personal services, or that a bank might be a customer's major or sole financier.[67] The reality is simply that financial affairs have traditionally been regarded as confidential, and will continue to be so. A company, unlike an individual, is obliged periodically to publish details of its financial status, but the financial affairs of both companies and individuals are treated as confidential regardless.

The obligation of confidentiality attaching to bankers is not absolute. There

63. [1924] 1 KB 461.

64. Scrutton LJ only dissented on the ground that the information in question was obtained not from the customer but a third party.

65. [1924] 1 KB 461, 480, 483.

66. [1924] 1 KB 461, 474.

67. Ellinger & Lomnicka, *Modern Banking Law* (2nd edn), pp 134–135. Neither explanation is convincing—banking is less and less a personal service, nor is a bank the agent of its customers in any meaningful way, and the obligation of confidentiality applies regardless of whether the bank is the only financier or one of numerous holding a minimal balance.

are four exceptions[68]: disclosure under compulsion of law; where there is a duty to the public[69]; where the interests of the bank require disclosure[70]; and where disclosure is made with the customer's express or implied consent.[70a] These are, however, very limited exceptions and, except in clear cases, relying on them will entail a degree of risk.

2.4.2 Are derivatives confidential?

The issue of whether derivatives are confidential is not susceptible of a clear, simple or uniform answer. It will depend upon the nature of the transaction and the nature of the relationship between the two parties to the contract. For example, if one party is a bank which, as part of wider banking services, offers its customer derivatives transactions to hedge foreign exchange or interest rate risk, that is likely to fall within the general obligation of confidentiality a bank owes to its customer. A bank would not, therefore, be free to reveal the existence of the transaction to any third party, still less of any default.

If, however, two financial institutions enter into a transaction at arm's length over the telephone, it is less obvious that there should be an obligation of confidence. In the traditional banking scenario, the obligation of confidence is owed by the bank to the customer, and the customer is free to reveal the state of its account at the bank if it wishes. In a trading situation, neither counterparty can properly be regarded as the customer of the other, and any obligation of confidentiality would have to be mutual rather than unilateral. This might point against there being any obligation, at least unless it was necessary to give business efficacy to a contract or where it is obvious from the factual matrix surrounding the contract that such a term was implicit. In the case of fast moving markets, it might be argued that the fact of two parties having entered into a particular deal on particular terms might of itself affect the market price, and therefore the ability of either party to close out the transaction at a profit or to hedge the position. This can, however, only justify some sort of temporary obligation of confidentiality, and the nature of open markets is that any particular market activity will rapidly be reflected in the market price. It may, therefore, be that there is no obligation of confidentiality as between market

68. *Tournier* v. *National Provincial and Union Bank of England* [1924] 1 KB 461, 473.

69. For example, where there is danger to the state (*Tournier* [1924] 1 KB 461, 473), but not merely because a customer is suspected of a crime (*Tournier* [1924] 1 KB 461, 474). This therefore seems to be a very limited exception.

70. For example, where a bank issues a writ claiming payment (*Tournier* [1924] 1 KB 461, 473). For these purposes, the interests of each company within a banking group must be regarded separately, and disclosure not made within the group: *Bank of Tokyo* v. *Karoon* [1987] 1 AC 45.

70a. In *Turner* v. *Royal Bank of Scotland* (unreported, 24 March 1999), the Court of Appeal held that giving a credit reference without a customer's consent was a breach of the bank's obligation of confidentiality. This was so notwithstanding that, at the material times (1986 to 1989), banks habitually did so. This usage was not, however, sufficiently notorious, certain and reasonable to pass into law.

counterparties, though the position is very far from clear.[71] It might, however, be that knowledge of what open positions one party has will affect its ability to close out those positions, or the price at which it can do so.

Between these two extremes there is potentially a range of situations where there might or might not be an obligation of confidentiality. In general, as between a financial institution and a party whose main business is something else, there should probably be a presumption that there is an obligation of confidentiality owed by the financial institution. Between market participants, it is less clear but arguable that there is no legal requirement to keep the existence or terms of a deal confidential, though it may be good practice to do so. For example, the London Code of Conduct provides that confidentiality "is essential for the preservation of a reputable and efficient market place", and states that principals and brokers share equal responsibility for maintaining confidentiality.[72] This does not, however, mean that it is necessary for the business efficacy of any particular transaction. In any event, the position of brokers is different from that of the principals to a transaction. At various times in a deal, a broker is likely to be the agent of one or other of the parties and, as a result, to owe a duty of confidentiality from that role rather than from any implication from the derivatives contract itself.

The consequences of any obligation of confidentiality would be, for example, that revealing the existence or terms of a transaction would be a breach of that obligation. This could occur if, for example, party A entered into a transaction with party B, and then entered into a back to back transaction with party C on terms that A would only pay to C sums equal to those it received from B. This would involve A telling C not only the terms of its contract with B but, more significantly, informing C if and when B defaulted on the transaction. If this led C to cross default other transactions with B, this could lead to a claim for damages.

71. It might be argued that market practice (see the next paragraph) imposes an obligation of confidentiality. In order to do this, the practice must be notorious, certain and reasonable, and not contrary to law (see *Chitty on Contracts* (27th edn), para 13–014). This requires an identification of the market in question, and then expert evidence on the practices of that market.

72. Para 41 of *The London Code of Conduct* (July 1995), issued by the Bank of England. This contrasts with, for example, pit trading where there is obviously very limited confidentiality.

CHAPTER 3

CAPACITY TO ENTER INTO DERIVATIVES TRANSACTIONS

3.1 INTRODUCTION

Bodies corporate have been most commonly created by statute or by royal charter.[1] Before the Joint Stock Companies Act 1844, it was necessary to obtain a private Act of Parliament in order to create a statutory body corporate for private purposes. This cumbersome and expensive process was undertaken by, for example, railway companies in need of compulsory purchase powers, which could only be granted by statute, in addition to separate legal personality. The Joint Stock Companies Act 1844 made incorporation far easier, allowing it merely by registration of certain particulars with the Registrar of Companies. This Act has long been replaced by a succession of Companies Acts but, because of its ease, the method of statutory incorporation which it introduced has become overwhelmingly the most common. Statutory incorporation by specific Act of Parliament is now in practice reserved for public bodies, such as local authorities.

Chartered corporations were used for commercial purposes,[2] but are now in general only created for educational, charitable and similar purposes. The simplicity of creating a body corporate by registration under the Companies Acts has rendered unnecessary the formality and expense of petitioning the sovereign for the grant of a charter.

Whatever the means by which a body corporate is created, the general approach in England has been to grant the "privilege"[3] of incorporation for one or more particular purposes and with certain express powers rather than by enabling the body to do whatever its management and members wish. This leads to the issue of who should bear the risk of the corporation's management acting

1. Certain corporations, such as bishops, exist at common law, but it seems unlikely that ecclesiastical office holders would wish to enter into derivatives transactions. The Mayor and Commonalty and Citizens of the City of London is also a corporation at common law.

2. Some, such as the Peninsular and Oriental Steam Navigation Company incorporated in 1840, still exist.

3. See, for example, *Ashbury Railway Carriage and Iron Company Limited* v. *Riche* (1875) LR 7 HL 653, 678 and 691.

outside the corporation's powers: the members and others who benefit from the incorporation, or third parties who deal with the corporation?

As far as chartered corporations are concerned, the answer to this question is that it is the members who bear the risk. A chartered corporation can do everything that an individual can do[4] unless restricted expressly or impliedly by statute.[5] A member may seek to restrain the corporation from acting improperly, or the crown may in those circumstances apply to the court to recall the charter, but contracts entered into with a third party remain valid and enforceable by the third party.[6]

The position of bodies incorporated by statute, whether under a private or public Act of Parliament or under the Companies Acts, is different. The courts regard the powers of a statutory corporation as being determined by the legislation which created it. They refused to draw the inference that Parliament intended to follow the legal position of chartered corporations and confer on a company all the powers of a natural person. The courts therefore concluded that a company only had those powers expressly or impliedly granted by statute.[7] In the words of Lord Cairns LC in *Ashbury Railway Carriage and Iron Company Limited* v. *Riche*,[8] "the existence, the coming into existence, of the company is to be an existence and to be a coming into existence for those objects [i.e. those set out in the company's memorandum of association] and for those objects alone." All actions and contracts outside these bounds are ultra vires and void. The risk arising from a corporation's management acting outside the limits of its constitutional documents was therefore placed on third parties dealing with the corporation rather than on the corporation's members. This same principle applies whether a corporation is created for public purposes (e.g. a local authority) or for private commercial purposes.

Despite imposing this risk on third parties, the courts have expressed the view that this rule is, in part at least, for the benefit of third parties.[9] Whilst a third party does, in theory at least, know[10] the nature of the business for which the company it is contracting with was incorporated (for example, whether it is high

4. *The Case of Sutton's Hospital* (1612) 10 Co Rep 1; *Baroness Wenlock* v. *River Dee Company* (1883) 34 Ch 674n, 685; *Bonanza Creek Gold Mining Company, Limited* v. *R* [1916] AC 566; *British South Africa Company* v. *De Beers Consolidated Mines Limited* [1910] 1 Ch 354, 374–376; *Jenkin* v. *Pharmaceutical Society of Great Britain* [1921] 1 Ch 392, 398.

5. *Hazell* v. *Hammersmith and Fulham London Borough Council* [1992] 2 AC 1, 43.

6. See the cases at note 4.

7. *Ashbury Railway Carriage and Iron Company Limited* v. *Riche* (1875) LR 7 HL 653.

8. (1875) LR 7 HL 653, 669.

9. See, for example, Lord Chelmsford in *Ashbury Railway Carriage and Iron Company Limited* v. *Riche* (1875) LR 7 HL 653, 679, and Lord Parker of Waddington in *Cotman* v. *Brougham* [1918] AC 514, 520. In the latter case, Lord Parker did recognise that "the narrower the objects expressed in the memorandum the less is the subscribers' risk, but the wider such objects the greater is the security of those who transact business with the company."

10. As a matter of common law, a third party is deemed to have notice of what is on the public register of a company: *Ernest* v. *Nicholls* (1857) 6 HLC 401. As far as companies incorporated under the Companies Acts are concerned, this rule will be abolished when (or if) section 711A of the Companies Act 1985 is brought into force.

risk, low risk or whatever), in practice this is unlikely to be of any significant value in assessing whether or not to enter into a contract. The ultra vires rule has instead generally been used by companies or their liquidators to seek to escape from the terms of contracts freely entered into. It has, however, been recognised that it is unattractive to allow company directors to use their own breach of duty in acting ultra vires to escape the consequences of a contract with a third party.[11] Two governmental committees on company law[12] recommended different ways to alleviate the effect of the rule on third parties, but nothing was done until impending membership of the European Community required reform, which was introduced in the European Communities Act 1972. This reform was the bare minimum the Government could get away with, and more radical reform had to await the Companies Act 1989.[13]

The effect of these reforms remains uncertain but their aim was to remove to a large extent the risk of the ultra vires rule from third parties dealing with companies incorporated under the Companies Acts. The reforms do not apply to other statutory bodies, such as local authorities. The ultra vires rule remains in full force for these bodies (as the financial institutions which entered into swaps and other transactions with local authorities will be only too well aware[14]).

Even where the ultra vires rule is, strictly speaking, not relevant, rules potentially to the same effect still exist. This is the case for, by way of example, insurance companies whose activities are closely regulated by statute. The remaining impact of the ultra vires rule on various types of body, and the provisions relating to bodies such as insurance companies, are discussed below.

11. See, for example, Lord Esher MR in *Baroness Wenlock* v. *River Dee Company* (1883) 36 Ch D 674n, 675. In *Bell Houses Limited* v. *City Wall Properties Limited* [1966] 2 QB 656, Danckwerts LJ observed (at p 685) that no one paid much attention to the memorandum "unless someone wishes to wriggle out of some obligation". In *Bell Houses*, one party to a contract argued that the contract was ultra vires its counterparty which could not therefore enforce the contract. Salmon LJ described the point as "conspicuously lacking in merit of any kind" (p 689), but the court left open the question of whether one party could rely on the fact that a contract was ultra vires its counterparty to escape its obligations (though Salmon LJ (p 694) clearly thought it could not). The conventional view, however, is that as ultra vires acts are void, neither the company nor its counterparty can enforce the contract: see Gower, *The Modern Law of Companies* (5th edn), p 168.

12. The Cohen Committee (1945 Cmnd 6659) and the Jenkins Committee (1962 Cmnd 1749).

13. The reforms are discussed in the section relating to companies below. These reforms followed a paper published by the Department of Trade and Industry, *Reform of Ultra Vires, a Consultative Document*, in which the Department recognised that the ultra vires rule "represents an obstacle to enterprise and works so capriciously that it is doubtful whether it offers any real protection to anyone".

14. For example, *Hazell* v. *Hammersmith and Fulham London Borough Council* [1992] 2 AC 1 (swaps) and *Credit Suisse* v. *Allerdale* [1996] 2 Lloyd's Rep 241 (guarantee).

3.2 COMPANIES INCORPORATED UNDER THE COMPANIES ACTS

The reforms introduced by the Companies Act 1989 did not abolish the ultra vires rule[15] but instead seek to mitigate its worst effects. The relevant issues when considering whether a company has (or had) power to enter into a particular derivatives transaction are: first, whether the transaction proposed is expressly or impliedly authorised by the company's memorandum of association; secondly, if so, whether there is any reason to believe that the directors are exercising the power to enter into the transaction for an improper purpose[16]; and, thirdly, if not, whether the transaction is nevertheless enforceable by virtue of sections 35, 35A and/or 35B of the Companies Act 1985.

3.2.1 The express terms of a company's memorandum of association

A company is obliged to state the purposes for which it is incorporated in the objects clause of its memorandum of association.[17] This clause may take one of two forms: the new form introduced by section 3A of the Companies Act 1985[18]; or the conventional form required since companies legislation was first passed in the mid-nineteenth century.

Section 3A of the Companies Act 1985 allows a company to state that its object is to carry on business as a "general commercial company", which means that the object of the company is to "carry on any trade or business whatsoever, and ... [that it] has power to do all such things as are incidental or conducive to the carrying on of any trade or business by it". The meaning of this has not been tested in the courts, but the aim is that in substance the ultra vires rule should not apply to the company. The effectiveness of section 3A to achieve this aim has been doubted (for example, is the giving of security for the debts of other companies or entering into gratuitous transactions the conduct of a trade or business or incidental or conducive to it?[19]), and what this section actually achieves remains uncertain. Objects clauses of this sort are therefore rare.

As far as entering into derivatives are concerned, however, these doubts are probably not relevant since it is possible for the entry into derivatives transactions to be either part of a trade or business or incidental or conducive to another trade or business.[20] If, therefore, a potential counterparty has an objects

15. The ultra vires rule has been abolished in certain Commonwealth jurisdictions, e.g. by section 7 of the Canada Corporations Act 1975: see Poole, 12 Co Law 43. Some, however, question whether the second EC Company Law Directive would allow abolition since it requires a company to have objects.

16. This is not strictly an issue going to whether the transaction is ultra vires the company but it can usefully be dealt with here.

17. Section 2(1)(c) of the Companies Act 1985.

18. The section was inserted in the Act by section 110(1) of the Companies Act 1989 with effect from 4 February 1991.

19. See, for example, Poole, 12 Co Law 43, 45 and Ferran, 13 Co Law 177, 183.

20. But see the discussion below about implied powers.

clause of this sort, it probably does have the corporate capacity to enter into a derivatives transaction.

The more usual, and until recently obligatory, form of the objects clause in a memorandum of association sets out the business for which the company has been incorporated (e.g. to build cars). The models for these clauses included in the legislation have been brief.[21] However, the practice has for many years been to extend them to cover as much as practicable in order to seek to evade the restrictions of the ultra vires rule. In addition to this sheer length, objects clauses usually also include powers (e.g. to borrow money) which could be used to achieve those objects.[22] The courts have grudgingly accepted that there was little they could do about these practices.[23] These practices have, therefore, been successful in widening the scope of what a company can do.

Does the fact that a company's objects clause expressly includes entering into derivatives transactions as an object or power mean that derivatives transactions are intra vires the company? The answer to this question is yes. The clearest expression of the position as it currently stands is in *Rolled Steel (Products) Holdings Limited* v. *British Steel Corporation*,[24] where Slade LJ set out six principles governing the area:

"(1) The basic rule is that a company incorporated under the Companies Acts only has the capacity to do those acts which fall within its objects as set out in its memorandum of association or are reasonably incidental to the attainment or pursuit of those objects. Ultimately, therefore, the question whether a particular transaction is within or outside its capacity must depend on the true construction of the memorandum.

(2) Nevertheless, if a particular act ... is of a category which, on the true construction

21. Formerly the clauses were in the legislation itself (such as Table B to the Companies Act 1948) but they are now set out in statutory instruments made under section 3 of the Companies Act 1985 (currently SI 1985 No 805 amended by SI 1985 No 1052). Table B to the Companies Act 1948 provided that the (hypothetical) company's objects were "the carriage of passengers and goods in ships or boats between such places as the company may from time to time determine and the doing of all such other things as are incidental or conducive to the attainment of that object". The version in the SI made under the Companies Act 1985 is the same but, reflecting the decline in Britain's fleet, refers instead to "the carriage of passengers and goods in motor vehicles".

22. Even if the objects clause in a memorandum of association includes powers and a clause stating that each clause should be construed independently and not as subsidiary to others (a clause inserted to escape the consequences of *Re German Date Coffee Company* (1882) 20 Ch D 169), a clause might still be construed as a mere power if it is incapable of existing as a separate object or if it can only be construed as a power ancillary to the other objects: *Rolled Steel* v. *British Steel Corporation* [1986] Ch 246, 306. In *International Sales* v. *Marcus* [1982] 3 All ER 551, Lawson J appeared to regard a power to sign cheques as only being ancillary to other objects (p 557).

23. *Cotman* v. *Brougham* [1918] AC 514. In *Cotman*, some members of the House of Lords were of the view that the use of long objects clauses fell outside the intention of the legislation and that the Registrar of Companies should not accept them (see, for example, Lord Finlay LC at p 519 and Lord Wrenbury at p 523). There was, however, nothing that they could do about the point in that case because section 17 of the Companies (Consolidation) Act 1908 (now section 13(7) of the Companies Act 1985) provided that the certificate of incorporation was conclusive evidence that the requirements for registration had been complied with. The Registrar of Companies appears to have remained of the view that long objects clauses are acceptable.

24. [1986] Ch 246.

of the company's memorandum, is *capable*[25] of being performed as reasonably incidental to the attainment or pursuit of its objects, it will not be rendered ultra vires the company merely because in a particular instance its directors, in performing the act in its name, are in truth doing so for purposes other than those set out in its memorandum. Subject to any express restrictions on the relevant power which may be contained in the memorandum, the state of mind or knowledge of the persons managing the company's affairs or of the persons dealing with it is irrelevant in considering questions of corporate capacity.

(3) While due regard must be paid to any express conditions attached to limitations on powers contained in a company's memorandum (e.g. power to borrow only up to a specified amount), the court will not ordinarily construe a statement in a memorandum that a particular power is exercisable 'for the purposes of the company' as a condition limiting the company's corporate capacity to exercise the power; it will regard it as simply imposing a limit on the authority of the directors ...

(4) At least in default of the unanimous consent of all the shareholders ... the directors of a company will not have actual power from the company to exercise any express or implied powers other than for the purposes of the company as set out in its memorandum of association.

(5) A company holds it directors out as having ostensible authority to bind the company to any transaction which falls within the powers expressly or impliedly conferred on it by its memorandum of association. Unless he is put on notice to the contrary, a person dealing in good faith with a company which is carrying on an intra vires business[26] is entitled to assume that its directors are properly exercising such powers for the purposes of the company as set out in its memorandum.[27] Correspondingly, such a person in such circumstances can hold the company to any transaction of this nature.

(6) If, however, a person dealing with a company is on notice that the directors are exercising the relevant power for purposes other than the purposes of the company, he cannot rely on the ostensible authority of the directors and on ordinary principles of agency, cannot hold the company to the transaction."[28]

In summary, this means that if a company has in its memorandum of

25. Slade LJ's emphasis. If on the true construction of a company's memorandum, a particular act is capable of being performed by the company for any reason, that act is within the company's *capacity*.

26. This qualification that the company must be carrying on intra vires business appears illogical and unnecessary. If all the company's business is ultra vires, but a third party dealing with the company does not, and has no cause to, know that, there seems no reason why the third party should not enforce a contract if the contract itself is within the company's capacity. This reference might have been included as a passing nod to Russell LJ's judgment in *Re Introductions* [1970] Ch 199 (see Slade LJ's judgment at 293–294). In *Rolled Steel*, Browne-Wilkinson LJ, though expressing his agreement with Slade LJ, did not include a similar qualification.

27. This is an expression of the rule in *Royal British Bank* v. *Turquand* (1856) 6 E & B 327. The rule, as expressed in para 980 of vol 7(1) of *Halsbury's Laws* (4th edn) and approved by Lord Simonds in the House of Lords in *Morris* v. *Kanssen* [1946] AC 459, 475, is that "persons dealing in good faith with a company may assume that acts within its constitution and powers have been properly and duly performed and are not bound to inquire whether acts of internal management have been regular."

28. [1986] Ch 246, 295. Similar views have been expressed in, for example, *Re David Payne & Co Limited* [1904] 2 Ch 608, 613 and 619, *Cotman* v. *Brougham* [1918] AC 514, 521 and *Charterbridge Corporation* v. *Lloyds Bank* [1970] Ch 62. In *Re Introductions* [1970] Ch 199, the Court of Appeal perhaps expressed the view that even if a power (e.g. to borrow) was expressly given in a memorandum, any exercise by the directors of that power for improper purposes would still be ultra vires and void. The doubts raised by that case were put to rest in *Rolled Steel*. The actual decision on the facts in *Re Introductions* is entirely consistent with the principles set out by Slade LJ in *Rolled Steel*.

association the express power to enter into derivatives contracts (i.e. the entry into a derivatives contract is within its capacity), doing so will not be ultra vires the company. A derivatives contract will not therefore be void. Although intra vires, a derivatives transaction might nevertheless be unenforceable by the counterparty if it was on notice that the company's directors were acting outside their powers. For this purpose, notice means not just actual notice; it is enough that the circumstances of the transaction are such as to put the counterparty on enquiry.[29] A counterparty might be put on enquiry by, for example, the volume of derivatives transactions undertaken where the power to enter into derivatives is expressed to be ancillary to another business rather than as a business on its own or the nature of the transaction itself. Ultimately, what is sufficient to put a counterparty on enquiry will depend upon all the particular circumstances.[30]

3.2.2 Implied powers

In addition to those matters referred to expressly in its memorandum of association, a company has implied power to do all acts incidental to or consequential upon those objects. As Lord Selborne LC said in *Attorney-General* v. *Great Eastern Railway*, the ultra vires doctrine "ought to be reasonably, and not unreasonably, understood and applied, and that whatever may fairly be regarded as incidental to, or consequential upon, those things which the legislature has authorised, ought not (unless expressly prohibited) to be held, by judicial construction, to be ultra vires".[31] In *Attorney-General* v. *Smethwick Corporation*, Lord Hanworth MR said that "the corporation have exercised their discretion within the area entrusted to them, and under those circumstances it seems impossible to hold that they are not authorised to take the further steps which prudence dictates and modern mechanism renders possible."[32]

As a result, if derivatives are not expressly mentioned in a memorandum of association, it may be that the company has the implied power to enter into derivatives transactions. To establish whether a company does have this implied power, it is first necessary to identify an express object or power in relation to which a derivatives transaction can be regarded as incidental or consequential. If, for example, a company is established to manufacture copper wire, that is probably sufficient to give the company the implied power to enter into copper futures transactions, at least in so far as the transactions can be used to hedge the risk of movements in the copper price. However, it is probably not sufficient to entitle the company to run a copper derivatives operation as a separate profit

29. *Rolled Steel* v. *British Steel Corporation* [1986] Ch 246, 284 (relying on *Morris* v. *Kanssen* [1946] AC 459, 475) and 306. This might, however, be affected by the "knowledge" requirement for constructive trusts, and the precise description of the state of knowledge required might follow a resolution of the uncertainties in that area: see pp 50–54 below.

30. *Rolled Steel* v. *British Steel Corporation* [1986] Ch 246, 285.

31. (1880) 5 App Cas 473, 478.

32. [1932] Ch 562, 578.

centre unrelated to its physical copper needs.[33] But even if, in this example, a copper derivatives operation were to be run as a separate and improper business operation, the principles set out by Slade LJ in *Rolled Steel* v. *British Steel Corporation*[34] are still applicable. This means that derivatives remain within the corporate capacity of the company, and a contract will only be unenforceable by a counterparty if the counterparty is on notice of the improper purpose for which derivatives are being used.

As far as purely financial transactions are concerned, the extent to which derivatives can be viewed as incidental to or consequential upon other corporate activities has never been tested in the courts. However, in *Hazell* v. *Hammersmith*,[35] the House of Lords did discuss whether interest rate swaps and other similar transactions[36] were "calculated to facilitate, or [are] conducive or incidental to the discharge"[37] of a local authority's power to borrow. In that case, Lord Templeman[38] was doubtful whether these transactions were calculated to facilitate or were conducive to borrowing, but he did appear to concede reluctantly that they might be capable of being incidental to borrowing.[39] In the *Hammersmith* case, however, Lord Templeman decided that whether a particular power is incidental to another had to be viewed in the light of the statutory provisions governing a local authority's borrowing power. He took the view that those provisions set out a comprehensive code defining and limiting a local authority's borrowing power, leaving no room for any incidental power to enter into swap transactions.[40] Companies are not in general surrounded by the same statutory restrictions as local authorities, and this objection is not, therefore, likely to apply.

Even if it is difficult as a matter of construction of a company's memorandum of association to imply the power to enter into derivatives transactions, there may be one other source for this power. It is common for a company to include in the objects clause of its memorandum of association a provision stating, for example, that a company may "carry on any other trade or business whatsoever which can, in the opinion of the board of directors, be advantageously carried on by the company in connection with or as ancillary to any of the above businesses

33. Many of the cases in which transactions have been held to be ultra vires (which in the twentieth century have generally concerned local authorities) have involved the establishment of separate business ventures: for example, *London County Council* v. *Attorney-General* [1902] AC 165, *Dundee Harbour Trustees* v. *D & J Nichol* [1915] AC 550 and *Attorney-General* v. *Fulham Corporation* [1921] 1 Ch 440.

34. [1986] Ch 246; see pp 43–44 above.

35. [1992] 2 AC 1.

36. Interest rate swap options, caps, collars, floors, forward rate agreements, gilt options and cash options; see [1990] QB 697, 739–741.

37. Section 111(1) of the Local Government Act 1972. This is a statutory embodiment of the position which would in any event be implied: [1992] 2 AC 1, 29.

38. With whom all the other members of the House of Lords agreed.

39. [1992] 2 AC 1, 29–30. Lord Templeman was, however, troubled by the fact that swaps could happen long after a loan had been taken.

40. [1992] 2 AC 1, 29–34.

of the company". In *Bell Houses Limited* v. *City Wall Properties Limited*,[41] the Court of Appeal accepted that as long as the directors have taken a bona fide decision about a particular activity in accordance with the clause, then that activity is intra vires the company. As Salmon LJ said:

"An object of the plaintiff company is to carry on any business which the directors genuinely believe can be carried on advantageously in connection with or as ancillary to the general business of the company. It may be that the directors take the wrong view and in fact the business cannot be carried on as the directors believe. But it matters not how mistaken the directors may be. Provided they form their view honestly, the business is within the plaintiff company's objects and powers."[42]

How does a counterparty know that the board of directors has formed the required honest view? According to Danckwerts LJ in *Bell Houses,* this "is a matter of internal management principally. Persons dealing with the company in the course of the trade or business are helped rather than hindered by a provision of this sort."[43] This is a reference to the rule in *Royal British Bank* v. *Turquand*[44] under which "persons dealing in good faith with a company may assume that acts within its constitution and powers have been properly and duly performed and are not bound to inquire whether acts of internal management have been regular."[45] A counterparty may, therefore, be entitled to assume that the directors have honestly reached a decision that a derivatives business can be carried on ancillary to the other businesses of the company. This does require the counterparty to be acting in good faith. The farther and more removed derivatives are from the company's other businesses, the less likely it is that the courts will accept that a counterparty is acting in good faith as opposed to shutting its eyes to the obvious fact that the directors are acting in breach of their duties to the company.

3.2.3 The enforceability of an ultra vires transaction

The need for the reform of the ultra vires law (as opposed to the desirability of reform) arose when the UK became a member of the European Community on 1 January 1973. Article 9 of the EC's First Council Directive on Company Law[46]

41. [1966] 2 QB 656. The clause quoted was that under consideration in the *Bell Houses* case.
42. [1966] 2 QB 656, 690. In his paper prepared for the Department of Trade and Industry and published in 1986 as an annexe to the Department's *Reform of the Ultra Vires Rule, a Consultative Paper*, Professor D D Prentice commented that "*Bell Houses* comes close to authorising a company to carry on whatever business it chooses provided its objects contain an appropriately worded 'subjective' objective clause."
43. [1966] 2 QB 656, 683–684. Sellers LJ agreed with Danckwerts LJ (p 672).
44. (1856) 6 E & B 327. *Turquand* was not in fact expressly cited in *Bell Houses*.
45. This quote is the rule as expressed in para 980 of vol 7(1) of *Halsbury's Laws* (4th edn) which was approved by Lord Simonds in *Morris* v. *Kanssen* [1946] AC 459, 475.
46. 1968, OJ 41.

required that acts done by the organs[47] of a company which are outside the company's objects should, nevertheless, be binding on the company. The Directive does, however, allow member states to provide that a company shall not be bound if the third party knew that the act was outside the company's objects or could not in view of the circumstances have been unaware of this. The Directive also provides that where an organ of a company does an act which is intra vires, limits on the power of that organ in the company's constitution may never be relied on as against third parties.

Parliament has made two attempts to give effect to this Directive: section 9(1) of the European Communities Act 1972 (later consolidated into the original section 35 of the Companies Act 1985); and, with effect from 4 February 1991, a new section 35, together with sections 35A and 35B, of the Companies Act 1985 inserted by section 108 of the Companies Act 1989. Despite these two attempts,[48] Parliament has yet to achieve a position which is either clear or coherent.

3.2.3.1 Corporate capacity

Section 35 of the Companies Act 1985 now provides that[49]:

> "(1) The validity of an act done by a company shall not be called into question on the ground of lack of capacity by reason of anything in the company's memorandum.
>
> (2) A member of a company may bring proceedings to restrain the doing of any act which but for subsection (1) would be beyond the company's capacity; but no such proceedings shall lie in respect of an act done in fulfilment of a legal obligation arising from a previous act of the company.
>
> (3) It remains the duty of the directors to observe any limitations on their powers flowing from the company's memorandum; and action by the directors which but for subsection (1) would be beyond the company's capacity may only be ratified by the company by special resolution.
>
> A resolution ratifying such action shall not affect any liability incurred by the directors or any other person; relief from such liability must be agreed separately by special resolution."

Section 35(1) of the Companies Act 1985 is accordingly clear that a company cannot on the grounds of ultra vires alone seek to escape from a transaction. This allows a counterparty to enforce an ultra vires transaction.

Section 35 is, however, not clear whether the company is also entitled to

47. "Organ" is not a term commonly used in England. The distinction appears to be between an agent of the company and an organ of the company, which can give the agent actual authority. An individual director will generally be an agent but the board of directors will be an organ.

48. The latter with the assistance of a report by an academic, Professor D D Prentice of the University of Oxford. Professor Prentice's report was published by the Department of Trade and Industry in 1986 as an annexe to a paper entitled *Reform of the Ultra Vires Rule: a Consultative Document*.

49. Omitting those parts dealing with charities, the position of which is different. The position of transactions between a company and a counterparty "connected" or "associated" with one of the company's directors is also different, and is discussed below.

enforce the transaction, at least without first obtaining a ratifying resolution from the company's shareholders. Section 35(1) suggests that neither the counterparty nor the company can call an act into question on the ground of ultra vires (it does not say "shall not be called into question *by the company* on the ground of lack of capacity"). However, if that is the correct interpretation, much of section 35(3) becomes otiose. A ratifying resolution would be pointless if the company could enforce the transaction anyway—it would not excuse the directors from any claims the company might otherwise have against them because section 35(3) is clear that an extra resolution is required for that purpose. As a result, it seems more likely that a company cannot enforce a transaction without first obtaining a resolution from its shareholders ratifying the transaction. This interpretation would also retain the orthodox view that neither party to an ultra vires transaction could (apart from section 35) enforce it because it is void, and not voidable,[50] and would credit section 35 with protecting the counterparty only but not automatically the company and its shareholders.[51] For a third party to take the point that whilst he could enforce a transaction against the company, the company could not enforce it against him is, however, likely to be viewed as highly unattractive.

3.2.3.2 Abuse of powers

Section 35 is not on its own enough to protect counterparties. A major difficulty with the 1989 reforms concerns the authority of the directors of a company to enter into ultra vires transactions. The directors of a company have no authority to bind the company to acts outside its corporate capacity,[52] and a counterparty is deemed to have notice of what is on the public record of the company,[53] and therefore to be aware of the directors' inability to bind the company. The counterparty cannot therefore contend that the transaction is that of the company. As a result of this problem, sections 35A and 35B of the Companies Act 1985 provide that:

> "35A(1) In favour of a person dealing with a company in good faith, the power of the board of directors to bind the company, or authorise others to do so, shall be deemed to be free of any limitation in the company's constitution.
>
> (2) For this purpose—

50. See, for example, the first instance decision in *Bell Houses* v. *City Wall Properties* [1966] 1 QB 207 (though this position was doubted by Salmon LJ in the Court of Appeal [1966] 2 QB 656, 693–694) and Gower, *The Modern Law of Companies* (5th edn), p 168.

51. The view that section 35 does not allow a company to enforce an ultra vires transaction without first ratifying it is taken by J Poole, 12 Co Law 43, and E Ferran, 13 Co Law 124 and 177. It is not, however, universally held; for example, the editors of *Gore-Browne on Company Law* (44th edn) do not agree, and contend that the company could enforce an ultra vires transaction without need for a ratifying resolution.

52. *TCB* v. *Gray* [1986] Ch 621, 636. See also *Meridian Global Funds Management Asia Ltd* v. *Securities Commission* [1995] 3 WLR 413, 418–419.

53. *Ernest* v. *Nicholls* (1857) 6 HLC 401. Section 711A of the Companies Act 1985 will, when (or if) brought into force, abolish this rule.

(a) a person 'deals with' a company if he is a party to any transaction or other act to which the company is a party;
(b) a person shall not be regarded as acting in bad faith by reason only of his knowing that an act is beyond the powers of the directors under the company's constitution; and
(c) a person shall be presumed to have acted in good faith unless the contrary is proved.

...

(5) [Subsection (1)] does not affect any liability incurred by the directors, or any other person, by reason of the directors exceeding their powers.

...

35B A party to a transaction with a company is not bound to enquire as to whether it is permitted by the company's memorandum or as to any limitation on the powers of the board of directors to bind the company or authorise others to do so."

Accordingly, a counterparty may treat the directors of a company as having power to bind the company to any act as long as the counterparty is acting in good faith. Knowing that the directors do not have power to bind the company is insufficient to establish bad faith—something else is required.[54] Section 35B provides that a counterparty is not bound to enquire whether a transaction is permitted by a company's articles of association, and therefore the failure to make that enquiry cannot of itself be bad faith.[55] Knowledge that the directors of the company are by the transaction intending to defraud the company is likely to be sufficient, but what, short of criminal acts, will suffice is not clear.[56]

3.2.3.3 *Constructive trusts*

But this is not the only problem with these sections.[57] In *International Sales* v. *Marcus*,[58] Lawson J decided that section 9(1) of the European Communities Act

54. In *Barclays Bank* v. *TOSG* [1984] BCLC 1, 18, Nourse J said that good faith for the purposes of section 9(1) of the European Communities Act 1972 was a subjective concept, and that it meant acting "genuinely and honestly in the circumstances of the case". As to whether it can be regarded as entirely subjective, see *Royal Brunei Airlines* v. *Tan* [1995] 2 AC 378 (a case about constructive trusts) and *International Sales* v. *Marcus* [1982] 3 All ER 551, 559 where Lawson J said (echoing the wording of article 9 of the EC's First Council Directive on Company Law) with regard to section 9(1) that it would be bad faith where "a person could not in view of all the circumstances, have been unaware that he was a party to a transaction ultra vires".
55. *TCB* v. *Gray* [1986] Ch 621, 636.
56. The position will be further complicated when (or if) section 711A of the Companies Act 1985 (inserted by section 142(1) of the Companies Act 1989) comes into force. Section 711A(1) provides that a person "shall not be taken to have notice of any matter merely because of its being disclosed in any document kept by the registrar of companies" but section 711A(2) goes on in contradictory fashion to provide that this "does not affect the question whether a person is affected by notice of any matter by reason of a failure to make such enquiries as ought reasonably to be made".
57. See the discussion by E Ferran, 13 Co Law 124 and 177.
58. [1983] 3 All ER 551.

1972[59] did not affect liability as a constructive trustee. Sections 35, 35A and 35B of the Companies Act 1985 do not appear to have changed this position; indeed section 35A(5), which specifically retains liability of the directors "and others" arising from breach by the directors of their powers, could be treated as confirming the point. As a result, there is a risk that even if a transaction is ultra vires but still enforceable by virtue of these provisions of the Companies Acts, the other party might be liable to the company as a constructive trustee.

Liability as a constructive trustee can arise in two ways: first, through the receipt of trust property transferred in breach of trust; and, secondly, through assisting a trustee in the breach of his fiduciary duties to the trust.[60] A company is not a trust, but directors are fiduciaries and that suffices for these purposes.[61] Neither assistance nor receipt is on its own enough to lead to liability as a constructive trustee; in addition, the receiver or assister must have "knowledge" of the breach of fiduciary duties.[62] There is, however, uncertainty as to what "knowledge" means for these purposes.[63]

With regard to "knowing assistance" (or "accessory liability"), in *Royal Brunei Airlines* v. *Tan*[64] the Privy Council decided that the requisite state of mind was dishonesty. Lord Nicholls said that:

> "... in the context of the accessory liability principle, acting dishonestly, or with a lack of probity, which is synonymous, means simply not acting as an honest person would in the circumstances. This is an objective standard. At first sight this may seem surprising. Honesty has a connotation of subjectivity, as distinct from the objectivity of negligence. Honesty, indeed, does have a strong subjective element in that it is a description of a type of conduct assessed in the light of what a person actually knew at the time, as distinct

59. Section 9(1) of the European Communities Act 1972 provided that: "In favour of a person dealing in good faith, any transaction decided on by the directors shall be deemed to be one which is within the capacity of the company to enter into, and the power of the directors to bind the company shall be deemed to be free of any limitation under the memorandum or articles of association; and a party to a transaction so decided upon shall not be bound to enquire as to the capacity of the company to enter into it or as to any limitation on the powers of the directors and shall be deemed to have acted in good faith unless the contrary is proved."

60. For a more detailed discussion than is appropriate here see, for example, Underhill & Hayton, *The Law Relating to Trusts and Trustees* (15th edn), pp 45ff.

61. *Selangor United Rubber Estates* v. *Cradock (No 3)* [1968] 1 WLR 1555; *Royal Brunei Airlines* v. *Tan* [1995] 2 AC 378, 386.

62. For this reason the two heads of liability as a constructive trustee have traditionally been called "knowing receipt" and "knowing assistance". However, in *Royal Brunei Airlines* v. *Tan* [1995] 2 AC 378, Lord Nicholls thought knowledge was better avoided in defining the ingredients of "knowing assistance", and favoured calling "knowing assistance" "accessory liability".

63. See the review of the authorities by S Gardner (1996) 112 LQR 56. The issue is whether actual knowledge of breach of trust is required or whether some sort of constructive knowledge or notice is enough, i.e. which of the following, in addition to actual knowledge, will suffice: (a) shutting one's eyes to the obvious, (b) wilfully and recklessly failing to make the enquiries a reasonable man would make, (c) knowledge of circumstances that would indicate the facts to a reasonable man, or (d) knowledge of circumstances that would put an honest and reasonable man on enquiry. (a) and (b) are often called constructive knowledge, (c) and (d) notice. With actual knowledge, this is the scale of knowledge put forward in *Baden* v. *Société Générale pour Favouriser* (note) [1993] 1 WLR 509 but which was disapproved by Lord Nicholls in *Royal Brunei Airlines* v. *Tan* [1995] 2 AC 378, 392 with regard to accessory liability.

64. [1995] 2 AC 378.

from what a reasonable person would have known or appreciated. Further, honesty and its counterpart dishonesty are mostly concerned with advertent conduct, not inadvertent conduct. Carelessness is not dishonesty. Thus for the most part dishonesty is to be equated with conscious impropriety. However, these subjective characteristics of honesty do not mean that individuals are free to set their own standards of honesty in particular circumstances. The standard of what constitutes honest conduct is not subjective. Honesty is not an optional scale, with higher or lower values according to the moral standards of each individual. If a person knowingly appropriates another's property, he will not escape a finding of dishonesty simply because he sees nothing wrong in such behaviour.

In most situations there is little difficulty in identifying how an honest person would behave. Honest people do not intentionally deceive others to their detriment. Honest people do not knowingly take others' property. Unless there is a very good and compelling reason, an honest person does not participate in a transaction if he knows it involves a misapplication of trust assets to the detriment of the beneficiaries. Nor does an honest person in such a case deliberately close his eyes and ears, or deliberately not ask questions, lest he learn something he would rather not know, and then proceed regardless. However in the situations now under consideration the position is not so straightforward ...

...

The only answer to these questions [what an honest person would do when there is doubt] lies in keeping in mind that honesty is an objective standard. The individual is expected to attain the standard which would be observed by an honest person placed in those circumstances. It is impossible to be more specific. Knox J captured the flavour of this, in a commercial setting, when he referred to a person who is 'guilty of commercially unacceptable conduct in the particular context involved' ... Acting in reckless disregard of others' rights or possible rights can be a tell-tale sign of dishonesty. An honest person would have regard to the circumstances known to him ..."[65]

The requirement of "knowledge" for the knowing receipt head of constructive trust liability may well now be the same as for accessory liability, though judicial expressions of the test have not been consistent.[66] In commercial transactions, the courts have often been concerned not to impose too onerous obligations on the recipients of money. As Millett J said in *El Ajou* v. *Dollar Land Holdings*: "A recipient is not expected to be unduly suspicious and is not to be held [to have notice] unless he went ahead without further inquiry in circumstances in which an honest and reasonable man would have realised that the money was trust money and was probably being misapplied."[67] In *Macmillan* v. *Bishopsgate Investment Trust*, Millett J went further and said that: "In order to establish constructive notice it is necessary to prove that the facts

65. [1995] 2 AC 378, 389–390.

66. In *Dubai Aluminium* v. *Salaam* (*The Times*, 4 September 1998), Rix J treated the test for knowing receipt as the same for accessory liability (or "dishonest assistance" as he called it). Prior to this and *Royal Brunei Airlines*, there were suggestions that the knowledge requirement for knowing receipt was less stringent than for accessory liability: see, for example, *El Ajou* v. *Dollar Land Holdings* [1993] 3 All ER 717, *Macmillan* v. *Bishopsgate Investment Trust* [1995] 1 WLR 978, *Eagle Trust* v. *SBC Securities* [1993] 1 WLR 484, *Cowan de Groot Properties* v. *Eagle Trust* [1992] 4 All ER 700, *Polly Peck International* v. *Nadir (No 2)* [1992] 2 All ER 769 and *Eagle Trust* v. *SBC Securities (No 2)* (unreported, 28 July 1994). The reported cases are discussed by S Gardner (1996) 112 LQR 56.

67. [1993] 3 All ER 717, 739.

known to the defendant made it imperative for him to seek an explanation, because in the absence of an explanation it was obvious that the transaction was probably improper."[68] In the light of these concerns, the courts have tended to impose liability only when a want of probity was present, the linguistic differences in how this is expressed having little relevance in practice.[69]

Whatever the final position for a knowing receipt constructive trust, a swap counterparty or arranger who knows that the company with whom it proposes to enter into an agreement has no legal capacity to do so is left in an unfortunate position. Section 35 of the Companies Act 1985 provides protection from an allegation that the transaction is ultra vires the company, and section 35A provides protection from an allegation that the directors had no authority to enter into the transaction on behalf of the company. Mere knowledge that the directors are acting outside their powers is not on its own sufficient to create bad faith for the purposes of the statute. The risk, nevertheless, remains that there could be liability as a constructive trustee. In *Royal Brunei Airlines* v. *Tan*,[70] Lord Nicholls said that reckless disregard of another's rights might be dishonesty for the purposes of accessory liability, and the position is unlikely to differ significantly for knowing assistance. Someone who knows that a derivatives transaction is not permitted by a company's memorandum of association is acting in disregard of the shareholders' rights to insist on the directors' observing limitations in the company's memorandum. The risk of being held liable as a constructive trustee is, therefore, real. If there were to be liability, it would, however, severely reduce the protection supposedly given in the 1989 reforms and render otiose section 35A(2)(b) of the Companies Act 1985 (which provides that for the purposes of that section, a person is not to be regarded as acting in bad faith by reason only of his knowing that an act is beyond the powers of the directors under the company's constitution). The company might not be able to object to the transaction on the ground that it is ultra vires, but the company might still be able to recover sums paid to its counterparty on the basis of a constructive trust. The party dealing with the company would therefore be in no improved position as a result of section 35A.

One argument against this result is that the Companies Act 1985 (as amended) defines dishonesty for the purposes of assessing whether someone is liable as a constructive trustee. Section 35A(2)(b) states that a person is not to be

68. [1995] 1 WLR 978, 1014.

69. In *Eagle Trust* v. *SBC Securities* (unreported, 28 July 1994), Arden J required actual knowledge, wilfully shutting one's eyes to the obvious or wilfully and recklessly failing to make such enquiries as an honest and reasonable man would have done. She did, however, say that this applied "where the receipt occurs in discharge of a lawful debt (at least one arising out of a transaction which does not itself constitute a breach of trust)". This restriction was probably raised in order to distinguish the Court of Appeal case of *Belmont Finance* v. *Williams (No 2)* [1980] 1 All ER 393 which arguably puts forward a lower threshold of "knowledge" than Arden J considered appropriate. This possible difference in approach, however, is not easy to sustain either in principle or on the authorities, and the matter might simply come down to the extent of suspicion a reasonable man is expected to show in the circumstances.

70. [1995] 2 AC 378.

treated as acting in bad faith, which is similar to, if not the same as, dishonesty, merely because he knows that an act is beyond the powers of the directors. If a person is not regarded by statute as being in bad faith, it is not for the courts to hold otherwise in the context of a constructive trust. This argument does not fall foul of section 35A(5) because that subsection only provides that section 35A(1) does not affect the liability incurred by reason of the directors of a company exceeding their powers, leaving the possibility that section 35A(2)(b) might do so.[71] This leaves open the possibility of a finding of some extra ingredient sufficient to create bad faith on the part of a counterparty and therefore to prevent the counterparty enforcing the transaction. This same extra ingredient could to lead to liability as a constructive trustee, whether or not there was actual receipt of the company's funds (for example, someone arranging an ultra vires swap to go with an intra vires bond issue could have constructive trust accessory liability even though it did not receive any payments on the swap).

3.2.4 Should a company's memorandum be inspected?

This ought to have been an easy question to answer in that the implementation of the EC's First Council Directive on Company Law should have rendered inspection unnecessary. The confused implementation of the (confusing) Directive does, however, make it difficult. Whatever arguments can be made, there remains a considerable degree of uncertainty over the whole matter and, therefore, of legal risk.

The safest course is probably to check the capacity of a company and the powers of its directors before each transaction, particularly bearing in mind that merely because a company has power to enter into one derivatives transaction or type of derivatives transaction does not mean that it has power to enter into many transactions or many types of transaction. If a company does not have the capacity to enter into derivatives transactions, no transaction should be entered into (at least until the company has changed its objects to allow it to enter into derivatives). Checking capacity before each transaction is likely to be impracticable in many cases, and would potentially increase transaction costs.

Should a counterparty therefore simply check the capacity whilst, say, negotiating a master agreement when the first transaction is entered into? If capacity is checked and found wanting, no further transactions should be entered into. Even if a company does have the capacity to enter into a particular type of derivative, constant monitoring is still necessary to ensure that future transactions remain within the permitted field, both in type and in scale. If they do not, the counterparty will have the company's memorandum of association and will therefore have corporate knowledge of its contents and restrictions. Whilst section 35A(2)(b) of the Companies Act 1985 provides that a person is

71. This is perhaps a somewhat strained interpretation as section 35A(2) starts "For this purpose", i.e. for the purpose of section 35A(1).

not to be regarded as acting in bad faith merely because he knows that an act is beyond the directors' powers, the counterparty still runs the risk of being held to be a constructive trustee.

If, however, a counterparty checks only the company's existence but not its capacity, it does not have the problem of actual knowledge of any lack of capacity.[72] Prima facie it can rely on section 35B of the Companies Act 1985 as a basis for not making any enquiry. If mere knowledge that the directors of a company are acting beyond their powers is not sufficient on its own to be bad faith, the absence of that knowledge when legislation provides that it is not necessary to obtain it similarly cannot be bad faith. With regard to the risk of being held to be a constructive trustee, the risk of being held to be in bad faith is perhaps less acute than if a counterparty was actually aware of the fact that the directors were acting outside the company's capacity. The most that could be said (absent special circumstances leading to doubts about capacity) is that the counterparty had failed to make enquiries which in all the circumstances it should have done. This is a harder argument upon which to base a constructive trust than actual knowledge of the directors' impropriety.[73]

Any decision not to consider a company's powers should, however, be a general one rather than taken on a case by case basis. A decision in an individual case not to check capacity is bound to excite suspicion that the counterparty was seeking to avoid actual knowledge of the impropriety it suspected.

3.2.5 Connected and associated parties

Section 322A of the Companies Act 1985[74] provides that notwithstanding anything in sections 35, 35A or 35B of the Act, a company may avoid a transaction in which, first, the directors of a company exceed their powers and, secondly, which has parties including a director of the company or its holding company, a person "connected" with the director, or a company with which the director is "associated". Even if the company does not avoid the transaction, section 322A(3) requires the director and anyone associated or connected with him to account to the company for any gain made directly or indirectly from the transaction and to indemnify the company for any loss or damage resulting from the transaction. If the company is indemnified for any loss arising from the transaction, it loses the right to avoid the transaction, as it does if rights which would be affected by avoidance are acquired bona fide for value by someone not a party to the transaction, if the company ratifies the transaction or if restitution

72. Fiches for individual companies provided by the Registrar of Companies include both a certificate of incorporation and the memorandum of association. If a counterparty has the fiche, it might have some difficulty in convincing others that it had only checked the company's existence and not looked at the objects.

73. Market practice may have some relevance as to what it is reasonable or proper to do in all the circumstances.

74. Inserted by section 109(1) of the Companies Act 1989 with effect from 4 February 1991.

of any money or other asset which was the subject matter of the transaction is no longer possible.

This right of the company to avoid the transaction applies even though there are also parties to the transaction who are not connected or associated with its directors, and would (apart from section 322A) be protected by section 35A of the Companies Act 1985. In those circumstances, however, the innocent party or the company can apply to the court which has power to affirm the transaction, sever it or set it aside on such terms as seem just.

Section 346 of the Companies Act 1985 defines who is connected or associated with a company for the purposes of section 322A. A person is connected with a director if he or she (a) is the director's spouse, child or step-child, (b) is a body corporate with which the director is associated, or (c) is a person who is acting as a trustee of any trust the beneficiaries of which include the director, his spouse, children or step-children or a body corporate with which he is associated. A company is associated with a body corporate if he and the persons connected with him are interested in one-fifth of the share capital.

Section 322A is intended to stop directors or those close to them taking advantage of the 1989 reforms to bind the company to transactions outside its powers. The range of the section is, however, relatively limited. For example, the fact that an employee of a financial institution is a director of another company which enters into an ultra vires transaction with the financial institution is not enough on its own to allow the company to avoid the transaction under section 322A.

3.2.6 The ultra vires risks in dealing with companies incorporated under the Companies Acts

The first risk in dealing with a company is assessing whether it is acting outside its powers. In some cases, this will clearly be the case (for example, where a company whose object is to trade in metals buys or sells coffee futures), but in other instances it may not be clear. If there is no express power to enter into derivatives contracts, the issue will be whether a power is to be implied. There is inevitably scope for a difference of opinion about whether a power to enter into derivatives transactions should be implied. Even where a power to enter derivatives will be implied, it does not necessarily apply to all derivatives. For example, a power to borrow may, in context, carry with it an implied power to enter into interest rate swaps and forward rate agreements, but it is less obvious that the company can also enter into gilt options even though they are relevant to interest rates.

If a company is acting outside its powers, the risk is then the extent to which the counterparty is protected by sections 35, 35A and 35B of the Companies Act 1985. The legislation is clearly intended to protect third parties, but is not necessarily entirely effective in achieving this aim. In most cases, it probably will provide protection, but this may, in part at least, depend on the knowledge of the counterparty of the company's activities. If a counterparty knows that a company is acting outside its powers, there is still an argument that the legislation gives protection, but the counterparty is unlikely to generate much sympathy from the courts in that situation, nor if it would have realised that something was wrong had it paused to consider the information readily available to it.

Even if a company is acting within the letter of its memorandum of association, there is still a question of whether those responsible at the company are using their powers for their proper purposes. For example, a company whose object is to trade in copper may have power to enter into copper futures to hedge its exposure to changes in the market price, but that does not necessarily give it the power to trade in copper derivatives as a separate profit centre. As long as the counterparty has no knowledge, and could have had no knowledge in the circumstances, that the company is using derivatives for an improper purpose, it will be protected under the doctrine espoused most clearly in *Rolled Steel*.[75] The difficulty in many cases will be to know when a company has sufficient knowledge of the facts leading to impropriety on the part of the company's officers to place it at risk of not being able to enforce a transaction and/or of being a constructive trustee. A company might, for example, know that a company only has power to use derivatives to hedge its exposure to certain market variables, but it might also know, or have means of knowledge, that the volume of transactions by the company exceeds a level which might reasonably thought to be hedging given the company's turnover. The difficulty is to put together the necessary pieces of information to assess the risk, in this case the purpose for which the company is empowered to enter into derivatives, the level at which it is doing so, and its underlying business need.

3.3 LOCAL AUTHORITIES

Local authorities in England are established under one of two statutes. Local authorities outside London are established under the Local Government Act 1972. Section 2(3) of this Act incorporates the elected council. As a body incorporated by statute, the council can only do those things which it is expressly or impliedly authorised by statute to do. Any transactions outside that area are void.

Local authorities in London are established under the London Government Act 1963. This provides for an unincorporated council but also allows the Queen to grant a charter of incorporation to the inhabitants of the borough.[76]

75. [1986] Ch 246.
76. Section 1(2) of the London Government Act 1963. Section 1(3) allows the Government to make an incorporation order if no royal charter is granted, but use of this section has not proved necessary.

London boroughs invariably have royal charters incorporating the inhabitants in the name of "The Mayor and Burgesses of the London Borough of" wherever. The purpose of the chartered corporation is to give the council a body corporate with perpetual succession which can enter into contracts, own land, etc without the difficulties which would be caused if the local authority could only act through an unincorporated council of elected, and therefore fluctuating, composition. In *Hazell* v. *Hammersmith* it was argued that, as a chartered corporation, the Mayor and Burgesses of the London Borough of Hammersmith and Fulham had all the powers of a natural person.[77] The House of Lords rejected this argument peremptorily.[78] Where a statute authorises the grant of a royal charter, the extent of the powers exercisable by the corporation depends upon the construction and intent of the statute. In this case, the statute did not intend to confer on the chartered corporation any powers beyond those enjoyed by the unincorporated council and by local authorities outside London.

As a result, a local authority, however established, will only have power to enter into derivatives if an express power to do so can be identified or, if no express power exists, there is an implied power to do so. In fact, there is no express power that enables local authorities to enter any kind of derivatives contract, and the main questions about local authorities are the extent to which powers can be implied and, even if power can be implied, whether there is any principle similar to that in *Rolled Steel* for companies incorporated under the Companies Acts[79] to offer some protection for third parties dealing with a local authority.

3.3.1 Implied powers

Section 111(1) of the Local Government Act 1972 codifies the powers which will be implied into the statutory functions given to local authorities. Section 111(1) provides that:

> "Without prejudice to any powers exercisable apart from this section but subject to the provisions of this Act . . . a local authority shall have power to do any thing (whether or not involving expenditure, borrowing or lending of money or the acquisition or disposal of property rights) which is calculated to facilitate, or is conducive or incidental to, the discharge of any of their functions."[80]

In *Hazell* v. *Hammersmith & Fulham London Borough Council*,[81] Hammersmith had entered into a large number of interest rate swaps, options,

77. [1992] 2 AC 1. It was accepted that the unincorporated council and monies raised by it through taxes were subject to the ultra vires rule in the normal way but it was argued that if the corporation had any other assets they could be used to meet liabilities which were ultra vires the council but intra vires the corporation.

78. [1992] 2 AC 1, 39–43. Lord Templeman described the argument as "absurd" (p 39).

79. See pp 43–45 above.

80. A local authority's functions "embraces all the duties and powers of a local authority; the sum total of the activities Parliament has entrusted to it": *Hazell* v. *Hammersmith* [1992] 2 AC 1, 29.

81. [1992] 2 AC 1.

forward rate agreements and similar derivatives transactions. Hammersmith's auditor contended that the council had no power to do so and, as a result, that all the transactions were void and unenforceable. It was accepted that there was no express power for local authorities to enter into derivatives transactions, but it was argued that the transactions were incidental, facilitated or conducive to a local authority's borrowing function. In the House of Lords, Lord Templeman was dismissive of the argument that swaps facilitated or were conducive to borrowing.[82] He paid greater heed to the argument that swaps were incidental to borrowing before concluding that Parliament had laid down in Schedule 13 to the Local Government Act 1972 a comprehensive code regulating local authority borrowing and, as a result, that there was no scope for implying powers. Section 111(1) had no application because it is expressly subject to the provisions of the Act. As there are no saving provisions like those in the Companies Acts,[83] all Hammersmith's derivatives transactions were void and unenforceable.[84]

The House of Lords therefore concluded that local authorities had no power to enter into interest rate related derivatives. This was, however, based on the borrowing powers set out in Schedule 13 to the Local Government Act 1972. That schedule was repealed by the Local Government and Housing Act 1989, but it was replaced by a more rigid and comprehensive financial code,[85] and there is no realistic possibility of the courts deciding that local authorities have power to enter into this kind of derivatives.

As far as other derivatives are concerned, the prospect of the courts using section 111(1) of the Local Government Act 1972 to imply powers is slight. The arguments used by Lord Templeman in *Hazell* v. *Hammersmith* have been applied to other instances. In *Credit Suisse* v. *Waltham Forest*,[86] Neill LJ commented that "where Parliament has made detailed provisions as to how certain statutory functions are to be carried out, there is no scope for implying the existence of additional powers which lie wholly outside the statutory code."[87] As a result of this approach, if the statutory framework is at all detailed, there is little chance of section 111(1) being applied to allow the use of derivatives. Even where the framework is not detailed, the courts have limited the applicability of section 111(1) by refusing to countenance actions which rather than being incidental to a function are only incidental to the incidental.[88] The scope of section 111(1) is therefore severely constrained.

82. [1992] 2 AC 1, 29–30.
83. See pp 43ff above.
84. See pp 75–76 below for the consequences of this. Interestingly, Lord Templeman was apparently prepared to countenance a local authority having the power to alter the interest rate on a borrowing from fixed to floating and vice versa as long as it was done by virtue of a power in the borrowing contract.
85. Sections 39–66 of the Local Government and Housing Act 1989.
86. [1996] 4 All ER 176.
87. [1996] 4 All ER 176, 184. See also *Sutton* v. *Morgan Grenfell* (1997) 6 Bank LR 156, 161.
88. *McCarthy & Stone* v. *Richmond* [1992] 2 AC 48; *Credit Suisse* v. *Allerdale* [1996] 4 All ER 129, 175; *Sutton* v. *Morgan Grenfell* (1997) 6 Bank LR 156.

3.3.2 The purpose for which functions are exercised

Even if it were possible to identify an express or implied power entitling a local authority to enter into a derivatives transaction, the courts require that local authorities take into account matters which they are obliged to take into account, disregard matters which they should not take into account and not reach a conclusion so unreasonable that no reasonable local authority could ever have come to it.[89] A counterparty will, however, seldom be in a position to assess whether a local authority has complied with these requirements. As far as companies are concerned, directors are obliged to act bona fide in the interests of the company but, if they fail to do so, counterparties can rely on the protection given by the principle laid down in *Rolled Steel*.[90] It is unclear whether this principle also applies to local authorities.

In *Credit Suisse* v. *Allerdale*,[91] Neill LJ felt constrained by authority to hold that this principle did not apply to local authorities. He considered that whether a local authority acted entirely outside the powers given to it by statute or whether it merely abused those powers, the result was the same, namely that the exercise of the power was void. Any transaction entered into was unenforceable by the counterparty regardless of whether it knew about any abuse. Hobhouse LJ took a bolder line and distinguished between public law and private law. In public law, abusing a power might entitle the courts in judicial review proceedings to quash the action, but the circumstances giving rise to that entitlement would not necessarily also provide a defence to the local authority in a private law action. In a private law action, such as an action on a contract, the principles in *Rolled Steel* dictate when a defence is available. As a result, if the counterparty did not know of any abuse of power by the local authority in entering into a contract, it might still be able to enforce the contract. The third judge in *Credit Suisse* v. *Allerdale* declined to express a view on this issue.[92]

Hobhouse LJ's views have much to commend them. They would restore a common framework to the ultra vires principle, and close one source of abuse in a very unsatisfactory area of the law.[93] They do, however, represent a radical approach and, in any event, the restrictive approach to the implication of powers which Hobhouse LJ and other members of the judiciary have taken probably means that, even if this approach does prevail, it will be of no assistance to local authorities which wish to enter into derivatives contracts or to their counterparties. The risks of doing so remain very considerable.

89. *Associated Provincial Picture Houses* v. *Wednesbury Corporation* [1948] 1 KB 223.
90. See pp 43–45 above.
91. [1996] 4 All ER 129.
92. Hobhouse LJ's views were supported by Cresswell J in *Merrill Lynch* v. *Municipality of Piraeus* [1997] 6 Bank LR 241.
93. In the same case Neill LJ was of the view, also expressed in cases on companies (see note 11 above), that the state of the law was unsatisfactory (p 159). In this case (at p 160) and in *Sutton* v. *Morgan Grenfell* (1997) 6 Bank LR 156, 162 Peter Gibson LJ expressed the same view.

3.3.3 The risks of dealing with local authorities

The legal risks of dealing with local authorities are very considerable. In the first instance, it is necessary to identify either an express power to enter into a specific derivatives transaction or a function in relation to which a derivative can be said to be incidental, conducive or facilitative within section 111 of the Local Government Act 1972. The limited scope given to section 111 by the courts makes it unlikely in most instances that a power to enter into derivatives transactions will be implied. Even if it were to be implied, or if there were an express power, there remains the risk, which is very difficult for a counterparty to assess, that the local authority may have exercised its powers for an improper purpose. If they have done this, there is a very real risk that the transaction would be void whether or not the counterparty had, or should have had, any knowledge of the impropriety.

3.4 BUILDING SOCIETIES

Building societies are incorporated under a specific statute, the Building Societies Act 1986 and its predecessors, for the "purpose or principal purpose of making loans which are secured on residential property and are funded substantially by its members".[94] As statutory corporations, they are subject to the full rigours of the ultra vires rule, and can only do those acts authorised by statute, namely, subject to statutory provisions, the powers conferred on them by their memorandum.[95] In order to enter into derivatives transactions, therefore, a building society must be given power by its memorandum—this raises the same issues as arise in connection with the memoranda of association of companies incorporated under the Companies Acts.[96] Sections 35 and 35A of the Companies Act 1985 do not apply to building societies but there are similar provisions in paragraphs 16 to 18 of Schedule 2 to the Building Societies Act 1986 (as amended by section 3(2) and Schedule 1 to the Building Societies Act 1997).

Even if a building society does have power in its memorandum to enter into derivatives transactions, there are additional legislative requirements. Section 9A of the Building Societies Act 1986, as amended by section 10 of the Building Societies Act 1997, provides that:

"(1) Subject to subsections (2) to (4) below, a building society shall not do, and shall secure that each of its subsidiary undertakings does not do, any of the following things, namely—

94. Section 5(1) of the Building Societies Act 1986, as substituted by section 1(1) of the Building Societies Act 1997. Incorporation is provided for by section 5(2).

95. See section 5(5) of the Building Societies Act 1986, as substituted by section 1(3) of the Building Societies Act 1997 (see also, for example, *Small* v. *Smith* (1884) 10 App Cas 119).

96. See pp 42ff above.

(a) act as a market maker in securities, commodities or currencies;
(b) trade in commodities or currencies; and
(c) enter into any transaction involving derivative instruments;

but a contravention of this subsection shall not invalidate any transaction or other act.
. . .

(4) Nothing in subsection (1)(c) above shall apply in relation to any transaction entered into by a building society, or subsidiary undertaking of a building society, if—

(a) it is entered into in the society's or undertaking's capacity as the manager of a collective investment scheme;
(b) it is entered into for the purpose of limiting the extent to which the society, or a connected undertaking of the society, will be affected by changes in any of the following factors, namely—
  (i) interest rates;
  (ii) exchange rates;
  (iii) any index of retail prices;
  (iv) any index of residential property prices; and
  (v) any index of prices of securities[97]; or
(c) it involves a [contract for differences] and it is entered into for the purpose of limiting the extent to which any person will be affected by changes in any interest or exchange rate applicable to—
  (i) a loan owed by him to;
  (ii) shares held by him in; or
  (iii) a deposit of his with,
  the society, or a connected undertaking of the society.
(d) Nothing in subsection (1)(c) above shall apply in relation to any transaction entered into by a subsidiary undertaking of a building society, if it is entered into in the undertaking's capacity—
  (i) a body authorised under section 3 or 4 of the Insurance Companies Act 1982[98] (authorised insurance companies) to carry on insurance business of a class specified in Schedule 1 to that Act (classes of long term business) . . ."

Building societies therefore have limited power to enter into derivatives contracts, and for this purpose derivatives are defined by reference to paragraphs 4, 7, 8 and 9 of Schedule 1 to the Financial Services Act 1986.[99]

The reforms introduced by the Building Societies Act 1997 improve very considerably the position of third parties. Before these reforms, there was uncertainty as to the extent of the powers of building societies, as to the effect on third parties of any breach by the building society of the legislation, and as to the impact on third parties of the powers of the Building Societies Commission in the event of breach by a building society. The Act is, however, now clear that the mere fact of a building society entering into a derivatives transaction in breach of the terms of the Act does not of itself invalidate the transaction.

This does not, however, mean that third parties are free to enter into any transactions with building societies without reference to the legislation. The issues faced by a third party are essentially the same as those faced by third

97. I.e. shares, stock, debentures, debenture stock, loan stock, bonds, units of a collective investment scheme and other securities of any description: section 9A(9) of the Building Societies Act 1986.

98. See pp 63ff below.

99. See pp 123ff below.

parties dealing with companies incorporated under the Companies Acts. As a result, prudence dictates that counterparties should ensure that transactions are capable of falling within the statutory limits.

3.5 INSURANCE COMPANIES

Unlike that for building societies, there is no special system of incorporation for insurance companies. If a body corporate,[100] an insurer must be incorporated under provisions of the general law, most commonly the Companies Acts. The questions which arise about the powers of any other body corporate to enter into derivatives transactions also therefore arise in relation to insurance companies. But, in addition to these questions, issues arise from the extensive regulation to which the insurance industry is subject, principally in the Insurance Companies Act 1982. This regulation is intended to safeguard the public and the solvency of insurance companies but in doing so it impacts upon the ability of insurance companies to enter into derivatives contracts and also upon the consequences of their having done so. Strictly the questions these regulations raise are not ones of capacity but rather of the lawfulness of an insurance company's activities. For most practical purposes, however, they are the same.

3.5.1 The ability of insurance companies to enter into derivatives transactions

It is a criminal offence to carry on insurance business in the United Kingdom unless authorised to do so by the Secretary of State, unless a branch of an insurance company incorporated under the law of another member state of the European Union, unless a member of Lloyd's or unless the activities fall within certain other limited exceptions.[101] Once a company obtains authorisation from the Secretary of State to undertake insurance business, section 16(1) of the Insurance Companies Act 1982 provides that it "shall not carry on any activities, in the United Kingdom or elsewhere, otherwise than in connection with or for the purposes of its insurance business".[102] As a result, even if an insurance company's memorandum of association gives it the widest power to enter into derivatives transactions, it is unlawful for it to do so unless those derivatives transactions are in connection with or for the purposes of its

100. Some insurers are still mutual societies, but this is now less commonly the case, particularly amongst big insurance companies.

101. Sections 2 and 14 of the Insurance Companies Act 1982.

102. This wording is (presumably intentionally) markedly different from, and wider than, section 111(1) of the Local Government Act 1972 ("calculated to facilitate, or . . . conducive or incidental to, the discharge of any of [the local authority's] functions") which was given a narrow interpretation in *Hazell* v. *Hammersmith* [1992] 2 AC 1 (see above).

insurance business. Unlike carrying on an insurance business without authorisation, it is not, however, a criminal offence for the company to act in breach of section 16(1).[103]

The principal question is, therefore, whether a specific derivatives transaction can be for the purposes of or in connection with the particular insurance company's insurance business and, if so, whether it is in fact for those purposes. The Insurance Companies Regulations 1994 make provision[104] for the valuation of certain derivatives contracts when considering an insurance company's assets and liabilities. This might be taken to indicate that insurance companies can enter into derivatives transactions as Parliament has passed a statutory instrument recognising the consequences of doing so in certain instances. The question of whether it is lawful for insurance companies to enter into derivatives contracts is, however, one of construction of section 16(1) of the Insurance Companies Act 1982, and the statutory instrument is not admissible as an aid to the construction of that section.[105] As a result, derivatives within the terms of the statutory instrument are not necessarily within the powers of an insurance company but nor are derivatives outside its terms necessarily outside those powers. The Department of Trade and Industry has also issued a guidance note[106] dealing with the use by insurance companies of derivatives, but that is still less an aid to the construction of the statute.

The obvious starting point to determine whether derivatives transactions can be entered into in connection with or for the purposes of an insurance business is the nature of insurance business itself. It is impossible to tell whether something can be done in connection with or for the purposes of a company's insurance business without knowing what that business is.

There is no statutory definition of insurance business[107] but section 1(1) of the Act provides that insurance business is divided into long-term business and general business, long-term business being insurance business of any of the classes specified in Schedule 1 to the Act, and general business being insurance

103. Section 71(7) of the Insurance Companies Act 1982.

104. SI 1994 No 1516, regulations 55 and 61.

105. In *Deposit Protection Board* v. *Dalia* [1994] 2 AC 367, 397 Lord Browne-Wilkinson (with whom all other members of the House of Lords agreed) said that: "Although there are occasions on which regulations can be used as an aid to construction of the Act under which they are made . . . that is only where the regulations are roughly contemporaneous with the Act being construed." See also *Hanlon* v. *Law Society* [1981] AC 124, 193–194. Regulations in a statutory instrument in 1994 are hardly contemporaneous with a statute of 1982. It is worth noting that section 9A(5) of the Building Societies Act 1986 seems to assume that insurance companies have power to enter into derivatives transactions.

106. Prudential Guidance Note 1995/3.

107. Though section 95 of the Insurance Companies Act 1982 states certain things which are included in insurance business. These include the effecting and carrying out, by a person not carrying on a banking business, of performance bonds, guarantees, and annuities, but it is not clear what this section adds to section 1(1) and Schedules 1 and 2 of the Act since all the matters mentioned in section 95 are covered in those schedules. The areas of business regulated are clearly those set out in these schedules.

business of any of the classes specified in Schedule 2 to the Act.[108] It is the activities in these schedules which are regulated by the Act. These schedules include contracts of insurance on human life, vehicles, aircraft property and vehicles. However, the schedules also refer to other business which prima facie does not involve insurance contracts; these include capital redemption contracts, managing the investments of pension funds, contracts to pay annuities on human life where the benefits are determined by reference to the value of property or an index of property, and performance bonds.

This wide statutory view of insurance business strongly suggests that insurance companies can enter into derivatives transactions. Where, for example, benefits are to be paid by reference to the index of particular property, it seems likely that a derivative could be entered into in connection with or for the purposes of that business in order, say, to hedge risks arising from that index. Similarly, an annuity involves receipt of a sum of money by an insurance company in consideration for the insurance company's undertaking to pay certain benefits over time. The insurance company must, as part of its insurance business, invest that sum, and there seems no reason why it should not enter into derivatives to hedge that investment.

Even as far as insurance contracts are concerned, it seems likely that derivatives can be entered into in connection with or for the purposes of the insurance business of which they are part. There is no statutory definition of what a contract of insurance is, but in *Prudential Insurance Co* v. *Inland Revenue Commissioners,* Channel J defined insurance as:

> "It must be a contract whereby for some consideration, usually but not necessarily for periodical payments called premiums, you secure to yourself some benefit, usually but not necessarily the payment of a sum of money, upon the happening of some event. Then the next thing that is necessary is that the event should be one that involves some amount of uncertainty. There must either be uncertainty whether the event will ever happen or not, or if the event is one which is certain to happen at some time there must be uncertainty as to the time at which it will happen. The remaining essential is that . . . the insurance must be against something. A contract which would otherwise be a mere wager may become an insurance by reason of the assured having an interest in the subject matter—that is to say, the uncertain event which is necessary to make the contract amount to an insurance must be an event which is prima facie adverse to the interest of the assured. The insurance is to provide for the payment of a sum of money to meet a loss or detriment which will or may be suffered upon the happening of the event."[109]

This emphasises the necessity for an uncertain event but, even with this focus, an insurance company must do something with the premiums it receives in return for taking the risk of an uncertain event. This will, for successful companies, be investment both to meet future claims and to increase profit.

108. By section 3(1) of the Insurance Companies Act 1982, the Secretary of State can authorise an insurance company to carry on some only of those classes of insurance.

109. [1904] KB 658, 663. See also, for example, *Re Sentinel Securities plc* [1996] 1 WLR 316 and *Fuji Finance* v. *Aetna* [1996] 3 WLR 871.

Insurance and investment have in any event long been regarded as complementary rather than mutually exclusive. In, for example, *Fuji Finance* v. *Aetna*,[110] the uncertain event element of a contract was of minimal, if not non-existent, significance but the Court of Appeal still held that it was an insurance contract. The contract, like many sold by insurance companies, was essentially one of investment rather than one to compensate for losses suffered as a result of the happening of an uncertain event. Indeed, category III of long-term insurance business referred to in Schedule 1 to the Insurance Companies Act 1982 specifically refers to life assurance and annuities where the benefits to be paid depend in whole or in part on the value of an index or fluctuations in the value of property. It would be a strange result if it was not part of that insurance business to invest in the relevant property or index.

If an insurance company possesses a portfolio of investments the return on part of which is dependent upon interest rates, it would be entirely linguistically consistent to say that the company can enter into a derivatives transaction in connection with or for the purposes of that portfolio in order to hedge its exposure to interest rate movements. Likewise, if an insurance company invests in other assets, it remains consistent for it to enter into other derivatives in connection with those investments. Further, credit derivatives might in some circumstances directly hedge credit insurance provided by an insurance company in the same way that reinsurance does.[111] It is therefore very likely that section 16(1) of the Insurance Companies Act 1982 does allow an insurance company to enter into derivatives transactions.

A contrary argument might be that investment can legitimately be carried on by an insurance company in connection with insurance business, but derivatives cannot because they are in connection with the activity carried out in connection with insurance business rather than themselves being in connection with insurance business.[112] This is, however, to mistake the nature of insurance. Investment is not merely an activity to be conducted in connection with, or for the purposes of, insurance business but is a central part of many insurance contracts.[113] Alternatively, it might be argued that derivatives are themselves investments. Whilst derivatives are within the definition of investments for the purposes of the Financial Services Act 1986 in order to bring them within the

110. [1996] 3 WLR 871.

111. Insurance classes 14 to 16 in Schedule 2 to the Insurance Companies Act 1982 relate to credit insurance, suretyship and miscellaneous financial insurance. Most of the categories of insurance in Schedules 1 and 2 to the Act start with the words "effecting and carrying out contracts of insurance ..."; some however do not (e.g. category VII in Schedule 1 which is "effecting and carrying out—(a) contracts to manage the investments of pension funds ...").

112. *McCarthy & Stone* v. *Richmond* [1992] 2 AC 48 in which the House of Lords decided that a local authority could not charge for pre-planning application advice because the advice was incidental to its planning function but charging was only incidental to the incidental, and therefore fell outside section 111(1) of the Local Government Act 1972. See also, for example, *Credit Suisse* v. *Allerdale* [1996] 4 All ER 129, 175 and *Sutton* v. *Morgan Grenfell* (1997) 6 Bank LR 156.

113. *Fuji Finance* v. *Aetna* [1996] 3 WLR 871, 880–881.

scope of regulation, many would not be considered as investments within the normal meaning of that term.[114]

Unless derivatives are themselves investments, it is doubtful whether an insurance company can run a derivatives portfolio as a profit-making activity independent of its investments. This might be regarded as using the strength of an insurance company's balance sheet to gain access to, and hopefully profit from, the derivatives markets, but it is further removed from the company's insurance business to which section 16(1) requires all activities to be linked. Insurance usually involves the collection and investment of premiums, but prima facie running a derivatives book does not depend on those premiums, unless it is using them to meet losses or adding to them through the return on the derivatives transactions. Running an independent derivatives book might be treated as the conduct of a separate business rather than an activity linked to insurance.[115]

As a result, although insurance companies probably are authorised under section 16(1) of the Insurance Companies Act 1982 to enter into derivatives transactions, that does not necessarily mean that the company can enter into them without restriction. Any individual derivatives transaction must be entered into in connection with or for the purposes of the particular insurance business carried on by a particular insurance company. The difficulty for the counterparty will be that, whatever warranties it takes, it is unlikely to know the nature of the insurance company's business and why it is entering into the derivatives transaction. There is therefore inevitably an element of uncertainty for a counterparty. This makes it important to consider the consequences for a derivatives contract of an insurance company acting in breach of section 16(1) of the Insurance Companies Act 1982.

3.5.2 The validity of transactions entered into unlawfully by insurance companies

This is a vexed issue which has troubled the courts. The modern starting point is probably the Court of Appeal's decision in *Phoenix General Insurance Co* v.

114. In *City Index Ltd* v. *Leslie* [1992] 1 QB 98, 105, Lord Donaldson of Lymington MR said that: "Whilst it may be thought to be a rather loose use of language to describe a bet as an investment, the word 'investment' is defined in section 1(1) of the [Financial Services] Act [1986] . . ." As a matter of law, absent section 63 of the Financial Services Act 1986, many derivatives contracts are gaming contracts: see pp 22ff above. This view also has consequences for section 38(1)(a) of the Insurance Companies Act 1982 which allows the Secretary of State to require an insurance company "not to make investments of a specified class or description". If a derivatives contract is not an investment, the Secretary of State cannot make an order about derivatives under this section. The section is, however, unusual in that the Act generally speaks of "assets", and a derivatives contract is capable of being an asset.

115. See note 33 above.

Halvanon Insurance Co.[116] This case concerned the predecessor of section 2(1) of the Insurance Companies Act 1982 rather than section 16(1). Section 2(1) provides that no person shall carry on insurance business in the United Kingdom unless authorised under the Act. The court considered whether a contract entered into in breach of the section was enforceable. It took the view that because insurance business is referred to in the Act as not only the effecting but also the carrying out of contracts of insurance, a contract entered into in breach of section 2(1) was unenforceable by both parties to it. Since the legislation expressly prohibited an insurance company from performing an insurance contract, the insured could not enforce that contract because to do so would require the insurer to do precisely what the statute forbade.

This decision was followed with reluctance in two further cases[117] but reversed by section 132 of the Financial Services Act 1986.[118] The question is whether the same logic that led the court to this conclusion on section 2(1) also applies to section 16(1) of the Insurance Companies Act 1982.

In *Fuji Finance* v. *Aetna*,[119] the Court of Appeal was faced directly with the issue of whether a contract in breach of section 16(1) was enforceable by the parties. Unfortunately, the court divided equally on the point. Morritt LJ considered that whilst section 2(1) prohibited the carrying out of insurance contracts, the wording of section 16(1), in particular the use of the general word "activities", did not carry the same necessary implication that a contract entered into in breach of the section was void. He concluded that, as a matter of statutory construction, a contract in breach of section 16(1) was enforceable. He gave three reasons for this.[120] First, the word "activities" is so wide that he found it difficult to ascribe to Parliament the intention to render void anything within its ambit. This was reinforced by the fact that acting in breach of section 16(1) is not a criminal offence.[121] Secondly, not only is there no criminal sanction in the statute but there is an impressive array of statutory remedies available to the Secretary of State for breach of section 16(1) which were more than sufficient to ensure compliance with the section. Thirdly, in limiting an insurance company's

116. [1988] QB 216. As the Court of Appeal recognised (p 267), the relevant part of their decision is obiter. There had been two earlier contradictory first instance decisions, *Bedford Insurance Co* v. *Instituto de Resseguros do Brasil* [1984] QB 966 and *Stewart* v. *Oriental Fire and Marine Insurance Co* [1985] QB 988.

117. *Re Cavalier Insurance Co* [1989] 2 Lloyd's Rep 430 and *DR Insurance Co* v. *Seguros America Banamex* [1993] 1 Lloyd's Rep 120.

118. In *DR Insurance Co* v. *Seguros America Banamex* [1993] 1 Lloyd's Rep 120, section 132 of the Financial Services Act 1986 was treated as having retrospective effect.

119. [1996] 3 WLR 871. The first instance decision by Sir Donald Nicholls V-C is at [1995] Ch 122. The relevant aspect of the Court of Appeal's judgment is obiter.

120. [1996] 3 WLR 871, 888.

121. Section 71(7) of the Insurance Companies Act 1982.

commercial activities, the section implemented two European Directives,[122] but it was not a necessary implication from that purpose that every contract entered into in breach was invalidated. This was especially so in view of the policy in section 35 of the Companies Act 1985 and its predecessors, themselves the result of European measures.[123]

Hobhouse LJ declined to express a view on this point but Sir Ralph Gibson reluctantly disagreed with Morritt LJ. He considered that the reference in section 16(1) to "activities" was apt to embrace the carrying out of a non-insurance contract as well as effecting the contract. He could therefore see no escape from the logic of the decision in the *Phoenix* case. He did not consider the regulatory steps available to the Secretary of State to be decisive; the legislation is to protect the public, in particular policy holders, and the invocation of regulatory steps after a breach of section 16(1) has occurred would not achieve that.

This is clearly a difficult issue, and there will remain uncertainty until the court finally resolves the issue or legislation is passed to clarify the position. However, probably the better view is that breach of section 16(1) of the Insurance Companies Act does not make contracts entered into in breach of its provisions unenforceable. In the case of section 2(1) of the Act, allowing someone to compel another to take steps which constitute a criminal offence is obviously unacceptable. That is not the case with section 16(1), breach of which is not a crime. The Act does not spell out what the consequences of breach of the section are, but it would unnecessarily attribute to Parliament a desire to create considerable injustice if the only penalty for breach of the section was that imposed on an innocent counterparty who found that he could not enforce a contract.

3.5.3 The risks of dealing with insurance companies

There is an unsatisfactory degree of uncertainty in the scope of section 16(1) of the Insurance Companies Act 1982 and the consequences of its breach. This entails the risk that insurance companies as a whole might not have power to enter into derivatives contracts and that, even if they do, the particular insurance company in question is not entering into the particular transaction in question in connection with or for the purposes of its insurance business under section 16(1). If the insurance company is not entering, or cannot enter into, a transaction within section 16(1), there is then uncertainty as to the effect of this. There are good arguments that the contract is nevertheless enforceable, but the risk remains that it will not be.

As a practical measure, the counterparty could obtain a contractual warranty

122. Articles 8(1)(b) of the First Council Non-Life Co-Ordination Directive (73/239/EEC) and of the First Council Life Co-Ordination Directive (79/267/EEC).

123. See pp 47ff above.

by the insurance company, both in any master agreement and in each confirmation, that each derivative transaction is being undertaken in connection with or for the purposes of its insurance business. This might be useful, but largely for the purpose of trying to ensure that a responsible person addresses the issue in connection with the transaction rather than as a means of obtaining financial recompense. If it does turn out that the contract was not entered into for this purpose and, as a result, that the transaction is void, it is unlikely to give rise to any claim for damages.[124] A representation (or indemnity) to the same effect from a third party, perhaps an officer of the insurance company or an inhouse lawyer, would be of value to ensure that a responsible person considered the issue but also as the basis of a financial claim provided that the person in question had sufficient insurance cover.

3.6 FOREIGN CORPORATIONS

"(1) The capacity of a corporation to enter into any legal transaction is governed both by the constitution of the corporation and by the law of the country which governs the transaction in question. (2) All matters concerning the constitution of a corporation are governed by the law of the place of incorporation."[125]

As a result, the question of whether a foreign corporation has the capacity to enter into a derivatives contract depends upon the constitution of the company interpreted in accordance with the law of the place of incorporation. It is therefore necessary to check this before entering into a transaction with a foreign corporation.

The relevance of the law of the place of incorporation is, however, limited to constitutional issues, including the existence and succession of the corporation, and does not extend to matters affecting the legality of the contract, which are governed by the law of the contract in question.[126] As a result, if a foreign corporation has the capacity to enter into a derivatives contract but to do so would be illegal under the law of its incorporation, the contract would, if governed by English law, be enforceable in the English courts.[127]

124. *Phoenix Insurance* v. *Halvanon Insurance* [1988] QB 216, 275. In this case, Kerr LJ did suggest that it might be possible for someone in these circumstances to sue on a collateral warranty given by the insurance company, but if the contract itself is void because it was not in connection with or for the purposes of insurance business, a warranty to the contrary is likely to fall foul of the same provision.

125. Dicey & Morris, *The Conflict of Laws* (12th edn), p 1111, approved by the House of Lords in *J H Rayner Limited* v. *Department of Trade* [1990] 2 AC 418, 509. See also *Merrill Lynch* v. *Municipality of Piraeus* [1997] 6 Bank LR 241 in which Cresswell J decided that, as a matter of Greek law, a Greek local authority did have power to enter into a loan and a related swap. See also pp 220–222 below in relation to foreign payment moratoria.

126. *Metliss* v. *National Bank of Greece and Athens* [1957] AC 509 and *Adams* v. *National Bank of Greece and Athens* [1961] AC 255.

127. Provided, of course, that performance of the contract would not necessarily involve the performance in the place of incorporation of an act which was illegal there.

The relevance of the law governing the contract is also that if, as a matter of English law, a particular contract is unenforceable, the fact that a foreign corporation had capacity to enter into the contract and that it would be enforceable under the law of its incorporation will not render it enforceable in England.

3.7 TRUSTS

Trusts are not bodies corporate and, therefore, are not subject to the ultra vires rule as such. However, one consequence of not being a body corporate is that a trust cannot itself enter into a contract—only legal persons can do so, and a trust has no legal personality.[128] For trust assets to be available to meet contractual liabilities, a trustee must personally enter into a contract in his capacity as trustee, and then rely on his right of indemnity from the trust fund for liabilities incurred in the execution of the trust.[129]

This right of indemnity is only available for liabilities properly incurred by the trustee,[130] and does not extend to liabilities outside the terms of the trust. If the trust fund is insufficient to meet the liability or if the trustee has acted outside his powers, the trustee has no right of indemnity but will remain, subject to the terms of any contract, personally liable. Further, if a trust fund is divided into parts for different purposes, the right of indemnity is only available against the part dedicated to the activity the trustee is undertaking, and not against the whole fund.[131] The trustee's right of indemnity does, however, take priority over the rights of beneficiaries.[132]

A trustee can limit his contractual liability to third parties to assets in his hands as trustee. Whether, and the extent to which, he has done this is a matter of contractual construction, but more is required than merely stating that a party is entering into a contract as trustee.[133] If a trustee's liability is limited to trust assets in the hands of the trustees, and the trust fund is insufficient or it has been disbursed, the counterparty will have no effective recourse against anyone. Similarly, if for some reason the trustee has lost or cannot make use of his right of

128. Section 75(8) of the Financial Services Act 1986 defines a unit trust as "a collective investment scheme under which the property in question [i.e. the investments] is held on trust for the participants".

129. The right of indemnity is now in section 30(2) of the Trustee Act 1925 (though it can be, but very rarely is, excluded by the terms of the trust: section 69(2)). It extends to liabilities in tort: *Re Raybould* [1900] Ch 199.

130. See, for example, *Holding and Management Ltd* v. *Property Holding and Investment Trust plc* [1989] 1 WLR 1313, 1324.

131. *Strickland* v. *Symons* (1884) 26 Ch D 245.

132. *Dowse* v. *Gorton* [1891] AC 190.

133. *Muir* v. *City of Glasgow Bank* (1879) 4 App Cas 337, particularly at pp 355, 368 and 388 (see also, more recently, *Martin Thompson & Evershed plc* v. *Benn* (unreported, 18 September 1997)). In *Williams* v. *Hathaway* (1877) 6 Ch D 544 and *Watling* v. *Lewis* [1911] Ch 415, it was said that whilst a trustee can limit his liability to trust assets in his hands at a particular time, any

indemnity, whether because the particular transaction is outside the terms of the trust or because the trustee owes money to the trust fund as a result of an unrelated transaction,[134] the counterparty will have no effective recourse against anyone.

When entering into a transaction with a trustee it is, therefore, first necessary to decide what is the credit risk being undertaken on the transaction. If the credit risk is that of the trust fund itself, then it is necessary to ensure that the transaction is within the terms of the trust[135] and that the trustee has not lost, and will not lose, his right of indemnity from the fund.[136] If the credit risk is that of the trustee, then, as long as he does not exclude personal liability, the terms of the trust itself may be irrelevant. However, if the counterparty receives money or other assets which are part of the trust fund in circumstances which might have put him on enquiry as to whether the trustees were acting improperly, he runs the risk of being found to be a constructive trustee.[137]

The primary right of a trustee's contractual counterparty is against the trustee.[138] If, however, the trustee does not pay because, for example, he is insolvent, the counterparty is subrogated to the trustee's right of indemnity against the trust fund.[139] If the trustee is insolvent, the counterparty's right of subrogation takes priority over the rights of the trustee's creditors,[140] but the counterparty can be in no better position than the trustee. As a result, if the trustee has, unknown to the counterparty, wrongly taken money from the trust fund and, as a result, is liable to reimburse the trust fund, the trustee cannot claim an indemnity (until he has made the trust fund whole again) and therefore has no right to which the counterparty can be subrogated.[141] Even if the transaction in which the counterparty is involved is entirely proper, the counterparty rather than the beneficiaries appears to take the risk that the trustee may as a result of unconnected transactions be indebted to the trust.[142] To mitigate this risk, where a trustee limits its liability to trust funds in its possession, a counterparty should seek a personal covenant from the trustee that

attempt wholly to exclude personal liability would be "repugnant and void". In *Watling*, Warrington J held that a term in a contract that trustees contracted "as such trustees, but not so as to create personal liability on the part of them or either of them" was void and therefore not effective to limit liability to the trust assets they held. In *Re Robinson's Settlement* [1912] Ch 717, 728–729, Buckley LJ (obiter) cast doubt on this decision.

134. *Re Evans* (1887) 34 Ch D 597.

135. This is a matter of construction of the terms of the documents establishing the trust. Ideally, there should be an express power to enter into derivatives.

136. Helpfully, it is common for a trust deed to have wide exclusions of trustees' liability: see *Armitage* v. *Nurse* [1997] 2 All ER 705.

137. See pp 50–54 above.

138. *Owen* v. *Delamere* (1872) LR 15 Eq 134.

139. *Re Johnson* (1880) 15 Ch D 545.

140. *Re Blundell* (1890) 44 Ch D 1.

141. *Re Evans* (1887) 34 Ch D 597. In this case, a creditor's right of subrogation was held to depend upon the general state of the account between the trustee and the trust fund.

142. Absent, at least, any provision in the trust instruments to the contrary. The law relating to this topic derives in the main from trusts set up in wills in the nineteenth century, and is in need of reconsideration in the light of the realities of modern trusts established for the purpose of trading.

it has not done and will not do anything which might limit its right of indemnity against the trust fund.

3.8 AUTHORITY

If a company does have the corporate capacity to enter into derivatives transactions, it must act through human agency in order to do so. This raises the question of whether the agent has the authority to commit his principal to a derivatives transaction. Agents can have either actual authority or apparent (or ostensible) authority to commit their principals.[143] If an agent has actual authority then, as the name suggests, the principal has given the agent the authority to bind it; if the agent has apparent authority, the principal has not in fact given the agent authority but is nevertheless still bound by the transaction to which the agent has committed it—the principal takes the risk of the agent acting outside his actual authority. In other circumstances, the third party with whom the agent deals takes the risk of the agent acting outside his authority.

3.8.1 Actual authority

Actual authority can be either express or implied.[144] Its source is an agreement between principal and agent.[145] It is clear when it is express, but it can be implied when it is inferred from the conduct of the parties and the surrounding circumstances.[146] So, for example, if someone acts as a managing director of a company, he will impliedly have the authority ordinarily associated with a managing director even if he is not formally appointed as such.[147] Actual authority must come from the company's organs authorised by its constitution to confer authority. This will usually be the directors, though they can usually delegate the power.

Even if an agent does not have actual authority, the principal can subsequently ratify a transaction.

143. For a more detailed consideration of this area than is appropriate here, see *Bowstead and Reynolds on Agency* (16th edn).

144. *Freeman & Lockyer* v. *Buckhurst Park Properties* [1964] 2 QB 480, 488.

145. *Freeman & Lockyer* v. *Buckhurst Park Properties* [1964] 2 QB 480, 502.

146. *Hely-Hutchinson* v. *Brayhead* [1968] 1 QB 549, 583 and 586–587. An aspect of the implied authority is "usual" authority, the implied authorisation to do what falls within the usual scope of a particular office (*Hely-Hutchinson* v. *Brayhead* at 583). This is not always (or at all) distinguishable from apparent authority (see below).

147. *Hely-Hutchinson* v. *Brayhead* [1968] 1 QB 549. The counterparty need not enquire whether the person acting as managing director was properly appointed as long as the company has the power to appoint one: *Royal British Bank* v. *Turquand* (1856) 6 E & B 327 and *Freeman & Lockyer* v. *Buckhurst Park Properties* [1964] 2 QB 480, 497.

3.8.2 Apparent authority

If someone acting as an agent does not have actual authority to commit his principal, the issue is who should bear the risk of the agent acting without authority. This risk is borne by the counterparty with whom the agent deals unless the principal has led the counterparty to believe that the agent has authority. In order for the principal to be liable in these circumstances, there must be a representation by the principal that the agent had authority to enter into on behalf of the principal a contract of the kind in question; the representation must be made by someone with actual authority to manage the business of the company generally or in respect of the matters to which the contract relates; and the counterparty must be induced by the representation to enter into the contract.[148] The most common form of representation will be by conduct, namely by permitting the agent to act in the management or conduct of the principal's business.[149]

If, to the knowledge of the counterparty, an agent does not have actual authority and there is nothing beyond the agent's own assertion that he has been given authority, the principal will not be bound.[150] An agent cannot in general give himself authority by merely asserting that he has authority,[151] but if the agent has apparent authority to communicate decisions of his seniors arising from his position, then, according to *First Energy (UK) Ltd* v. *Hungarian International Bank Ltd*, his statement that he has been given authority can lead to his principal being bound.[152] These cases on the law of apparent authority are not easy to reconcile, the judiciary being inclined at one time to protect the principal from the excesses of its agent and at others the counterparty, and a significant reform of the law may be necessary to bring reconciliation and commercial sense.[153]

If an agent warrants that he has authority which he does not in fact have, he may be liable on the warranty of authority every agent gives when purporting to act for another if the counterparty relies on that warranty and suffers loss as a result.[154] Whether this claim is worth pursuing will depend on the resources of the agent, usually whether he has insurance.

148. *Freeman & Lockyer* v. *Buckhurst Park Properties* [1964] 2 QB 480, 506.
149. *Freeman & Lockyer* v. *Buckhurst Park Properties* [1964] 2 QB 480, 505.
150. *Armagas Ltd* v. *Mundogas SA* [1986] 1 AC 717.
151. The assertion of authority must come from someone with actual authority. In *BBME* v. *Sun Life* [1983] 2 Lloyd's Rep 9, BBME knew that an agent did not have authority and therefore wrote to the "general manager" seeking confirmation of authority. They received confirmation from the "branch manager" (there was no general manager). The House of Lords held that the branch manager had no actual authority to commit Sun Life, which was therefore not bound. It is difficult to see, however, what more BBME could have done in the real world.
152. [1993] 2 Lloyd's Rep 195. Steyn LJ referred particularly to banks in this context, commenting that it would be absurd to suggest that the counterparty should communicate with the board of directors of the bank as a whole (p 204). This decision is not easy to reconcile with either *Armagas* or *BBME* (see the previous two notes).
153. See, for example, I Brown [1994] JBL 360.
154. *Colleen* v. *Wright* (1857) 8 E & B 647.

3.8.3 The risk of lack of authority

In an ideal world, there should be a clear chain of authority from the board of directors to the person who actually purports to enter into a transaction on behalf of a corporate counterparty. This does not mean that the board has actually to sanction the transaction in question, but rather that it should give authority to someone to bind the company to transactions of the type in question. In a less than ideal world, authority should be obtained from someone senior to the person who actually transacts the business at the least, unless that person is in a position, such as managing director, to have apparent authority to bind the company. The sanction of a second person also adds the comfort that the business being transacted is not merely the frolic of one individual within the organisation. The more unusual the transaction, the more important it is to ensure that there is actual authority from on high.

3.9 RESTITUTION

In the event that someone does enter into a derivatives contract which is beyond the powers of its counterparty, what remedies does that person have? The contract itself cannot be enforced because it will be void,[155] but there will in most cases be a restitutionary remedy based on the principle of unjust enrichment.[156] This will restore to the parties the net benefits[157] they have paid to the other on the basis that there has been no consideration (or that the consideration has failed[158]) or on the basis of money paid under a mistake.[159] A restitutionary remedy is not dependent upon showing loss, and therefore the remedy is available no matter how profitable or unprofitable the contract had been or

155. Subject to section 35A of the Companies Act 1985; see above.

156. For a detailed description of the law relating to restitution, see Goff and Jones, *The Law of Restitution* (4th edn).

157. At least if those benefits are monetary, in which case the net payer can recover the net sum paid on a transaction. Benefits in kind raise more complex issues.

158. The Court of Appeal in *Westdeutsche Landesbank* v. *Islington* [1994] 1 WLR 938 decided that case on the basis of no consideration because the consideration was the promise to pay certain sums, and that promise was void. Though not necessary for their decision, the House of Lords in the same case preferred failure of consideration ([1996] AC 669, 683 and 710; see also the Privy Council in *Goss* v. *Chilcott* [1996] 3 WLR 180, 188 which similarly referred to failure of consideration), and in *Guinness Mahon* v. *Kensington & Chelsea* [1998] Lloyd's Rep Bank 109, the Court of Appeal divided over whether the basis should properly be described as total failure of consideration or absence of consideration (see pp 114, 119 and 125). The House of Lords in *Westdeutsche* also decided that, in general, there will be no equitable remedy.

159. *Kleinwort Benson* v. *Lincoln City Council* [1998] 4 All ER 513. It makes no difference whether the mistake is one of fact or law. In most cases, the mistake will be as to the capacity of the counterparty to enter into the transaction and, as a result, as to the binding nature of the contract. If, however, a party is aware of the risks involved and still makes a payment, recovery will be more difficult.

would have turned out to be either on its own or in the context of a derivatives business run by one of the parties,[160] nor does it matter that the contract has run its full course.[161]

One defence to a restitutionary claim is change of position, i.e. that the recipient has in good faith changed its position in reliance on the payment,[162] but the change of position must, save in exceptional circumstances, take place after receipt of the payments in question rather than before.[163] In particular, the recipient cannot rely, for example, on other contracts entered into in the belief that the contract was valid because, ex hypothesi, it is not. In practical terms therefore, the defence is of limited value because in most cases a change of position will be made in reliance on the enforceability of the derivatives "contract" by entering into other transactions to balance the risk on a portfolio rather than in reliance on a payment subsequently made under the "contract".

160. *Kleinwort Benson* v. *South Tyneside* [1994] 4 All ER 972 and *Kleinwort Benson* v. *Birmingham* [1996] 3 WLR 1139.

161. *Guinness Mahon* v. *Kensington & Chelsea* [1998] Lloyd's Rep Bank 109 and *Kleinwort Benson* v. *Lincoln City Council* [1998] 4 All ER 513.

162. *Lipkin Gorman* v. *Karpnale* [1991] 2 AC 548.

163. *Westdeutsche Landesbank* v. *Islington* [1994] 4 All ER 890 and *South Tyneside* v. *Svenska* [1995] 1 All ER 545.

CHAPTER 4

MISREPRESENTATION

4.1 INTRODUCTION

English law has no general theory of lender or counterparty liability, suitability or a duty of good faith in contractual negotiations.[1] The principal control on contractual negotiations is the law of misrepresentation. This does not impose a general duty to make any representation or disclosure in the course of contractual negotiations,[2] but if a representation is made it must be accurate. The law on misrepresentation is, however, of considerable complexity, both as regards what constitutes an actionable misrepresentation and the remedies. In outline, the possibilities arising from a pre-contractual misrepresentation, even if it becomes a term of the contract,[3] are as follows:

1. if the representation is by a contractual party and is fraudulent, (a) damages, and (b) rescission of the contract;
2. if the representation is by a contractual party and is negligent, (a) damages calculated as if the representation were fraudulent under section 2(1) of the Misrepresentation Act 1967 and/or on the lesser basis in the tort of negligent misrepresentation, and (b) rescission of the contract or damages in lieu under section 2(2) of the Misrepresentation Act 1967;

1. The closest English law comes to a duty of good faith is, perhaps, the comment by Stuart-Smith LJ in *Commission for New Towns* v. *Cooper* [1995] Ch 259, 281 that "where A intends B to be mistaken as to the construction of the agreement, so conducts himself that he diverts B's attention from discovering the mistake by making false and misleading statements, and B in fact makes the very mistake that A intends, then notwithstanding that A does not know, but merely suspects, that B is mistaken, and it cannot be shown that the contract was induced by any misrepresentation, rectification may be granted. A's conduct is unconscionable and he cannot insist on performance in accordance with the strict letter of the contract; that is sufficient for rescission." See also *Good Faith and Fault in Contract Law* edited by Beatson and Friedman.
2. See, for example, *Peek* v. *Gurney* (1873) LR 6 HL 377, 403, and *Davies* v. *London and Provincial Marine Insurance Company* (1878) 8 Ch D 469, 474. A duty to disclose will exist where the contracting party is a trustee contracting with his beneficiary or if the contract is one of insurance and therefore requires the utmost good faith from both parties.
3. Section 1(a) of the Misrepresentation Act 1967.

3. if the misrepresentation is by a contractual party and is innocent,[4] (a) damages calculated on the limited basis provided by section 2(2) of the Misrepresentation Act 1967 or (b) rescission of the contract;
4. if the representation is by someone other than a contractual party and is fraudulent, damages;
5. if the representation is by someone other than a contractual party and is negligent, damages in the tort of negligent misrepresentation, but on a narrower basis than in fraud; and
6. if the representation is by someone other than a contractual party and is innocent, nothing.[4a]

The number and variety of causes of action and remedies stems from the historical development of the law on this topic. Before 1964, the law on misrepresentation comprised an amalgam of strands from common law and equity. Damages were granted for fraudulent misrepresentation, rescission being the only remedy for other forms of misrepresentation, whether negligent or entirely innocent (though a form of equitable compensation might be recovered as part of the rescissionary process in order to restore the parties to the position as if the contract had never been made). Rescission was only available if the misrepresentation was by the other contractual party or his agent. In 1964, the House of Lords in *Hedley Byrne* v. *Heller & Partners*[5] recognised for the first time that damages could be awarded for negligent misrepresentation, whether by a contractual party or by another party owing a duty of care. In 1967, the Misrepresentation Act, a significant part of which was probably unnecessary in the light of *Hedley Byrne*, built upon the pre-*Hedley Byrne* law by providing that, in addition to rescission, a party entering into a contract could recover damages for negligent misrepresentation by the other party, though probably calculated on a different, and more generous, basis than on *Hedley Byrne* principles. In addition, the Misrepresentation Act 1967 gave the court discretion to award damages instead of rescission for innocent misrepresentation.

The differing sources and courses of development, and the major legislative and judicial reforms in the 1960s, mean that the law of misrepresentation is anything but straightforward. In order to try to assess the risk of a claim under any particular head, it is necessary to identify the particular requirements of that head. In discussing this, it is probably most useful to start with the nature of a representation upon which a cause of action may be founded before turning to the remedies that this may give rise to.

4. I.e. neither fraudulent nor negligent. Cases before 1964, and some afterwards, sometimes draw a distinction between innocent misrepresentation, meaning negligent and entirely innocent, and fraudulent misrepresentation.

4a. In addition, it appears that if A is induced by a misrepresentation by B to enter into a transaction with C, A has an equity against B to set aside the transaction. If C has actual or constructive notice of the misrepresentation, C may be bound by the equity, enabling A to rescind the contract: *Barclays Bank* v. *O'Brien* [1994] 1 AC 180, 195–196.

5. [1964] AC 465.

4.2 WHAT CAN BE MISREPRESENTED?

4.2.1 Fraud and rescission

For there to be liability, a representation must be inaccurate. As a result, a representation must be of a material fact[6] rather than of opinion for there to be liability other than in fraud. If an opinion is not actually held by the person offering it, that constitutes fraud; but if the opinion is held, no matter how unreasonable it may be to do so, it is not possible to say that a representation that the opinion is held is inaccurate.

However, a representation of opinion may often also involve a representation of fact, principally that there are facts to justify holding that opinion.[7] Whether an expression of opinion will be treated as carrying with it a representation of fact depends on the circumstances. For example, if the facts are equally well known to both parties, no additional representation is likely to be implied, but if the facts are within the knowledge or expertise of one party only it is likely that it will be implied that the representor knows facts to support his opinion.[8] The cases on this topic are, however, hard to reconcile,[9] and *Chitty on Contract*[10] suggests forcefully that the fundamental principle underlying them is that a representation should not give rise to a cause of action if it is unreasonable for the representee to rely on the statement. As a result, casual remarks, sales puff, will not give rise to liability.

If this is the correct principle, it is linked to the requirement that a representation be "material". A representation is material if its natural and probable result is to induce the representee to act on the faith of it in the kind of way he did in fact act[11]; a representation which it is unreasonable to rely on is probably not material.

It is also often said that no action for misrepresentation can lie for a statement of law.[12] This "rule" stems from a time when, absent fraud or contract,[13] the

6. For example, *Brown* v. *Raphael* [1958] 1 Ch 636, 637, 641.

7. *Smith* v. *Land and House Property Corporation* (1884) 28 Ch D 7, 15 and, more recently, *Bankers Trust* v. *Dharmala* (unreported, 29 November 1995).

8. *Smith* v. *Land and House Property Corporation* (1884) 28 Ch D 7, 15.

9. For example, in *Smith* v. *Land and House Property Corporation* (1884) 28 Ch D 7 a representation that someone was a most desirable tenant was held to import a representation of fact and in *Thomas Witter* v. *TPB Industries* [1996] 2 All ER 573, 594–595 a profit forecast was also held to import a representation of fact; but in *Bissett* v. *Wilkinson* [1927] AC 177 a representation that land could carry a certain number of sheep was held not to import a representation of fact.

10. 27th edn, para 6.006, cited with approval in *Bankers Trust* v. *Dharmala* (unreported, 29 November 1995) and *Sumitomo Bank* v. *BBL* [1997] 1 Lloyd's Rep 487, 515.

11. *Downs* v. *Chappell* [1997] 1 WLR 426, 434. As Millett J pointed out in *Lonrho* v. *Fayed (No 2)* [1992] 1 WLR 1, 6 this is closely related to the requirement that the representation must in fact have induced the representee to act as he did.

12. For example, *Beesly* v. *Hallwood Estates* [1960] 1 WLR 549, 560.

13. A fraudulent misrepresentation of law is an actionable misrepresentation: *West London Commercial Bank* v. *Kitson* (1884) 13 QBD 360, 362–363. A cause of action would also lie if there was a contractual obligation to advise as to the law as, for example, when a lawyer is consulted and paid for his services.

only remedy was against the other contracting party (rarely a lawyer) for rescission. In those circumstances, a statement of law would in general be a statement of opinion which it would be unreasonable for the representee to rely on; both the parties could be expected to have equal knowledge (or ignorance) of the law. Even within this "rule", a statement of private rights, as opposed to public law, was treated as a representation of fact rather than of law. Private rights are likely to be within the knowledge of one of the parties only, though the difference between private rights and public law is often not easy to see.[14] This "rule" is therefore consistent with the position that the real issue is whether it is reasonable for the defendant to rely on the representation.

There is no requirement that a representation be in any particular form. A representation can be in writing, oral or implied from conduct[15] but an omission will not in general be enough unless there is an obligation to make disclosure because the contracting party is a trustee contracting with his beneficiary or the contract is one of insurance and therefore of the utmost good faith.[16] If, however, there is "such a partial and fragmentary statement of fact, as that the withholding of that which is not stated makes that which is stated absolutely false",[17] then the combined effect of the active statement and the omission can give rise to an actionable misrepresentation. A representation must, however, be more than a mere unfulfilled promise; for a promise to be actionable, it must be in the form of a contract.[18]

A representation once made continues until the contract to which it relates is entered into. As a result, if a representation is true at the time it was made but

14. *Cooper* v. *Phibbs* (1867) LR 2 HL 149, 170 and *Brikom Investments* v. *Seaford* [1981] 1 WLR 863, 869.

15. In *Ray* v. *Sempers* [1974] AC 370, sitting down in a restaurant and ordering food was held to be a continuing representation of an intention to pay such that a change of mind in the middle of the meal constituted an offence. In *Re Shackleton* (1875) LR 10 Ch App 446, it was accepted that ordering goods and taking them constituted a representation of intention to pay but the court held that, as long as there was an intention to pay, the fact that the buyer had outstanding against him a bankruptcy petition, which ultimately he did not contest, did not give rise to any representation because a man is not bound to tell all his affairs to those with whom he deals. In *Richardson* v. *Silvester* (1873) LR 9 QB 34, placing an advertisement for the sale of a farm was held to involve the representation that the advertiser did have power to sell the farm. See also *The Lutetian* [1982] 1 Lloyd's Rep 140 (approved by the Court of Appeal in *Banque Keyser* v. *Skandia (UK) Insurance* [1990] 1 QB 665, 786–787).

16. See note 2 above.

17. *Peek* v. *Gurney* (1873) LR 6 HL 377, 403. See also *Atlantic Lines & Navigation Co Inc* v. *Hallam Ltd* [1983] 1 Lloyd's Rep 188, 198.

18. *The Zephyr* [1985] 2 Lloyd's Rep 529, 528–529, *Tudor Grange Holdings Ltd* v. *Citibank* [1992] Ch 53, 67 and *Thomas Witter* v. *TPB Industries* [1996] 2 All ER 573, 589. However, in *Bankers Trust* v. *Dharmala* (unreported, 29 November 1995), Mance J said that a statement of intention may imply the absence of any facts or known facts which would prevent the fulfilment of the intention, and in *Box* v. *Midland Bank* [1979] 2 Lloyd's Rep 391, a bank was held liable for the opinion of one of its employees that the credit committee would grant credit approval even though the relevant employee did not himself have authority to do so.

becomes untrue before the contract is made, there is a duty to correct the statement failing which it will be actionable by someone relying on it.[19]

4.2.2 Negligent misrepresentation

In general, the principles determining what misrepresentations can give rise to a claim for rescission and fraud are also applicable to negligent misrepresentation, but it is likely that range of possible representations which can give rise to liability may be somewhat wider. This is discussed further below in the context of negligent misrepresentation.

4.2.3 Risks

In practical terms, a representation that, say, interest rates were likely to rise would probably not constitute an actionable misrepresentation if made by one banker to another. It would be an expression of opinion made by one person to another with equal knowledge of the underlying facts and, therefore, unreasonable to rely on. The same representation made by a banker to a client in the context of trying to interest the client in hedging products, however, probably would include a representation that the banker knew facts to support this view. In those circumstances it might well be reasonable for the client to rely on the representation—a banker might be expected to have special knowledge of potential movements in interest rates.[20] This alone is not enough to give the customer a cause of action if there was in fact no reasonable basis for taking this view,[21] but there is clearly a risk attached to any form of representation, particularly in the context of marketing. These risks can be mitigated by the use of exclusion clauses in contracts and other documents,[22] but there is an inescapable tension between, on the one side, a desire to persuade a client to enter into a derivatives (or any other sort of) contract and, on the other, a desire to minimise risks.

4.3 RESCISSION

The basic remedy for a pre-contractual representation is rescission of the contract. In order to give a contractual party the possibility of rescinding a contract, there must be: first, a representation of material fact (discussed above); secondly, the representation must be untrue; and, thirdly, in entering into the

19. *Davies* v. *London and Provincial Marine Insurance Company* (1878) 8 Ch D 469, 475 and, more recently, *McCullagh* v. *Lane Fox* [1996] PNLR 205. Where the representation is of a current intention, however, a subsequent change in that intention does not make the representation untrue: *Tudor Grange Holdings Ltd* v. *Citibank* [1992] Ch 53, 68.
20. In *Esso* v. *Mardon* [1976] QB 801, a forecast led to liability.
21. The further requirements of a cause of action are discussed below.
22. Discussed in Chapter 8.

contract the other party must have been induced by reliance on the representation.[23] The representation may be innocent, negligent or fraudulent but that does not affect the contractual party's ability to rescind a contract induced by the misrepresentation. It is a question of fact as to whether someone was induced by a misrepresentation to enter into a contract, but a representor cannot escape the consequences of misrepresentation by arguing that the other party had the means of information available and would not have been misled had he been careful.[24] Once a misrepresentation has been made, the onus is on the representor to show that the representee was not in fact misled.[25]

Rescission is an equitable remedy, the effect of which is to lead to a contract being treated as if it had never existed.[26] Until the right to rescind is exercised or lost, a contract is voidable, not void, the rescission taking effect when notice of rescission is given to the other party—rescission does not depend upon a court order.[27]

The right to rescind can be lost in four[28] circumstances: first, if the contract is affirmed with knowledge of the right to rescind; secondly, through the lapse of time; thirdly, because it is impossible to restore the parties to the position they were in before the contract was entered into; and, fourthly, because of the effect on third parties. In addition, the court has power under section 2(2) of the Misrepresentation Act 1967 to award damages instead of rescission if the representation is not fraudulent.

4.3.1 Affirmation of the contract

Any right to rescind a contract will be lost if the contract is affirmed with knowledge both of the facts leading to the right to rescind and of the entitlement to rescind.[29] Once the innocent party has this knowledge, he does not have to act precipitately but can take a reasonable time to consider his options as long as in that period he does not do something unequivocal to affirm the contract.[30] Affirmation can be by words or conduct, as long as it is unequivocal.[31] The lapse of time may, however, be evidence of affirmation,[32] and it also runs the risk that a third party may gain rights under the contract which may be a further bar to

23. *Brown* v. *Raphael* [1958] 1 Ch 636, 641.
24. *Smith* v. *Land and House Property Corporation* (1884) 28 Ch D 7, 16–17.
25. *Torrance* v. *Bolton* (1872) 8 Ch App 118, 123.
26. *Johnson* v. *Agnew* [1980] AC 367, 393.
27. *Reese River* v. *Smith* (1869) 4 HL 64. In rare circumstances where it is impracticable to communicate with the other contractual party, as where he is a fraudster who is trying to escape the authorities, other manifestations of the intention to rescind will suffice: *Car & Universal Finance* v. *Caldwell* [1965] 1 QB 525.
28. There was arguably a fifth bar to rescission, performance or execution of a contract, but, if this was ever a ground as opposed to an aspect of *restitutio in integrum* (see *Senenyake* v. *Chang* [1966] AC 63, 82–83), it was abolished by section 1 of the Misrepresentation Act 1967.
29. *Peyman* v. *Lanjani* [1985] 1 Ch 457, 487 and 494.
30. *Senenyake* v. *Chang* [1966] AC 63, 78–79.
31. *Peyman* v. *Lanjani* [1985] 1 Ch 457, 501.
32. *Clough* v. *London & North Western Railway Co* (1871) LR 7 Ex 26, 34.

rescission (see below). So, for example, exercising rights under a contract, whether an option or making or receiving a payment, with knowledge of the right to rescind might well be taken as an affirmation of the contract because it is inconsistent with treating the contract as if it had never existed.[33]

4.3.2 Lapse of time

Lapse of time shades into affirmation, but even where the innocent party has no knowledge of the right to rescind the lapse of time can act as a bar to rescission. In one case, a lapse of five years between a purchase and finding out about a misrepresentation was held on its own to be sufficient to bar rescission on the basis that there must be certainty in transactions at some point.[34]

4.3.3 Impossibility of restoring the parties to their pre-contractual position

The effect of rescission is to treat a contract as if it had never existed. As a result, a requirement is that it is possible to restore the parties to the position they were in before the contract was entered into. This does not require precise restoration but the ability to do what is "practically just" in the circumstances.[35] This will not involve the payment of compensation calculated on contractual or tortious principles but can take the form of an account of profits and an indemnity against losses and other expenses.[36]

There is some doubt as to the extent to which the court will adjust rights and liabilities in order to allow rescission, but the general trend appears to be towards flexibility. For example, partnerships have been unwound with appropriate indemnities against liabilities to third parties,[37] and items returned even though they were less valuable than when transferred on the basis that the reduction in value was inherent in what was transferred.[38] However, in relation to derivatives contracts, restoring the parties to their pre-contractual position will in most cases pose no difficulties. The repayment of money paid by the parties is in general straightforward,[39] at least if the contract is unconnected with other transactions. If the connection to other transactions is merely that a

33. However, in *Abram Steamship Co* v. *Westville Shipping Co* [1923] AC 773, assent to minor variations in the specification of a vessel was held not to be an affirmation of the purchase contract.

34. *Leaf* v. *International Galleries* [1950] 2 KB 86, 90 and 92.

35. *Erlanger* v. *New Sombrero Phosphate Company* (1878) 3 App Cas 1218, 1279 (Lord Blackburn), quoted with approval many times subsequently (e.g. *Spence* v. *Crawford* [1939] 3 All ER 271, 279 and 288 and *O'Sullivan* v. *Management Agency* [1985] 1 QB 428, 449–450 and 466).

36. *Newbigging* v. *Adam* (1886) 34 Ch D 582, per Bowen LJ. Cotton LJ took a rather more expansive view as to what was possible but his approach appears not to have been followed: see, for example, *Whittington* v. *Searle-Hayne* (1900) 48 LT 49.

37. *Senenyake* v. *Chang* [1966] AC 63.

38. *Spence* v. *Crawford* [1939] 3 All ER 271, 279. In *Smith New Court Ltd* v. *Scrimgeour Vickers* [1997] AC 254, 262, Lord Browne-Wilkinson suggested that it would still be possible to grant rescission even if the fungible security the subject of the contract in question had been sold because an identical security could be purchased on the market, and it would be enough to return that.

39. In the local authority swaps cases, restitution proved no problem: see pp 75–76 above.

contract forms part of a bank's portfolio, and the portfolio will become unbalanced if the contract is removed, that will not be sufficient to prevent the restoration of the parties to their pre-contractual position.[40] If, however, the derivatives contract is an integral part of a structured financing, at least if third parties are involved, it is more arguable that the parties cannot be restored to the position they were in before the contract was made. The removal of one part of a structure may affect very significantly what remains. If third parties are not involved, rescission could include the unwinding of the whole structure if it either is treated as one with the derivatives transaction or the misrepresentation induced all the limbs of the structure.

4.3.4 Third party rights

Rescission is an equitable remedy which leads to a contract being treated as if it had never existed. The contract remains in existence until the right to rescind is exercised. If during the contract's existence, a third party has acquired rights under it, the courts will not allow rescission because it would penalise an innocent party.[41] As a result, if the benefit of a contract has been assigned or if others have acted in reliance on its existence, rescission will not be possible.

4.4 FRAUD

Fraud[42] is an element in the tort of deceit, or fraudulent misrepresentation. To succeed in deceit it is necessary to show that a false representation has been made (1) knowingly, (2) without belief in its truth or (3) recklessly, careless as to whether it is true or false. If a statement is made in this way, it does not matter that there was no intention to cheat or injure the person to whom the representation was made.[43] A representation does not have to be made directly to the person who relies on it—it is enough if, for example, it is in a newspaper advertisement.[44] As fraud depends upon the state of mind of the representor, if a

40. "The mere fact that the party making the representation has treated the contract as binding and has acted on it does not preclude relief": *MacKenzie* v. *Royal Bank of Canada* [1934] AC 468, 476.

41. For example, *Senenyake* v. *Chang* [1966] AC 63, 80 and *Society of Lloyd's* v. *Lyons* (*The Times*, 11 August 1997).

42. This is common law fraud, not equitable fraud as described in *Nocton* v. *Lord Ashburton* [1914] AC 932 and *Armitage* v. *Nurse* [1997] 2 All ER 705, 710–711 and 712.

43. *Derry* v. *Peek* (1889) 14 App Cas 337, 374. In *Standard Chartered Bank* v. *PNC* [1995] 2 Lloyd's Rep 365, 373, Clarke J said that it was necessary to have an intention to deceive but not to defraud. In *Thomas Witter* v. *TPB Industries* [1996] 2 All ER 573, 586–587, Jacob J considered that the test was dishonesty, and the issue was whether, in that case, the representor had been so reckless as to be considered dishonest.

44. *Richardson* v. *Silvester* (1873) LR 9 QB 34 and *Swift* v. *Winterbotham* (1873) LR 8 QB 244. Nor is it necessary to know the identity of the person acting on the representation: *Brown Jenkinson* v. *Percy Dalton* [1957] 2 QB 621.

representation is ambiguous, the representor must have no honest belief in the statement in the sense that he intended it even if, on an objective construction, it does not bear that sense.[45] But if the representor knows that a statement is ambiguous and one of the possible meanings is false, it is no defence to argue that the representee should have attributed the other, correct, meaning to the statement[46]; nor is it a defence to show that the representee made a mistake as long as the representation was actively present in his mind when he acted in the manner which caused loss.[47]

A principal is liable for the fraud of his employee if that employee is acting within the actual or apparent scope of his authority, even if the fraud is only for the benefit of the employee and not the employer.[48]

With one exception, there is no requirement as to the form in which an actionable fraudulent representation can be made. The one exception is under section 6 of the Statute of Frauds Amendment Act 1828 (Lord Tenterden's Act). This provides that an action in deceit can only be brought on a credit reference if the reference is in writing and signed.

If fraud is proved, the courts show very little sympathy. They will, for example, be more flexible in restoring the parties to the position they were in before the contract was entered into in order to allow rescission,[49] and the measure of damages is more generous than for breach of contract or for negligent misrepresentation. Damages under both those heads depend upon foreseeability of the loss, but in deceit the damages recoverable are as follows:

"(1) the defendant is bound to make reparation for all the damage flowing directly from the transaction; (2) although such damage need not have been foreseeable, it must have been directly caused by the transaction; (3) in assessing such damage, the plaintiff is entitled to recover by way of damages the full price paid by him but must give credit for any benefits which he has received as a result of the transaction; (4) as a general rule, the benefits received by him include the market value of the property acquired as at the date of acquisition; but such general rule is not to be inflexibly applied where to do so would prevent him obtaining full compensation for the wrong suffered; (5) although the circumstances in which the general rule should not apply cannot be comprehensively stated, it will not normally apply where either (a) the misrepresentation has continued to operate after the date of acquisition of the asset so as to induce the plaintiff to retain the asset or (b) the circumstances of the case are such that the plaintiff is, by reason of the fraud, locked into the property. (6) In addition, the plaintiff is entitled to recover consequential losses caused by the transaction; (7) the plaintiff must take all reasonable steps to mitigate his loss once he has discovered the fraud."[50]

45. *Akerhielm* v. *De Mare* [1959] AC 789.

46. *Smith* v. *Chadwick* (1884) 9 App Cas 187, 201.

47. *Edgington* v. *Fitzmaurice* (1885) 29 Ch D 459, 483. Contributory negligence has no role in deceit: *Alliance & Leicester Building Society* v. *Edgestop* [1994] 2 All ER 38.

48. *Lloyd* v. *Grace Smith* [1912] AC 716 and, for example, *Credit Lyonnais Nederland* v. *ECGD* [1999] 2 WLR 540. In *Breiss* v. *Woolley* [1954] AC 333, a principal was held liable for a fraudulent misrepresentation of an agent made before he was appointed agent because there was a continuing duty to correct that misrepresentation.

49. *Spence* v. *Crawford* [1939] 3 All ER 271, 288.

50. *Smith New Court Ltd* v. *Scrimgeour Vickers* [1997] AC 254, 267 (Lord Browne-Wilkinson).

4.5 MISREPRESENTATION ACT 1967

The Misrepresentation Act 1967 built upon the pre-*Hedley Byrne* law relating to misrepresentation by making two major changes: first, it allowed the court to award damages for a negligent misrepresentation in addition to granting rescission; and, secondly, it allowed the court to award damages in lieu of rescission in the case of innocent misrepresentation.

4.5.1 Negligent misrepresentation

Section 2(1) of the Misrepresentation Act 1967 provides that:

> "Where a person has entered into a contract after a misrepresentation has been made to him by another party thereto and as a result thereof he has suffered loss, then, if the person making the misrepresentation would be liable to damages in respect thereof had the misrepresentation been made fraudulently, that person shall be so liable notwithstanding that the misrepresentation was not made fraudulently, unless he proves that he had reasonable grounds to believe and did believe up to the time the contract was made that the facts represented were true."

As a result, the test for liability under this section is: would the representor have been liable had the misrepresentation been made fraudulently; if so, can the representor prove[51] that he had reasonable grounds to believe that the facts[52] represented were true. Although this liability is clearly based on the negligence of the representor, the section provides for damages as if the misrepresentation had been made fraudulently. The damages are therefore calculated on the fraud basis[53] even though that is significantly wider than the damages which can be recovered in the tort of negligent misrepresentation. Despite this fiction of fraud, damages can be reduced if there is contributory negligence on the part of the representee.[54]

4.5.2 Innocent misrepresentation

Damages can be granted under section 2(1) of the Misrepresentation Act 1967 in addition to rescission, but under section 2(2) the court has a discretion to

51. The burden of proof is on the representor: *Howard Marine* v. *Ogden* [1978] 1 QB 574, 596.

52. In *Lancaster City Council* v. *Unique Group* (unreported, 15 December 1995), Jonathan Parker J considered that section 2(1) was only applicable if there was a representation of fact, and an opinion was not enough even if it carried a representation that the representor knew facts to support it. In *Sumitomo* v. *Banque Bruxelles Lambert* [1997] 1 Lloyd's Rep 487, 514, Langley J expressed the view that this was incorrect. Langley J's view is to be preferred.

53. *Royscott Trust* v. *Rogerson* [1991] 2 QB 310. In *Smith New Court Ltd* v. *Scrimgeour Vickers* [1997] AC 254, 267 Lord Browne-Wilkinson said that he expressed no view as to the correctness of this, but in *South Australia Asset Management Corp* v. *York Montague* [1997] AC 191, 216 Lord Hoffmann supported the position as he had done as Hoffmann LJ in *William Sindall plc* v. *Cambridgeshire CC* [1994] 3 All ER 932, 954. Writers (e.g. Professor Treitel in *The Law of Contract*, 9th edn) take a different view. It is, however, hard to interpret the wording of the statute any other way even though the result is manifestly unjust.

54. *Gran Gelato* v. *Richcliff* [1992] Ch 560.

award damages instead of rescission as long as the misrepresentation is not fraudulent (damages can be awarded under section 2(1) and under section 2(2), though if that occurs section 2(3) requires any award under section 2(2) to be taken into account when assessing damages under section 2(1)). Section 2(2) provides:

"Where a person has entered into a contract after a misrepresentation has been made to him otherwise than fraudulently, and he would be entitled, by reason of the misrepresentation to rescind the contract, then, if it is claimed, in any proceedings arising out of the contract, that the contract ought to be or has been rescinded the court or arbitrator may declare the contract subsisting and award damages in lieu of rescission, if of opinion that it would be equitable to do so, having regard to the nature of the misrepresentation and the loss that would be caused by it if the contract were upheld, as well as to the loss that rescission would cause to the other party."

Damages under section 2(2) are, it seems, awarded on a narrower basis than under section 2(1),[55] and perhaps even than under the tort of negligent misrepresentation. The measure of damages is far from obvious from the section, but it may be that under section 2(2) the damages are concerned only with the difference in value between the item acquired and its actual value, and do not include any consequential losses.[56] The award is, however, discretionary, and if it does not lead to satisfactory compensation that might be a ground for allowing rescission rather than awarding damages in lieu. The court can award damages in lieu of rescission and restore the contract even if the contract has already been rescinded by self-help means.[57] The court has, according to one case, a discretion to award damages even if by the time it does so rescission is barred on one of the grounds discussed above[58] though this makes it hard to take into account the loss rescission would cause, one of the factors section 2(2) requires the court to take into account in exercising its discretion to award damages.

4.6 NEGLIGENT MISREPRESENTATION

Damages for fraud and rescission have been part of the English legal landscape for many years. Damages for negligent misrepresentation, whether by a contractual party or by someone else, is a far more recent innovation, and the principles which govern it are still being worked out. The tort has a wider ambit than rescission (other than in fraud) because it can apply to parties whether or not they enter into a contract, but the remedy is confined to damages.

The conditions which must be fulfilled for liability in the tort of negligent misrepresentation (or negligent misstatement) are as follows: first, the defendant

55. *William Sindall plc* v. *Cambridgeshire CC* [1994] 3 All ER 932, 954.
56. *Thomas Witter* v. *TPB Industries* [1996] 2 All ER 573, 591.
57. *Atlantic Lines & Navigation Co Inc* v. *Hallam Ltd (The "Lucy")* [1983] 1 Lloyd's Rep 188.
58. *Thomas Witter* v. *TPB Industries* [1996] 2 All ER 573, 588–591; but see (1995) 111 LQR 385.

must owe the plaintiff a duty of care; secondly, the defendant must have acted in breach of that duty; and, thirdly, the plaintiff must have suffered damage as a result of that breach of duty. Although easily stated, each of these three conditions (though particularly the first[59]) raises difficult issues. They are also inter-related; for example, a duty of care does not exist in the abstract—it exists in respect of a particular kind of loss that the plaintiff might suffer.[60] As a result, although logically the first question is whether there is a duty of care, before that question can be answered it is necessary to know what loss the plaintiff has suffered.[61] Nevertheless, the courts treat each requirement separately, and this is probably the only practical way of determining the risk of liability attaching in the tort of negligent misrepresentation as a result of any particular course of action.

4.6.1 When does a duty of care arise?

In 1932, Lord Atkin made one of the most famous statements in English law. He said that "[y]ou must take reasonable care to avoid acts or omissions which you can reasonably foresee would be likely to injure your neighbour", that is "persons who are so closely and directly affected by [your] act that [you] ought reasonably to have them in contemplation as being so affected".[62] This broad principle, aimed at providing a common basis for the then disparate incidence of the law of negligence, has never, however, applied where the loss suffered by the plaintiff is purely economic or financial. The courts have always been concerned that applying this principle, based on the foreseeability of harm only, would open up indeterminate liability to an indeterminate class, and thereby impede legitimate activity.[63] The courts have therefore looked for additional criteria to limit the scope of liability for negligent misstatement.

Until 1963, the additional criterion applied was simply to deny any liability for negligent misrepresentation. Tortious liability for misrepresentation could only be in fraud.[64] This position was changed in *Hedley Byrne & Co Ltd* v.

59. Markesinis and Deakin (1992) 55 MLR 619, record the large number of cases which had gone to the House of Lords on the issue of whether a duty of care was owed up to the time of their article. The number of cases reaching the highest court in the land on this issue has not slowed since.

60. *South Australia Asset Management Corporation* v. *York Montague Ltd* (on appeal from *BBL* v. *Eagle Star*) [1997] AC 191, 211 (see also *Nykredit Mortgage Bank* v. *Edward Erdman* [1997] 1 WLR 1627 and *Platform Home Loans* v. *Oyston Shipways* [1999] 2 WLR 518).

61. For example, in *South Australia Asset Management Corporation* v. *York Montague Ltd* [1997] AC 191, the courts below the House of Lords treated the main issue in the case as being one of the quantification of damages but the House of Lords treated it as concerning the type of loss for which the duty of care was owed.

62. *Donoghue* v. *Stevenson* [1932] AC 562, 580.

63. For example, in *Candler* v. *Crane Christmas & Co* [1951] 2 KB 164, 194, Asquith LJ expressed the fear that if marine hydrographers were liable for loss caused by the negligent preparation of charts, people would think twice before making maps. "Cartography would become an ultra-hazardous activity."

64. *Candler* v. *Crane Christmas & Co* [1951] 2 KB 164. There could also be liability if there was a fiduciary relationship or if there was a contract.

Heller & Partners Ltd,[65] where the House of Lords accepted that there could be liability for a negligent misrepresentation. The courts have, however, remained concerned to ensure that liability for negligent misrepresentation is constrained within proper limits, but the judiciary has been divided as to what, in addition to foreseeability that a misstatement might cause damage, the appropriate limiting factor should be.

This issue has not been resolved; indeed, the swing in judicial attitude has led some to abandon attempts to identify any real principle behind the imposition of a duty of care. Instead, each case is to be treated on its facts, the only guide being whether a duty of care has been imposed in the same or similar facts in the past. Pragmatism,[66] with the benefit of judicial hindsight, is the determining factor.

The absence of any practical guiding principle as to when a duty of care will arise makes it difficult to determine the extent of any risks that a particular activity might entail. This is especially so in relatively novel areas such as derivatives. Assessing and controlling risks in this area is, therefore, not always easy. If someone is prepared to accept the risk of liability in negligent misstatement (e.g. by accepting an advisory mandate), and to put in place quality control measures to try to reduce the prospect of liability actually arising, then there may be no particular difficulty. If, however, someone does not wish to accept the risk of liability in negligent misstatement, defining safe areas of activity is not necessarily easy.

4.6.2 The development of the criteria to establish the existence of a duty of care

To understand the current legal position with regard to negligent misstatement, it is necessary to go into the chequered development of the tort since it was recognised in *Hedley Byrne*.

4.6.2.1 *From Hedley Byrne to Anns v. Merton—the search for a limiting principle*

In *Hedley Byrne & Co Ltd* v. *Heller & Partners Ltd*[67] itself, the members of the House of Lords expressed the criteria necessary to establish the existence of a duty of care giving rise to liability for a negligent misrepresentation in various different ways. These included: a duty of care will arise if "expressly or by implication from the circumstances the speaker or writer has undertaken some responsibility"; "if A assumes a responsibility to B to tender him deliberate

65. [1964] AC 465. Stapleton (1991) 107 LQR 249 argues that *Hedley Byrne* may have been the wrong turn in the law.

66. See, for example, *Rowling* v. *Takaro Properties Ltd* [1988] AC 473, 501, *Caparo plc* v. *Dickman* [1990] 2 AC 605, 638 and 633, and *Bankers Trust* v. *Dharmala* (unreported, 29 November 1995), transcript, p 87.

67. [1964] AC 465.

advice"; if "a person . . . takes it upon himself to give information or advice to, or allows his information or advice to be passed on to, another person who, as he knows or should know, will place reliance upon it"; "if someone possessed of a special skill undertakes, quite irrespective of contract, to apply that skill for the assistance of another person who relies on such skill"; where the relationship is " 'equivalent to contract', that is, where there is an assumption of responsibility in circumstances in which, but for the absence of consideration, there would be a contract"; and "if persons holding themselves out in a calling or situation or profession take on a task within that calling or situation or profession, they have a duty of skill and care. In terms of proximity one might say that they are in particularly close proximity to those who, as they know, are relying on their skill and care".[68]

Though expressed in different ways, the common theme in the speeches in *Hedley Byrne* is that, in order for there to be a duty of care, the additional factor over and above foreseeability of harm is an assumption of responsibility by the defendant towards the plaintiff, a relationship equivalent to contract except for the absence of consideration. In *Anns* v. *Merton London Borough Council*[69] this limiting approach was not pursued, and an attempt was made to unify all aspects of the law of negligence by imposing common criteria based initially only on the foreseeability of harm. Lord Wilberforce said that in order to establish the existence of a duty of care, it should no longer be necessary to bring the facts of that situation within those of previous situations in which a duty of care has been held to exist. Instead, he proposed a two-stage test: first, there must be a sufficient relationship of proximity between the plaintiff and defendant such that the defendant could reasonably foresee that carelessness on his part may be likely to cause damage to the plaintiff—if so, a prima facie duty of care arises; secondly, there should be no policy considerations to negative or to limit or reduce the scope of the duty or the class of person to whom it is owed or the damages to which a breach of it may give rise.[70] The limiting factor on liability was therefore public policy, but with the burden apparently on the defendant to show why public policy should exonerate him.

The judicial reassertion that, where economic loss is concerned, foreseeability should not alone be sufficient even to impose a prima facie duty of care was not long in coming,[71] and Lord Wilberforce's approach was finally overruled in

68. The quotes are from, respectively, [1964] AC pp 483 (Lord Reid), 494 (Lord Morris), 502–503 (Lord Morris), 503 (Lord Morris), 529 (Lord Devlin) and 538 (Lord Pearce). In *Henderson* v. *Merrett* [1995] 2 AC 145, 178, Lord Goff said that the governing principles from *Hedley Byrne* "are perhaps now perceived to be most clearly stated in the speeches of Lord Morris of Borth-y-Gest (with whom Lord Hodson agreed) and of Lord Devlin".

69. [1978] AC 728.

70. [1978] AC 728, 751–752. See also *Dorset Yacht Co* v. *Home Office* [1970] AC 1004, 1026–1027 and *Junior Books* v. *Veitchi* [1983] AC 520, 539.

71. For example, *Tate & Lyle* v. *GLC* [1985] 2 AC 509, *Peabody* v. *Sir Lindsay Parkinson* [1985] 1 AC 210, *Candlewood* v. *Mitsui* [1986] 1 AC 1, *Leigh & Sillavan* v. *Aliakmon* [1986] 1 AC 785, *Yuen Kun Yeu* v. *Attorney-General of Hong Kong* [1988] 1 AC 175 and *D&F Estates* v. *Church Commissioners* [1989] 1 AC 177.

Murphy v. *Brentwood Council*.[72] Liability for negligent misstatement was treated as a special area where, in accordance with *Hedley Byrne*, it was necessary to show an assumption of responsibility.[73] In 1989 and 1990, however, two major cases on negligent misrepresentation questioned whether even this was the basis upon which liability should be imposed.

4.6.2.2 Smith v. Bush and Caparo v. Dickman—the abandonment of the search for a principle

In *Smith* v. *Eric S Bush*, *Harris* v. *Wyre Forest District Council*,[74] surveyors carried out valuations of modest properties for a mortgagee. In one case, the valuation contained a disclaimer but the mortgagee was sent a copy of the valuation; in the other, the valuation was stated to be for the sole benefit of the mortgagee and was not sent to the mortgagor. Both valuations were negligently prepared, and in both cases the valuers were found liable to the mortgagors.[75] The members of the House of Lords took two different approaches to reach the conclusion that the surveyors were liable.

Lord Templeman, with whom Lords Keith and Brandon agreed, considered that the surveyor assumed responsibility to the mortgagor by agreeing to carry out a valuation for mortgage purposes knowing that the valuation fee was to be paid by the mortgagor and that the valuation would probably be relied on by the mortgagor. This, however, stretches the concept of an assumption of responsibility beyond breaking point. The surveyors carried out the survey on the instructions, and for the benefit, of the mortgagee, not the mortgagor. Merely because it was likely the mortgagor would not have his own survey done does not mean that there was any intention on the part of the surveyor to assume liability to the mortgagor. If the mortgagor had paid an appropriate fee, doubtless the surveyor would have been happy to make that assumption.[76] No fee was paid by the mortgagor in his own right (as opposed to reimbursing the mortgagee its expenses of the transaction), and it is hard to resist the conclusion that, whether judged subjectively or objectively, the surveyor had no conceivable intention of assuming any responsibility to the mortgagor. Any talk of assumption of responsibility in these circumstances is a legal fiction based on the foreseeability of damage and the desire to impose liability.

72. [1991] 1 AC 398.
73. *Yuen Kun Yeu* v. *Attorney-General of Hong Kong* [1988] 1 AC 175, 192 and 197.
74. [1990] 1 AC 831.
75. All the members of the House of Lords considered that the disclaimers in the valuation reports were unreasonable and therefore void under the Unfair Contract Terms Act 1977.
76. The risk a surveyor undertakes to a mortgagee is different from that undertaken to a mortgagor: the surveyor is liable to the mortgagor if his survey is negligently prepared; but he is only liable to the mortgagee if the survey is negligently prepared and the mortgagor defaults on repayments.

Lord Griffiths, with whom Lords Keith and Brandon also agreed, took a different approach. He recognised the deficiencies of any concept of assumption of responsibility in the context of that case,[77] and, furthermore, thought the concept was unlikely to be a helpful or realistic test in most cases.[78] Instead, Lord Griffiths proposed a three-stage test: first, is it foreseeable that if advice is negligent the recipient would suffer damage; secondly, if so, is there a sufficiently proximate relationship between the parties; and, thirdly, is it just and reasonable to impose liability.[79] This is, therefore, very similar to the test proposed by Lord Wilberforce in *Anns* v. *Merton* but with the addition of a requirement of "proximity". Lord Griffiths went on to say that the necessary proximity arose from the surveyors' knowledge that the overwhelming probability was that the purchaser would rely on the valuation, i.e. it arose from foreseeability.

Smith v. *Bush* probably turns upon its facts—the House of Lords felt that the purchasers of modest[80] houses should be able to rely on valuations which they had indirectly paid for even though the valuations were carried out for their mortgagees. Although the decision was made at a time when the approach of the House of Lords to the imposition of a duty of care was generally restrictive,[81] in this particular case the reluctance to impose a duty of care was overcome even though the most commonly cited basis for doing so was not present.

The other major case is *Caparo Industries plc* v. *Dickman*,[82] a case concerning company auditors' liability to shareholders. In this case, the House of Lords gave up any attempt to establish the criteria over and above foreseeability which give rise to a duty of care for a negligent misrepresentation. Lord Bridge[83] repeated the three-stage test put forward by Lord Griffiths in *Smith* v. *Bush*, but said that concepts of proximity and fairness were not susceptible of any definition which would give them practical utility as tests, and he therefore preferred an incremental approach. Instead of identifying a principle, he, and the other members of the House of Lords, preferred to rely on previous factual situations where the courts have decided that a duty of care exists and to develop novel categories incrementally and by analogy with those estab-

77. Lord Griffiths in the same case recognised that the "phrase 'assumption of responsibility' can only have any real meaning if it is understood as referring to the circumstances in which the law will deem the maker of the statement to have assumed responsibility to the person who acts upon the advice": [1990] 1 AC 831, 862. In wishing to find the surveyors liable he had no real choice but to take this line. Lord Jauncey also referred to the issue as being whether the facts disclosed a sufficiently proximate relationship between surveyors and mortgagors that the surveyors would be deemed to have assumed responsibility to the mortgagors (p 871).

78. In *Caparo* v. *Dickman* [1990] 2 AC 605, 628 and 637 Lords Roskill and Oliver took a similar view of the utility of treating assumption of responsibility as a test for liability for negligent misstatement.

79. [1990] 1 AC 831, 865.

80. Lord Griffiths in particular was keen to stress that the houses in question were modest.

81. See the cases cited at note 71 above, *Murphy* v. *Brentwood Council* [1991] 1 AC 398 and Stapleton (1991) 107 LQR 249.

82. [1990] 2 AC 605.

83. [1990] 2 AC 605, 617–618.

lished categories.[84]

Lord Oliver considered that assumption of responsibility was of no value as a test for the existence of a duty of care,[85] but suggested that liability might attach for a negligent misrepresentation if: first, advice is required for a specific or general purpose known to the adviser at the time the advice was given; secondly, the adviser knows either that his advice will be communicated to the advisee, either specifically or as the member of an ascertainable class; thirdly, it is known that the advice is likely to be acted upon without further enquiry for that purpose; and, fourthly, it is so acted upon by the advisee to his detriment.[86]

Caparo v. *Dickman* identified the problem, but failed to offer an answer. Citing sufficient proximity or neighbourhood as a necessary ingredient in the existence of a duty of care just begs the question, as the House of Lords recognised, of whether that relationship arises on a particular set of facts.[87] The House of Lords answered this question with the instruction to look at existing cases to see whether the courts have already determined that a duty of care exists and, if not, whether imposing a duty would be an incremental or analogous extension of those cases. *Smith* v. *Bush* is, however, neither incremental nor analogous to existing categories, and therefore adds a random factor to the issue.

4.6.2.3 *The current position—assumption of responsibility*

In the mid-1990s the House of Lords revisited on several occasions the circumstances which give rise to a duty of care. These have confirmed the three-stage test for liability in negligent misrepresentation,[88] namely that the loss in question should be foreseeable as the result of the negligent act, that there should be sufficient proximity between the plaintiff and the defendant, and that it should be fair, just and reasonable to impose liability upon the defendant.

This still begs the question as to what circumstances give rise to sufficient

84. [1990] 2 AC 605, 618 and 633–634. In *Junior Books* v. *Veitchi* [1983] AC 520, 539, Lord Roskill considered that principle should determine the existence of a duty of care, but in *Caparo* he impliedly recanted in favour of incrementalism from established categories.

85. [1990] 2 AC 605, 637.

86. [1990] 2 AC 605, 638. In each of the first three conditions stated by Lord Oliver, knowledge included both actual and inferential knowledge.

87. In *Morgan Crucible* v. *Hill Samuel* [1991] Ch 295, 317, the Court of Appeal recognised that: "Proximity is a somewhat uncertain concept, representing as it does, no more than a description of the kind of relationship between the parties which courts consider capable of giving rise to a duty of care. It is closely bound up with the no less uncertain concept of justice and reasonableness, and it may give rise to difficult problems in cases such as the present, where the facts are not precisely covered by previous authority." Similar sentiments were expressed in *James McNaughton* v. *Hicks Anderson* [1991] 2 QB 113, 123–124.

88. For example, *Marc Rich* v. *Bishop Rock Marine* [1996] 1 AC 211, 235 and *Spring* v. *Guardian Assurance* [1995] 2 AC 296, 335 and 342. In *Marc Rich*, Lord Steyn said that the three-stage test was applicable to all claims in negligence but in *Williams* v. *Natural Life Health Foods* [1998] 1 WLR 830, 834 he said that if there was an assumption of responsibility there was no need to look at whether it is fair, just and reasonable to impose liability.

proximity between the plaintiff and the defendant. For this purpose, the test of assumption of responsibility has been revived[89] as potentially the key test in most negligent misrepresentation cases.[90] If there is an assumption of responsibility, there is no need to consider the third limb of the three-stage test—it will be assumed that it is fair, just and reasonable to impose liability.[91] Whether someone has assumed responsibility is to be determined objectively in the light of what the defendant has said or done in his dealings with the plaintiff,[92] and the assumption in question is an assumption of responsibility for a task, not the assumption of legal liability; the assumption of responsibility for the task creates the special relationship to which the law attaches a duty to carry out carefully the task assumed.[93] However, in *White* v. *Jones*, which concerned whether a solicitor owed a duty of care to potential legatees, as well as to the testator, in preparing a will, the House of Lords accepted that the case did not on ordinary principles give rise to an assumption of responsibility but was prepared to enlarge the concept by holding that the assumption of responsibility to the testator should be held in law to extend to the legatee.[94] The concept is therefore in itself sufficiently flexible to meet circumstances which might not be thought to fall within its terms.

However, assumption of responsibility is probably not the sole basis upon which the necessary proximity between plaintiff and testator can be established for the purposes of negligent misstatement. In *Spring* v. *Guardian Assurance*,[95]

89. *Spring* v. *Guardian Assurance* [1995] 2 AC 296, 316, *Henderson* v. *Merrett* [1995] 2 AC 145, 180–181 and 205, *White* v. *Jones* [1995] 2 AC 207, 262, 268 and 274, and *Williams* v. *Natural Life Health Foods* [1998] 1 WLR 830.

90. In, for example, *Peach* v. *Slater* [1998] BCC 139, Morritt LJ in the Court of Appeal treated assumption of responsibility as the "touchstone" of liability. See also, in the Court of Appeal, *McCullagh* v. *Lane Fox* [1996] PNLR 205, and *Gold Coin Joaillers* v. *United Bank of Kuwait* [1997] 6 Bank LR 60.

91. In *Henderson* v. *Merrett* [1995] 2 AC 145, 181, Lord Goff suggested that if there was an assumption of responsibility there was no need to consider whether it was fair, just and reasonable to impose liability but in *White* v. *Jones*, which Lord Goff treated as a case of assumption of responsibility, he considered policy issues without suggesting that there was no need to do so. In *Williams* v. *Natural Life Health Foods* [1998] 1 WLR 830, 834 Lord Steyn, with whom the other members of the House of Lords (including Lord Goff) agreed, stated expressly that if there was an assumption of responsibility there was no need to look to the other limbs.

92. *Henderson* v. *Merrett* [1995] 2 AC 145, 181, *ADT* v. *Binder Hamlyn* (unreported, 6 December 1995), *Peach* v. *Slater* [1998] BCC 139 and *Williams* v. *Natural Life Health Foods* [1998] 1 WLR 830. In *Electra Private Equity Partners* v. *KPMG* (unreported, 23 April 1999), the Court of Appeal confirmed that the text is objective but indicated that actual intention may be a strong indicator of a duty of care.

93. *White* v. *Jones* [1995] 2 AC 207, 273, applied in *Gold Coin Joaillers* v. *United Bank of Kuwait* [1997] 6 Bank LR 60, *McCullagh* v. *Lane Fox* [1996] PNLR 205 and *Peach* v. *Slater* [1998] BCC 139. In *Machin* v. *Adams* (unreported, 7 May 1997) Sir Brian Neill described what was required as a "conscious" assumption of responsibility for the task but it is doubtful whether this is consistent with the objective assessment of the assumption: see *Electra Private Equity Partners* v. *KPMG* (unreported, 23 April 1999).

94. [1995] 2 AC 207, 268 (Lord Goff, with whom Lords Browne-Wilkinson and Nolan agreed). See also *Goodwill* v. *British Pregnancy Advisory Service* [1996] 2 All ER 161, *Trusted* v. *Clifford Chance* (unreported, 17 May 1996) and *Carr-Glynn* v. *Frearsons* [1998] 4 All ER 225.

95. [1995] 2 AC 296.

which concerned the liability of a company to a former member of its staff in respect of a negligently given reference, the majority of the House of Lords considered that the case did not fall within the *Hedley Byrne* principle of assumption of responsibility. They still held the company liable, apparently as a measured extension of the existing factual categories where liability might accrue. They appear to have treated this as being in accordance with the incremental approach to extensions of liability referred to above.[96] Indeed, the Court of Appeal has suggested that it may be useful to look in turn at any new set of facts using each of the three main approaches—assumption of responsibility, incrementalism, and the three-stage approach—and said, somewhat implausibly, that if the facts are properly analysed and the policy considerations correctly evaluated, the several approaches will yield the same result.[97]

The issue of liability in negligent misrepresentation appears in reality to be governed by the judicial "impulse to do practical justice"[98] regardless of existing cases or the principles expounded in them. This impulse can lead both to liability[99] and to the refusal to impose liability,[100] but has led to disagreement amongst the senior judiciary and inevitably involves uncertainty among those who have to assess the risk of there being liability from a certain course of action and different views amongst the judiciary.

4.6.3 How can responsibility be assumed?

In practice, the principal risk of incurring liability for negligent misrepresentation is from the doctrine of assuming responsibility to another for a task. The fact of entering into a derivatives contract, or even merely negotiating a derivatives contract, does not give rise to any assumption of responsibility outside the terms of the contract, but if an explanation is given of the transaction reasonable care must in general be taken.[101] No comprehensive list of the factors

96. [1995] 2 AC 296, 332–334, 344 and 353. Lord Goff referred to the incremental approach derived from *Caparo* v. *Dickman* [1990] 2 AC 605, but considered there to be one broad category (assumption of responsibility) to which, apparently, the incremental approach was not necessary. This approach was followed in *Williams* v. *Natural Life Health Foods* [1998] 1 WLR 830.

97. *BCCI* v. *Price Waterhouse and others* [1998] Lloyd's Rep Bank 85, 98–99.

98. *White* v. *Jones* [1995] 2 AC 207, 259. In *Williams* v. *Natural Life Health Foods* [1998] 1 WLR 830, 837, Lord Steyn said that "coherence must sometimes yield to practical justice".

99. As in *White* v. *Jones* [1995] 2 AC 207 (Lords Keith and Mustill dissenting) and *Spring* v. *Guardian Assurance* [1995] 2 AC 296 (Lord Keith dissenting).

100. As in *Marc Rich* v. *Bishop Rock Marine* [1996] 1 AC 211 (Lord Lloyd dissenting).

101. *Williams & Glynn's* v. *Barnes* (1980) 10 *Legal Decisions Affecting Bankers* 220, *Redmond* v. *Allied Irish Banks, Financial Times*, 15 July 1987, *Lloyds Bank* v. *Cobb* (unreported, 18 December 1991), *Barclays Bank* v. *Khaira* [1992] 1 WLR 623, *National Westminster Bank* v. *McIntyre* (unreported, 12 May 1995), *Bankers Trust* v. *Dharmala* (unreported, 29 November 1995, transcript, p 20), and *Morgan* v. *Lloyds Bank* (unreported, 3 March 1998). A possibly dissenting voice is Kerr LJ in *Cornish* v. *Midland Bank* [1985] 3 All ER 513, 522–523, but his comments are probably best viewed as legitimate concern about a wife executing a mortgage in favour of a bank for her husband's debts before the decision in *Barclays Bank* v. *O'Brien* [1994] 1 AC 480 made it clear that in those circumstances for reasons outside the law of negligence a bank has a duty to advise a

likely to be taken into account in determining whether one party has assumed responsibility to another is possible, but the principal areas are probably those discussed below though in reality all merge into one another without any clear dividing lines. Essentially, it is a matter of the relationship between the parties[102]; the closer the relationship the greater the risk.

4.6.4 Who can assume responsibility?

The cases, particularly the early ones, have references to a requirement for the person assuming responsibility to be engaged in a calling requiring special skill or knowledge.[103] The position now is probably that anyone can assume responsibility whether or not he has a special skill if, on the facts, he has accepted responsibility to another for a particular state of affairs. It is, however, more likely that someone will be treated as having assumed responsibility if it relates to something peculiarly within his knowledge or in respect of which he claims special knowledge, whether it involves advice, information or opinion.[104] The suitability, nature and effect of a derivatives transaction unquestionably involve information, advice or opinion in respect of which it is possible to assume liability to the counterparty or others. In this connection, advertising literature which emphasises the expertise of a financial institution is capable of being used to show the special nature of the skills in question and to reinforce any alleged assumption of responsibility, though in most cases it is likely only to be of marginal relevance.[105]

4.6.5 To whom will responsibility be assumed?

The concern of the courts has been that words, written or spoken, can travel far beyond those within the original contemplation of the maker and, as a result, cause loss to many. The courts always sought to avoid liability for negligent

wife to take independent legal advice. In *ICS* v. *WBBS* (unreported, 15 January 1999), Evans-Lombe J said that "without more, there is no sufficient proximity between a banker and his customer to place on the banker a duty of care to advise the customer as to the terms, effect or commercial prudence of a transaction of loan which the customer might be about to enter into with the bank." None of these cases concern instances where regulation required any advice or assessment of the suitability of the transaction for the counterparty (for the relevant regulations, see chapter 6); the existence of regulations should not of themselves give rise to a duty of care, but might make it easier for the courts to infer that responsibility to warn a counterparty had been taken on.

102. See, for example, *Caparo* v. *Dickman* [1990] 2 AC 605, 636, *Henderson* v. *Merrett* [1995] 2 AC 145, 180 and *Davis* v. *Radcliffe* [1990] 1 WLR 821, 826. Flowing from this, a conflict of interest between the parties is likely to show that there is no proximity between the parties: *Chapman* v. *Barclays Bank* [1997] 6 Bank LR 315, 318.

103. For example, *Candler* v. *Crane Christmas & Co* [1951] 2 KB 164, 180 and *Hedley Byrne* v. *Heller* [1964] AC 465, 502 and 538.

104. For example, *Hedley Byrne* v. *Heller* [1964] AC 465, 531, and *Henderson* v. *Merrett* [1995] 2 AC 145, 180.

105. As Millett LJ pointed out in *James* v. *Barclays Bank* (unreported, 27 October 1994), whatever promotional literature says, the issue is what the bank did in a particular case.

misstatements being incurred to an indeterminate class of people; they have, however, struggled with where to draw the line to prevent this. The result of the courts' deliberations appears to be that a statement put in more or less general circulation will not give rise to a duty of care—a duty of care will only arise if the recipients are more readily definable. It is not necessary to be able to identify individually every recipient of the relevant misstatement, but it must be reasonably foreseeable that a statement will be communicated to the particular person claiming that a duty of care is owed to him, either as an individual or as the member of an identifiable class.[106]

The size of the relevant class is more difficult. If, say, a circular is sent generally to clients or potential clients, then that may well give rise to a duty of care to each of those clients even though they may be large in number.[107] If a circular is individually addressed to each client, then that will almost certainly give rise to a duty of care, provided the other requirements for liability in negligent misstatement are met.

4.6.6 In respect of what will responsibility be assumed?

Responsibility is not assumed in the abstract, it is assumed for something. As a result, for there to be a duty of care it is not enough merely for the recipient of the information, advice or opinion to be identifiable; in addition, the adviser must know, or reasonably foresee, the purpose for which the recipient wants the advice or the nature of the transaction the recipient has in contemplation.[108] So, for example, a representation made in the course of contractual negotiations can readily give rise to a duty of care because the nature of the transaction will be obvious.[109] For representations outside the context of a specific transaction, it is

106. *Caparo* v. *Dickman* [1990] 2 AC 605, 621 and 638. In, for example, *Brostoff* v. *Clark Kenneth Levethal* (unreported, 11 March 1996) a letter to one person was, unknown to the author, shown to another: Dyson J held that any duty of care was owed only to the addressee of the letter. A similar result was arrived at in *Omega* v. *Wright, Son & Pepper* (unreported, 17 December 1996) and in *Machin* v. *Adams* (unreported, 7 May 1997).

107. In *Possfund* v. *Diamond* [1996] 1 WLR 1351 the class in question (purchasers of shares in the after-market following a public issue) was potentially very large.

108. *Caparo* v. *Dickman* [1990] 2 AC 605, 621 and 638 (see also *Western Trust & Savings Ltd* v. *Strutt & Parker*, unreported, 9 July 1998).

109. *Esso* v. *Mardon* [1976] QB 801. Even within a contractual context, it is necessary to assess carefully what assumption of responsibility is being undertaken. In *Peach* v. *Slater* [1998] BCC 139, a seller's accountant who confirmed the accuracy of accounts in a meeting was held only to have assumed responsibility to his own client so the client could give a contractual warranty rather than having assumed liability to the buyer. In *Gold Coin Joaillers* v. *United Bank of Kuwait* [1997] 6 Bank LR 60, a bank was held to have assumed responsibility for a reference but not as to the identity of the person who had asked them to provide the reference. In *Machin* v. *Adams* (unreported, 7 May 1997), an architect wrote a letter to his client commenting on the quality of works undertaken to a building and on the cost of further works. Even if he should have foreseen that the letter would be shown to someone buying the property from his client, it was held that he did not owe the buyer a duty of care because he could not be taken to have undertaken to guard the buyer against any harm (see *South Australia Asset Management* v. *York Montague* [1997] AC 191) or to have signalled to her that she could purchase without further enquiry.

more difficult. If advice is given that interest rates are likely to rise, that could lead to any number of possible transactions—swaps, loans, options, caps, etc. A range of possible transactions in this way will make it less likely that a duty of care will arise, but the more specific the advice the greater the probability that this requirement will be fulfilled.

4.6.7 What sort of representation is necessary?

For there to be a duty of care, it must be reasonably foreseeable that a representation will be relied by the recipient as the basis for a decision without further enquiry.[110] As a result, no assumption of responsibility will arise for what have been variously described as casual, social or perfunctory remarks,[111] perhaps also "off-the-cuff" advice over the telephone,[112] but in practice it should be made clear that this is all that is being offered.[113] The mere fact that someone is bounced into offering advice without adequate notice will not enable them to escape liability. The options in these circumstances are to refuse to answer, to answer but apply a disclaimer or just to answer. If the last course is taken, then there can be an assumption of responsibility for the content of the statement.[114]

Whether it is reasonable to foresee reliance will depend upon the circumstances. If, for example, the recipient of a misstatement has sufficient skill, or holds himself out as having this skill, to assess the relevant matter himself, then it is unlikely to be treated as foreseeable that he would rely on a statement at all, still less without further enquiry.[115] Similarly, if the state of parties' knowledge on the relevant matter is the same, it is unlikely to be reasonable for one to rely on the other. The existence of other advisers is also likely to count against any reliance and the reasonableness of doing so,[116] as is the possibility of obtaining adequate protection for the risk in question through other means.[117]

110. *Caparo* v. *Dickman* [1990] 2 AC 605, 621 and 638.

111. *Candler* v. *Crane Christmas* [1951] 2 KB 164, 180, and *Hedley Byrne* v. *Heller* [1964] AC 465, 495 and 539.

112. *Howard Marine* v. *Ogden* [1978] QB 574, 591–592.

113. If this is all that is being offered, there may still be a duty to express an honest opinion (*Hedley Byrne* v. *Heller* [1964] AC 465, 504) or a duty to pass on accurately information held (*Royal Bank* v. *Pampellone* [1987] 1 Lloyd's Rep 218).

114. *Hedley Byrne* v. *Heller* [1964] AC 465, 486 and *ADT* v. *Binder Hamlyn* (unreported, 6 December 1995).

115. As in *Bankers Trust* v. *Dharmala* (unreported, 29 November 1995), which turned largely on this point.

116. *James McNaughton* v. *Hicks Anderson* [1991] 2 QB 113, 128, and as in *Peach* v. *Slater* [1998] BCC 139 and *Young* v. *Clifford Chance* (unreported, 21 December 1995). In *Peach*, Morritt LJ was firm that the doctrine of caveat emptor was not dead and that in commercial transactions one party did not merely rely on another's advisers without more, and in *BCCI* v. *Price Waterhouse* [1998] Lloyd's Rep Bank 85, 99, Sir Brian Neill accepted that there was an important difference between cases where advisee and adviser were dealing at arm's length and where they were acting on the same side of the fence. In *Electra Private Equity Partners* v. *KPMG* (unreported, 23 April 1999), Auld LJ saw no reason why auditors could not owe a duty of care to an investor even though the investor had instructed its own investigating accountants to whom the auditors supplied information.

117. *Leigh & Sillavan* v. *Aliakmon* [1986] 1 AC 785, 819. Also Stapleton (1995) 111 LQR 301.

There has been debate about the nature of a representation which can give rise to liability. In general, the principles determining what representations give rise to claims for rescission and fraud are also applicable to negligent misrepresentation, but it is likely that the range of possible representations is somewhat wider in negligent misrepresentation. For claims in rescission and fraud, it is necessary to identify a specific misrepresentation and show that it is incorrect. In negligent misrepresentation, the question is usually for what has someone assumed responsibility. If someone has made a specific representation, it is easy to conclude that they have assumed responsibility for the content of that representation. But it is also possible to assume responsibility for a wider area. For that reason, omissions can give rise to liability if within the area of assumption of responsibility.[118] A mere failure to warn of the possible consequences of a transaction will not, however, lead to liability unless there has been an assumption of responsibility for the consequences of the transaction.[119] In practice, though, it is more difficult to show an assumption of responsibility which requires a statement to be made rather than one attaching to a statement which has been made. If, however, a statement is made which, before being acted upon by the recipient, is found by the maker to be incorrect, it will usually be necessary to correct it in order to avoid liability.[120]

The intention of the maker of the statement may also be relevant to liability. If a statement is made with the intention of persuading someone to enter into a contract, then it will in practice be impossible to say that it was unreasonable for that person to rely on it, at least unless the context or content shows the statement to have been an inconsequential sales puff. Even where a statement is made to a very wide group in circumstances which would not in normal circumstances give rise to an assumption of responsibility, it can lead to liability if the intention of the maker, objectively ascertained and reasonably inferred by the recipient, was that the recipient should rely on it in entering into

118. *White* v. *Jones* [1995] 2 AC 207, 268. See Logie [1989] CLJ 113.

119. However, when dealing with complex derivatives transactions, it may be easy to conclude that a financial institution has taken on the role of adviser to someone without experience, certainly if an individual, as in *Morgan Stanley* v. *Puglisi* (unreported, 29 January 1998). In that case, Longmore J said that the "whole point of Mr Puglisi coming to Morgan Stanley in the first place ... was so that he could be advised as to how he could sensibly and suitably invest his funds. Even if Mr Puglisi never said so in terms, there can have been no other basis upon which he would transfer to Morgan Stanley considerable sums of money ... The fact that a serious financial institution can make such a submission [i.e. that it did not give Mr Puglisi advice] shows, in my judgment, a serious under-appreciation of the Financial Services Act ..."

120. In *McCullagh* v. *Lane Fox* [1996] PNLR 205, Hobhouse LJ took the view that a representation continued up to the time it was relied on and, as soon as it was reasonably foreseeable that it might cause loss, the maker had a duty to avoid that loss by correction. He considered that by the time the statement was relied on in that case, the recipient knew that the maker was not assuming responsibility for it and therefore it was unreasonable to rely on it. Sir Christopher Slade took the view that there was no obligation to correct an innocent misrepresentation unless either there was an assumption of responsibility at the time the statement was made or the maker became aware of its inaccuracy before it was acted upon.

transactions.[121] The intention of the maker of a statement alone will not of itself be enough to give rise to liability if the recipient was not aware of the intention.

4.6.8 The effect of a disclaimer

In *Hedley Byrne* v. *Heller & Partners* itself, the House of Lords would have found a bank which gave a credit reference liable for its negligent misstatement but for the existence of a disclaimer which the House of Lords considered negated what would otherwise have been an assumption of responsibility. A disclaimer can still have this effect, but only if it is reasonable in accordance with the Unfair Contract Terms Act 1977, if applicable.[122] If it is unreasonable, it will be ignored in considering whether there has been an assumption of responsibility.

The opportunity of the adviser to issue a disclaimer may also be relevant to the question of whether a duty of care will arise—if there is no opportunity to do so, it is less likely that a duty of care will arise, but if the adviser has the opportunity but does not take it then that may be evidence of an assumption of liability.[123]

4.6.9 The influence of a contract

A contract may affect liability in negligent misstatement in three ways. First, a disclaimer in a contract applicable to a negligent misstatement made before the contract was entered into may operate to negate any assumption of responsibility (see above).

Secondly, if the activity alleged to constitute negligent misstatement was done pursuant to a contract (e.g. a mandate to act as an adviser on a particular issue), then the contract may provide the only remedies available to the contractual counterparty. The mere fact of there being a contract will not be sufficient to prevent liability in negligence—an assumption of responsibility can take place under a contract, and negligence represents the general law out of which the parties can contract if they wish.[124] If there is no express exclusion of the law of negligent misstatement, the question becomes whether the alleged tortious duty is so inconsistent with the contract that the parties must be taken to have agreed that the tortious remedy was to be limited or excluded.[125] Where an assumption of responsibility is made under a contract, the tortious duty cannot extend beyond the contractual duty,[126] but the fact that there is a contract does not

121. *Possfund* v. *Diamond* [1996] 1 WLR 1351. In this case, which concerned liability for representations made in a prospectus to those who purchased in the after market, there was only one sort of transaction possible, namely the acquisition of shares. If there is a wider range of possible transactions, it may be more difficult to establish liability.

122. *Smith* v. *Bush* [1990] 1 AC 831 and *McCullagh* v. *Lane Fox* [1996] PNLR 205. For the application of the Unfair Contract Terms Act 1977, see chapter 8 below.

123. *BCCI* v. *Price Waterhouse* [1998] Lloyd's Rep Bank 85, 99.

124. *Henderson* v. *Merrett* [1995] 2 AC 145, 193.

125. *Henderson* v. *Merrett* [1995] 2 AC 145, 194.

126. *Saigol* v. *Cranley Mansions Limited* (unreported, 6 July 1995).

mean that responsibility cannot be assumed for activities outside the scope of the contract and involving wider duties than under the contract.[127] So, for example, if responsibility is assumed by carrying out work or answering questions outside the scope of a contract, then there could be separate tortious liability in respect of that additional work. Even where the tortious duty is the same as the contractual duty, it is possible that the limitation periods on the claims on contract and tort could differ as could the rules on the remoteness of damages, which are less strict in tort than in contract.[128]

The third area where a contract could be of influence is where a claim is brought in respect of a statement made by an adviser of the other party to a transaction as, for example, where the bidder for a company claims against the accountant acting for the target company. This turns upon whether in all the circumstances the maker of the statement has assumed responsibility to the other party as well as to his client. There are cases on similar facts which both impose liability and which decide that there was no duty of care, but the trend appears to be that the existence of a contractual responsibility to one party makes it less likely that responsibility will be treated as also being assumed to another, particularly where there would be a conflict in the duties concerned.[129] Ultimately, however, it is likely to come down to a question of whether one person has on the facts assumed responsibility to another.

4.6.10 Agents

The mere fact that someone may be acting as the agent of another does not prevent him assuming responsibility. The issue in each case is whether the person in question has himself assumed personal responsibility for the matter in question.[130] As a result, insurance brokers arranging a policy which they knew

127. *Holt and Holt* v. *Payne Skillington* [1996] PNLR 179.

128. *Henderson* v. *Merrett* [1995] 2 AC 145, 185.

129. In, for example, *James McNaughton* v. *Hicks Anderson* [1991] 2 QB 113, the accountant acting for the target company was held not to have assumed responsibility to the bidder for draft accounts; the same result was reached in *Galoo* v. *Bright Grahame Murray* [1994] 1 WLR 1360, *Peach* v. *Slater* [1998] BCC 139 and, in a different context, in *Simaan* v. *Pilkington (No 2)* [1988] 1 QB 758. However, there was liability in *Morgan Crucible* v. *Hill Samuel* [1991] Ch 295 and *ADT* v. *Binder Hamlyn* (unreported, 6 December 1995). Stapleton (1995) 111 LQR 301 suggests that some of the cases where there was no liability should be treated as cases where the recipient had adequate alternative means of protection, as in *Saigol* v. *Cranley Mansions* (unreported, 6 July 1995). In *Red Sea Tankers* v. *Papachristidis* (unreported, 30 April 1997), Mance J held that a contractual party should be held to a "deliberately constructed contractual framework" as a result of which an employee did not owe a duty of care in tort to his employer's contractual counterparty. In *Abbott* v. *Armstrong* (unreported, 22 May 1998), Ferris J found it incomprehensible that a person (X) who makes a statement or gives advice to another (Y) for the purpose of assisting Y to make representations to a third party (Z), should be regarded as owing a duty of care to Z when the participation of X in the preparation of Y's statement is unknown to Z. But where the participation is known, a duty of care may be owed: *Electra Private Equity Partners* v. *KPMG* (unreported, 23 April 1999).

130. *McCullagh* v. *Lane Fox* [1996] PNLR 205 and *Williams* v. *Natural Life Health Foods Ltd* [1998] 1 WLR 830. There may be particular exceptions as in *Gran Gellato* v. *Richcliffe* [1992] Ch 560 where a conveyancing solicitor acting for a seller was held not to owe a duty of care to the buyer: this decision was cited in the House of Lords without apparent disapproval in *White* v. *Jones* [1995] 2 AC 207, 256 but was questioned by Hobhouse LJ in *McCullagh* v. *Lane Fox*.

would be assigned to a bank were held to owe a duty of care to the bank in performing their function.[131] Similarly, an employee owes a duty of care to a client as well as to his employer if he has assumed personal responsibility towards the plaintiff and the plaintiff reasonably relies on the individual without regard to the corporate character of the employer, perhaps even to the extent of relying on the individual's financial standing.[132] In practice, however, it is likely to be very difficult to show that an employee has personal liability for a negligent misstatement.

4.6.11 The nature of any duty assumed

If there is a duty of care in the tort of negligent misstatement, the duty does not entail, for example, a warranty that a statement made is correct. A warranty must be contractual. Instead, the duty is to take reasonable care in the performance of the relevant task. The level of skill required is that of the

> "ordinary skilled man professing to have that special skill. A man need not possess the highest skill; it is well established that it is sufficient if he exercises the ordinary skill of an ordinary competent man exercising that particular art . . .
>
> [A person] is not guilty of negligence if he has acted in accordance with a practice accepted as proper by a responsible body of . . . men skilled in that particular art . . . Putting it the other way round, a man is not negligent, if he is acting in accordance with such a practice, merely because there is a body of opinion who would take a contrary view."[133]

In some circumstances this test is, however, not of great value. For example, if the issue of liability concerns an explanation of the effect of a derivative, the party professing enough expertise to explain can in most circumstances be expected to get it right; but if the matter turns upon a forecast of interest rates, then the issue of whether the forecast was one a reasonably competent economist or banker could have made arises. In this context, the obligation is not to make a forecast which falls in the centre of the band of forecasts made by others but to make one which is not outside the band that can be considered reasonable.[134] A forecast might turn out to be wrong, but still be

131. *Punjab National Bank* v. *de Boinville* [1992] 1 WLR 1138.

132. *Williams* v. *Natural Life Health Foods* [1998] 1 WLR 830, following the Canadian decisions in *London Drugs Ltd* v. *Kuehne & Nagel* (1992) 97 DLR (4th) 261 and *Edgeworth Constructions Ltd* v. *ND Lea & Associates Ltd* (1993) 107 DLR (4th) 169. There were shades of this approach in *Ministry of Housing* v. *Sharp* [1970] 2 QB 223, 291. In *Red Sea Tankers* v. *Papachristidis* (unreported, 30 April 1997), Mance J considered that the plaintiff should be held to the "contractual framework which was deliberately negotiated" and could not circumvent that by alleging tortious duties on the part of employees who, in any event, could not be treated as personally having undertaken responsibility in respect of the substantial commercial risks in the particular transaction in question. Some comments in *Punjab National Bank* v. *de Boinville* [1992] 1 WLR 1138 (e.g. at p 1154) may need to be reconsidered in the light of *Williams*.

133. *Bolam* v. *Friern Hospital Management Committee* [1957] 1 WLR 582, 586–587, described by Lord Browne-Wilkinson in *Bolitho* v. *City & Hackney Health Authority* [1997] 3 WLR 1151, 1156 as the "locus classicus" on the topic. See also *Whitehouse* v. *Jordan* [1981] 1 WLR 246.

134. But damages will be calculated by reference to the mean forecast: *Lion Nathan Limited* v. *CC Bottlers Limited* [1996] 1 WLR 1438.

perfectly reasonable.

Since the test cited above depends upon the standard of the ordinary skilled man, the market standards within the relevant area are clearly relevant. It is, however, possible that the market has, as a whole, adopted lax standards in which case the court will not be bound by those standards but rather by the standards it considers the market should have set.[135] Similarly, the standards set by professional bodies are likely to be relevant in assessing what is reasonable.

4.6.12 Loss[136]

4.6.12.1 The general principle

Negligence is not actionable per se; a cause of action only arises if and when loss is suffered as a result of the negligence. In general, the measure of damages recoverable for negligent misstatement is: "that sum of money which will put the party who has been injured, or who has suffered, in the same position as he would have been if he had not sustained the wrong for which he is now getting his compensation".[137]

This requires there to be a causal link between the negligence and the loss—if there is not, then the party who has suffered the wrong would have been in the same position regardless of whether or not the wrong had been committed. This generally requires reliance on the representation in question; if there is no reliance—if the defendant would have acted in the same way whether or not the representation had been made—then the loss will not have been caused by the misrepresentation.[138]

As a factor in reliance, the question often arises as to what the defendant would have done if the representation made had in fact been accurate. It is probably the case that a plaintiff must show that he would not have acted as he

135. *Professional Negligence* by Jackson & Powell (3rd edn), p 39, approved in *Deeny* v. *Gooda Walker* [1994] CLC 1224. See, for example, *Edward Wong Finance Co Ltd* v. *Johnson Stokes & Master* [1984] 1 AC 296 for a case in which the court considered that generally adopted professional conduct was negligent. In *Bolitho* v. *City & Hackney Health Authority* [1997] 3 WLR 1151, 1160, Lord Browne-Wilkinson considered, in the context of medical negligence, that it would very seldom be right for a judge to conclude that views held by a competent expert are unreasonable.

136. For a more detailed treatment see, for example, *Professional Negligence* by Jackson and Powell (3rd edn) and *Damages* by MacGregor (16th edn).

137. *Livingstone* v. *Rawyards Coal Co* (1880) 5 App Cas 25, 39.

138. In general, causation is to be established by applying common sense rather than strict rules: *Galoo* v. *Bright Grahame Murray* [1994] 1 WLR 1360, 1375. Reliance is not always necessary (for example, *White* v. *Jones* [1995] 2 AC 207 and *Spring* v. *Guardian Assurance* [1995] 2 AC 296) but in the vast bulk of cases it will be, including where there is an assumption of responsibility: *Williams* v. *Natural Life Health Foods* [1998] 1 WLR 830.

did if the representation had been accurate,[139] but it is necessary to consider carefully what is meant by an accurate representation. In *Downs* v. *Chappell*,[140] an accountant made a representation as to the accuracy of profit figures put forward by someone selling a business. In fact he had no basis to make any representation at all as the true figures were not available for over a year. The Court of Appeal considered that the accurate representation would have been that the true figures were not known rather than the representation that would have been made if the true figures had been available. If this representation had been made, the buyer would not have proceeded with the transaction and, therefore, the necessary causal link was established. On this basis, in some cases the accurate representation will be that no representation can be given, in which case the question is whether the plaintiff would still have acted as he did.

In addition to causation, there are two limiting factors to the damages which can be recovered under the general proposition that the plaintiff should be put in the same position as if he had not suffered the wrong. These are: first, the scope of the duty undertaken[141]; and, secondly, that the loss is reasonably foreseeable.

4.6.12.2 Scope of the duty

As to the scope of the duty undertaken, it is necessary to identify for what kind of loss the defendant has assumed a duty to the plaintiff. If the duty is to provide information to enable someone else to decide on a course of action, the duty is to take reasonable care to ensure that the information is correct and to be responsible for all the foreseeable consequences of the information being wrong. If the duty is to advise on what course of action to take, the responsibility is for all foreseeable consequences of the course of action being taken. In *South Australia Asset Management Corp* v. *York Montague*,[142] valuers gave negligent mortgage valuations to mortgagees. The mortgagors defaulted but in addition

139. *Downs* v. *Chappell* [1997] 1 WLR 426 was thought to have established (at least for courts below the House of Lords) that the plaintiff only had to show that he relied on the representation and not that he would have acted differently if the representation had been accurate: see *Downs* v. *Chappell* at p 441 and *Bristol & West Building Society* v. *Mothew* [1997] 2 WLR 436, 443 and 445. In *Swindle* v. *Harrison* [1997] 4 All ER 705, 728, Hobhouse LJ, the judge who gave the only reasoned judgment in *Downs* v. *Chappell*, explained that this was incorrect. It was necessary to consider what the plaintiff would have done had the representation been correct.

140. [1997] 1 WLR 426—this is the explanation of the judgment given in *Swindle* v. *Harrison*: see the previous note.

141. Logically, this comes before assessment of damages under the principle in *Livingstone* v. *Rawyards Coal Co* (1880) 5 App Cas 25 (see above). If the loss does not fall within the scope of the duty, no question of assessment can arise: *BCCI* v. *Price Waterhouse (No 3)* (unreported, 24 March 1998).

142. [1997] AC 191 (see also *Nykredit Mortgage Bank* v. *Edward Erdman* [1997] 1 WLR 1627 and *Platform Home Loans* v. *Oyston Shipways* [1999] 2 WLR 518). In a speech to the Chancery Bar Association on 3 June 1998, Lightman J said of this case: "... the pyrotechnics of the reasoning of the House of Lords in [this case] limiting valuers' liability in damages are spellbinding, but the guidance provided to less elevated minds advising in or deciding other cases is less clear cut, and so it has spawned its own shoal of litigation."

there was a significant and unforeseen fall in the property market which increased the loss suffered by the mortgagees. The issue was whether the mortgagees could recover the whole of their loss, including that part due to the fall in the property market, on the basis that they would not have lent at all had a reasonable valuation been given. The House of Lords decided that they could not. The valuers had only provided information to enable the mortgagees to make a decision and were therefore only liable for the difference between the actual valuation given and a reasonable valuation, subject to a cap of the actual loss suffered.

Applying this to derivatives, if the representation is as to the likely movement in interest or exchange rates and the plaintiff enters into a transaction in reliance on that representation, the loss recoverable is not the whole loss suffered on the transaction but only, in effect, the difference between the actual representation and a reasonable representation.[143] But if advice is given to enter into a derivatives transaction, the damages could be all the consequences which flow from having done so.[144]

4.6.12.3 *Remoteness*

The second limiting factor is the foreseeability of the loss in question. A defendant is only liable for damages which were reasonably foreseeable by him at the time of the negligence, but it seems that even most unusual occurrences are foreseeable for this purpose.[145] It is the kind of damage which must be foreseeable rather than the extent of the damage. So, for example, if loss of profits is reasonably foreseeable, then damages can be recovered in respect of the profits even if the extent of the loss was not specifically foreseeable.[146]

4.6.12.4 *Contributory negligence*

Finally in connection with loss, it is necessary to mention contributory negligence. At common law, if a plaintiff's injuries were caused partly through his own negligence and partly through the negligence of the defendant, the plaintiff's contributory negligence acted in effect as a complete defence for the defendant. This position was reversed by the Law Reform (Contributory Negligence) Act 1945. Section 1(1) of this Act provides:

> "Where any person suffers damage as the result partly of his own fault and partly of the fault of any other person or persons, a claim in respect of that damage shall not be defeated by reason of the fault of the person suffering the damage, but the damages

143. Damages are not assessed by reference to the lowest possible reasonable valuation. The court has to form a view as to the most likely figure to have been put forward, i.e. the mean of the range of reasonable valuations: *Lion Nathan Ltd* v. *CC Bottlers Ltd* [1996] 1 WLR 1438 and *South Australia Asset Management Corp* v. *York Montague* [1997] AC 191, 221–222.

144. Subject to limitations arising from remoteness, etc.

145. *The Wagon Mound (No 1)* [1961] AC 388 and *The Heron II* [1969] AC 350, 385. Intended consequences are never too remote: *Quinn* v. *Leatham* [1901] AC 495, 537.

146. *H Parsons (Livestock) Ltd* v. *Uttley Ingham & Co Ltd* [1978] QB 791.

recoverable in respect thereof shall be reduced to such an extent as the court thinks just and equitable having regard to the claimant's share in the responsibility for the damage."

The standard expected from the plaintiff in his own protection is the same as in negligence itself.[147] In assessing the extent to which the plaintiff's damage should be reduced, the plaintiff's blameworthiness and the extent to which his negligence caused the damage must be taken into account.[148]

4.6.13 The risk of liability in negligent misstatement

The principal risk of liability in negligent misstatement is of failing to take reasonable care in making a representation, expressing an opinion or giving advice of any sort. If reasonable care is taken, then no liability will arise. If a decision is made to accept the risk of liability in negligent misstatement by, for example, taking advisory roles, it is clearly prudent to ensure that those concerned understand their responsibilities and that checks are in place to ensure that due care is taken. Even if the decision is taken to seek to avoid the risk of negligent misstatement wherever possible, it is still sensible to ensure that people understand the risks, and that checks are in place to ensure that reasonable care is taken.

In addition to this elementary step in reducing the risk of liability, if the wish is to avoid the risk of liability, the next aspect is not to undertake activities which might give rise to a duty of care. The risk of a duty of care comes from the relationship with the potential claimant—the closer the relationship, the greater the risk. This can, perhaps, be split into general relationships and transaction-specific relationships.

A general relationship might involve, for example, sending market reports to clients to seek to interest them in possible transactions, to warn them of movements that might have an adverse affect or to raise possible ideas or strategies with them. These might be either general to all clients or specific to particular clients. A general relationship might also involve discussing over the telephone recent movements in, say, interest, currency or commodity rates. A general relationship does involve the risk of duty of care arising if reasonable care is not taken, but in most cases the risk is unlikely to be very high. Leaving aside the effect of any disclaimers,[149] in order for there to be a duty of care it has to be reasonably foreseeable that the recipient of the information, opinion or advice will rely on it without further enquiry in entering into a transaction of a reasonably foreseeable sort. The more general the information given, the less likely it is that these elements will be fulfilled. A client of any sophistication will probably see this as sales orientated information and, in any event, is likely to receive similar information from a number of sources. The more specific the

147. *Billings* v. *Ridden* [1958] AC 240.
148. *Stapley* v. *Gypsum Mines* [1953] AC 663, 682.
149. As to which, see Chapter 8.

advice or information given, however, the more likely it is that these requirements will be fulfilled and, therefore, that there will be a duty of care.

A general relationship of this sort is usually intended to lead to a transaction (whether or not with the person giving the advice or information). The risk of a duty of care arising increases the closer a transaction is, and the more transaction-specific the relationship becomes. It will be clear what transaction the recipient has in mind to enter into, and it will also be clear whether the recipient is relying on the advice in doing so. Even if the original representation was made in circumstances which did not give rise to a duty of care, a representation made in the course of negotiations about a specific transaction probably will give rise to a duty of care. In these circumstances, there is an obvious tension between the desire to secure the transaction and the desire to minimise the risk of liability should any statement be made without reasonable care. This requires a careful balancing exercise as to extent of the risk that someone is prepared to accept in seeking to secure a transaction. Disclaimers can seek to mitigate the risk, but they cannot remove it completely.

CHAPTER 5

FIDUCIARY DUTIES

5.1 INTRODUCTION

"The fiduciary relationship is concept in search of a principle."[1] Despite the uncertainty which this quotation correctly indicates surrounds fiduciary relationships, it is relatively easy to enter a fiduciary relationship in a financial context, but in most cases it will not matter.[2] Not every breach of duty by a fiduciary is a breach of fiduciary duty[3]—so, for example, if a fiduciary is negligent or acts in breach of contract, it is the law of negligence or contract which is relevant, not the law relating to fiduciary obligations. It is only those obligations specific to a fiduciary which raise questions of breach of fiduciary duty. Even then, the content of fiduciary duties will vary from case to case, and will be affected by, for example, the terms of a contract—fiduciary obligations cannot be prayed in aid to enlarge the scope of contractual obligations,[4] and similarly a contract can restrict fiduciary obligations which might otherwise arise.[5]

Difficult questions can nevertheless arise in any particular case as to who is a fiduciary, and what the fiduciary obligations in that case are. English law has been primarily concerned with particular categories of people who are considered to be fiduciaries without more, and has developed little by way of a generalised theory of fiduciary relationships. The lack of specific guidance can increase the legal risks arising from a particular relationship, absent a well drafted contract.

1. Sir Anthony Mason, "Themes and Prospects", in P D Finn (ed), *Essays in Equity*, p 246. Also, see generally Millett, *Equity's Place in the Law of Commerce* (1998) 114 LQR 214.

2. Cf *Fiduciary Duties and Regulatory Rules*, para 2.4.6 (Law Commission Consultation Paper No 124). See also Tjio, [1997] JBL 350.

3. *Bristol & West Building Society* v. *Mothew* [1997] 2 WLR 436, 448.

4. *Clark Boyce* v. *Mouat* [1994] 1 AC 428, 437.

5. *Kelly* v. *Cooper* [1993] AC 205.

5.2 WHO IS A FIDUCIARY?

The Law Commission divided fiduciaries into two categories, status-based fiduciaries and fact-based fiduciaries.[6] English law has focused mainly on status-based fiduciaries, people who by virtue of their involvement in certain relationships (such as solicitor and client, agent and principal, and director and company) are considered fiduciaries without more. Fact-based relationships have received less attention. In *Bristol & West Building Society* v. *Mothew* (a case about solicitors), Millett LJ said that:

"A fiduciary is someone who has undertaken to act for and on behalf of another in a particular matter in circumstances which give rise to a relationship of trust and confidence. The distinguishing obligation of a fiduciary is the obligation of loyalty. The principal is entitled to the single-minded loyalty of his fiduciary. This core liability has several facets. A fiduciary must act in good faith; he must not make a profit out of his trust; he must not place himself in a position where his duty and interest conflict; he may not act for his own benefit or the benefit of a third person without the informed consent of his principal. This is not meant to be an exhaustive list, but it is sufficient to indicate the nature of fiduciary obligations. They are the defining characteristics of a fiduciary. As Dr Finn pointed out in his classic work *Fiduciary Obligations* (1977), p 2, he is not subject to fiduciary obligations because he is a fiduciary; it is because he is subject to them that he is a fiduciary."[7]

The essential element is, therefore, that a fiduciary is entrusted by his principal with a job, for example, the negotiation of a contract on his behalf and for his benefit, and the principal relies on the fiduciary to procure the best terms available.[8]

A fiduciary relationship will not generally arise in an arm's length commercial transaction. This is particularly so where the expectation is that the other party will form his or her own independent view as to the matter under consideration, especially if he or she has independent advice.[9] For the most part, the expectations in a commercial relationship will be unrelated to any consideration of loyal service; they will demand no more than honesty, frank disclosure, and care and skill. The legal responsibilities will therefore in general arise in the law of contract and tort, or, perhaps, equity unrelated to the law relating to

6. *Fiduciary Duties and Regulatory Rules*, para 2.4.3 (Law Commission Consultation Paper No 124).

7. [1997] 2 WLR 436, 449. In *Indata Equipment Supplies* v. *ACL* (unreported, 31 July 1997), Otton LJ referred with approval to the Law Commission's definition that a "fiduciary relationship is one in which the person undertakes to act on behalf of or for the benefit of another often as an intermediary with a discretion or power which affects the interests of the other who depends on a fiduciary for information or advice" (*Fiduciary Duties and Regulatory Rules*, Law Commission Report No 236). Sir Peter Millett has also commented that the "search for a single, all embracing definition [of a fiduciary] is doomed to failure" (1998) 114 LQR 214, 219. He went on to identify three intertwined types of fiduciary relationship: trust and confidence (to which he said *Mothew* belonged and with which this chapter is concerned); undue influence; and confidentiality.

8. *Reading* v. *The King* [1949] 2 KB 232, 236.

9. See, for example, *Commonwealth Bank* v. *Smith* (1991) 102 ALR 453, 476–477.

fiduciaries.[10] A fiduciary relationship can, however, arise in some commercial circumstances. Finn has suggested that a bank is unlikely to be found to owe fiduciary obligations beyond the following three circumstances:

"(1) Where the course of the relationship can found the expectation, not only that advice will be given but that, where appropriate, it will be given adversely to the bank's interests. (2) Where the bank has created the expectation that it is advising or will advise in the customer's interest in a matter because its own interest therein is represented to be formal, nominal or technical ... And (3) where the bank, though expected to act in its own interest in the actual dealing *inter se*, has created the expectation that it will otherwise advise in the customer's interests, for example, on the wisdom of an investment proposal in respect of which a loan application is made."[11]

Fiduciary obligations arise where there is an obligation of loyalty. Where a commercial counterparty has a clear interest itself in a transaction, this will rarely be the case. If, however, there is an obligation of loyalty, it can apply to one part of a relationship but not all—"a person ... may be in a fiduciary position quoad a part of his activities and not quoad other parts: each transaction, or group of transactions must be looked at."[12] Thus, for example, in *Ata* v. *American Express Bank*,[13] a bank entered into foreign currency and gold transactions with a client. The bank was held not in general to have been in a fiduciary relationship with the customer. For part of the relationship, however, the bank had discretionary management of the customer's positions, and for that aspect the bank was held to owe fiduciary obligations.

The closer the relationship with a customer, the greater the risk of a fiduciary relationship arising. However, as far as derivatives are concerned, a principal to principal trading relationship will seldom give rise to fiduciary obligations. Only if the institution has an obligation of loyalty will it arise, and then (as discussed in the next section), the obligations only have any impact if there is a breach of that obligation of loyalty. It is possible for an advisory relationship to lead to fiduciary obligations, but in most cases breach of the obligations in the relationship will give rise to liabilities in contract or tort rather than liability as a fiduciary.

10. Finn, "Fiduciary Law and the Modern Commercial World", pp 10–12, in *Commercial Aspects of Trusts and Fiduciary Obligations* by McKendrick (ed). According to Otton LJ in *Indata Equipment Supplies* v. *ACL* (unreported, 31 July 1997), "the law has been reluctant to find [commercial] relationships creating fiduciary duties". In that case, the Court of Appeal refused to find a fiduciary relationship between a broker and finance house. In *Woods* v. *Martins Bank* [1959] 1 QB 55, Salmon J did hold that a bank which advised a plaintiff which was indebted to it owed a fiduciary duty to its debtor. This was necessary in order to find the bank liable for negligent misrepresentation since it was before *Hedley Byrne* v. *Heller & Partners* [1964] AC 465 (see pp 88ff above) and therefore there could be no liability without this finding. The case is best treated as depending on its facts or as an example of negligent misrepresentation.

11. "Fiduciary Law and the Modern Commercial World", p 12, in *Commercial Aspects of Trusts and Fiduciary Obligations* by McKendrick (ed).

12. *New Zealand Netherlands Society* v. *Kuys* [1973] 1 WLR 1126, 1130.

13. Unreported, 7 October 1996 (Rix J) and 17 June 1998 (Court of Appeal).

5.3 WHAT DUTIES DOES A FIDUCIARY HAVE?

> "The phrase 'fiduciary duties' is a dangerous one, giving rise to a mistaken assumption that all fiduciaries owe the same duties in all circumstances. That is not the case. Although, so far as I am aware, every fiduciary is under a duty not to make a profit from his position (unless such profit is authorised) ... the extent and nature of the fiduciary duties owed in any particular case fall to be determined by reference to the underlying contractual relationship between the parties."[14]

Nevertheless, the basic obligations of a fiduciary have been stated by the Law Commission as the "no conflict" rule, the "no profit rule", the "undivided loyalty" rule, and the duty of confidentiality.[15] This differs slightly from what Millett LJ said in *Bristol & West Building Society* v. *Mothew* were the "several facets" of the "core liability": good faith; no profit; no conflict of duty to one person with duty to another; and no conflict of duty and interest.[16] In practice there may be little difference.

Before turning to these, however, it is important to emphasise the role of the background and any agreement in determining the existence and extent of any fiduciary obligations. Fiduciary obligations cannot be prayed in aid to enlarge the scope of contractual duties,[17] nor can they be used to evade the obvious. For example, it is obvious to anyone instructing an estate agent that the agent sells competing properties and may hold confidential information about them; in those circumstances, there cannot be a duty to disclose the confidential information or to preclude the agent from acting for rival sellers.[18] Similarly, if a bank has a discretionary power on behalf of a client to trade with itself, it is obvious that the bank will seek to make a profit on those trades, and cannot therefore be under an obligation to account for that profit.[19] Again, where someone instructs a solicitor he knows to be acting for another party with a potentially conflicting interest in a transaction, that person cannot complain of

14. *Henderson* v. *Merrett* [1995] 2 AC 145, 206, per Lord Browne-Wilkinson.

15. *Fiduciary Duties and Regulatory Rules*, para 2.4.9 (Law Commission Consultation Paper No 124).

16. [1997] 2 WLR 436, 449. Millett LJ broadly follows the description given by Finn in *Fiduciary Obligations*.

17. *Clark Boyce* v. *Mouat* [1994] 1 AC 428, 437.

18. *Kelly* v. *Cooper* [1993] AC 205, 215. At pp 213–214, Lord Browne-Wilkinson put it on the basis that there was an implied term in the contract that the estate agent could act in this way, and the fiduciary relationship must accommodate itself to the terms of the contract. The degree of obviousness, or usual practice, required has been stated in various ways (see paragraphs 3.4.7–3.4.10 of *Fiduciary Duties and Regulatory Rules* (Law Commission Consultation Paper 124)).

19. *Ata* v. *American Express Bank* (unreported, 7 October 1996 and 17 June 1998).

breach of the double employment rule—the potential for conflict is of its own making.[20]

5.3.1 Undivided loyalty

This rule in turn has a number of different aspects, described by Millett LJ in *Bristol & West Building Society* v. *Mothew* as "double employment", "the duty of good faith", "the no inhibition principle" and "the actual conflict rule".[21] All are, however, different aspects of the fundamental obligation of loyalty owed by a fiduciary.

The "double employment rule" prevents a fiduciary acting as such for two parties whose interests *may* conflict without their informed consent. Informed consent means consent given in the knowledge that there is a conflict and that, as a result, the fiduciary may not be able to disclose to each party the full knowledge he possesses or may not be able to advise one party where there is a conflict. Breach of this rule automatically constitutes a breach of fiduciary duty, whether or not an actual conflict arises.[22]

The "actual conflict" rule means that a fiduciary must take care not to find himself in a position where there is an actual conflict of duty so that he cannot fulfil his duty to one without breach of his obligations to the other. If this situation does occur, the fiduciary will have no option but to cease to act for one, and usually both, parties—the fact that fulfilling his duty to one will give rise to a breach of the obligations to the other does not absolve the fiduciary from liability.

The duty of good faith means that a fiduciary must not allow his duties to one principal to influence his relationship with the other. The no inhibition rule means that a fiduciary must not be inhibited by his obligations to one principal in the performance of his duties for the other. This requires that a breach must be intentional, though it need not be dishonest.[23]

As far as derivatives are concerned, no problem will arise from the undivided loyalty rule in normal principal to principal dealing—it requires fiduciary obligations to be owed to two parties. Merely because an institution has the power to act for two different principals will not of itself give rise to a breach of the double employment rule, but the institution must take care to treat

20. *Bristol & West Building Society* v. *Mothew* [1997] 2 WLR 436, 450. There has been debate as to whether there is a core set of obligations which a fiduciary or trustee could not exclude. Leaving aside the extent to which someone can be considered a fiduciary if they have not undertaken the core obligations, in *Armitage* v. *Nurse* [1997] 3 WLR 1046, 1056 Millett LJ considered a trustee's core duty was to perform the trusts honestly and in good faith for the benefit of the beneficiaries, and anything else could be excluded. It seems likely that the same would apply to fiduciaries.

21. *Bristol & West Building Society* v. *Mothew* [1997] 2 WLR 436, 450–451. See also Finn, *Fiduciary Obligations* pp 252–258.

22. See, regarding this paragraph, *Clark Boyce* v. *Mouat* [1994] 1 AC 428, 435, *Bristol & West Building Society* v. *Mothew* [1997] 2 WLR 436, 450, and *Bristol & West Building Society* v. *Fancy & Jackson* [1997] 4 All ER 582, 614.

23. *Bristol & West Building Society* v. *Mothew* [1997] 2 WLR 436, 450–451.

principals in a like position equally to avoid preferring one over another.[24] It is the impact of one relationship on another which leads to breach. So, for example, an institution which has a discretionary power to enter into transactions on behalf of two principals will be in breach of the rule if it arranges a transaction between those two principals; even if the institution, or some other institution, is interposed between the two principals, there is still a real risk of breach of this rule.

5.3.2 No conflict

Related to the undivided loyalty principle is the requirement that a fiduciary must not place himself in a position where his interests conflict with those of his principal, at least without the consent of the principal. If a fiduciary enters into a transaction with his principal, this will breach this principle because the fiduciary's obligation is to secure the best terms for his principal but that obligation is clearly compromised if there is self-dealing. The fact that the fiduciary carries on the same or a similar business as his principal is unlikely in general to give rise to a conflict in this way since in many derivatives there is a large and liquid market; if, however, there is a limited market in a particular product at a particular price such that only the fiduciary or his principal could enter into a transaction, it would be a breach of fiduciary duty for the fiduciary to enter into the transaction to the exclusion of his principal.

5.3.3 No profit

A fiduciary can make a profit from his office, but only if it is authorised by the principal.[25] If the profit is not authorised, then the fiduciary is liable to account to the principal for it. In the context of derivatives, an unauthorised profit might arise from, say, entering into a transaction with the principal, unless the principal had, or must be taken to have, consented to this.[26] It would also be a breach of this obligation to accept commission, or any other payment, from any third party in return for entering into a transaction on behalf of a principal. So, for example, an arranger or broker who owes fiduciary obligations to his principal cannot request or accept commission from the other party unless prior disclosure is made to the principal.

24. Prudence nevertheless requires that any discretionary mandate, or documentation governing a relationship which might be considered fiduciary, expressly states that the institution can act for others.

25. E.g. *Dale* v. *IRC* [1954] AC 11, 27.

26. As in *Ata* v. *American Express Bank* (unreported, 7 October 1996 and 17 June 1998).

5.3.4 Good faith

It is not clear whether a duty of good faith is a distinct obligation on fiduciaries or whether it is the overriding obligation of which the other obligations are particular examples. In *Fiduciary Obligations*, Finn treats the specific duties mentioned as each being a duty of good faith, but Millett LJ in *Bristol & West* v. *Mothew*[27] appears to treat it as a distinct head. In practice there may not be much difference, as it is seldom likely to be the case that breach of some abstract duty of good faith does not also fall within another category of obligation.

5.3.5 Breach of confidence

Breach of confidence is an equitable obligation closely related to other fiduciary duties as it depends on an obligation of loyalty with regard to the confidential information. It has, however, a relatively independent existence, and often arises in circumstances which do not give rise to any other fiduciary obligations.[28] It is considered above in connection with contractual obligations of confidentiality.[29]

5.4 THE PROBLEMS OF BEING A FIDUCIARY

If a derivatives business were considered in isolation, fiduciary obligations would in most cases not pose any significant problem. It will only be on rare occasions that a fiduciary obligation will arise, and seldom inadvertently. An advisory role will rarely give rise to fiduciary obligations, but any agency or discretionary power to act on the principal's behalf is likely to lead to fiduciary obligations. These situations will in general arise under a contract and, as stressed above, the courts have recognised that fiduciary obligations cannot expand the scope of a contract. It is therefore important that the contract addresses the issues by defining the obligations that are undertaken in order to prevent the imposition of fiduciary obligations which were not intended. If there is no pre-existing fiduciary duty, then the contract should be free to define the parties' rights and obligations. If, however, there is a pre-existing fiduciary relationship and the contractual terms are being agreed within the scope of the contractual relationship, the position is more difficult. In these circumstances,

27. [1997] 2 WLR 436, 449.
28. In *Indata Equipment Supplies* v. *ACL* (unreported, 31 July 1997), Otton LJ said that "the mere fact that the confidant may have received confidential information from the confider does not create a fiduciary relationship".
29. See pp 35ff.

the principal's informed consent is required.[30]

In general terms, the issues which a contract establishing a fiduciary relationship will need to cover, if appropriate, include the following: first, that the fiduciary can deal with the principal and need not account for any profits made[31]; secondly, the fiduciary need not use for the benefit of its principal any information regarding which it owes an obligation of confidentiality to a third party; thirdly, the fiduciary may act for others, and for itself, even if its interests and those of the others conflict with that of the principal, subject to the establishment of Chinese walls[32]; and, fourthly, that all other parts of the business of the institution should be treated as if they were a separate legal entity with the intention that knowledge acquired by those parts of the institution should not be treated as knowledge of the fiduciary unless actually acquired by those responsible for the relationship with the principal.[33]

The issues arising for an arranger or broker owing fiduciary obligations are similar, but are likely to concern specifically accepting commission from the other party to the transaction. An improper payment to a fiduciary is usually described as a bribe, whether or not it also constitutes a criminal offence. In this context:

"... a bribe means the payment of a secret commission, which only means (i) that the person making the payment makes it to the [fiduciary] of the other person with whom he is dealing; (ii) that he makes it to that person knowing that that person is acting as the [fiduciary] of the other person with whom he is dealing; and (iii) that he fails to disclose to

30. Paragraphs 3.4.4–3.4.9 of *Fiduciary Duties and Regulatory Rules* (Law Commission Consultation Paper 124). What constitutes informed consent is a question of fact depending on the circumstances of each case (*Re Pauling* [1962] 1 WLR 86, 108), and in *Commonwealth Bank* v. *Smith* (1991) 102 ALR 453 it was considered that telling the principal of the conflicting relationship was not enough—the fiduciary should have told his principal to take independent advice.

31. But the clearer the basis of dealing is defined the better in order to limit any difficulties should things go wrong. For example, if the price to be charged to the principal is a certain spread over a quoted index or price, the principal can have no area of complaint.

32. Absent Chinese walls, there is a risk that acting for different principals or in the interests of the institution itself would conflict with the fundamental obligation to act honestly and in good faith for the benefit of the principal: see note 30. The efficacy of Chinese walls had been questioned in cases about solicitors (see, for example, *David Lee* v. *Coward Chance* [1991] Ch 259, 268 and 270, and *Re a Firm of Solicitors* [1992] 1 All ER 353, 363), but they have been recognised both by statute (section 48(2)(h) of the Financial Services Act 1986) and by the SFA's rules (rule 5–3, following the core rules issued by the SIB); there had, however, been doubt whether these provisions modify the general law on use of information (see also *Fiduciary Duties and Regulatory Rules* (Law Commission Consultation Paper 124), paragraphs 5.3.16–5.3.22 and 5.4.1). In *Prince Jefri Bolkiah* v. *KPMG* [1999] 2 WLR 215, the House of Lords recognised the efficacy of institutional Chinese walls, but apparently rejected Chinese walls set up after the event without the consent of all relevant parties. In *Young* v. *Robson Rhodes* (unreported, 30 March 1999), Laddie J accepted a Chinese wall set up on the merger of two accountancy firms on the basis that it was sufficient to prevent there being any greater risk of leakage of information than before the merger.

33. Failing this, there is a danger that an institution could be caught by the aspect of the principle of loyalty which requires it to use all the information available to it for the benefit of the principal. The extent of this principle of attribution of knowledge is open to doubt (see *Harrods* v. *Lemon* [1931] 2 KB 157, *Lloyds Bank* v. *Savory* [1933] AC 201, *Armstrong* v. *Strain* [1952] 1 KB 232, *Meridian* v. *Securities Commission* [1995] 2 AC 500 and *Mahli* v. *Abbey Life* [1995] 4 Re LR 305), but it is better to avoid the issue if possible.

the other person with whom he is dealing that he has made the payment to the person whom he knows to be the other person's [fiduciary]."[34]

The central issue is whether the payment gives rise to a conflict of interest on the part of the fiduciary, i.e. where his own interests conflict with his duties[35] because the principal is entitled to honest and disinterested service from the fiduciary.[36]

If, for example, a broker's task is to obtain a price from one or more particular potential counterparties, it is unlikely that any fiduciary obligations would be owed because the principal is not dependent upon the singleminded loyalty of the broker but merely on the accurate reporting of conversations. If, however, the broker's obligation is to obtain for its customer the best price available in the market, the broker is likely to owe fiduciary duties to that customer because the customer will be dependent on the singleminded loyalty of the broker in establishing what that price is. If, through negligence, the broker fails to find the best, the customer's remedies will lie in the tort of negligence or in contract; if, however, the broker accepts commission from the other party to the transaction without making full disclosure to the principal, that will constitute a breach of fiduciary duty. The broker will be liable to the principal either for the amount of the commission or for any damages the principal can show that it suffered, but not both although the principal need not make an election between the remedies until the time comes for judgment to be entered.[37] As a result, the principal in effect has a choice between the amount of the bribe and, if higher, damages, and does not have to make that choice until it knows the amount of the damages it can recover.

The way for a broker or arranger to avoid this risk is to make full advance disclosure to its customer. This could be, for example, in the contract establishing the relationship. Absent express disclosure, if it can be shown that it is the usual practice in the relevant market for the broker to be remunerated by the other party as well as the principal, and the principal is aware, actually or impliedly, of this and does not enquire further, then the payment may be unexceptionable.[38] An alternative, but related, concept which may mitigate this risk is through the incorporation of a trade custom into the contract between third party and principal. Trade customs can be incorporated into a contract if they are certain and uniform, notorious, are considered legally binding, and are

34. *Industries & General Mortgage Co Ltd* v. *Lewis* [1949] 2 All ER 573, 575. The word used by Slade J was "agent" rather than "fiduciary" but an agent is a fiduciary (see, for example, article 1(1) of *Bowstead and Reynolds on Agency* (16th edn) which states that "Agency is a fiduciary relationship").

35. *Anangel Atlas Compania Naviera SA* v. *Ishikawajima-Harima Heavy Industries Co Ltd* [1990] 1 Lloyd's Rep 167, 171.

36. *Panama and South Pacific Telegraph Company* v. *India Rubber, Gutta, Percha, and Telegraph Works Company* (1875) LR 10 Ch App 515, 528.

37. *Mahesan* v. *Malaysia Housing Corporation* [1979] AC 374, 383.

38. Paragraphs 3.4.7–3.4.10 of *Fiduciary Duties and Regulatory Rules* (Law Commission Consultation Paper No 124).

reasonable.[39] This is likely to be hard to prove in a market as relatively novel and fast-moving as off-exchange derivatives. Further, in order to be reasonable, there are some suggestions that a trade custom must not contradict a vital principle of fiduciary law.[40] If a payment is made without the knowledge of the principal with a risk of an agent's fundamental duty of loyalty being compromised, a trade custom, even if it could be proved, might be held to be unreasonable.

5.5 THE PROBLEM OF DEALING WITH A FIDUCIARY

In most cases, dealing with a fiduciary will not pose any particular difficulties. Problems can, however, arise when a third party deals with a fiduciary who is acting in breach of his fiduciary obligations. This brings with it a risk of constructive trusteeship (which is discussed elsewhere[41]). The main problem, however, is the risk of being treated as putting a fiduciary in a position of conflict, a risk which will arise most commonly when a payment is made to the fiduciary; if a payment is made, it is immaterial whether the agent requested the payment, whether it is made by the other party to the transaction or whether he merely assisted the agent or an associate to obtain it.[42]

This risk is discussed above in the context of a payment being accepted by a fiduciary, but the fiduciary is at least in a position to assess whether it does in fact owe any fiduciary obligations and, if so, the extent to which they have been modified by contract. Someone dealing with a broker or an arranger who might owe fiduciary obligations is in a more difficult position because it will not know what the relationship is. In the decided cases, it has generally been clear that the payment was being made to the agent of the other even if it was not appreciated that the payment should not be made. In many cases involving derivatives, however, it will not be clear whether, for example, a broker is a fiduciary since that will involve an analysis of the relationship between the broker and the other party, something which it will not be practicable to undertake. In these circumstances, the test of knowledge of the fiduciary relationship has been said to be the same as for accessory liability in constructive trusts,[43] namely that the

39. *Nelson* v. *Dahl* (1879) 12 Ch 568. See also paragraphs 3.2.2–3.2.7 of *Fiduciary Duties and Regulatory Rules* (Law Commission Consultation Paper No 124).

40. *Anglo-African Merchants* v. *Bayley* [1970] 1 QB 311, 323–324. A slightly less strict approach was taken in *North and South Trust* v. *Berkeley* [1971] 1 All ER 980.

41. See pp 50ff above.

42. *Logicrose* v. *Southend United FC* [1988] 1 WLR 1256, 1261.

43. *Logicrose Ltd* v. *Southend United FC* [1988] 1 WLR 1256, 1261. With the development of the law relating to constructive trusts, the current test is not the same as stated by Millett J in *Logicrose*.

payment must be one that an honest person would not have made in the circumstances.[44]

As a result, if there is any dealing with an agent acting for the other party to the transaction, and that agent requests a payment, there is a real risk that, absent disclosure to the principal,[45] the payment will be characterised as a bribe, and the consequences of this are severe. The person making the payment cannot escape these consequences by asserting that he believed that the agent would make or had made disclosure to the principal—if someone takes the "hazardous course" of paying a sum to someone acting for another and does not communicate it himself, he must accept the risk of the agent's not doing so.[46]

Once a payment is made with the requisite knowledge, it is an irrebuttable presumption that it was made to induce the agent to act favourably to the payer, whatever the real motive, and that the agent was influenced by the payment.[47] The principal is entitled to rescind the contract *ab initio* or, if that is no longer possible, to terminate the contract for the future.[48] Where the contract involves payments of money, rescission will usually be possible and will require the return of all payments made under it, restoring the parties to the position they were in before the contract.[49] As an alternative to rescission, the principal can recover from the other party to the agreement the amount of the bribe (if not recovered from the agent), together with any additional damages the principal can prove that it has suffered.[50] If the principal recovers the amount of the bribe from the agent, he does not need to bring this into account when returning payments in the event of rescission.[51]

The primary way to remove the potential risks of dealing with a fiduciary is to ensure that the principal is aware of any payment to the agent before the transaction is entered into. The best way of making a principal aware of a payment is to tell him expressly. If that is not practicable, a clause covering this might be incorporated expressly into a contract. There is no reason why contractual terms, whether agreed orally or included in a confirmation or master agreement, cannot allow one party to pay commission to the other's agent but the more express the term is as to the amount of the commission the better the disclosure is likely to be. Absent disclosure, the party may be able to rely on market practice in the same way that a fiduciary can in order to show that there has in fact been no breach of fiduciary duty, but a third party could also take a

44. *Royal Brunei Airlines* v. *Tan* [1995] 2 AC 378, 389; see pp 51–52 above. Where a payment is made by an employee, it is enough that he is acting in the course of his employment for the bribe to be attributed to the employer: *Armagas Ltd* v. *Mundogas* [1986] 1 AC 717, 743.

45. See pp 115–116 above.

46. *Grant* v. *The Gold Exploration and Development Syndicate Ltd* [1900] 1 QB 233, 248–249.

47. *Shipway* v. *Broadwood* [1899] 1 QB 369 and *Industries & General Mortgage Co Ltd* v. *Lewis* [1949] 2 All ER 573, 576–577.

48. *Armagas Ltd* v. *Mundogas* [1986] 1 AC 717, 742–743.

49. See pp 81ff above.

50. *Mahesan* v. *Malaysia Housing Corporation* [1979] AC 374, 383. The remedies available in equity are potentially more wide ranging even than this.

51. *Logicrose Ltd* v. *Southend United FC* [1988] 1 WLR 1256, 1263–1264.

warranty from a potential fiduciary that the payment of commission to him is not improper.

5.6 CRIMINAL LIABILITY

There could also in some circumstances be the possibility of the crime of bribery under section 1(1) of the Prevention of Corruption Act 1906. This provides that:

"... if any person corruptly gives or agrees to give or offers any gift or consideration to an agent as an inducement or reward for doing or forbearing to do ... any act in relation to his principal's affairs or business, or for showing or forbearing to show favour or disfavour to any person in relation to his principal's affairs or business he shall be guilty of an offence."

The essence of the offence is corruption, but it is not clear what this means.[52] Whilst corruption is not the same as dishonesty,[53] it may not be wholly different.

52. See paragraphs 2.29 and 2.30 of the Law Commission's paper entitled *Legislating the Criminal Code: Corruption* (Law Com No 248).

53. *Cooper* v. *Slade* (1857) 6 HL Cas 746.

CHAPTER 6

THE REGULATION OF DERIVATIVES

6.1 INTRODUCTION[1]

Sections 3 and 4 of the Financial Services Act 1986 (in this chapter called "the Act") make it a criminal offence for anyone to carry on or purport to carry on investment business in the United Kingdom unless that person is authorised or exempted under the Act. The Act has been affected by the Banking Coordination (Second Council Directive) Regulations 1992[2] (in this chapter called the "2BCD Regulations") and the Investment Services Regulations[3] (in this chapter called the "ISD Regulations"). These Regulations implement the European "single passport" for investment services, that is, they allow a firm authorised in one member state of the European Economic Area[4] to carry on some or all of the activities covered by the European Union directives[5] in any other member state without further authorisation. The 2BCD and ISD Regulations do this by providing that many of the provisions of the Act do not apply to these European investment firms.

Carrying on investment business in the United Kingdom in breach of the Act is not only a criminal offence. In addition, an agreement is unenforceable against the other party if entered into by a person who is neither authorised nor exempted in the course of carrying on investment business to which the Act applies.[6] Even if an agreement is entered into by an authorised or exempted person, if it is done in consequence of anything said or done by a person in the course of carrying on an illegal investment business, the agreement is also unenforceable against the other party.[7] In both these cases, the other party is also

1. The regulation of the financial markets is to undergo considerable change in the light of proposals and draft legislation, the Financial Services and Markets Bill, published by the Government in July 1998 and, in revised form, in June 1999.

2. 1992 SI No 3218.

3. 1995 SI No 3275.

4. Most of Western Europe except Switzerland.

5. The Second Council Directive on the coordination of laws, regulations and administrative provisions relating to the taking up and pursuit of business by credit institutions and amending the First Council Directive (No 89/646/EEC), and the Council Directive on investment services in the securities field (No 93/22/EEC).

6. Section 5(1)(a) of the Act.

7. Section 5(1)(b) of the Act.

entitled to recover any money or property transferred under the agreement, together with compensation for loss suffered by him as a result of having parted with it.[8] The court may, however, allow an agreement to be enforced if it is just and reasonable to do so (or for money paid under it to be retained) as long as the person reasonably believed he was not contravening the Act or, where an authorised or exempted person enters into an agreement as a consequence of anything said or done by someone else who is carrying on an illegal investment business, he did not know that the agreement was entered into in this way.[9]

In addition to the rights given to the other party to an agreement entered into in the course of investment business to which the Act applies and which is neither exempt nor authorised, the Secretary of State (whose powers for these purposes have been delegated to the Financial Services Authority[10]) has power to seek an injunction to stop the continuation of an illegal investment business. It can also seek orders that the person carrying on that business, or anyone else knowingly concerned in the contravention, restore the parties to the position they were in before the agreement was entered into.[11] As a result of this reference to others knowingly concerned in the contravention, the Act does not just affect the person acting in breach of the Act (in most cases likely to be a corporate entity) but also extends, for example, to the directors of, or solicitors acting for, a company in breach of the Act; they can also be ordered to restore a third party to the position he was in before the agreement entered into in breach of the Act, whether or not they have actually received or hold the other party's money.[12]

The Act and the regulations and rules made under it are long and complex, and the position is further complicated by the effect of the 2BCD and ISD Regulations. The issues arising will, however, in general be: first, whether a particular transaction is subject to the Act; secondly, if so, which part of the fragmented regulatory system set up by the Act applies to the transaction; and, thirdly, whether there has been any breach of the relevant rules. This first question in turn depends on the nature of "investments" as defined in the Act, the nature of the transactions involving investments, by whom they were carried out, and the link between the transaction and the United Kingdom.

8. Section 5(1) of the Act.

9. Section 5(3) of the Act.

10. See p 134 below. The Financial Services Authority was formerly called the Securities and Investments Board but, for convenience, will be referred to throughout this chapter as the Financial Services Authority.

11. Sections 6(1) and (2) of the Act. In addition, section 61 gives the Secretary of State similar powers for breach of sections 47 (misleading statements and practices), 56 (unsolicited calls), 57 (restrictions on advertising), or 59 (employment of prohibited persons).

12. *Securities and Investments Board* v. *Pantell (No 2)* [1993] Ch 256. The solicitors in *Pantell* were alleged to have operated a bank account for those acting in breach of the Act and collected investors' cheques (see pp 273–274).

6.2 THE SCOPE OF THE ACT

As mentioned above, the Act prohibits anyone carrying on investment business in the United Kingdom unless that person is an authorised or exempted person. This begs the questions of what is an investment, what is investment business, and when is it carried on in the United Kingdom.

6.2.1 Investments

6.2.1.1 The definition of derivatives

Section 1(1) of the Act provides that an "investment" is "any asset, right or interest falling within any paragraph in Part I of Schedule 1 to this Act". As far as derivatives are concerned, the relevant paragraphs of Part I of Schedule 1 are paragraphs 7 to 9.[13] These provide in full as follows:

"**Options**

7. Options to acquire or dispose of—
(a) an investment falling within any other paragraph of this Part of this Schedule;
(b) currency of the United Kingdom or of any other country or territory;
(c) gold, palladium, platinum[14] or silver; or
(d) an option to acquire or dispose of any investment falling within this paragraph by virtue of (a), (b) or (c) above.

Futures

8. Rights under a contract for the sale of a commodity or property[15] of any other description under which delivery is to be made at a future date and at a price agreed upon when the contract is made.

Notes

(1) This paragraph does not apply if the contract is made for commercial and not investment purposes.
(2) A contract shall be regarded as made for investment purposes if it is made or traded on a recognised investment exchange or made otherwise than on a recognised investment exchange but expressed to be as traded on such an exchange or on the same terms as those on which an equivalent contract would be made on such exchange.

13. "Derivatives" are defined by reference to these three paragraphs in the rules of the Securities and Futures Authority, following the core definitions issued by the Financial Services Authority. Section 2 of the Act allows its scope to be extended or restricted by order made under that section: this has been done on a number of occasions.

14. The reference to palladium and platinum were added by the Financial Services Act 1986 (Extension of Scope of Act and Meaning of Collective Investment Scheme) Order 1988, 1988 SI No 496.

15. Paragraph 28(1)(a) of the Act provides that "'property' includes currency of the United Kingdom or any other country or territory."

(3) A contract not falling within Note (2) above shall be regarded as made for commercial purposes if under the terms of the contract delivery is to be made within seven days.
(4) The following are indications that any other contract is made for a commercial purpose and the absence of any of them is an indication that it is made for investment purposes—
  (a) either or each of the parties is a producer of the commodity or other property or uses it in his business;
  (b) the seller delivers or intends to deliver the property or the purchaser takes or intends to take delivery of it.
(5) It is an indication that a contract is made for commercial purposes that the price, the lot, the delivery date or the other terms are determined by the parties for the purposes of the particular contract and not by reference to regularly published prices, to standard lots or delivery dates or to standard terms.
(6) The following are indications that the contract is made for investment purposes—
  (a) it is expressed to be traded on a market or on an exchange;
  (b) performance of the contract is ensured by an investment exchange or a clearing house;
  (c) there are arrangements for the payment or provision of margin.
(7) A price shall be taken to have been agreed upon when a contract is made—
  (a) notwithstanding that it is left to be determined by reference to the price at which a contract is to be entered into on a market or exchange or could be entered into at a time and place specified in the contract; or
  (b) in a case where the contract is expressed to be by reference to a standard lot and quality, notwithstanding that provision is made for a variation in the price to take account of any variation in quantity or quality on delivery.

Contracts for differences etc

9. Rights under a contract for differences or under any other contract the purpose or pretended purpose of which is to secure a profit or avoid a loss by reference to fluctuations in the value or price of property of any description or in an index or other factor designated for that purpose in the contract.

Notes[16]

(1) This paragraph does not apply where the parties intend that the profit is to be obtained or the loss avoided by taking delivery of any property to which the contract relates.
(2) This paragraph does not apply where the rights are under any contract under which money is received by the Director of Savings as deposits or otherwise in connection with the business of the National Savings bank or raised under the National Loans Act 1968 under the auspices of the Director of Savings or under which any money raised is treated as having been so raised by virtue of section 11(3) of the National Debt Act 1972."

The other paragraphs of Part I of Schedule 1 refer to, for example, shares, bonds and other instruments creating or evidencing debt, and debentures.

16. The heading was added, and the existing text numbered as shown, by the Financial Services Act 1986 (Extension of Scope of Act and Meaning of Collective Investment Scheme) Order 1990, 1990 SI No 349.

The aim of these paragraphs is to identify financial transactions rather than commercial ones; as with the uncertainty relating to the Gaming Acts,[17] however, this is not always an easy distinction to make. To assist in this, the statute uses "notes" to paragraphs 8 and 9 of Schedule 1 to the Act. In some instances, such as notes (2) and (3) to paragraph 8, these notes provide mandatory deeming provisions,[18] but in others it is merely an indication as to which side of the line a transaction might fall.

Futures, covered by paragraph 8 of Schedule 1, pose particular difficulties, and have been the subject of guidance from both the Government and the Financial Services Authority.[19] The problem is to ensure that the Act does not cover genuine commercial transactions which provide, as is commonly the case, for delivery in the future. Equally, the fact that delivery is not intended or is not likely to take place does not as a matter of course divide financial from commercial transactions—delivery can take place with, for example, transactions on the London Metal Exchange even though it is far more common for a transaction to be closed out by another transaction. The Act provides, through Note (2), that all transactions on a recognised investment exchange, such as the LME or LIFFE, or on exchange terms fall within the scope of the Act, but for transactions unrelated to an exchange the position is more difficult.[20]

To be a "futures" contract within paragraph 8, it seems that the contract must provide for delivery. This appears to be the view taken by Thomas J in *Larussa-Chigi* v. *CS First Boston*,[21] a case concerning foreign exchange transactions. Thomas J took the view that because the contract did not contemplate delivery of the currencies, the transactions were not futures contracts within paragraph 8. Thomas J also considered that if delivery had been contemplated, the value date would have been the delivery date and the contracts would prima facie have been futures contracts within paragraph 8. However, because the value date was within seven days of the contract date, the transaction would fall outside the scope of the Act as a result of the statutory presumption in Note (3).

On this basis, it is possible to run a foreign exchange book outside the scope of the Act as long as the contract provides for delivery within seven days. If the contract allows for delivery after seven days, the position is more uncertain. The notes appear to be directed in the main to exchange traded transactions rather

17. See pp 22ff above.

18. *Larussa-Chigi* v. *CS First Boston* (unreported, 18 December 1997).

19. A statement by a Government Minister, the Hon Francis Maude MP, on 19 January 1988, and guidance notes GR3 of March 1988 and GR1 of February 1996. The guidance issued by the Financial Services Authority was given under section 206 of the Act.

20. The heading of paragraph 8 of Schedule 1 to the Act is "Futures", but it clearly covers both futures and forwards.

21. Unreported, 18 December 1997. The problem with this approach is Note (4)(b) which appears to contemplate a contract being a futures contract within paragraph 8 because delivery is not intended. If delivery is not intended, the contract is likely to be a contract for differences within paragraph 9, but there seems no reason why it could not fall within both paragraphs. This does, however, extinguish any real difference between paragraphs 8 and 9.

than off-market ones, and a court would be faced with the problem of distinguishing between transactions for investment and commercial purposes on the basis of the notes to paragraph 8. Where not concerned with exchange related transactions, the two most relevant notes are (4)(a), which deals with the use of the commodity or other property in the business of one or both of the parties, and (5), which deals with the terms of the contract. Where the commodity or other property is, say, copper, it may be obvious whether one party uses it in the course of its business; where the commodity or other property is, say, money,[22] this will not be so. The guidance issued by the Financial Services Authority treats hedging as a commercial rather than an investment activity[23]—if that is so, a forex deal entered into by a company as a hedge for, say, export exposure will not be within the scope of the Act, but the counterparty will in many cases not know what the purpose of the transaction is and therefore whether it is within the scope of the Act.

In *Larussa-Chigi* v. *CS First Boston*, Thomas J decided on the facts that delivery of the currency was never intended, and therefore the transactions were contracts for differences within paragraph 9. He took this view because the contracts provided for settlement to take place by an offsetting transaction and payment of the net sums only. As a result, contracts which might usually be described as forward transactions might well be categorised as contracts for differences under the Act. Note (1) to paragraph 9 of Schedule 1 to the Act provides that a transaction cannot be a contract for differences if delivery is intended, but it is not clear how this intention can be expressed. A contract might allow for delivery even if the parties do not in fact expect there to be delivery. The cases on delivery generally relate to the Gaming Acts,[24] where, latterly at least, the courts have tended to try to make financial contracts enforceable and have therefore looked no further than a contractual obligation to deliver or a right to require delivery which was not a sham. The Act has a different aim, and the courts might be more inclined to find an intention not to deliver if that brought a transaction within the scope of the Act. Nevertheless, in *Larussa-Chigi* v. *CS First Boston*, Thomas J looked at the contractual terms in order to discern the intention of the parties.[25]

Contracts for differences are a very wide category. Not only do they potentially include futures contracts where delivery is not intended to take place, but they can also include other transactions which would not normally be

22. Paragraph 28(1)(a) of Schedule 1 to the Act states that "property" includes the currency of the United Kingdom or any other country or territory.

23. Paragraph 6 of the guidance in GR1 of February 1996.

24. See pp 22ff above.

25. This perhaps ignores the distinction between note (4)(b) to paragraph 8 and note (3). Note (3) refers to the contractual terms whereas note (4)(b) refers to the parties' intention. It is possible for the contract to provide for delivery but for the parties to intend, without the contract being a sham, that delivery will not in fact take place.

considered to be derivatives. *Morgan Stanley* v. *Puglisi*[26] concerned Principal Exchange Rate Linked Securities (PERLS). PERLS are fixed rate bonds where the redemption value of the bond is dependent on the movement of currencies; in one of the transactions in question, the redemption value was the original US dollar amount plus twice the spot exchange rate at maturity of the US dollar against the Italian lira less twice the spot exchange rate of the Swiss franc against the US dollar. If, therefore, (contrary to market expectation) the Italian lira gained against the Swiss franc, the redemption value of the bond increased, but if (as actually happened) the Italian lira weakened against the Swiss franc, the redemption value decreased. Longmore J decided that this variable redemption value meant that PERLS were contracts for differences. This was not because the payment was linked to an exchange rate but because the payment was made by reference to fluctuations in different exchange rates, the Italian lira and the Swiss franc. Longmore J did, however, leave open the possibility that a transaction linked only to one exchange rate could still be a contract for differences as being dependent on an "index or other factor" within paragraph 9.

The PERLS also contained an embedded option, the term that the redemption value of the PERLS would never be negative—a form of floor. In *Morgan Stanley* v. *Puglisi*, Longmore J rejected the argument that this made PERLS options within paragraph 7 of Schedule 1 to the Act. The documentation included this embedded option in the form of a proviso that the redemption amount due on the bonds would not be negative. Longmore J considered that because it was not expressed in terms of an option but rather as a proviso, it could not be an option. This is a rather limited approach—looking at form rather than substance—but is probably correct in this case. An option is usually considered as the right but not the obligation to take a certain step. The proviso in this case did not confer any rights which the buyer of the PERLS could choose to exercise or not; it was part of the definition of the redemption value. As such, although economically the same as an option, it is not so legally.

6.2.1.2 *Common forms of derivative*

Where do common forms of derivative fit into Schedule 1 to the Act? Futures, forwards and the problems they pose have been discussed above. Interest rate swaps are generally contracts for differences in that their purpose or pretended purpose is to secure a profit or avoid a loss by reference to fluctuations in the value or price of property.[27] This is the case whether or not gross payments or net payments are made. For the same reason, currency, equity, commodity, and total return swaps are likely also to be contracts for differences.

An interest rate swap option might fall within paragraph 7 of Schedule 1, and/or possibly within paragraph 9 if it provides for cash settlement. Paragraph

26. Unreported, 29 January 1998.
27. *Morgan Grenfell* v. *Welwyn Hatfield* [1995] 1 All ER 1, 12.

7 is, however, limited in the options it covers. It expressly refers to currency options and to gold, palladium, platinum and silver options, but not to options to buy, for example, copper. To avoid the scope of the Act, however, the option must be on a contract where delivery is intended—if it is not, the transaction is likely to be a contract for differences within paragraph 9. Similarly, an option to enter into a copper future or forward would generally fall within the Act as being an option under paragraph 7(a) to acquire or dispose of an investment falling within another paragraph of Schedule 1, namely a futures contract under paragraph 8 or a contract for differences under paragraph 9.

A credit default swap or a credit spread option which gave the buyer the right to transfer the underlying asset would also be an option provided that the underlying asset fell within one of the other paragraphs in Schedule 1 to the Act. The paragraphs most likely to apply are paragraph 1 ("shares and stock in the share capital of a company"), paragraph 2 ("debentures, including debenture stock, loan stock, bonds, certificates of deposit and other instruments[28] creating or acknowledging indebtedness . . ."), and paragraph 3 ("loan stock, bonds and other instruments creating or acknowledging indebtedness issued by or on behalf of a government, local authority or public authority").

6.2.2 Investment business

Part I of Schedule 1 to the Act defines investments, but it is investment business which is regulated by the Act. Investment business constitutes the activities set out in Part II of Schedule 1 (i.e. paragraphs 12 to 16) unless excluded by Part III.[29] Paragraph 12 covers "buying, selling, subscribing for or underwriting investments or offering or agreeing to do so, either as principal or as agent". For these purposes, an offer includes an invitation to treat, buying and selling includes any acquisition or disposal for valuable consideration, and disposal includes creating an investment or granting the rights or interests of which the investment consists.[30] Paragraph 13 covers making or offering or agreeing to make arrangements for others to carry on the activities in paragraph 12 (i.e. broking), paragraph 14 covers managing investments, and paragraph 15 covers advice on investments.

With regard to advice, in *Re Market Wizard Systems (UK) Ltd*,[31] Carnwath J decided that the sale of computerised trading systems did constitute advice on the part of the supplier. He said that:

"I have no doubt that the signals generated by the use of the System constitute the kind of advice with which paragraph 15 [of Schedule 1 to the Act] is concerned. The signals provide guidance as to the course of action which the user should take in relation to the buying and selling of the investments. Such guidance, in the ordinary use of English, is

28. An instrument does not have to be a document: paragraph 28(1)(c) of Schedule 1 to the Act.
29. Section 1(2) of the Act.
30. Paragraphs 28(1)(c) and (d) and 28(2) of Schedule 1 to the Act.
31. *The Times*, 31 July 1998.

'advice on the merits' of purchasing those investments. It matters not that the user is free to follow or disregard the advice, nor that he may receive further advice from his broker before making a final decision ...

[Counsel for the company] submitted that the System is 'simply a matter of calculation based on historical data and the updates put in by the customer ...' The submission would have some substance if all the program purported to do was to provide a convenient means of extracting and analysing data as to historical movements in the market, without offering any interpretation of that information as a guide to future action. But such a limited function would be quite inconsistent with the sense of the brochure ...

It is to be noted that the Act requires that the advice should be on the merits of purchasing 'an investment'. General advice on the merits of a category of investment, for example on the merits of investment trusts as opposed to unit trusts, is not caught. By contrast the System gives specific signals directed to the merits of buying or selling options in each of the 12 selected companies ... Nor in my view does it make any difference that the purchaser is warned that what he is receiving is not intended to be treated as investment advice. If, on an objective view, it is investment advice within the meaning of the statute, the agreement of the parties cannot make it something different ...

The only arguable issue, in my view, is whether it is the company which is 'giving or offering to give' the advice ... The only time at which any advice is given on the merits of a particular investment is at the point at which the user generates a signal. At that point the company does nothing ... The question is whether the company is carrying on the business of giving investment advice. It is not necessary to identify a particular point in time at which advice is given. It is enough, in my view, that it is providing the customer with a medium by which its purported expertise in the analysis of historical trading patterns is communicated in the form of advice related to a particular investment."

Investment business is, therefore, very wide. It is hard to think of an activity involving derivatives which does not prima facie fall within Part II of Schedule 1. Indeed, even carrying out one transaction might well fall within the scope of the Act. Section 1(3) says that "'investment business' means the business of engaging" in those activities. The section could simply have said that investment business means engaging in those activities; using the phrase "business of engaging" must therefore add something, but it seems likely that it will be given a fairly liberal interpretation[32] given that the aim of the Act is to provide a framework of regulation to protect users of financial instruments from the unscrupulous, the incompetent and, on occasions, themselves. In *Morgan Grenfell* v. *Welwyn Hatfield*, which concerned the words "by way of business" in section 63 of the Act, Hobhouse J said that it was probable that those words were a reiteration of what is already to be found in Schedule 1, and went on:

"I see no reason, whether on a consideration of the policy of the Act or the wording used, to place a narrow meaning on the word 'business'. It clearly should not be given a technical construction but rather one which conforms to what in ordinary parlance would be described as a business transaction, as opposed to something personal or casual ...

... Regularly entering into a certain type of transaction for the purpose of profit is a

32. In *Town Investments* v. *Department of Environment* [1978] AC 359, 386, Lord Diplock commented that the "word business is an etymological chameleon; it suits its meaning to the context in which it is found. It is not a term of legal art ..."

good indication that the party doing so is doing so by way of business. But it is equally possible that the very first time it enters into such a contract it is doing so by way of business because it is doing so as part of its overall business activities."[33]

In these circumstances, "business" will perhaps only be treated as distinguishing between those activities within the scope of the Act and those undertaken in a private, non-commercial capacity. Any company which enters into a derivatives transaction or carries out any of the other activities in Part II of Schedule 1 will therefore prima facie fall within the scope of the Act unless it comes within one of the exceptions in Part III and elsewhere.

The activities in Part III of Schedule 1 to the Act (paragraphs 17 to 25) are excluded from the definition of investment business. As far as derivatives are concerned, paragraph 17(4) provides that paragraph 12 (entering into transactions) does not apply to a transaction which relates or is to relate to an investment within paragraphs 7 to 9 (derivatives), which is entered into as a principal, and which is entered into with or through an authorised person, an exempted person or an offshore office of the other party as long as that other party's head office is outside the UK and its business would otherwise be within Part II. This is a more limited exemption for someone dealing as a principal than for other investments,[34] and provides essentially that one of the parties to a derivatives transaction must be a professional, whether authorised or exempted (this will depend on the nature of the transaction), or offshore, or the transaction must be arranged by a professional.

In addition to this exemption, there are also exemptions for derivatives related to the supply of goods or services by someone whose main business is the supply of those goods or services and not investment business.[35] So, for example, a copper producer could sell copper and at the same time enter into a derivatives contract with the buyer for the purposes of or in connection with that sale or a related sale. Similarly, investment advice otherwise within paragraph 15 is excluded if given in the course of a profession or business not constituting investment business and giving it is a necessary part of other advice or services.[36]

6.2.3 Investment business in the United Kingdom

Investment business must have a geographical link to the United Kingdom to fall within the scope of the Act. This is provided by section 1(3) of the Act which provides that a person carries on investment business in the United Kingdom if he:

33. [1995] 1 All ER 1, 13–14.
34. Paragraph 17(1) provides that, for other investments, paragraph 12 only applies to those dealing as a principal if, in summary, they do so as market makers or dealers or they solicit members of the public.
35. Paragraphs 19(1) and (2) of Schedule 1 to the Act.
36. Paragraph 24 of Schedule 1 to the Act.

"(a) carries on investment business from a permanent place of business maintained by him in the United Kingdom; or
(b) engages in the United Kingdom in one or more of the activities which fall within the paragraphs of Part II of [Schedule 1] and are not excluded by Part III or IV of that Schedule and his doing so constitutes the carrying on of a business in the United Kingdom."

Section 1(3)(a) therefore requires, first, a permanent place of business to be maintained in the United Kingdom, and, secondly, investment business to be carried on from that place. In the Companies Act 1985 and its predecessors, overseas companies are required to register with the Registrar of Companies if they have an "established place of business"[37] in the United Kingdom which "connotes not only setting up a place of business at a specific location, but a degree of permanence or recognisability as being a location of the company's business".[38] A permanent place of business is presumably more than this—if not the draftsman would have used the same phrase—it requires greater than merely a "degree" of permanence. Further, the place of business has to be maintained by the relevant person, but this probably means no more than that it must be the place of business of the person in question—it would be curious if the Act did not apply, for example, because the place of business was maintained by its parent in the sense that the parent owned or leased the property and paid all expenses.

A company within section 1(3)(a) of the Act will commit a criminal offence if it carries on investment business from the place even if that business is carried on wholly overseas. Section 1(3)(b) deals with business carried on in the United Kingdom even if from a place of business outside the United Kingdom. Section 1(3)(b) applies if someone engages in one or more of the activities in Part II of Schedule 1 in the United Kingdom which are not excluded by Parts III or IV.[39] Paragraph 12 of Schedule 1 applies to buying and selling investments, i.e. entering into derivatives contracts. To do so in the United Kingdom presumably requires the contract to be made in the United Kingdom, which is not necessarily the case just because one of the parties is, say, an English company.[40] When a contract is entered into through correspondence transmitted by post, a contract is made where the letter of acceptance is posted,[41] but when a contract is made by instantaneous communication—such as telephone, fax or e-mail—the contract is made where the offeror receives notice of the acceptance.[42] This could make it a lottery whether any particular business transaction is entered into in the United Kingdom. With regard to post, it comes down to ensuring that the contract is only formed when the offshore party posts its acceptance, but with

37. Section 691 of the Companies Act 1985.
38. *Re Oriel* [1986] 1 WLR 180, 184.
39. Part IV is discussed below in the context of overseas companies.
40. It is also possible to take a more purposive interpretation and look at the transaction in the round rather than where, according to artificial rules, it was consummated.
41. *Wansborough Paper Co* v. *Laughland* [1920] WN 344. The same is true of a contract made by telegram: *Cowan* v. *O'Connor* (1880) 20 QBD 640.
42. *Entores* v. *Miles Far East Corporation* [1955] 2 QB 327.

regard to fax it is the reverse. For telephone conversations, it requires what will often be an artificial dissection of the conversation to see who made the offer and who accepted it.

Business can now also be transacted through internet sites.[43] An internet site, even if hosted on a computer in the United Kingdom, is unlikely to be a permanent place of business within section 1(3)(a) of the Act—this must refer to a physical location where business can physically be carried on. A contract formed through the internet is likely to be treated as a contract made by instantaneous communications and therefore formed where the offeror receives acceptance. In reality, this is where the offeror carries on business rather than where the computer holding an internet site is situated.

Paragraph 12 also applies to offering to buy or sell investments, and paragraph 13 applies to making or offering to make arrangements for another to enter into an investment.[44] It is possible to make an offer, or to make arrangements, in the United Kingdom even if the agreement is subsequently made overseas, but it is not clear whether the offeror has to be in the United Kingdom or whether it is enough that the offeree is. In *SIB* v. *Pantell*, Sir Nicolas Browne-Wilkinson V-C held that there was an arguable case that sending circulars from outside the United Kingdom to those within was a breach of the Act by offering to deal or arrange deals in investments,[45] in the light of which it is likely that a generous interpretation of the Act would be taken. Sir Nicolas Browne-Wilkinson V-C also considered that there was an arguable case that sending an investment advertisement to people within the United Kingdom was offering to give investment advice in the United Kingdom within paragraph 15 of Schedule 1 to the Act. This accords with the general view that advice is given where the recipient of the advice is located and acts on the advice rather than where the adviser is located.[46] As a result, advising on the telephone someone in England might well fall within the Act.

This approach is also in line with section 207(3) of the Act, which provides that an advertisement or other information issued outside the United Kingdom is to be treated as issued in the United Kingdom if it is directed to persons in the United Kingdom or is made available to them otherwise than in a newspaper or

43. In Board Notice 416, the SFA comments that "the global structure of the internet raises a number of complex jurisdictional issues which will take some time to resolve." See also the Financial Law Panel's *Report on Jurisdiction and the Regulation of Financial Services on the Internet*.

44. Paragraphs 12 and 13 also apply to agreeing to buy or sell an investment or arrange for another to do so.

45. [1989] 1 All ER 673, 676. In *SIB* v. *Vandersteen* [1991] BCLC 206, Harman J agreed, but put his decision more on the basis of section 57 of the Act ("no person other than an authorised person shall issue ... an investment advertisement in the United Kingdom ...") than on section 3 (see also section 207(3)).

46. *Diamond* v. *Bank of London & Montreal* [1979] QB 333 and *The Albaforth* [1984] 2 Lloyd's Rep 91. In *Domicrest* v. *Swiss Bank Corporation* [1999] 2 WLR 364, Rix J decided that, for the purposes of article 5(3) of the Lugano Convention, the harmful event occurred for the tort of negligent misrepresentation, where it was made rather than where it was received. This was, however, applying an independent meaning to a treaty governing jurisdiction between a large number of parties rather than applying English domestic law.

periodical published and circulating principally outside the United Kingdom or in a sound or television broadcast transmitted principally outside the United Kingdom. This is a very wide description, and indicates that, for example, an advertisement on the internet would be treated as issued in England if accessible from England,[47] at least unless it is in a language other than English and states expressly that it is not available to English residents, though even that might not be enough.

The curious feature of section 1(3)(b) of the Act is the last requirement, that engaging in the United Kingdom in one or more of the activities in Part II of Schedule 1 must constitute the carrying on of business in the United Kingdom. This may be just an over-cautious repetition of the requirement in section 1(2) that the transaction must be a business transaction. It certainly did not appear to trouble the court in *SIB* v. *Pantell*[48] that all the Swiss company had done was send advertisements from Switzerland to England and did not appear to have any other business presence in the United Kingdom. It may, however, add a further test so that, for example, someone who simply makes a contract in the United Kingdom does not necessarily fall within section 1(3)(b). The further nature of this test is, however, far from clear.

The requirement for a connection with the United Kingdom is not therefore stringent. Any business conducted from a permanent place of business in the United Kingdom falls within the Act. More significantly, any business with someone in the United Kingdom at the time the business is conducted runs the risk of falling within the Act, unless it is within one of the exemptions for overseas institutions discussed below. The Act is aimed at protecting investors in the United Kingdom from unscrupulous or incompetent financial advisers and counterparties, and investors anywhere in the world from unscrupulous or incompetent financial advisers and counterparties operating from the United Kingdom. As such, the Act is likely to be given a generous interpretation.

6.3 AUTHORISATION

Sections 3 and 4 of the Act make it a criminal offence to carry on investment business in the United Kingdom unless, amongst other things, a person is authorised to do so. What constitutes authorisation for the purposes of the Act is set out in sections 7 to 33 of the Act (Chapter III of Part I of the Act), but the most important section is section 7. This provides that "a member of a self-regulating

47. This is the line taken by the SFA in its guidance on the internet issued on 25 April 1998 (Board Notice 416) and by the Financial Services Authority in its guidance (Guidance 2/98). The FSA's guidance threatens enforcement action against not only those responsible for the content of a web site but also "those who are the sponsors or advisers to such persons (or otherwise knowingly concerned with a breach of the Act)" (para 15).

48. [1989] 1 All ER 673.

organisation [an 'SRO'] is an authorised person by virtue of his membership of that organisation".

The structure of regulation under the Act is that the lead regulator is the Secretary of State, but he has delegated most of his powers under the Act to the Financial Services Authority,[49] including the power to recognise SROs. An SRO is a body "which regulates the carrying on of investment business of any kind by enforcing rules which are binding on persons carrying on business of that kind either because they are members of that body or because they are subject to its control".[50] In order to become a recognised SRO under the Act, an SRO must meet certain criteria laid down in the Act and a recognition order must be made by the Financial Services Authority.[51] Once an SRO is recognised, members of the SRO are authorised to carry on investment business of the type which that SRO regulates; so, for example, for distinct kinds of investment business one institution may have to belong to two, or possibly all three, SROs.[52] As far as derivatives are concerned, the relevant SRO is the Securities and Futures Authority (the "SFA").

Each SRO has criteria for membership, rules regulating the conduct of business, financial status, and financial reporting, and disciplinary provisions for breach of the rules and other applicable laws and regulations. An SRO's rules themselves encompass "core rules" issued by the Financial Services Authority under section 63A of the Act in order to provide a common framework for regulation. Outside the SRO's rules, there are certain rules made by the Financial Services Authority which are applicable to members of all SROs,[53] and also the Authority's Statements of Principle, wide and general principles governing the conduct of investment business.[54]

For most institutions wishing to carry on a derivatives business, it will be necessary to become a member of an SRO. Outside this area, there are certain other means of obtaining authorisation to carry on investment business. These are: authorisation from a recognised professional body, namely a body regulating a profession where practitioners do not wholly or mainly carry out investment business[55]; insurance companies authorised under the Insurance

49. The power to delegate is in section 114 of the Act. The delegation orders made under that section are 1987 SI No 942, 1988 SI No 738, 1991 SI No 200, and 1991 SI No 1256.

50. Section 8(1) of the Act.

51. Sections 9 and 10, and Schedule 2 to the Act.

52. The number of SROs has now dwindled to three, the SFA, the Investment Management Regulatory Organisation, and the Personal Investment Authority. Under the Government's proposals for the reform of the regulation of financial services, it will diminish to one, the Financial Services Authority.

53. Such as the Common Unsolicited Calls Regulations made under section 56 of the Act.

54. For example, Principle 2 is that a "firm should act with due care, skill, and diligence". The SFA's rules and the principles are discussed at pp 150–156 below.

55. Sections 15 to 21 of the Act. Such bodies include, for example, the Law Society for solicitors.

Companies Act 1982 so far as they are allowed to carry out investment business as part of their insurance business[56]; friendly societies authorised under the Friendly Societies Act 1992[57]; operators of collective investment schemes recognised under section 86 of the Act[58]; investment companies with variable capital so far as investment business consists in operating the collective investment scheme constituted by the company[59]; persons directly authorised by the Financial Services Authority[60]; and persons authorised in other states subject to various conditions.[61]

6.4 EXEMPTION

Investment business can be carried out not only by those authorised under the Act but also by those exempted from its provisions. These include the Society of Lloyd's and persons permitted by the Council of Lloyd's to act as underwriting agents at Lloyd's as respects investment business carried out in connection with or for the purposes of insurance business at Lloyd's.[62] They also include the Bank of England.[63] More significantly, exempted persons include recognised investment exchanges,[64] such as LIFFE, but this exemption does not extend to members of an exchange which must be authorised independently according to the nature of their businesses or ensure that the business they carry out does not require authorisation.[65]

The widest group of exempt persons are those for the time being on a list maintained by the Financial Services Authority for the purposes of section 43 of the Act, but only "in respect of, and of anything done for the purposes of, any transaction to which Part I or Part II of Schedule 5 to [the] Act applies and in respect of any arrangements made by him with a view to other persons entering into a transaction to which Part III of that Schedule applies". The Bank of England, as predecessor in this role to the Financial Services Authority,[66] has published two papers setting out the standards it expects of those on the list it maintains, *The London Code of Conduct* and *The Regulation of the Wholesale*

56. Section 22 of the Act. As to the power of insurance companies to enter into derivatives, see pp 63–70 above.
57. Section 23 of the Act.
58. Section 24 of the Act.
59. Section 24A of the Act.
60. Sections 25 to 30 of the Act. Very few institutions are directly regulated in this way.
61. Sections 31 to 34 of the Act. The provisions relating to overseas bodies are discussed at pp 140–146 below.
62. Section 42 of the Act.
63. Section 35 of the Act.
64. Sections 36 to 41 of the Act.
65. For example, those dealing only as principals on a recognised investment exchange fall within the exception in paragraph 17(4) of Schedule 1 to the Act.
66. By section 21(b)(i) of the Bank of England Act 1998, the Financial Services Authority took over the Bank of England's functions under section 43 of the Act.

Cash and OTC Derivatives Markets (in sterling, foreign currency and bullion),[67] which are discussed further below.[68] Section 43 is directed at large transactions in the wholesale markets.

Exempt transactions under section 43 fall into two categories: transactions not subject to monetary limit; and those which are subject to monetary limit. Exempt derivatives transactions which are not subject to monetary limit are as follows:

1. an option, neither made nor expressed to be made on a recognised investment exchange, on a debenture, loan stock, bond, certificate of deposit, or other instrument creating or acknowledging indebtedness which is issued by someone other than a government, local authority or public authority and which requires repayment not later than five years from the date of issue[69];
2. an option, neither made nor expressed to be made on a recognised investment exchange, on loan stock, bonds or other instruments creating or acknowledging indebtedness which is issued by a government, local authority or public authority and which requires repayment not later than one year from the date of issue or, if issued by a local authority in the United Kingdom, not later than five years from the date of issue[70];
3. an option, neither made nor expressed to be made on a recognised investment exchange, on the currency of the United Kingdom or of any country or territory, or on gold or silver[71];
4. a futures contract made for investment purposes,[72] and neither made nor expressed to be made on a recognised investment exchange, for the sale of a debenture, loan stock, bond, certificate of deposit, or other instrument creating or acknowledging indebtedness which is issued by someone other than a government, local authority or public authority and which requires repayment not later than five years from the date of issue[73];
5. a futures contract made for investment purposes,[74] and neither made nor expressed to be made on a recognised investment exchange, for the sale of loan stock, bonds or other instruments creating or acknowledging indebtedness which is issued by a government, local authority or public authority and which requires repayment not later than one year from the

67. Published most recently in July 1995 and December 1995 respectively.
68. See pp 146–149 below.
69. Paragraphs 2(1) and 2(2)(f)(i) of Part I of Schedule 5 to the Act.
70. Paragraphs 2(1) and 2(2)(f)(i) of Part I of Schedule 5 to the Act.
71. Paragraphs 2(1) and 2(2)(f)(ii) and (iii) of Part I of Schedule 5 to the Act.
72. See pp 125–126 above.
73. Paragraphs 2(1) and 2(2)(g)(i) of Part I of Schedule 5 to the Act.
74. See pp 125–126 above.

date of issue or, if issued by a local authority in the United Kingdom, not later than five years from the date of issue[75];

6. a futures contract made for investment purposes,[76] and neither made nor expressed to be made on a recognised investment exchange, on the currency of the United Kingdom or of any country or territory, or on gold or silver[77];
7. a contract for differences,[78] neither made nor expressed to be made on an recognised investment exchange, by reference to fluctuations in any of the contracts referred to in paragraphs 1 to 6 above, the investments underlying those contracts, a warrant entitling the investor to subscribe for those underlying investments, or any other rights to or interests in those underlying investments[79];
8. a contract for differences,[80] neither made nor expressed to be made on a recognised investment exchange, by reference to fluctuations in the currency of the United Kingdom or of any other country or territory or in a rate of interest in any of those currencies or an index of those rates[81];
9. an option, neither made nor expressed to be made on a recognised investment exchange, to acquire any of the investments referred to above.[82]

These transactions are only exempt if entered into by one listed institution with another or with the Bank of England.[83] As a result, two listed institutions dealing on the wholesale markets fall outside the scope of the Act. If, however, they deal through a recognised investment exchange, they are subject to the rules of that exchange. Similarly, if they deal with a person who is not listed under section 43, they must be authorised through membership of the SFA and are subject to its rules.

These transactions are all off exchange transactions—on exchange transactions are not between two listed institutions once adopted by the exchange, but even before that they fall outside the scope of exempt transactions. The transactions cover forwards on short or medium-term debt and on currencies, but not, for example, commodity or equity forwards or swaps (except on gold and silver). Interest rate and currency swaps are included within the scope of exempt transactions.

Exempt transactions by persons listed under section 43 which are subject to monetary limit are as follows:

75. Paragraphs 2(1) and 2(2)(g)(i) of Part I of Schedule 5 to the Act.
76. See pp 125–126 above.
77. Paragraphs 2(1) and 2(2)(g)(ii) and (iii) of Part I of Schedule 5 to the Act.
78. See pp 126–127 above.
79. Paragraphs 2(1) and 2(2)(h)(i) of Schedule 5 to the Act.
80. See pp 126–127 above.
81. Paragraphs 2(1) and 2(2)(h)(ii) and (iii) of Schedule 5 to the Act.
82. Paragraphs 2(1) and 2(2)(i) of Schedule 5 to the Act.
83. Paragraph 1 of Schedule 5 to the Act.

(a) an option within paragraphs 1, 2, or 3 above where the value or price of the property in respect of which the option is granted is at least £500,000[84];
(b) a futures contract under paragraphs 4, 5 or 6 above where the price payable under the contract is not less than £500,000[85];
(c) a contract for differences under paragraphs 7 or 8 above where the value or price of the fluctuation in which, or the amount of the fluctuation in the interest on which, is relevant for the purposes of the contract is not less than £500,000[86]; and
(d) an option within paragraph 9 above (options on the above) where the requirements in paragraphs a, b or c are satisfied with regard to the underlying investment to which the option relates.[87]

The transactions are therefore the same as those for which there are no monetary limits. The monetary limits apply at the time the transaction is entered into.[88] Unlike the transactions which have no monetary limit, these apply to transactions between a listed person and an unlisted person (except the Bank of England).[89] This regime therefore applies, for example, to transactions between a bank on the section 43 list and a corporate. The rationale behind the exemption is clearly that the transactions are of such a size that only those who can or should be considered relatively sophisticated, or at least have access to sophisticated advice, can enter into them.

Once a person on the section 43 list has entered into a transaction within the monetary limits described above with someone who is not on the list, for 18 months after that the monetary limits no longer apply to transactions between the two.[90] This provision means that the non-listed person can be treated in effect as if it were listed for 18 months after the last transaction within the monetary limits. The listed party therefore needs only to watch the calendar rather than each transaction to see what rules apply to it.

Transactions arranged by a listed institution which fall within one of the two sets of criteria above are also exempt.[91] Essentially this means that a broker who arranges a transaction which, as between the two parties, falls within the exemptions in Schedule 5, will not be committing an offence.

Section 43 of the Act provides that a listed person is exempted in respect of transactions which fall within Schedule 5 and also in respect of anything done

84. Paragraph 5(4) of Schedule 5 to the Act.
85. Paragraph 5(5) of Schedule 5 to the Act. The reference to the "price" payable under the contract is potentially confusing if the futures contract is cash to be settled. To make sense, the reference must be to the nominal price of the underlying contract.
86. Paragraph 5(6) of Schedule 5 to the Act.
87. Paragraph 5(7) of Schedule 5 to the Act.
88. Paragraph 8 of Schedule 5 to the Act.
89. Paragraph 4 of Schedule 5 to the Act.
90. Paragraph 6 of Schedule 5 to the Act
91. Paragraphs 9 and 10 of Schedule 5 to the Act.

for the purposes of the transaction. In *CS First Boston* v. *Larussa-Chigi*,[92] Thomas J held that a listed person was exempted for all steps preparatory to an exempt transaction even though at the time of those steps details of the transaction were not known and it was not therefore known whether it would be large enough to be within the exemptions. In that case, Mrs Larussa-Chigi could not rely on alleged breaches of the SFA's rules before any transactions were carried out because the transactions which she in fact entered into were exempt, though at the time of the steps in question CS First Boston did not know that the transactions would be exempt. Nevertheless, the only prudent approach in these circumstances is either to assume that the transactions which will be entered into are likely to fall outside the exemptions or to ensure that only exempt transactions are entered into.

The preparatory steps in that case were essentially documenting the relationship. It is less clear that advice about a transaction would constitute "anything done for the purposes of" a transaction in Schedule 5. The Act treats advice as being a distinct activity from a transaction—entering into a transaction is within paragraph 12 of Schedule 1 and advice is in paragraph 15. Nevertheless, advice in the form of a representation in the course of a negotiation between a corporate and a financial institution (for example, "in our view, interest rates will fall over the next year") could on a wide view be given for the purposes of the transaction subsequently entered into, and there are practical difficulties in being required to treat the same counterparty as both subject to the SFA's rules in case advice is given but otherwise within the section 43 regime. This is, however, an area of real risk in that advice in the course of a transaction might fall outside the exemption. Though not a transaction within the section 43 regime, the transaction under consideration in *Morgan Stanley* v. *Puglisi*[93] was large in scale. Longmore J nevertheless brushed aside the suggestion that Morgan Stanley had not given advice to Mr Puglisi: "The whole point of Mr Puglisi coming to Morgan Stanley in the first place . . . was so that he could be advised as to how he could sensibly and suitably invest his funds. Even if Mr Puglisi never said so in terms, there can have been no other basis on which he would transfer to Morgan Stanley considerable sums of money . . . The fact that a serious financial institution can make such a submission [i.e. that it did not give Mr Puglisi investment advice] shows, in my judgment, a serious under-appreciation of the Financial Services Act . . ."

92. Unreported, 18 December 1997.
93. Unreported, 29 January 1998. For the transaction, see p 127 above.

6.5 OVERSEAS INSTITUTIONS

There are two principal exemptions for overseas institutions: first, in Part IV of Schedule 1 to the Act; and, secondly and more importantly, the European passport regime introduced by the ISD and 2BCD Regulations.

6.5.1 Part IV of Schedule 1 to the Act

Paragraph 26(1) of Schedule 1 to the Act provides that paragraph 12 of the Schedule (buying or selling investments or offering or agreeing to do so) does not apply to a transaction entered into by a person who does not have a permanent place of business maintained by him in the United Kingdom at which he does investment business provided that the transaction is with an authorised or exempted person. As a result, as long as, say, a US institution has no permanent place of business in the United Kingdom, that institution is free to enter into transactions with authorised or exempted persons even if this is done on visits to the United Kingdom, from any non-permanent place of business, or on the telephone. This also applies to institutions which do have a permanent place of business in the United Kingdom as long as the permanent place of business is not used to carry on investment business, but it is questionable if it applies to someone with a permanent place of business in the United Kingdom at which investment business is carried on but the business is in fact done through an offshore office.

Paragraph 26(2) of Schedule 1 to the Act provides that paragraph 13 of Schedule 1 (broking) does not apply if the arrangements are made with someone who does not have a permanent place of business in the United Kingdom as long as the arrangements are made by an authorised or exempted person.

Finally, paragraph 27 of Schedule 1 provides that paragraphs 12 to 15 of that Schedule do not apply to a transaction with someone without a permanent place of business in the United Kingdom as long as the transaction was made as the result of an approach to the overseas person by the onshore person and the approach was not solicited or, if it was solicited, was not solicited in a way that contravened sections 56 and 57 of the Act,[94] or the approach has been made by the overseas person in a way that does not contravene either of those sections.

6.5.2 The ISD and 2BCD Regulations

The ISD and 2BCD Regulations introduce additional complexity to the regime under the Act, which is in any event far from straightforward. In summary, however, these regulations implement European directives which require

94. Unsolicited calls and advertising; see pp 163–164 below.

member states to impose authorisation requirements for certain types of investment business (though not everything covered by the Act). By obtaining authorisation[95] in its home[96] state, an institution acquires a "passport" which entitles it to carry on that same business, home regulated business, in any other member state without being authorised in that other state. In the United Kingdom, this is implemented by regulation 9 of the ISD Regulations which provides that the prohibition in sections 3 and 4 of the Act does not prevent a passported firm from carrying on in the United Kingdom any activities to which the Regulations apply.[97]

The distinction between the ISD and the 2BCD Regulations, and the European directives which underlie them, is that the latter apply essentially to banks whilst the former apply to other credit institutions. An institution is covered by either one or the other of the directives, but not by both. If, therefore, an overseas institution accepts deposits from the public, then it must gain authorisation under the regime established by the Second Banking Coordination Directive even if it also carries on, say, trading in futures and options.[98]

Even if it has a passport, an overseas institution can still take advantage of the regime in Part IV of Schedule 1 to the Act if applicable (and other exemptions under the Act), and does not therefore need to rely on its passport. This can be of significance because those relying on the passport remain obliged to comply with many of the provisions of the Act and the rules made under it, but these do not apply where Part IV of Schedule 1 is concerned. Where, however, a passported institution is also, for example, a member of the SFA and carries out a transaction which is both subject to the SFA's rules and falls within the passport, the passport in effect trumps the SFA's rules and the institution will,

95. For the purposes of an outgoing passport (i.e. United Kingdom firms wishing to carry on business in other member states), authorisation covers those authorised under the Act but also persons exempted under section 43 of the Act: regulation 18(2) of the ISD Regulations.

96. Regulation 2(1) of the ISD Regulations provides that "'home state' in relation to (a) an investment firm which has no registered office, means the EEA State in which the firm's head office is situated; and (b) an investment firm which has a registered office, means the EEA State in which that office is situated". This differs slightly from the definition in article 1(6) of the Investment Services Directive, but it appears that, for most purposes, the distinction is between natural persons, to whom (a) applies, and legal persons (corporations), to whom (b) applies and for whom the home state will almost always be the place of incorporation.

97. In addition, regulations 4 and 5 of the 2BCD Regulations provide that a passported credit institution is not prevented by sections 3 or 4 of the Act from carrying on investment business regulated by the Act which it is authorised to carry on in its home state. The 2BCD Regulations apply to "... 7. Trading for own account or for account of customers in: (a) money market instruments (cheques, bills, CDs, etc); (b) foreign exchange; (c) financial futures and options; (d) exchange and interest rate instruments; (e) transferable securities ... 10. Money broking" (the Annex to the Second Banking Coordination Directive which is quoted in Schedule 1 to the 2BCD Regulations).

98. Accepting deposits from members of the public falls within the Second Banking Coordination Directive only, while futures and options fall within both directives.

therefore, be treated as entering into the transaction by virtue of its passport and not its membership of the SFA.[99]

6.5.2.1 *Investments and activities governed by the ISD and 2BCD Regulations*

The investments governed by the ISD Regulations are set out in section B of the Annex to the Investment Services Directive,[100] which is quoted in Schedule 1 to those Regulations. They are:

> "1. (a) Transferable securities.[101]
> (b) Units in collective investment undertakings.
> 2. Money market instruments.[102]
> 3. Financial futures contracts, including equivalent cash-settled instruments.[103]
> 4. Forward interest-rate agreements (FRAs).
> 5. Interest-rate, currency and equity swaps.
> 6. Options to acquire or dispose of any instruments falling within this section of the Annex, including equivalent cash-settled instruments. This category includes in particular options on currencies and on interest rates."[104]

The drafting style of this is markedly different to Part I of Schedule 1 to the Act, though it covers similar ground. Since the United Kingdom is obliged to have a regime requiring authorisation for business involving these investments, Part I of Schedule 1 needs to be at least as wide as the Annex to the Investment Services Regulations in order to avoid the United Kingdom being in breach of its

99. Regulation 21 of the ISD Regulations, which provides that a passported institution is not to be treated as authorised by virtue of its membership of an SRO for any business to which the passport applies. On the same lines, paragraph 26 provides that inclusion in the list under section 43 of the Act does not make a passported firm exempt for any business to which the passport applies.

100. 93/22/EEC.

101. Defined in article 1(4) of the Investment Services Directive as "shares in companies and other securities equivalent to shares in companies, bonds and other forms of securitised debt which [in the case of either the shares or bonds] are negotiable on the capital market, and any securities normally dealt in giving the right to acquire any such transferable securities by subscription or exchange or giving rise to a cash settlement excluding [in any of these cases] instruments of payment". Transferable securities is also defined in the recitals to the Directive as "those classes of securities which are normally dealt on the capital market, such as government securities, shares in companies, negotiable securities giving the right to acquire shares by subscription or exchange, depositary receipts, bonds issued as part of a series, index warrants and securities giving the right to acquire such bonds by subscription".

102. Defined in article 1(5) of the Investment Services Directive as "those classes of instruments which are normally dealt with on the money market". It is also defined in the recitals to the Investment Services Directive as "those classes of instruments which are usually dealt with on the money market such as treasury bills, certificates of deposit and commercial paper".

103. The recitals to the Investment Services Directive provides that an " 'instrument equivalent to a financial futures contract' means a contract which is settled by a payment in cash calculated by reference to fluctuations in interest or exchange rates, the value of any instrument listed in Section B of the Annex or an index of any such instruments".

104. The scope of the 2BCD Regulations is set out in note 91 above.

obligations. The Government has presumably taken the view that it is, but this comes down to the construction of the two schedules. Both the European Directive on which it was based and the ISD Regulations post-date the Act[105] and therefore are not an aid to the construction of the Act,[106] but the European Court of Justice might refer to the Act in considering the meaning of the Directive. To the extent that Schedule 1 to the Act is wider than the Annex, then a passported firm will also require authorisation or exemption under the terms of the Act if it wishes to carry on Schedule 1 activities which are not within the Annex; to the extent that section B of the Annex is wider, the United Kingdom is in breach of its treaty obligations, but there is no direct effect for individual firms carrying on investment business.

As far as derivatives are concerned, the reference to futures almost certainly includes forwards, and faces the difficulty confronted more overtly by the Act in seeking to distinguish financial contracts from ordinary commercial transactions. Paragraph 3 states expressly that it includes cash-settled instruments, which, unless this reference is treated as defining rather than clarifying its scope, indicates that a contract for delivery can be within the scope. In practice, the scope of the Act is likely to be the same as under the ISD Regulations with the possible exception of the statutory presumption in note (3) to paragraph 8 of Schedule 1 to the Act that contracts providing for delivery within seven days are commercial. This presumption does not apply to the Regulations, and it is therefore possible that some currency trading could fall outside the scope of the Act but within the Regulations. The recitals to the Investment Services Directive do, however, state that the Directive cannot be used to provide spot and forward foreign exchange services other than as services connected with the provision of investment services.

For swaps, the ISD Regulations refer only to interest rate, currency and equity swaps. This appears to omit commodity swaps and some kinds of credit derivatives (such as total return swaps though, for example, certain credit default swaps could be options rather than swaps). Similarly, there could be questions as to whether some more complex swaps fall within the terms of the Regulations. A European court can, however, be expected to take a purposive approach to the construction of the list of instruments and not be too hidebound by technicalities.

6.5.2.2 Activities covered by the ISD and 2BCD Regulations

As with the Act, it is not particular investments which are subject to the Regulations but rather activities involving those investments. These are set out in section A of the Annex to the Investment Services Directive, and cover:

105. The Directive was made on 10 May 1993, and the ISD Regulations on 18 December 1995 (though they did not come into force until 1 January 1996).

106. See p 64 above.

"1. (a) Receipt and transmission, on behalf of investors, of orders in relation to one or more of the instruments listed in section B.
(b) Execution of such orders other than for own account.
2. Dealing in any instruments listed in section B for own account.
3. Managing portfolios of investments in accordance with mandates given by investors on a discretionary basis, client-by-client basis where such portfolios include one or more of the instruments listed in section B.
4. Underwriting in respect of issues of any of the instruments listed in section B and/or the placing of such issues."

This, again, is a markedly shorter list than that in Part II of Schedule 1 to the Act, though probably not significantly different in effect. The area possibly omitted which does fall in Part II is arranging deals, broking, which falls within paragraph 13 of Schedule 1.[107] Broking might arguably come within 1(a) or (b), but this is not entirely clear. A traditional broker introduces parties and, whilst he might become an agent for the purpose of passing names and the terms on which the parties are prepared to deal, that would, in a case where the broker has both parties on the telephone simultaneously, not generally be considered the reception and transmission of orders or executing those orders. However, the recitals to the Investment Services Directive state that "the reception and transmission of orders also includes bringing together two or more investors thereby bringing about a transaction between those investors". This indicates that the Annex is meant to cover broking.

In addition to the services quoted above, section C to the Investment Services Directive, quoted in Schedule 1 to the ISD Regulations, includes certain "non-core" services which institutions may carry on alongside their core services to which the passport applies. These include investment advice on any of the instruments in section B. The difference between the core activities in section A and the non-core activities is that each state is required by the Investment Services Directive to authorise core activities, and may alongside core activities also authorise non-core activities. Authorisation is not required by a home state for non-core activities, though it is permitted. The passport does, therefore, cover authorised non-core activities in case a home state does not impose authorisation requirements.

6.5.2.3 *United Kingdom regulation of passported firms*

The fact of having a passport from a European state under the Investment Services Directive entitles the firm to carry on investment business in the United Kingdom without further authorisation, but does not mean that the firm falls outside the United Kingdom regulatory regime. Before a passported firm can

107. In paragraph 29 of *The London Code of Conduct*, the Bank of England describes a broker as an arranger who "bring[s] together counterparties on mutually acceptable terms and pass[es] names to facilitate the conclusion of a transaction".

carry on business in the United Kingdom, due notification must be given to the United Kingdom authorities. This requires the supervisory authority in the home state to be notified of the firm's wish to carry on business in the United Kingdom, and for that authority to pass on notification to the United Kingdom authorities.[108] Further, breach of the Act or any rules or regulations made under it ultimately entitles the Financial Services Authority to revoke the passport and prohibit the firm carrying on investment business in the United Kingdom, though first the Authority must require the investment firm in writing to remedy the situation, the firm must fail to do so, the firm's home regulator must be notified, and that regulator must refuse or fail to procure a remedy or take inadequate measures for that purpose.[109]

The United Kingdom is forbidden by the Investment Services Directive from imposing additional authorisation requirements on passported firms, and capital requirements remain the province of the home state. Outside this sphere, article 11 of the Directive requires member states to draw up rules of conduct which investment firms must observe at all times. The Act represents English law on this point, and those carrying on business in the United Kingdom must adhere to it. In particular, paragraph 9 of Schedule 7 to the ISD Regulations expressly provides that passported firms are obliged to comply with the statements of principle issued by the Financial Services Authority under section 47A of the Act,[110] and paragraph 10 of Schedule 7 obliges them to comply with the conduct of business rules issued by the Authority under section 48 of the Act. These form the core of the regulations governing institutions which are authorised in the United Kingdom—the statements of principle are directly applicable to authorised persons, and the conduct of business rules are for most purposes implemented through the SFA's rules. A passported firm which is a member of an SRO for its non-passported business, as it is likely to be, is subject to an SRO and its disciplinary regime, subject to matters reserved to the home state,[111] in the same way that a non-passported firm is.[112]

To emphasise the similarity of the rules applicable to passported and other firms, the Financial Services (European Institutions) Instrument 1993, issued by

108. Regulation 6(1) of, and paragraph 1 of Schedule 3 to, the ISD Regulations. Even if entitled to a passport, it is a criminal offence for a firm to carry on investment business in the United Kingdom without due notification: paragraph 7 of the ISD Regulations.

109. Regulations 9 to 11 of the ISD Regulations.

110. Article 11 of the Investment Services Directive sets out certain principles which member states are obliged to implement, and these are very similar to the statements of principle issued by the Financial Services Authority.

111. SFA rule 1-14 sets out what SFA rules apply to passported institutions; as far as disciplinary proceedings are concerned, issues of their fitness and properness do not apply to passported institutions as these are matters for their home states.

112. Similarly, regulation 15 of the 2BCD Regulations allows the Financial Services Authority to prohibit an institution covered by those Regulations from carrying on investment business if it has contravened or is likely to contravene any provision of the Act or any rules or regulations made under the Act (including the rules of any SRO of which the institution is a member). Before doing so, regulations 15 to 17 of the 2BCD Regulations require the Authority to go through procedures similar to those in regulations 9 to 11 of the ISD Regulations (see above).

the Financial Services Authority, provides in rule 5.01 that where an institution listed under section 43 of the Act does business under its passport in respect of which, but for its passport, it would be an exempted person under section 43, the Authority's statements of principle and rules do not apply to that business. But for this provision, passported institutions would be in a worse position than other listed institutions in having to comply with the Authority's rules when others were subject to the Bank of England's lighter non-statutory regime for the wholesale markets.[113]

6.6 THE REGULATION OF THE WHOLESALE MARKETS

Section 43(2) of the Act allows the Financial Services Authority, with the approval of the Treasury, to impose conditions for admission to the list maintained by the Authority under that section[114] (until 1 June 1998, section 43(2) required the list to be maintained by the Bank of England, but these functions were transferred to the Financial Services Authority by section 21(b)(i) of the Bank of England Act 1998). The Act does not expressly allow the Authority to regulate the conduct of business within the market in the manner required of SROs,[115] but the rules for listing state that listed institutions are expected to comply with rules of conduct it has laid down, and threaten removal from the list in the event of failure to comply.[116] The listing requirements are in the Bank's paper on *The Regulation of the Wholesale Cash and OTC Derivatives Markets (in sterling, foreign currency and bullion)*,[117] commonly known as the Grey Paper, and the rules for conduct within the market are in *The London Code of Conduct*.[118]

The aim of *The London Code of Conduct* is to "set out in a clear and concise manner the principles and standards which broking firms and their employees, and 'core principals' in the wholesale markets (i.e. banks, building societies plus financial institutions supervised under the Financial Services Act 1986) should

113. See pp 135–139 above and 146–149 below. By regulation 26(1) of the ISD Regulations, a listed institution is not treated as listed in respect of home regulated investment business (i.e. activities to which its passport applies).

114. See pp 135–139 above.

115. Schedule 2 to the Act provides that an SRO must have fair and reasonable rules and practices for disciplining members (para 2) and have rules to which its members are subject as well as investigatory powers into its members (para 3).

116. Paragraph 31 of *The Regulation of the Wholesale Cash and OTC Derivatives Markets* (December 1995). Paragraph 10 of *The London Code of Conduct* (July 1995) is to the same effect.

117. The most recent edition is dated December 1995.

118. The most recent edition is dated July 1995. Both the Grey Paper and the Code continue to apply despite the transfer of responsibility for the section 43 regime by virtue of paragraph 1 of Schedule 4 to the Bank of England Act 1998.

observe".[119] The Code is a mixture of general exhortation to high standards,[120] guidance as to good practice,[121] and warnings to market participants.[122] It assumes that those able to deal in the wholesale markets are in a position to make independent decisions as to whether they wish to enter into a particular transaction and are not dependent on others, including their counterparties, for this[123]; as such, those in the wholesale markets do not get the protection which those dealing with, for example, institutions authorised under the Act receive.[124] The prime rule in the wholesale markets appears to be that before dealing with a new counterparty who will be a wholesale counterparty and therefore outside the main protection of the Act for (at least) 18 months,[125] a listed institution must give a full written explanation of this, including sending a copy of the Code.[126] In the Annex to the Grey Paper, the Bank of England supplies a draft of a letter suitable for this purpose.

The main theme of the Code is that the wholesale markets are for professionals, and participants are expected to look after their own interests. Core principals will generally assume that their counterparties, whether or not also professionals, have the capability to make independent decisions; all principals should assess for themselves the risks of dealing in the wholesale markets.[127] The other side of this emphasis on the professional nature of the wholesale markets is concern about the giving of advice.[128] The Code urges those who are not market professionals and who want advice to retain a market professional in writing and to set forth the exact nature and extent of the reliance it will place on that professional.[129] At the same time, the Code warns

119. Foreword to *The London Code of Conduct*.

120. For example, the preamble to Section II, General Standards, states that core principals and broking firms should observe not only the letter but also the spirit of the Code in undertaking, arranging or advising on transactions in the wholesale markets, and paragraph 13 states that firms should ensure that they and all other parties act in a manner consistent with the Code to maintain the highest reputation for the wholesale markets in London.

121. For example, paragraph 22 states that it is good practice for principals, "subject to their own legal advice, to alert counterparties to any legal or tax uncertainties which they know are relevant... in order that the counterparty may seek its own advice if it so wishes". What the phrase "subject to their own legal advice" means is not clear; presumably if a principal (i.e. not a broker) can find lawyers to advise that it is better not to alert the counterparty to any such thing because of the risks of misrepresentation, there is no need to do so. Paragraph 31 contains guidance as to considerations salespersons should take into account before dealing with new customers (e.g. legal capacity).

122. For example, paragraph 30 warns brokers of some of the dangers of giving advice, and paragraph 31 draws attention to some legal risks arising in transactions.

123. Paragraph 21 of the Code.

124. See, for example, pp 157–161 below.

125. See p 138 above.

126. Paragraph 70 of the Grey Paper and paragraph 6 of the Code. Paragraph 70 concedes that an oral warning may exceptionally be given as long as it is followed up in writing.

127. Paragraph 21 of the Code.

128. This mirrors concern expressed by the Bank of England in its annual report published on 25 May 1994 about the risks to merchant banks acting as advisers on major takeovers, new issues and corporate restructurings. The Bank's concern was driven by high profile litigation against merchant banks arising from this role.

129. Paragraph 21 of the Code.

professionals that small investors (i.e. individuals and small businesses) might want advice but, where they do, they should not automatically be granted a dealing line for the relevant product. If advice is given and the product is a derivative or leveraged, the Code provides that it is in the interests of listed institutions for them to have in place a written agreement which makes clear the extent to which reliance can be placed by the small investor on the advice given.

Setting out the terms of business on paper is in the interests of a bank wishing to limit or control the legal risks it runs. Whether it is realistic in advance of a transaction may be a different matter. If a listed institution is prepared to allow its counterparty or those for whom it arranges transactions to rely on its advice, or the counterparty is prepared to accept that it can only place limited reliance on what the institution says, there may be no problems. But if the institution is marketing itself based on its expertise in the markets, it might sit ill with this to present at the same time a document stating that the counterparty cannot rely on what the institution says. Marketing in this way runs a risk of legal responsibility in any event,[130] but the more usual course, though less satisfactory legally, is to seek to include in the terms of any contract a term to the effect that neither party has relied on the other.[131]

The Bank of England always had a close relationship with money brokers, and a significant part of the Code is devoted to emphasising the limited role played by brokers.[132] Paragraph 29 of the Code states that the typical role of a specialist wholesale market broker is to act as an arranger of deals, bringing together parties on mutually acceptable terms and passing names to facilitate the conclusion of the transaction (hence they are sometimes described as name-passing brokers). Brokers are paid commission by one or both of the parties for effecting the introduction, and are not permitted to act as principal in a transaction.[133] Brokers are urged to tell new clients of their limited role,[134] and the Code expressly states that brokers do not have sufficient information to be qualified to advise principals on the creditworthiness of specific counterparties and to do so is not their role.[135] Though it absolves brokers from credit assessments, if a broker makes a representation as to the nature of the

130. See p 96 above.

131. See pp 258–259 below.

132. Money brokers in the role they play in London are peculiar to the London money markets.

133. The Code reveals two exceptions to this rule: specialist inter-dealer brokers, primarily involved in US Treasury bills, which act as matched principals; and when name passing-brokers are investing their own money, in which case they must make clear that they are acting as principals.

134. Paragraph 17 of the Code.

135. Paragraph 30 of the Code. If, however, a broker were to offer advice on the creditworthiness of a counterparty, there is no reason in principle why it could not be liable if negligent, *a fortiori* if fraudulent (see Chapter 4). Paragraph 27 of the Code emphasises that it is for a principal to decide what credence, if any, to give any information or comment made by a broker, and that responsibility for assessing the creditworthiness of a counterparty rests on the principal alone. In making this

transaction[136] as to interest rate or other price movements, there is no reason why the broker cannot be liable in accordance with normal principles.[137]

The Code notes that confidentiality is essential for the preservation of a reputable and efficient market,[138] deals with the location of back offices,[139] the taping of conversations,[140] dealing at non-current rates, with unidentified principals and after hours,[141] and generally with best practice when dealing.[142] If there is an alleged breach of the Code, the Code urges that it be resolved amicably if at all possible but, if not, the Authority will investigate.[143] If it finds that there has been a breach, it does not fine offending institutions in the way that SROs do; rather it may publicly reprimand those involved, it may restrict a listed institution's activities or it may remove the institution from the section 43 list.[144]

Breach of the Code does not automatically lead to a right to damages on the part of the other party as it does for private investors where there has been breach of an SRO's rules[145] (unless an institution has incorporated the Code into the contract with the counterparty—use of the standard form of letter set out in the Annex to the Grey Paper may have this result[146]). The Code merely comments somewhat obscurely that an institution will be "expected to consider making appropriate redress to any damaged party or parties, bearing in mind the legal implications of so doing".[147] The Authority is prepared to act as an arbitrator in disputes between firms it supervises about the application of the Code, or current market practice, to specific transactions in wholesale market products.[148]

assessment, there is nothing in the Code to stop a principal from taking into account what a broker has said and relying on its accuracy. Where a core principal is concerned, it might, however, often be difficult to argue convincingly that it did, and that it was reasonable for it to rely on a broker, at least unless what the broker said could be considered within the broker's knowledge but not that of the core principal.

136. Paragraph 24 of the Code says that great care must be taken not to misrepresent the nature of any transaction.

137. See Chapter 4.

138. Paragraph 41 of the Code.

139. Paragraph 46 of the Code.

140. Paragraph 48 of the Code.

141. Paragraphs 50–54 of the Code.

142. Paragraphs 66–127 of the Code.

143. Paragraph 9 of the Code.

144. Paragraph 10 of the Code.

145. Sections 62 and 62A of the Act.

146. In *Larussa-Chigi* v. *CS First Boston* (unreported, 18 December 1997), CSFB wrote that transactions "will be governed by the Code of Conduct established by the Bank of England, to which we will adhere". Other than the last five words, this follows the wording in the Bank's form of risk warning letter set out in the Annex to the Grey Paper. Thomas J held that "the words 'the transactions will be governed by the Code of Conduct established by the Bank of England' are amongst the clearest words that could be chosen by the parties to indicate that the transactions in question were governed by the Code". The decision is nevertheless rather harsh in this aspect.

147. Paragraph 11 of the Code.

148. Paragraph 120 of the Code.

6.7 THE REGULATION OF AUTHORISED PERSONS

The regulation of authorised persons, for current purposes members of SROs, comes in tiers, with different consequences for breach of the various tiers. At the top are the statements of principle issued by the Financial Services Authority under section 47A of the Act; breach of the principles does not of itself give rise to any cause of action on the part of anyone injured by breach but can give rise to disciplinary and related powers.[149]

Secondly, are the rules of the SROs themselves[150]; breach of these rules can in some circumstances give rise to a cause of action on the part of a person who suffers loss as a result of contravention of the rules[151] and can lead to disciplinary action by the SRO. An SRO's rules are binding on members as a matter of contract only, and not as a matter of general law. Alongside an SRO's rules are certain rules of general application which the Financial Services Authority has power to make under the Act; these are binding as a matter of general law. These include conduct of business rules under section 48, but these have been covered by the rules of the SROs and the general rules disapplied to members of SROs.[152] The Financial Services Authority has, however, made rules under section 55 of the Act relating to the holding of clients' money.

Thirdly, are codes of practice which the Financial Services Authority has power to issue under section 63C of the Act, a power it has not in fact exercised.

Finally, under section 206 of the Act the Financial Services Authority may issue information and advice with regard, amongst other matters, to the operation of the Act and the statements of principle. This is not binding, and breach does not give rise to any disciplinary consequences; disobedience to guidance given by the Authority runs a risk, however, of leading to disciplinary action, though in any action it is always open to argue that the guidance is wrong.

6.7.1 The Statements of Principle

Section 47A of the Act provides that the Financial Services Authority[153] may issue statements of principle with respect to the conduct and standing expected of persons authorised to carry on investment business. The principles are therefore only applicable to authorised, and not to exempted, persons. They do not, therefore, apply to institutions listed under section 43 of the Act. Paragraph 9 of Schedule 7 to the ISD Regulations does, however, require passported firms

149. Section 47A(3) of the Act.

150. Paragraph 3(1) of Schedule 2 to the Act requires an SRO to have rules governing the carrying on of investment business and paragraph 4(1) requires an SRO to have adequate arrangements for the enforcement of compliance with those rules.

151. Sections 62 and 62A of the Act: see pp 159–162 below.

152. Rule 1.02(1) of the Conduct of Business Rules.

153. The Secretary of State has transferred to the Financial Services Authority his powers under this section under section 114 of the Act subject to limited exceptions, including under this section: see p 134 above.

to comply with the principles unless, but for the passport, the firm would be exempt.[154] The statements of principle are intended to be a "straightforward and universal statement of the conduct expected, which will: (a) encapsulate, express and build on current best practice; (b) be readily understood by all those involved in financial markets, not merely compliance experts; (c) be sufficiently general to apply readily to new situations, without the need for frequent amendment and updating which has dogged the [SRO's] rulebooks so far".[155]

Section 47A(3) of the Act provides that a failure to comply with the principles is a ground for taking disciplinary action or exercising powers of intervention, but does not of itself give rise to any right of action by investors. Section 47A(4) then goes on to define the disciplinary action which can be taken for breach of the principles; this includes the withdrawal of authorisation for those directly authorised by the Financial Services Authority and the issue of a public reprimand under section 60 of the Act. Section 47A(4) does not mention the imposition of fines by an SRO, and, therefore, as a matter of general law an SRO is not entitled to fine for breach of the principles.

However, the rules of the SFA set out the principles, and state expressly that the principles are available for the purposes of discipline and intervention.[156] As a result, although the SFA is not as a matter of general law entitled to fine for breach of the principles, it is entitled to do so by virtue of the contract between members and the SFA set out in the rules unless section 47A can be construed as removing that power. It would be curious if this were the case, but it is certainly arguable from its wording that section 47A(4) sets out a comprehensive list of the sanctions arising for breach of the principles. The principles are expressed to be applicable to authorised firms, and it would have been easy for section 47A(4) to refer to an SRO's general disciplinary powers arising on breach of its rules. Nevertheless, in view of the purposive approach to the construction of statutes now increasingly prevalent in the courts,[157] this interpretation is unlikely to prevail.

The statements of principle themselves are statements of a high degree of generality as to the conduct expected of authorised persons. They divide broadly into principles of general application and those concerning an authorised firm's

154. See pp 145–146 above. The application of the principles to passported institutions excludes provisions as to the fitness and properness of the firm to carry on investment business, and other matters reserved to the home state, principally regarding capital.

155. Paragraph 14 of the Consultative Paper on *The Proposed Principles for Investment Business* issued by the Financial Services Authority (then called the Securities and Investments Board) in January 1990.

156. Paragraph 3 of the Introduction to the Statements of Principle in form issued by the Financial Services. The definitions in paragraph 9-1 of the SFA's rules also state that the "rules" include the statements of principle, and chapter 7 of the SFA's rules is clear that disciplinary action can be taken for breach of the "rules".

157. In *Inland Revenue Commissioners* v. *McGuckian* [1997] 1 WLR 991, 999, Lord Steyn said: "During the last 30 years there has been a shift away from literalist to purposive methods of construction. Where there is no obvious meaning of a statutory provision the modern emphasis is on a contextual approach designed to identify the purpose of the statute and to give effect to it."

relations with the market, with customers, and with regulators. Their very generality inevitably creates a degree of uncertainty about their meaning.[158]

6.7.1.1 General principles

Principle 1 provides that: "A firm should observe high standards of integrity and fair dealing." This carries moral overtones. Integrity and fair dealing have little to do with competence—extreme incompetence could call into question integrity, but it is quite possible to act fairly and with integrity but negligently. Fairness and integrity require honesty and sincerity, and not favouring one client over another (though this adds little to principle 6). The standard required is not the highest standard or a reasonable standard, but a high standard[159] which presumably lies between the two. What is a high standard for these purposes is also presumably to be measured by reference to standards expected of the financial services industry. This industry often handles other people's money and has been subjected to special regulation by Parliament and the European Union, and can therefore be expected to have standards higher than certain other industries and perhaps than the general population.[160]

This principle could have application in dealings between market professionals as it is of general application. For example, as a matter of English law there is no general duty of good faith in pre-contractual negotiations[161] or any requirement that a contract be performed in good faith,[162] but principle 1 might be taken to impose a regulatory requirement of good faith even if breach of that duty does not of itself give rise to an action in civil law—negotiating other than in good faith might well fall short of high standards of integrity. Where there is no element of this sort, however, it is hard to believe that the principle requires the parties to ensure that the terms of a contract are "fair" to the other party. In a deal between professionals, the parties are best placed to determine whether the terms are fair to them.

While principle 1 deals with the moral rectitude of authorised persons, principle 2 deals with competence. Principle 2 provides that: "A firm should act with due skill, care and diligence." One issue on this principle is what degree of skill, care and diligence is "due" in any given circumstances. It might arguably vary from situation to situation, but as far as the general law is concerned duties

158. Some have the appearance of the Football Association's standard charge of "bringing the game into disrepute".

159. This also points against this principle having anything to do with competence, which is invariably defined in terms of acting reasonably.

160. This principle could be related to the requirement that authorised persons are fit and proper to carry on investment business (see, for example, paragraph 1(1) of Schedule 2 to the Act which requires the rules of an SRO to be such as to secure that its members are fit and proper persons to carry on investment business).

161. See p 77 above.

162. Unlike, for example, in the USA, where the Restatement (Second) of Contracts provides: "Every contract imposes upon each party a duty of good faith and fair dealing in its performance and enforcement."

of this sort are usually defined in terms of what is reasonable for someone professing the expertise of the person in question,[163] an approach likely to be followed in this principle. There is no obligation to be right all the time, but only to take reasonable care in the circumstances.

As a matter of general law, duties such as those referred to in principle 2 are usually owed to a particular person or persons rather than being stated in abstract terms.[164] This principle clearly applies where there would be a common law duty of care, and adds to the threat of civil proceedings the possibility of regulatory action. But the principle could also be invoked by a regulator if a firm was negligent in the conduct of its own affairs regardless of whether a third party was damaged by this negligence (even though the fact of this will usually be sufficient punishment for the firm concerned without any additional regulatory action).

6.7.1.2 Market principles

Principle 3 states that:

> "A firm should observe high standards of market conduct. It should also, to the extent endorsed for the purpose of this principle, comply with any code or standard as in force from time to time and as it applies to the firm either according to its terms or by rulings made under it."

This imposes two obligations: high standards of market conduct and compliance with designated codes.

As to standards of market conduct, like principle 1 this again refers to "high", rather than highest or reasonable, standards. Market conduct presumably means conduct whilst trading on a market, but "market" in this context should be interpreted in a broad sense. Dealing between professionals even though over the telephone rather than in one location (which would probably be an exchange in any event) could well for these purposes be dealing on a market. Factors pointing to the existence of a market might include one or more of: the existence of a published market price for the transaction in question; regular dealings in a particular transaction; an identifiable group of institutions which deal in a particular type of product; and established terms of business for a particular product. In general, the more standard the transaction, the more likely it is to be made on a market. A transaction tailored specifically to the needs of one party is unlikely to be a market transaction for the purposes of this principle even if it involves elements which could be traded on a market.

The fact of there being a market in a particular kind of transaction does not mean that all such transactions are necessarily made on that market. Where a transaction is between two parties, both of whom can be considered market participants, the transaction will be on the market. Where, however, one party is

163. See p 102 above.
164. See pp 96–97 above.

an outsider, the position is less clear. Whether a transaction between a market professional and an outsider is a market transaction perhaps depends upon the nature of the market. If it is a market in which professionals deal with each other, whether to lay off non-market transactions or for other reasons, then a deal with an outsider will not be a market transaction; if, however, the market is one where outsiders come to deal with professionals, then the transaction is likely to be a market transaction.

If a market transaction can be identified, it is then necessary to determine what the standards of the relevant market are. Market standards vary, and this principle cannot have been intended to impose uniform standards on each market or to treat it as if there was only one financial market. It is possible, however, that the general standards in a market could be unacceptable such that everyone in the market is in breach of principle 2 even if behaving in the usual way within that market.

The second element of principle 2 is compliance with designated codes or standards. Only one code has been designated for this purpose, the Takeover Code.[165]

6.7.1.3 Customer principles

Principles 4 to 7 deal with relations between an authorised person and a customer. For these purposes, a customer is unlikely to include a market counterparty.[166] Principle 4 and the main part of principle 5 only apply if the authorised institution advises a customer, but the principles do not themselves impose a duty to advise. Principle 4 states that:

> "A firm should seek from customers it advises or for whom it exercises discretion any information about their circumstances and investment objectives which might reasonably be expected to be relevant in enabling it to fulfil its responsibilities to them."

A firm cannot therefore simply rely on a customer to reveal information which might be relevant. If a firm is in an advisory relationship with the customer, this principle imposes a positive obligation to seek information about circumstances and investment objectives. It is only obliged to do so in order to enable it to fulfil its responsibilities to the customer, but the principle does not define what those responsibilities are. The responsibilities must be those undertaken in the advisory relationship, which requires an investigation into the nature of the advisory relationship in question.

Principle 5 states:

> "A firm should take reasonable steps to give a customer it advises, in a comprehensible

165. This was designated by the Financial Services (Statements of Principle) (Endorsement of Codes of Conduct and Standards) Instrument 1995 issued by the Financial Services Authority (then called the Securities and Investments Board).

166. Though not directly relevant, the Financial Services Core Glossary (3rd edn) (issued by the Financial Services Authority) defines a customer as including a potential customer but excluding a market counterparty.

and timely way, any information needed to enable him to make a balanced and informed decision. A firm should similarly be ready to provide a customer with a full and fair account of the fulfilment of its responsibilities to him."

This imposes two obligations, one during the course of advice and one after acting for a customer, whether or not advice has been given. The first of these obligations flows on from principle 4. Principle 4 requires a firm to seek relevant information from an advisee, and principle 5 requires the advice given in the light of that information to be given in a comprehensible and timely way and to be such as to enable the advisee to make a balanced and informed decision. That advice should be comprehensible and timely is largely self-evident.[167] The information required to enable a customer to make a balanced and informed decision depends upon what that decision is and what advice is sought in relation to that decision. If a customer is clear that he is only seeking advice on one limited aspect of a wider decision, then the information given need, as a result of this principle, only be concerned with that limited aspect; prudence requires, however, that advice records that it is limited and that it does not cover other areas which might be relevant.

The latter part of principle 5 requires that a customer be given a full and fair account of the fulfilment of the firm's responsibilities to the customer. Though this is not confined to an advisory relationship, it does first require an assessment of what the firm's responsibilities are. If it is as a counterparty only, those responsibilities might not be onerous but it does require an account as to the fulfilment of the firm's contractual obligations. If a dispute arises, this might oblige a firm to give rather fuller information to the counterparty than it would otherwise be inclined to give. For example, the information given must also be fair, which might mean that the firm cannot suppress relevant but adverse information and, if it concludes that it has acted in breach of contract, it might arguably be obliged to say so.[168]

Principle 6 states that:

"A firm should either avoid any conflict of interest arising or, where conflicts arise, should ensure fair treatment of all its customers by disclosure, internal rules of confidentiality, declining to act, or otherwise. A firm should not unfairly place its interests above those of its customers and, where a properly informed customer would reasonably expect that the firm would place his interests above its own, the firm should live up to that expectation."

This principle accepts that conflicts of interest can arise without a firm being in breach of the principles as a matter of course. In many respects the obligations under this principle are less than arise as a matter of law if there is a fiduciary relationship,[169] but on the wording they apply whether or not there is a fiduciary

167. What is timely will depend on the circumstances. If advice is as to rapidly moving markets, "timely" might be almost instantaneous.

168. But if saying so would or could lead to civil liability which might be covered by insurance, this requires careful handling. Admitting liability without an insurer's consent will often invalidate insurance cover.

169. See Chapter 5 above.

relationship. However, if a firm is acting as a counterparty only, without any advisory relationship, it is hard to see what application this principle has. One of two contracting parties can hardly be supposed to place the other party's interests above its own—looking after its own interests is not unfair in these circumstances, and it will be clear to the counterparty that the firm must do this in order to stay in business.

Principle 7 relates to the segregation of customer's assets from a firm's own assets.

6.7.1.4 *Regulator principles*

Principles 8 and 9 require a firm to have adequate financial resources to meet its commitments and to withstand the risks to which its business is subject, and to have proper control of its internal affairs.

Principle 10 requires that a firm be open and cooperative in its dealings with its regulator, and that it keep the regulator informed of anything concerning the firm that the regulator might reasonably expect to be disclosed.[170] Principle 10 is of particular relevance when something goes wrong, particularly if it might involve breach of the regulatory scheme. Principle 10 requires the firm to inform the regulator of this, rather than to keep quiet in the hope that the regulator will not find out, which is probably the natural inclination. The difficulty is in deciding at what stage the obligation to inform the regulator comes into play. Mere suspicion that something is wrong should not give rise to an obligation under this principle, but more than this might do even if it is not certain.[171]

6.7.2 The rules of self-regulating organisations

One way to carry on investment business in the United Kingdom without committing a criminal offence is to be a member of an SRO. Membership of an SRO entails a contractual relationship between the member and the SRO in question which obliges the member to comply with the SRO's rules. Breach of the rules of an SRO potentially involves some statutory and some contractual consequences. The contractual consequences are in the disciplinary powers of the SRO, which are discussed further below.[172] The statutory consequences arise from sections 61 and 62 of the Act.

Section 61(1) of the Act allows the Financial Services Authority or, in some

170. None of the principles apply to the conduct of the regulators themselves (as opposed to the regulated), but paragraph 6.5 of the consultation draft dated May 1998 produced by the International Organisation of Securities Regulators on *Objectives and Principles of Securities Regulation* states that in exercising its powers and discharging its functions, a regulator should adopt processes which are consistently applied, comprehensible, transparent to the public, and fair and equitable.

171. There are difficulties in deciding the safest method of giving information to a regulator. These are discussed at p 300 below.

172. See pp 161ff above.

circumstances, the Treasury[173] to seek from the court an injunction restraining breach of an SRO's rules on the part of a person in breach or where there is a reasonable likelihood that he will breach the SRO's rules.[174] They may also seek an order that the person in breach, and any other person knowingly concerned in the breach, take steps to remedy it. The Financial Services Authority and the Treasury can only seek orders under section 61(1) if it appears that the SRO is unable or unwilling to take steps itself.[175] This power is, therefore, in effect a fall-back power in the event of failure or inability on the part of the SRO to take necessary steps.

It is significant that the court is given express power to make orders not only against the member of the SRO but also against others knowingly concerned in the breach, such as directors and other officers of the company, and also professionals acting for the company. In *SIB* v. *Pantell (No 2)*, the Court of Appeal decided that an order under section 61(1) to remedy a breach was a form of statutory rescission and, whilst it had to be directed at remedying a contravention and not to providing compensation, was not dependent upon the person against whom the order was made having received assets from an investor. The same orders could be made against the person in breach of the SRO's rules and anyone knowingly concerned in the breach. The difference between remedying a breach and compensating is not always an easy one, and they will often cover the same ground.[176]

Sections 61(3), (4) and (5) also allow the court, on the application of the Financial Services Authority, to make certain orders if it is satisfied that profits have accrued to any person as a result of breach of the SRO's rules or investors have suffered loss or otherwise been adversely affected as a result of breach. The orders the court may make are that a sum be paid into court or to the Financial Services Authority, that sum being such as appears just in the light of the profits and/or losses suffered[177]; the court can also appoint a receiver to recover the sum. The orders can be made against the member of the SRO in breach, but, it

173. See two delegation orders, SI 1987 No 942 and SI 1991 No 200, and the Transfer of Functions (Financial Services) Order 1992, SI 1992 No 1315.

174. The court can also grant a Mareva injunction in support of an application under section 61 (*SIB* v. *Pantell* [1989] 2 All ER 673, 678) but will not in general order the applicant to give an undertaking in damages when seeking a Mareva injunction (*SIB* v. *Lloyd-Wright* [1993] 4 All ER 210).

175. Section 61(2) of the Act.

176. [1993] Ch 256, particularly pp 275–277. The basis for treating a provision aimed at remedying a breach as statutory rescission is far from clear (unlike, for example, applications under section 6 of the Act which require the court to restore parties to the same position they were in before a transaction was entered into), but the relation between remedying the position under section 61(1) and orders under section 61(4) is also far from clear.

177. This allows the court to award compensation or to confiscate profits but, it appears, not to impose penalties.

appears, cannot be made against anyone else.[178] Any amount recovered under section 61 is to be paid to those who have entered into the transactions leading to the profits or causing the loss.[179]

Whilst section 61 of the Act gives powers to the senior regulators and a discretion to the court, section 62 gives a limited category of investors a specific cause of action entitling them, if successful, to damages as of right.[180] These investors may seek damages from a member of an SRO for loss suffered as a result of breach of the SRO's rules[181] (but the rules do not, for these purposes, include the statements of principle issued under section 47A of the Act[182]) subject to the defences and other incidents applying to actions for breach of statutory duty. There is no requirement to show that the member of the SRO has failed to take reasonable care; liability is strict if there is a breach of the rules, though it may require negligence to be in breach of the rules. Breach of statutory duty is subject to the law relating to contributory negligence and, as a result, any sums an investor might otherwise be entitled to can be reduced if the damage is partly caused by the investor's fault.[183] Nevertheless, where a statute has been enacted to protect a certain class of people, the standards of self-protection that are to be expected of them may not be very high.[184] The Financial Services Act 1986 was undoubtedly passed to protect investors, and therefore a significantly greater onus is likely to be placed on the firm than on the investor in protecting the investor.

The most difficult problems with an action for breach of statutory duty are

178. *SIB* v. *Pantell (No 2)* [1993] Ch 256, 262 (Sir Nicolas Browne-Wilkinson V-C). This is not, however, entirely clear from the wording which, in section 61(4), allows orders to be made against "the person concerned". This might be treated as referring back to the person in breach in section 61(3)(a) who, presumably, can only be the member of the SRO.

179. Sections 61(6) and (7). Action by the regulators does not affect the right of others to bring proceedings in respect of the matters to which section 61 applies: section 61(9) of the Act.

180. Section 62(1) refers to contravention being "actionable", and therefore the court could also grant an injunction in appropriate circumstances.

181. But only if those rules could have been made under sections 47 to 63C of the Act in relation to an authorised person who is not a member of an SRO: section 62(2). In practice this restriction is of little consequence in view of the wide rule-making power under those sections. For these purposes, however, an SRO's rules do not include rules which could have been made under section 49 of the Act. Section 49 deals with financial resources: the only way breach of that rule could in most cases lead to loss to an investor is if funds were not available to complete a transaction, but this would in most circumstances lead to a cause of action in any event or at least the right to claim in insolvency proceedings.

182. Section 47A(3) of the Act. This is the case even if the principles are incorporated in an SRO's rules (see p 151 above) because they are not "rules" which could have been made under Chapter V of Part I of the Act in relation to an authorised person. For example, section 48 allows for conduct of business "rules" and section 59 for financial resources "rules", but section 47A allows for "statements of principle".

183. Section 1(1) of the Law Reform (Contributory Negligence) Act 1945 provides that: "Where any person suffers damage as a result partly of his own fault and partly of the fault of any other person or persons, a claim in respect of that damage ... shall be reduced to such extent as the court thinks just and equitable having regard to the claimant's share of responsibility for the damage ..." Section 4 defines "fault" as including breach of statutory duty.

184. See, for example, *Staveley Iron & Chemical Co Ltd* v. *Jones* [1956] AC 627, 648 and *Quintas* v. *National Smelting* [1961] 1 WLR 401, 408.

usually whether the statute gives rise to a private right of action and, if so, to whom it gives that right. These areas are, however, covered expressly by the Act. This leaves the requirements that the investor suffers damage, that it is the kind of damage contemplated by the statute,[185] and that the damage is caused by the breach of the SRO's rules.[186] Causation will be determined by applying common sense rather than strict rules.[187] Since the statute is concerned with the regulation of the financial services industry, the type of damage within the contemplation of the statute will be economic rather than physical.

Section 62A of the Act provides that those entitled to bring actions under section 62 are private investors, except in circumstances specified by the Secretary of State. Section 62A also provides that the Secretary of State may define who is a private investor for these purposes. The regulations made under this section[188] define a private investor as

"an investor whose cause of action arises from anything he has done or suffered—(a) in the case of an individual, otherwise than in the course of carrying on an investment business; and (b) in the case of any other person, otherwise than in the course of carrying on business of any kind."[189]

As a result, an individual (including a partnership or non-corporate trustee since neither has any corporate personality) carrying on a business who enters into a derivatives transaction during which there is a breach of an SRO's rules has a cause of action under section 62 for any damage caused by that breach; this is so even if the individual enters into the transaction as part of a business, as long as it is not investment business,[190] and is a sophisticated investor (though if so, the individual may have trouble in proving a causal link between the breach and the loss). A company, whether a charity or a commercial concern, will not have a cause of action under section 62 even if it suffers a loss as a result of a breach of an SRO's rules provided that it enters into the transaction in the course of carrying on a "business of any kind". "Business" is a flexible word, but the words of emphasis after it and the fact that public bodies are expressly excluded from the scope of the section suggest that it should be given a wide meaning.[191]

In the regulations made under section 62A, the Secretary of State has laid

185. For example, *Gorris* v. *Scott* (1874) LR 9 Ex 125 and *Peabody Donation Fund* v. *Sir Lindsay Parkinson* [1985] 1 AC 210 .

186. For example, *X* v. *Bedfordshire CC* [1995] 3 All ER 353, 364.

187. *Galoo* v. *Bright Grahame Murray* [1994] 1 WLR 1360, 1375.

188. The Financial Services Act 1986 (Restriction of Right of Action) Regulations 1991, SI 1991 No 486.

189. Regulation 2 of the Financial Services Act 1986 (Restriction of Right of Action) Regulations 1991, SI 1991 No 486. Government, local authorities and public authorities are expressly excluded from the definition.

190. Since the regulations say "otherwise than in the course of carrying on investment business" and not "an" investment business, an individual will have a cause of action in the unlikely event that he does carry on investment business but the transaction in question is in respect of part of his business which is not investment business.

191. This is consistent with the approach taken by Hobhouse J in *Morgan Grenfell* v. *Welwyn Hatfield* [1995] 1 All ER 1, 13 in relation to the meaning of business for the purposes of section 63 of the Act (gaming contracts): see pp 27 and 129 above.

down four circumstances in which someone other than a private investor may bring an action under section 62. These are:

1. If "the contravention in question is not a contravention of a kind mentioned in section 62(1) or (2) of the Act".[192] This ensures for the avoidance of doubt that causes of action given in other parts of the Act by reference to section 62[193] are not subject to the same restrictions as the cause of action given by section 62 itself.
2. If the contravention in question is a contravention of a rule prohibiting a person from seeking to make provision excluding or restricting any duty.[194] As a result, if in breach of an SRO's rules a firm includes in a contract a disclaimer excluding or limiting liability in circumstances where the counterparty would otherwise have had a cause of action (whether on the contract, in negligence or whatever), the inclusion of the disclaimer will provide a statutory cause of action to the counterparty. The loss which will flow from the inclusion of the disclaimer will be the loss the counterparty could have recovered if the disclaimer had not been there.[195]
3. If the contravention in question is a contravention of any rule directed at ensuring that transactions are not effected with the benefit of unpublished information which, if made public, would be likely to affect the price of the investment.[196] As a result, breach of rules and regulations concerning insider trading[197] gives rise to a statutory cause of action in addition to any other consequences.
4. If the action must be brought by someone acting in a fiduciary or representative capacity and the cause of action arises as a result of anything done or suffered at a time when the beneficiary was a person who would have had an action of his own as a private investor.[198] This protects beneficiaries with professional trustees, but also indirectly protects those trustees because the beneficiary has, through the trustee, a cause of action when he might otherwise sue the trustee. In these circumstances, however, it might be difficult for the trustee to show that the beneficiary had suffered any loss as a result of the breach if the trustee would have done the same even if it had known of it.

Section 62(4) of the Act expressly provides that contravention of the rules to

192. Regulation 3(a) of the Financial Services Act 1986 (Restriction of Right of Action) Regulations 1991, SI 1991 No 486.

193. For example sections 71(1), 91(4) and 104(4) of the Act.

194. Regulation 3(b) of the Financial Services Act 1986 (Restriction of Right of Action) Regulations 1991, SI 1991 No 486.

195. See Chapter 8 concerning disclaimers.

196. Regulation 3(c) of the Financial Services Act 1986 (Restriction of Right of Action) Regulations 1991, SI 1991 No 486.

197. See pp 167ff below.

198. Regulation 3(d) of the Financial Services Act 1986 (Restriction of Right of Action) Regulations 1991, SI 1991 No 486.

which section 62(1) applies does not invalidate any transaction. The provision giving a cause of action for breach of an SRO's rules is, however, section 62(2), but it does so by applying section 61(1) to a breach of an SRO's rules; breach of an SRO's rules probably does, therefore, benefit from this express saving, but it is not entirely clear. Even if this is wrong, section 62(4) cannot be read as impliedly invalidating any transactions to which section 62(2) applies. Unless, therefore, there is any common law provision invalidating contracts in breach of an SRO's rules, the transactions are valid. An SRO's rules take effect as a contract between the member and the SRO, and entering a contract (the second contract) in breach of another contract (the first contract) does not, as between the parties to the second contract, invalidate the second contract.[199]

6.7.2.1 *The SFA's rules*

The SRO to which most firms carrying on investment business in derivatives belong is the SFA. This is not the place for a detailed description of the SFA's conduct of business rules,[200] most of which are of general application in any event. In brief, however, the fundamental distinction in the rules is between private customers and the rest. Private customers are individuals or small business investors not acting in the course of carrying on an investment business.[201] For example, rule 5-15 allows written communications with another person to promote the sale of investment services (including derivatives) only if the member can show that it believes on reasonable grounds that the communication is fair and not misleading; but in addition, when dealing with a private investor, the member must take reasonable steps to ensure that the written communication is presented fairly and clearly. A private customer must also be given three days' written notice before assets are realised to meet a default.[202]

199. For example, *Linden Gardens* v. *Lenesta Sludge* [1994] 1 AC 85, 108 regarding an attempt to assign rights under a contract which prohibited such an assignment. Lord Browne-Wilkinson said "a prohibition against assignment normally only invalidates the assignment as against the other party to the contract so as to prevent the transfer of the chose in action: in the absence of the clearest words it cannot operate to invalidate the contract as between assignor and assignee and even then it may be ineffective on the grounds of public policy". Few contracts will actually be in breach of SRO's rules (as opposed to performance being in breach), but in any event invalidating the contract might damage the investor more than the SRO member in breach.

200. Which would in any event be largely just a repetition of the rules. The rules are of considerable length and detail.

201. A small business investor is a person (including a trustee) not large enough to be treated as an ordinary business investor. An ordinary business investor is defined as being over a certain size. A private customer can be treated as a non-private customer if the firm can show that it believes on reasonable grounds that the customer has sufficient experience and understanding to waive the protection given to private customers, if it has given written warning to the customer of the protection he will lose (the SFA provides a precedent for this warning) and if the customer has given his written consent. It is, of course, a private investor who also has a cause of action under section 62 of the Act for breach of an SRO's rules (though the definitions of private investor and private customer are not identical).

202. SFA rule 5-26.

Specifically with regard to derivatives, where a member of an SRO provides investment services to a private customer involving contingent liability transactions, the member must do so under a two-way customer agreement, unless the customer is ordinarily resident outside the United Kingdom and the member believes on reasonable grounds that the customer does not wish an agreement to be used.[203] A contingent liability transaction is a derivatives transaction under which the customer will or may be liable to make future payments when the transaction falls to be completed or upon the earlier closing out of his position.[204] A contingent liability transaction therefore encompasses most derivatives which could involve payments in both directions but not, for example, the purchase by the customer of a cash-settled option as this will, in practice, confer the right to receive payments but not an obligation to make any. A two-way customer agreement is a signed agreement which the customer has had proper opportunity to consider[205] and which must contain certain matters, including a statement of the services to be provided (i.e. the terms of the transaction in most cases), the customer's investment objectives except in the case of an execution-only service[206] and a statement of the basis upon which a contingent liability may be incurred, including any margining requirement and the consequences of failure to provide margin.[207]

A firm which effects a contingent liability transaction with or for a private customer must require the customer to pay any margin which is payable and, in the case of an on exchange transaction, the margin must be the same as the exchange requirements.[208] A firm may not effect a contingent liability transaction with a private customer unless it can show on reasonable grounds that the private customer understands the circumstances in which he may be required to provide margin, the form in which it may be provided, the steps that may be taken if he fails to provide the margin, that his position may be closed out if he fails to provide margin and will be closed out after a default of five days, and the other circumstances which may lead to the customer's position being closed out.[209] These matters must be covered in a two-way customer agreement.[210] A firm must close out a private customer's position where he has failed within five

203. SFA rule 5-23(2).
204. SFA rule 9-1.
205. SFA rule 9-1.
206. Execution only is not defined by the SFA (a curious omission since their rules are drafted in the main by reference to the very long list of definitions in rule 9-1). Appendix 42 to the SFA's rules gives guidance as to execution-only business. It states that execution-only business is a dealing-only arrangement where the customer knows the transaction before approaching the firm. With regard to derivatives, the SFA comments that where standardised products exist, such as exchange contracts, the question to be addressed is whether or not the customer chose the product himself or had it suggested to him in response to a question as to a particular end. The SFA also says that it is unlikely that a firm will be able to effect or arrange an OTC derivative without it or another person having given advice to the customer.
207. SFA rule 5-28(3).
208. SFA rule 5-28(1).
209. SFA rule 5-28(2).
210. SFA rule 5-28(3).

business days to meet a margin call, though it can lend a private customer the sums required for a margin call provided the maximum amount of the loan has been set out in writing following an assessment of the customer's financial standing and the suitability of the arrangements.[211]

Until relatively recently,[212] the SFA prohibited off-exchange derivatives transactions with private customers. That prohibition no longer has effect, but before recommending, arranging or executing, or acting as a discretionary manager in respect of, a derivatives transaction with respect to a private customer, a firm is required by SFA rule 5-30(2) to send the customer a derivatives risk warning notice and obtain a signed copy back in circumstances where the member is satisfied that the customer has had a proper opportunity to consider it. As a result, no risk warning notice is required for execution-only derivatives business with a private customer, but the SFA considers that it is unlikely that a firm will be able to arrange or effect a derivatives transaction with a private customer without the firm or another person having given advice to the customer. The risk warning statement is in Appendix 15 of the SFA's rules and emphasises the risks attaching to derivatives.

In addition to sending a risk warning notice, SFA rule 5-31 requires a firm to take reasonable steps to ensure that it does not make a personal recommendation to a private customer or effect or arrange a discretionary transaction for any customer unless the recommendation or transaction is suitable for the customer having regard to the facts disclosed by the customer and other relevant facts of which the firm is or should be aware. The SFA's guidance on this rule states that in assessing the suitability of an OTC derivative, the firm must have regard to the customer's understanding of the nature of the risks involved. The suitability of an OTC derivatives transaction for a private customer is said to depend, amongst other matters, on the customer's financial standing, and firms are required to consider whether the transaction could materially impair that standing.

6.7.3 General rules

In addition to the rules of SROs, there are also certain core rules of general application. These do not, however, affect derivatives specifically. These are: the client money regulations made under section 55 of the Act and which protect clients' funds held by firms; section 56 of the Act and the unsolicited calls regulations made under it which protect largely private investors in relation to investment agreements entered into as a result of unsolicited calls; and sections 57 and 58 of the Act and SFA rules 5-9 to 5-12 which place restrictions on who may issue advertisements for investments and the contents of those advertisements. Making an unsolicited call in breach of the regulations is not a criminal

211. SFA rules 5-28(5) and (6) and 5-27.
212. SFA Board Notice 303 of 19 February 1996 which confirmed the deletion of rule 5-44.

offence, but an investment agreement entered into as a result of such a call may not be enforceable and any sums paid under it, together with loss as a result of having parted with those sums, may be recoverable by the investor.[213] Issuing an advertisement in breach of the Act is, however, a criminal offence.[214]

6.7.4 Misleading statements and practices

Section 47 of the Act creates a number of criminal offences carrying a maximum of seven years' imprisonment and/or a fine.[215] The offences can only be prosecuted by or with the consent of the Director of Public Prosecutions or the Treasury.[216]

6.7.4.1 *Deceptive statements and omissions*

Section 47(1) of the Financial Services Act 1986 creates three criminal offences,[216a] all of which can be committed either by individuals or corporations.[217] The first offence requires[218]:

1. a statement, promise or forecast;
2. which is misleading, false or deceptive;
3. which the maker knows to be so;
4. which is made either (a) for the purpose of inducing another person (whether or not it is the person to whom the statement, promise or forecast is made) to enter or offer to enter into, or refrain from entering into, an investment agreement, or to exercise or refrain from exercising any rights conferred by an investment agreement, or (b) reckless as to whether it may induce a person in this way; and
5. which is made in or from the United Kingdom, or the person on whom the inducement is intended or may have effect is in the United Kingdom,

213. Section 56(2) of the Act.

214. Section 57(3) of the Act.

215. Someone guilty of insider dealing cannot recover losses suffered as a result of his conduct from a solicitor alleged to have advised him negligently, and nor can he recover those losses on a contractual indemnity: *Page* v. *DP Robert Hughes & Denye* (unreported, 24 April 1998). It seems likely that the same applies to offences under section 47 of the Act.

216. Section 201(1) of the Act.

216a. In *Aldrich* v. *Norwich Union* (unreported, 23 November 1998), the Court of Appeal considered it arguable that breach of section 47(1) also gives rise to a claim in damages for breach of statutory duty. The first instance decisions to the contrary, by Rix and Rimer JJ, are more persuasive.

217. For a corporation to be liable, the conventional view is that both the relevant act (the *actus reus*) and the mental state (*mens rea*) must be that of the "directing mind and will" of the company, i.e. very senior officers: *Lennard's Carrying* Co v. *Asiatic Petroleum* [1915] AC 705, 713 and *Tesco Supermarkets* v. *Natrass* [1972] AC 153. In the light of *Meridian Global Funds* v. *Securities Commission* [1995] 2 AC 500, this could arguably no longer be the case, the question of whether an act is to be attributed to the company depending on the construction of the relevant statute.

218. See sections 47(1) and (4) of the Act.

or the investment agreement is or would be entered into or the rights are or would be exercised in the United Kingdom.

Taking these elements in turn, a statement, promise or forecast does not include an omission (the third offence deals with omissions) but the phrase seems apt to cover any positive assertion, whether of a current state of affairs or a forecast of the future. This statement, promise or forecast must be misleading, false or deceptive. This is potentially complicated for a forecast as to the future. A forecast can turn out to be false, indeed many forecasts concerning, for example, interest rates are false in this sense, but within the meaning of the statute a forecast probably represents the forecaster's belief in the forecast rather than its ultimate accuracy. In this way, "misleading" may not add much to "deceptive" as a deceptive statement is one which is made to induce a person to believe a thing true which is false, or vice versa, contrary to the belief of the person practising the deceit.[219] Although this offence does not deal with omissions, the provision that an offence can be committed if the statement is misleading could take into account an omission. For example, a statement could be literally true but through an omission still be misleading.[220]

The statement, promise or forecast must also be known to the maker to be misleading, false or deceptive. This must take into account the audience to which the statement is made. A statement can be misleading to one person because he does not know certain background information but not so to another, but the fact that someone intends to mislead is likely to lead to an inference that it was successful in its aim.

It is not knowingly making misleading, false or deceptive promises, statements or forecasts in the abstract which creates an offence. They must be made for the purpose of inducing another person to enter into or refrain from entering into, or to offer or refrain from offering to enter into, an investment agreement, or to exercise or refrain from exercising any rights under an investment; alternatively, the maker may be reckless as to whether it would have this effect. The statement can be made to someone other than the person to whom the inducement is directed; so, for example, the statement can be made to an intermediary, such as a broker, even though it is the broker's client who might be induced to enter into an investment agreement. Recklessness for these purposes probably means doing an act which creates an obvious risk and either giving no thought to that risk or recognising the risk but nevertheless going ahead.[221]

For the purposes of this section, an investment is a product to which the Act applies,[222] and an investment agreement means any agreement the making or

219. *Re London & Globe Finance Limited* [1903] 1 Ch 728, 732 and *Welham* v. *DPP* [1961] AC 103, 126–127.
220. For example, *R* v. *Kylsant* [1932] 1 KB 442.
221. *R* v. *Caldwell* [1982] AC 341, 354.
222. Section 1 of the Act: see pp 123ff above.

performance of which by either party constitutes an activity which falls within Part II of Schedule 1 to the Act or would do but for the exclusions in Parts III and IV.[223] This means that an agreement resulting from any investment business is an investment agreement, but without the benefits of the exclusions in Parts III and IV (which include, for example, dealing as a principal[224] or without a permanent place of business in the United Kingdom[225]).

The link with the United Kingdom required to commit this offence is not very strong. It is enough if the subject of the deception is in the United Kingdom even if the statement is made from outside the United Kingdom. Similarly, it is enough if the agreement is entered into in the United Kingdom, something which can be a matter of chance.[226]

The second offence created by section 47(1) of the Act is the same as the first offence except that, instead of knowing that the statement, promise or forecast is misleading, false or deceptive, the maker is reckless (whether dishonestly or otherwise) as to whether it is misleading, false or deceptive. A person is reckless for these purposes if the statement was a rash statement to make and the maker had no real basis of facts on which he could support the statement.[227]

The third offence created by section 47(1) of the Act is again the same as the first, but instead of making a statement, promise or forecast involves dishonestly concealing material facts. A person acts dishonestly if he realises that his conduct is dishonest according to the ordinary standards of reasonable and honest people.[228]

6.7.4.2 Misleading impressions

Section 47(2) creates an offence, again which can be committed by an individual or a corporation, which requires:

1. an act or course of conduct;
2. which creates a false or misleading impression as to the market in or the price or value of an investment;
3. which is done or engaged in in the United Kingdom or the false or misleading impression is created in the United Kingdom;
4. which is done for the purpose of creating that impression;
5. and, thereby, of inducing another person to acquire, dispose of, subscribe for or underwrite those investments or to refrain from doing so or to exercise, or refrain from exercising, any rights conferred by those investments.

223. Section 44(9) of the Act: see pp 128ff above.
224. Paragraph 17 of Schedule 1 to the Act: see p 130 above.
225. Paragraph 26 of Schedule 1 to the Act: see pp 130–133 above.
226. See pp 131–132 above.
227. *R* v. *Grunewald* [1963] 1 QB 935 and *R* v. *Page* [1996] Crim LR 821.
228. *R* v. *Ghosh* [1982] QB 1053. Even where the conduct concerned takes place in a particular market place, the test remains the standards of ordinary people rather than those operating in that market: *R* v. *Lockwood* [1986] Crim LR 244.

It is, however, a defence for the person doing the act or engaging in the conduct to show that he reasonably believed that his act or conduct would not create an impression which was false or misleading.[229]

It is open to question what mental element is required for this offence. It requires the fact of an act or course of conduct which creates a false or misleading impression, but it is not clear whether the act or course of conduct must be done for the purpose of creating the false or misleading impression or whether it is enough that it is done for the purpose of creating a particular impression which is false or misleading even though the fact that it was false or misleading was unknown to the relevant person. In view of the defence of a reasonable belief that a false or misleading impression would not be created, it seems likely that the former is correct, and an offence is committed if a false or misleading impression is created unless there is a reasonable belief that the act or conduct would not create a false or misleading impression. The defence presumably covers the situations where it is accepted that the impression created was false or misleading but it is claimed that the relevant person reasonably believed that that impression would not be created or that he reasonably believed that the impression created was not false and misleading.

6.7.5 Insider dealing

The law relating to insider dealing is of considerable complexity[230] and is set out largely in 13 sections and two schedules of the Criminal Justice Act 1993. The legislation, implementing an EEC Directive,[231] creates three categories of offences: insider dealing, encouraging others to do so, and disclosing inside information. The offences can only be committed by an individual but not by a company.[232] The three offences are:

(1) dealing in price-affected securities on a regulated market or in reliance on, or as, a professional intermediary when in possession as an insider of information in relation to the securities[233];
(2) when in possession of information as an insider, encouraging another to deal in price-affected securities (whether or not the other knows they are price-affected securities), knowing or having reasonable cause to believe that the dealing would take place on a regulated market or in reliance on, or as, a professional intermediary[234];

229. Section 47(3) of the Act.
230. Which is doubtless one reason why it has proved singularly difficult for the authorities to obtain convictions for insider dealing.
231. Council Directive 89/592/EEC.
232. Though if an employee of a company is guilty of insider dealing, the company may be in breach of regulatory requirements: see p 160 above.
233. Section 52(1) of the Criminal Justice Act 1993.
234. Section 52(2)(a) of the Criminal Justice Act 1993.

(3) disclosing information held as an insider other than in the performance of the functions of his employment, office or profession.[235]

There are various defences, both general and specific, which apply to these offences, but first it is necessary to consider the requirements common to all offences. These concern the securities covered by the legislation, and the source of that information.

6.7.5.1 *Securities*

The first general requirement of the offences is that they should concern securities covered by the legislation, and that the securities should be dealt with on a regulated market or through a professional intermediary.

6.7.5.1.1 SECURITIES

For an offence to be committed, there must be price-affected securities.[236] The relevant securities are defined in Schedule 2 to the Criminal Justice Act 1993. The definition starts with shares and stock ("shares") in a company, any instrument creating or acknowledging indebtedness issued by a company or public sector body ("debt"), warrants to subscribe for either shares or debt ("warrants"), or depositary receipts issued in relation to shares, debts or warrants.[237] These do not concern derivatives, but securities are also defined to include:

(1) options to acquire or dispose of shares, debts, warrants and the futures and contracts for differences referred to below[238];
(2) rights under a contract for the acquisition or disposal of shares, debts, warrants, the options mentioned above or the contracts for differences mentioned below under which delivery is to be made at a future date and at a price agreed when the contract is made or determined in accordance with the contract (i.e. futures)[239]; and
(3) rights under a contract which does not provide for delivery of securities but whose purpose or pretended purpose is to secure a profit or avoid a loss by reference to fluctuations in a share index or other

235. Section 52(2)(b) of the Criminal Justice Act 1993.

236. Section 52(2)(b), dealing with disclosing information, does not actually mention securities, but in context the section only makes sense if the disclosure is of information which affects the price of securities.

237. Paragraphs 1 to 4 of Schedule 2 to the Criminal Justice Act 1993. A company for these purposes is a body (whether or not incorporated and wherever incorporated or constituted) which is not a public sector body, and a public sector body is the government of the United Kingdom, of Northern Ireland or of any country or territory outside the United Kingdom, a local authority in the United Kingdom or elsewhere, an international organisation the members of which include the United Kingdom and another state, the Bank of England, and the central bank of any sovereign state.

238. Paragraph 5 of Schedule 2 to the Criminal Justice Act 1993.

239. Paragraph 6 of Schedule 2 to the Criminal Justice Act 1993.

similar factor connected with shares, debts, warrants or the options or futures mentioned above, the price of particular shares, debts, warrants, or the options or futures mentioned above, or the interest rate offered on money placed on deposit (i.e. contracts for differences).[240]

These definitions are very similar to the definitions in paragraphs 7, 8 and 9 of Schedule 1 to the Financial Services Act 1986,[241] but are tied to shares, debts or warrants. As a result, commodity and currency derivatives are, for example, not caught by the definition but equity and credit derivatives generally will fall within the definition as long as they are linked to shares, debts or warrants.

The reference, in the definition of contracts for differences, to the interest rate offered on money placed on deposit is somewhat curious. The other securities with which the insider dealing legislation is concerned are securities issued by a particular person, but this definition is not. It seems, therefore, that any interest rate swap, option or future is subject to the insider dealing legislation.[242] As a result, acting on insider information as to movements in interest rates by entering into any of these transactions may be a criminal offence, as long as the other requirements of the offence are met. It is arguable, however, that the interest rate in question is not the general interest rate as set by the Bank of England but the interest rate in debt securities issued by a particular person which could well be influenced by information about the issuer.

6.7.5.1.2 REGULATED MARKETS AND PROFESSIONAL INTERMEDIARIES

Not all securities which might, however, fall within the definition in Schedule 2 to the Criminal Justice Act 1993 are covered by the Act. Section 52(3) provides that the offence is only committed if the acquisition or disposal of the securities takes place on a regulated market or the person dealing relies on a professional intermediary or is himself acting as a professional intermediary. For these purposes, regulated markets comprise the London Stock Exchange, LIFFE, OMLX, Tradepoint, and the principal European stock exchanges.[243]

A professional intermediary is someone who carries on business consisting of

240. Paragraph 7 of Schedule 2 to the Criminal Justice Act 1993.

241. See pp 123ff above.

242. Paragraph 7(1) of Schedule 2 to the Criminal Justice Act 1993 does provide for "Rights under a contract which does not provide for the delivery of securities but whose purpose or pretended purpose is to secure a profit or avoid a loss by reference to fluctuations in— ... (c) the interest rate offered on money placed on deposit". The reference to a contract not providing for the delivery of "securities" might be taken to mean that the contract must have something to do with securities as defined in the schedule. That is not so, however, as section 54(1) defines securities as those securities referred to in Schedule 2 except where the reference is actually in Schedule 2. The reference to securities in paragraph 7(1) therefore means anything that can properly be called a security.

243. Section 60(1) of the Criminal Justice Act 1993 and the Insider Dealing (Securities and Regulated Markets) Order 1994, SI 1994 No 187, as amended by the Insider Dealing (Securities and Regulated Markets) (Amendment) Order 1996, SI 1996 No 1561.

acquiring and disposing of securities (whether as principal or agent) or acting as an intermediary between persons taking part in dealing with securities, and who holds himself out to the public or any section of the public as willing to engage in any such business or as an employee of a person who does so.[244] It is both the carrying on of this business and the holding out which is necessary for someone to become a professional intermediary for these purposes, and the holding out must be as to a willingness to engage in any such business. This cannot mean that the person is prepared to enter into securities transactions with anyone—no one would do so because, for example, some of the deals might be long term and the identity of the counterparty could raise real credit concerns—but probably means a holding out of a willingness to consider any relevant transactions. The holding out only needs be to a section of the public, including a section of the public constituted by persons such as himself. It is therefore likely that anyone who carries on a business of dealing in any of the securities covered by the insider dealing legislation would be a professional intermediary for these purposes.

A professional intermediary who himself deals in securities on the basis of inside information could, subject to the other requirements of the Act, commit an offence. In addition, a person who deals in reliance on a professional intermediary, whether or not on a regulated exchange, can commit an offence. For these purposes, someone relies on a professional intermediary in dealing in securities if the professional intermediary acquires or disposes of securities (whether as principal or agent) or acts as an intermediary between persons doing so.[245] The professional intermediary therefore has to do the deal—whether with the person dealing on the basis of inside information or on his behalf—in order for an offence to be committed.

6.7.5.2 *Inside information*

The offences created by the legislation require the use of information in relation to securities that is held as, or obtained from, an insider. What constitutes "information" is not defined in the Criminal Justice Act 1993, but insider information must be something that relates to particular securities or to a particular issuer of securities and not to securities generally or to issuers of securities generally, it must be specific or precise, it must not have been made public, and it must be something that would, if made public,[246] have a significant

244. Section 59 of the Criminal Justice Act 1993. A person is not a professional intermediary if the activity is incidental to another activity or merely because he occasionally conducts one of those activities: section 59(3).

245. Section 59(4) of the Criminal Justice Act 1993.

246. Section 58 of the Criminal Justice Act 1993 gives a non-exhaustive definition of when information is made public, and provides that information may be treated as made public even though it can only be acquired by a person exercising diligence or expertise, is communicated to a section of the public and not the public at large, can only be acquired by observation, is communicated only on payment of a fee, or is published only outside the United Kingdom.

effect on the price or value of securities.[247] Securities are price-effected securities, if the information, if made public, would have a significant effect on the price or value of the securities.[248]

What constitutes information must also be considered in the light of the requirement that the information is inside information. The offences under the Act require a person to have information as an insider. A person has information as an insider if and only if he has inside information, he knows it is inside information and he has it, and he knows that he has it, from an inside source.[249] A person has information from an inside source if and only if he has it through being a director, employee or shareholder of an issuer of securities, through having access to the information by virtue of his employment, office or profession, or indirectly through one of those sources.[250]

6.7.5.3 *The offences*

The three offences have been mentioned above; in summary, they are dealing in price-affected securities, encouraging others to do so, and disclosing inside information.

6.7.5.3.1 DEALING

A person is guilty of insider dealing if he has information as an insider, and deals in price-affected securities on a regulated exchange or through, or in reliance on, a professional intermediary. From the definition of inside information, this requires knowledge, not merely suspicion, that it is inside information.[251] Dealing includes acquiring or disposing of securities, whether as principal or agent, agreeing to do so, or procuring, directly or indirectly, the acquisition or disposal of securities by another person.[252] A person procures the acquisition or disposal of securities if it is done through a person who is his agent, nominee or acting at his direction.[253]

It is a defence to a charge of insider dealing that the dealer did not expect the dealing to result in a profit, or the avoidance of loss, attributable to the fact that the information in question was price-sensitive information in relation to the securities, that he believed on reasonable grounds that the information had been disclosed widely enough to ensure that none of those taking part would be prejudiced by not having the information, or that he would have done as he did

247. Sections 56(1) and (3) of the Criminal Justice Act 1993.
248. Sections 56(2) and (3) of the Criminal Justice Act 1993.
249. Section 57(1) of the Criminal Justice Act 1993.
250. Section 57(2) of the Criminal Justice Act 1993.
251. Dealing where there is a suspicion that information was inside information would, however, be singularly unwise.
252. Sections 55(1) to (3) of the Criminal Justice Act 1993.
253. Section 55(4) of the Criminal Justice Act 1993, though this definition of procuring is not exhaustive: section 55(5).

even if he had not had the information.[254] As a result, if a dealer has inside information, it is not an offence to deal with a customer on exchange related terms and to enter into a back to back deal on the exchange, the profit being a commission on the exchange price, as that profit will not in general be attributable to the fact that he had inside information, at least unless the dealer encouraged his customer to deal, but that is a separate offence.

6.7.5.3.2 ENCOURAGING

A person is also guilty of an offence if he has information as an insider and he encourages another to deal in price-affected securities, knowing or having reasonable cause to believe that the dealing would take place on a regulated exchange or through, or in reliance on, a professional intermediary. Having information as an insider again requires knowledge, but it is enough to have reasonable cause to believe that the dealing will take place in the manner regulated by the legislation. This offence does not require the person encouraged to know that he would be dealing in price-affected securities, or indeed to deal at all.

It is a defence to a charge of encouraging insider dealing that the dealer did not expect the dealing to result in a profit, or the avoidance of loss, attributable to the fact that the information in question was price-sensitive information in relation to the securities, that he believed on reasonable grounds that the information had been disclosed widely enough to ensure that none of those taking part would be prejudiced by not having the information, or that he would have done as he did even if he had not had the information.[255]

6.7.5.3.3 DISCLOSING

A person is guilty of an offence if he discloses inside information to another person other than in the proper performance of the functions of his employment, office or profession. This requires the person to have information as an insider, which requires knowledge that it is inside information and that it comes from an inside source, but the disclosure does not have to be related to any dealing or anticipated dealing in securities.

It is, however, a defence to a charge of disclosing insider information if the person disclosing the information did not expect any person, because of the disclosure, to deal in securities on a regulated market or as, or in reliance on, a professional intermediary, or, although he expected dealing to take place in this

254. Sections 53(1)(a) to (c) of the Criminal Justice Act 1993. This is rather curious because anyone dealing without price-sensitive information is disadvantaged in some way, but presumably it means that the market price has already taken into account the information even if the other party is not aware of it.

255. Sections 53(2)(a) to (c) of the Criminal Justice Act 1993.

way, he did not expect the dealing to result in a profit, or the avoidance of loss, attributable to the fact that the information was price-sensitive information.[256]

6.7.5.4 *Special defences*

In addition to the defences mentioned above which relate to specific offences, there are also general defences applicable to market makers, market information and price stabilisation.

6.7.5.4.1 MARKET MAKERS

An individual is not guilty of insider dealing or encouraging if he acted in good faith in the course of a business as a market maker.[257] A market maker is someone who holds himself out at all normal times in accordance with the rules of a regulated market or an approved organisation[258] as willing to acquire or dispose of securities and is recognised as doing so under those rules.

6.7.5.4.2 MARKET INFORMATION

An individual is not guilty of insider dealing or encouraging if he shows that the information he had as an insider was market information and it was reasonable for an individual in his position to have acted as he did despite having that information as an insider.[259] Market information is information consisting of facts relating to the acquisition or disposal of particular securities,[260] and in determining whether it is reasonable for a market maker to act it is necessary to take into account the content of the information, the circumstances in which he first had the information, and the capacity in which he acted.[261]

It is also a defence to insider dealing or encouraging if the acting is in connection with an acquisition or disposal, or series of acquisitions or disposals, which was then under consideration, with a view to facilitating the accomplishment of acquisitions or disposals, or a series of acquisitions and disposals, and the information in question was market information[262] arising directly out of his involvement in those acquisitions or disposals.[263] This allows, for example, someone making a takeover bid, which is itself price-sensitive information, to buy shares before announcing the bid.

256. Section 53(3)(a) and (b) of the Criminal Justice Act 1993.
257. Paragraph 1(1) of Schedule 1 to the Criminal Justice Act 1993.
258. An approved organisation is an international self-regulating organisation recognised under paragraph 25B of Schedule 1 to the Financial Services Act 1986.
259. Paragraph 2(1) of Schedule 1 to the Criminal Justice Act 1993.
260. Paragraph 4 of Schedule 1 to the Criminal Justice Act 1993.
261. Paragraph 2 of Schedule 1 to the Criminal Justice Act 1993.
262. See the previous paragraph.
263. Paragraph 3 of Schedule 1 to the Criminal Justice Act 1993.

The use of derivatives in the context of a takeover is controversial,[264] but, at best, there is a real risk that this defence would not be available if, for example, a contract for differences were entered into with regard to the shares in question before a takeover bid was announced. For these purposes, a contract for differences is a contract which does not provide for the delivery of securities[265] (i.e. is cash settled only), whether a swap, an option or a future; in these circumstances, it is hard to argue that the swap is with a view to facilitating the accomplishment of the acquisition of the shares because all it can do is make a profit or loss as a result of share movements and does not in itself lead to the acquisition of shares. The position might be different with, for example, an option or future which does expressly provide for delivery because in those circumstances it is easier to argue that the transactions do facilitate the accomplishment of the acquisition.[266]

6.7.5.4.3 PRICE STABILISATION

A person does not commit the offence of insider dealing or encouraging if he acts in conformity with price stabilisation rules made by the Financial Services Authority under section 48 of the Financial Services Act 1986. Section 48(2)(i) expressly allows rules to be made as to the circumstances and manner in which and the time when or the period during which action may be taken for the purpose of stabilising the price of investments of any description.

264. The Financial Services Authority (then the SIB) has issued guidance, GR4 of 1996, on this topic pointing out amongst other matters that even if a criminal offence is not committed, there could still be a breach of the Principles.

265. Paragraph 7 of Schedule 2 to the Criminal Justice Act 1993. The position is *a fortiori* if the derivative relates to an index rather than an individual option.

266. On this topic, see, for example, [1995] 4 JIBL N-79.

CHAPTER 7

THE OTC DERIVATIVES CONTRACT

7.1 FORMING A CONTRACT[1]

A derivatives contract is capable of being created in the same way as any other general contract, namely without formality.[2] For there to be a contract enforceable at law, there must be an agreement, there must be consideration, and there must be an intention to create legal relations. These last two elements will seldom pose any difficulty. Consideration will exist where, in return for a promise, there is some detriment to the promisee or some benefit to the promisor; this will usually come in the form of mutual promises, such as by one party to pay on a floating rate basis and the other to pay a fixed rate.[3] In an ostensibly commercial transaction, it will be very hard to show that there was no intention to create legal relations.[4]

Where a derivatives contract is made in writing, that will set out the terms of the agreement. Most derivatives contracts are, however, agreed in the course of a telephone conversation, either direct or through a broker, and this can lead to some difficulties in determining whether and, if so, on what terms, a contract has been made. Whether an agreement has been reached is determined largely objectively, not according to the subjective views of the parties.[5] Thus, for example, in *OTC Africa Line Limited* v. *Vickers plc*[6] solicitors offered £155,000 in settlement of a case when they meant to offer $155,000. The recipients of the offer accepted it, and Mance J held that a contract was formed despite the mistake. If, however, a recipient knew, or ought reasonably to have known, of the mistake, no contract would be formed. This

1. This is not the place for a detailed treatment of the law on the formation of contracts. For a detailed treatment, see, for example, *Chitty on Contracts* (27th edn), chapters 2 and 3.

2. English law imposes formal requirements for contracts in very few cases. These include contracts for the disposition of land, guarantees, and various consumer protection measures.

3. "A defence of no consideration rarely has merit": Donaldson J, *Thoresen* v. *Weymouth Portland Borough Council* [1977] 2 Lloyd's Rep 614, 619.

4. *Edwards* v. *Skyways* [1964] 1 WLR 349, 355.

5. In *Hofflinghouse* v. *C-Trade* [1986] 2 Lloyd's Rep 132, Parker LJ even suggested that if, objectively, an agreement has been reached, there will be a binding contract even if the parties neither realised this nor intended such a result. It is, however, hard to see how there can be a contract if neither party intended it as there will be no intention to create legal relations.

6. [1996] 1 Lloyd's Rep 700.

"is capable of including circumstances in which a person refrains from or simply fails to make enquiries for which the situation reasonably calls and which would have led to the discovery of the mistake. But there would have, at least, to be some real reason to suppose the existence of a mistake before it would be incumbent on one party ... in the course of negotiations to question whether another party ... meant what he or she had said."[7]

In the light of this, if one party offers, say, a rate which is marginally off what it intended, that offer is capable of leading to a contract if accepted; if, however, the offer is sufficiently off the market rate that the offeree should have realised that it must be a mistake, no contract will be formed.

To determine whether the parties have reached an agreement, the courts usually look to see whether there has been an offer and an acceptance.[8] An offer is an expression of willingness to contract made with the intention, actual or apparent, that it shall become binding on the person making it as soon as it is accepted by the person to whom it is addressed; and an acceptance is an unqualified expression of assent to the offer, both determined objectively as discussed above.[9] The acceptance of an offer must be communicated to the offeror. So, for example, if an offer is accepted but the offeror does not hear and asks for it to be repeated, which is not done, there is no contract; if, however, the offeror does not hear because of, say, a crackle on the line but does not bother to request a repetition, then a contract will be formed because he is estopped from saying that he did not receive the acceptance.[10]

In some conversations it will be clear that there is an offer and acceptance, or at least that the parties have reached agreement and intend to be bound by it. Where it is not so clear, the courts will not look at each sentence in isolation to determine whether it is an offer and whether it has been accepted, but rather will look at the whole of what took place.[11] In doing so, it might be that the parties have concluded an agreement but one or both of them then seek to resile from it or amend the terms; it might be that the parties were in agreement on the terms but had not yet agreed to contract on those terms; or it might be that the parties have not agreed at all, whether through some misunderstanding or muddle or deliberately. In this last case, the parties remain in negotiations.[12] In determining what happened in the course of a telephone call, absent a tape of the

7. *OTC Africa Line Limited* v. *Vickers* [1996] 1 Lloyd's Rep 700, 703.

8. *Gibson* v. *Manchester City Council* [1979] 1 WLR 294, 297. Lord Diplock accepted that there were exceptional types of contract which did not fit easily into the normal analysis as being constituted by an offer and acceptance but he did not consider that the contract in that case, made by exchange of correspondence, was one of those exceptions.

9. *Chitty on Contracts* (27th edn), paragraphs 2-002 and 2-016.

10. *Entores* v. *Miles Far East* [1955] 2 QB 327, 332–333.

11. *Hussey* v. *Horne-Payne* (1879) 4 App Cas 311, 316. The case actually concerned an exchange of correspondence with offer and counter-offer, but the approach of the courts to the transcript of a telephone conversation should be the same.

12. See *Pagnan* v. *Granaria* [1986] 2 Lloyd's Rep 547, 548.

conversation, the content will have to be decided in the main in the light of evidence from the participants. If, however, there is a tape or other recording of the conversation, that is admissible as evidence before the English courts.[13]

To be enforceable, an agreement must also be both complete and certain. Where the courts have formed the view that the parties did intend to be bound, they have been reluctant to hold that the contract was void for want of certainty or completeness.[14] As far as derivatives are concerned, the need for a confirmation covering specific items should make it relatively easy to ensure that an agreement is complete.[15] Nevertheless, if, say, the length of a swap is omitted, then that is likely to make the swap void for uncertainty, at least unless the term is obvious from the matters which have been agreed; similarly, if payment dates are not agreed, then an agreement is likely to be void; again, if the credit events applicable to a credit default swap are not agreed, then the agreement is likely to be void for want of certainty. The fact that other terms which are not essential to the transaction have not been agreed will not prevent the transaction being enforced.

If, however, the price of an option is omitted, the agreement might just survive if it can be interpreted as an agreement to deal at a reasonable price or some other price not too uncertain to be enforced.[16] The failure to specify a price is more likely to be treated as an indication that the parties did not intend to be bound at that point or as rendering the agreement too uncertain to be enforced since the court cannot complete a contract for the parties.[17] A failure to agree a

13. A tape is hearsay evidence but is admissible under section 1(1) of the Civil Evidence Act 1995, subject to service of a hearsay notice under CPR part 33, and can be proved by the procedures for business records in section 9 of the Act.

14. For example, *Brown* v. *Gould* [1972] Ch 53, 57–58. In *Rafsanjan Pistachio Producers Co-Operative* (unreported, 19 December 1997), Rix J said that, in his judgment, there "is a tension between two principles of equal validity and importance. The first is that the law should be the upholder and not the destroyer of bargains which parties have intended to make. The second is that the law is unwilling to give legally binding force to agreements which are too uncertain, and in this connection agreements to agree are viewed as an archetypal case of uncertainty."

15. In *Pagnan* v. *Feed Products* [1987] 2 Lloyd's Rep 601, 619, Lloyd LJ analysed the possible positions if an agreement is incomplete: the parties may intend that the agreement shall not become binding until a further condition is fulfilled or some further terms are agreed; or they may intend to be bound forthwith even though there are further terms to be agreed; and if they fail to reach agreement on these further terms, the contract is not invalidated unless the failure to reach agreement on the further terms renders the agreement as a whole unworkable or void for uncertainty.

16. See, for example, *Hillas & Co* v. *Arcos* (1932) 147 LT 503, *Way* v. *Latilla* [1937] 3 All ER 759, and *Voest Alpine* v. *Chevron* [1987] 2 Lloyd's Rep 547. It seems unlikely that an option is a contract for services leading to the statutory implication of an agreement to pay a reasonable charge under section 15 of the Supply of Goods and Services Act 1982.

17. As in, for example, *Scammell & Nephew Ltd* v. *Ouston* [1941] AC 251 and *Rafsanjan Pistachio Producers Co-Operative* (unreported, 19 December 1997). In the latter case, Rix J commented that no case had been cited to him in which a contract for the agreement of an essential term such as price in an executory contract had been enforced. Performance of a contract is, therefore, likely to add to the court's inclination to uphold a contract.

term differs from leaving that term to be agreed at a future date; in this case, unless the parties have agreed the criteria by which the price is to be determined or some machinery for determining it, the agreement will be treated as an agreement to agree and, therefore, unenforceable.[18]

The aim of market transactions like derivatives is not to buy disputes but rather for the events which trigger payments to be as clear and obvious as possible. Where, for example, the payment is dependent upon a particular interest rate published on a certain page of a financial news service, this is unlikely to pose any difficulty.[19] Anything which refers, for example, to a material change or consideration or depends upon reasonableness without defining what these terms mean is likely to lead to uncertainty, as it is possible, quite reasonably, to hold conflicting views on an issue as to what is material or reasonable.[20]

7.1.1 Confirmations

Even though a derivatives contract is generally concluded over the telephone, it is usual to send a confirmation of the terms. A confirmation is merely evidence of an existing transaction rather than a variation of the terms of the transaction agreed on the telephone—though the parties are free to agree additional terms at any time and commonly do so in negotiation over the precise terms of a confirmation which is then signed by the parties to confirm their agreement to those terms. Absent any fresh agreement over the terms set out in a confirmation or intention to vary terms previously agreed, if one or both parties send a confirmation to the other which is wrong (e.g. reversing floating and fixed rate payers), even if the recipient does not advise of the error (though it would be prudent to do so), it will not have the effect of varying the contract. This will, however, be affected by the terms of any master agreement applicable to the transaction, and in this respect IFEMA and ICOM differ significantly from ISDA's Master Agreement. It could also in some limited circumstances give rise to an estoppel which prevents the parties from denying the accuracy of the confirmation.

18. See, for example, the cases in note 16 and *Walford* v. *Miles* [1992] 2 AC 128.
19. Though it is always wise to add a fall back in case the price source fails, moves or changes.
20. Credit derivatives can pose particular difficulties in this area. If the issue is whether a company has gone into liquidation, this will generally be objectively ascertainable, as will whether the price of its bonds has been downgraded by a particular credit reference agency. Where, however, the events in question require "publicly available information" to support (as in ISDA's 1997 standard credit swap confirmation) there is further scope for uncertainty since, for example, the press will rarely report that a company is insolvent unless it has been officially confirmed, for fear of libel proceedings, but they might hint at the point. Similarly, the press might not be rigorous in their research, enabling one party to plant favourable information without being cited as the source.

7.1.1.1 *The effect of a master agreement*

Section 9(e)(ii) of the ISDA Master Agreement provides that a confirmation shall be entered into as soon as practicable after a transaction has been agreed but the parties are to be bound from the moment they agree terms. Nevertheless, the precise status of a confirmation under a master agreement is not entirely clear. ISDA's standard form of confirmation expressly requests that the recipient "confirm that the foregoing correctly sets forth the terms of our agreement". This is the language of recognition of an existing agreement rather than the creation of a new one, nor does it purport to vary an existing agreement. This is reinforced both by section 9(e)(ii) of the ISDA Master Agreement, which provides that the parties "intend that they are legally bound by the terms of each Transaction from the moment they agree those terms (whether orally or otherwise)", and by the opening words of the Master Agreement, which define a "Confirmation" as "the documents and other confirming evidence ... exchanged between the parties confirming those transactions".[21]

However, there are also indications in the Master Agreement that a confirmation is to be regarded as a contractual document. First, section 1(c) provides that the Master Agreement and all confirmations (not the transactions set out in the confirmations) form "a single agreement between the parties", which is defined as "this Agreement". Secondly, section 9(e)(ii) refers to a confirmation as "being entered into" and "executed and delivered", terms normally only applicable when a contract is being formed. Thirdly, section 9(a) provides that "this Agreement [i.e. Master Agreement and all confirmations] constitutes the entire agreement and understanding of the parties with respect to its subject matter and supersedes all oral communication and prior writings with respect thereto." This could mean that a confirmation, once signed, supersedes the oral agreement; section 9(a) does, however, only say that it supersedes "oral communications and prior writings", not prior agreements.

The better view is probably that the effect of section 9(a) of ISDA's Master Agreement is that a confirmation once signed supersedes the prior oral agreement, or at least prevents the parties bringing forward evidence that the confirmation does not set out the whole agreement.[22] Unless section 9(a) does have this effect, it is probably irrelevant.[23] It is unlikely, however, to prevent rectification of a confirmation if one of the parties can show that the confirmation did not reflect the true agreement.[24]

21. Similarly, section 1.2 of the 1991 ISDA Definitions which defines a "Confirmation" as "one or more documents exchanged between the parties which, taken together, confirm all of the terms of a Swap Transaction". (See also pp 190–192 below.)

22. *McGrath* v. *Shaw* (1989) 57 P&CR 452.

23. It does not cover prior misrepresentations: *Thomas Witter Ltd* v. *TPB Industries* [1996] 2 All ER 573, 595–597 and *Deepak Fertilisers* v. *ICI Chemicals & Polymers Ltd* [1999] 1 Lloyd's Rep 387.

24. See pp 180–181 below.

Section 2.3 of IFEMA[25] provides that the parties shall promptly confirm a transaction, but the failure to do so does not prejudice or invalidate the terms of the transaction. It goes on to provide in section 8.15 that unless a party objects to the terms contained in a confirmation, or sends a corrected confirmation within three business days[26] of receipt, the terms of the confirmation shall be deemed correct and accepted absent manifest error.[27] Unlike ISDA, IFEMA, therefore, does not require a confirmation to be independently agreed. This could potentially lead to a battle of confirmations: if only one party sends a confirmation, which elicits no response from the other party, that confirmation is prima facie binding; but if both parties send confirmations but they are not the same, prima facie it is the second sent that is binding unless the first objects or sends a further confirmation within three business days; if a further confirmation is sent within that period, and no objection or further confirmation is sent within three business days, it is that final confirmation which is prima facie binding.

If one party sends a confirmation which it knows to be wrong, that is likely to be considered fraudulent and therefore would not be binding on the recipient. Absent fraud, however, there seems no reason that an errant confirmation should not be binding if that is what the parties have agreed. Whilst there is an obligation on the parties to send a confirmation, it is hard to construe sending a confirmation which is incorrect as a breach of contract giving rise to a claim in damages since that would defeat the purpose of section 8.15. It is unlikely that the party sending the confirmation would be under any extra-contractual duty of care. In these circumstances, a confirmation could be binding on the parties even if wrong. This is, however, subject to two qualifications: first, rectification, and, secondly, estoppel.

7.1.1.2 Rectification

Rectification applies only to written instruments, and can be granted in two circumstances: first, where the parties have a common intention continuing up to the time the written contract is executed in regard to a particular provision or aspect of an agreement but the written contract does not conform with that common agreement[28]; or, secondly, one party is under a mistake as to the terms of the written contract, the other party has knowledge[29] of that mistake but

25. Section 2.3 of ICOM is to the same effect (and section 11.15 has the same requirement to correct a confirmation as appears in section 8.15 of IFEMA).

26. It is not absolutely clear from the drafting that the three business days applies both to objection and to sending a corrected confirmation, but it is likely that it does.

27. Manifest errors are "oversights and blunders so obvious as to admit of no difference of opinion" (Potter J in *Heald Foods Ltd* v. *Hyde Dairies Ltd*, unreported 19 August 1996).

28. *Joscelyne* v. *Nissan* [1970] 2 QB 86.

29. For these purposes, knowledge means actual knowledge, wilfully shutting one's eyes to the obvious, and wilfully and recklessly failing to make such enquiries as an honest and reasonable person would make: *Commission for New Towns* v. *Cooper* [1995] Ch 259. In this case, Stuart-Smith LJ took the view that "... where A intends B to be mistaken as to the construction of the

omits to mention it, and the mistake is calculated to benefit the other party.[30] It requires cogent evidence to obtain rectification because of the inherent probability that the written instrument truly represents the parties' intentions.[31] There seems no reason why a confirmation under IFEMA or ISDA could not be rectified under this doctrine[32] provided that there are no bars to rectification. These bars include the ability to put the parties into the position they would have been in but for the mistake, and undue lapse of time,[33] but the mere fact that a contract has been performed is not of itself a bar to rectification.[34]

If the recipient of an incorrect confirmation knows it to be wrong but does nothing to draw this to the sender's attention, that cannot be fraud,[35] but it could form the basis of an estoppel by acquiescence to prevent the recipient relying on the confirmation.[36]

7.1.1.3 Estoppel

Even if a confirmation is not stated under the terms of a master agreement to be binding or if no confirmation is sent, then, absent fraud, there could still be an estoppel which prevents that confirmation being challenged. There are essentially three varieties of estoppel which could be relevant: promissory estoppel (and its close relatives, waiver[37] and estoppel by acquiescence); estoppel by representation; and estoppel by convention. Estoppel is, however, a difficult

agreements, so conducts himself that he diverts B's attention from discovering the mistake by making false and misleading statements, and B in fact makes the very mistake that A intends, then notwithstanding that A does not actually know, but merely suspects, that B is mistaken, and it cannot be shown that the mistake was induced by any misrepresentation, rectification may be granted. A's conduct is unconscionable and he cannot insist on performance in accordance to the strict letter of the contract; that is sufficient for rescission. But it may also not be unjust or inequitable to insist that the contract be performed according to B's understanding, where that was the meaning that A intended that B should put upon it" (p 280).

30. *Thomas Bates & Son Ltd* v. *Wyndhams (Lingerie) Ltd* [1981] 1 WLR 505. With regard to the last requirement for this head of rectification (benefit to the party which is not mistaken), this is the view taken by Buckley LJ, with whom Brightman LJ agreed (pp 516 and 521). Eveleigh LJ took the view that it was enough that the mistake was detrimental to the mistaken party whether or not it also benefited the other party (p 521).

31. *Thomas Bates & Son Ltd* v. *Wyndhams (Lingerie) Ltd* [1981] 1 WLR 505, 514 and 521.

32. "Courts of Equity do not rectify contracts: they may and do rectify instruments purporting to be made in pursuance of the terms of contracts": James V-C in *MacKenzie* v. *Coulson* (1869) LR 8 Eq 369, 375 (see also, for example, *Craddock* v. *Hunt* [1923] 2 Ch 136, 159 to the same effect). Even instruments recording contracts required to be evidenced in writing can be rectified: *Craddock* v. *Hunt* [1932] Ch 136 and *USA* v. *Motor Trucks* [1924] AC 196.

33. See pp 82–84 above where this is discussed in connection with rescission for misrepresentation.

34. *Craddock* v. *Hunt* [1923] 2 Ch 136, 151.

35. "Mere silence, however morally wrong, will not support an action of deceit": *Bradford* v. *Borders* [1941] 2 All ER 205, 211.

36. See pp 181–183 below.

37. *Woodhouse AC Israel Cocoa Ltd* v. *Nigerian Produce Marketing Ltd* [1972] AC 741, 762C. Promissory estoppel goes under various other names, including equitable estoppel and the rule in *Hughes* v. *Metropolitan Railway* (1877) 2 App Cas 439.

area where the authorities are not always easy to reconcile; reliance on an estoppel is always likely to carry significant risks.[38]

7.1.1.3.1 PROMISSORY ESTOPPEL

The requirements for promissory estoppel are: (1) that there should be a legal relationship between the parties; (2) that there should be a representation, express or implied, by one party that he will not enforce his strict legal rights against the other; and (3) reliance by the representee (whether by action or by omission to act) which renders it inequitable, in all the circumstances, for the representor to enforce his strict rights, or at least to do so until the representee has been restored to his former position.[39] The representation must be clear and unequivocal.[40] Promissory estoppel cannot create a cause of action in that if the only ground for claim the representee has is the non-contractual promise and his reliance on it, then his action will fail.[41] If, however, the representee can rely on another cause of action, promissory estoppel can be used to prevent the representor relying on a defence which might otherwise be available. The effect of promissory estoppel may only be suspensory or it may prevent a cause of action being relied on at all.[42]

The requirement that a representation be clear and unequivocal means that silence cannot be the basis of a promissory estoppel unless there is a duty to

38. "... as is common with an expanding doctrine [the sequence of cases based on promissory estoppel since the war] do raise problems for coherent exposition which have never been systematically explored" (Lord Hailsham LC in *Woodhouse AC Israel Cocoa Ltd* v. *Nigerian Produce Marketing Ltd* [1972] AC 741, 758).

39. *BP Exploration* v. *Hunt (No 2)* [1979] 1 WLR 783, 810 (Robert Goff J, affirmed without reference to this point by the House of Lords) and *Motor Oil Hellas (Corinth) Refineries* v. *Shipping Corporation of India* [1990] 1 Lloyd's Rep 391, 399 (Lord Goff). The principle stems originally from *Hughes* v. *Metropolitan Railway* (1877) 2 App Cas 439, but was "rediscovered" by Denning J in *Central London Property Trust* v. *High Trees House* [1947] 1 KB 130. There has been some debate as to whether the reliance by the representee must be to his detriment, but the better view is that detriment is one ground likely to make it inequitable for a representor to rely on his strict legal rights, but it is not necessarily the only one: *The Post Chaser* [1982] 1 All ER 19, 27 and *WJ Alan* v. *El Nasr Export* [1972] 2 QB 189, 213–214. It has also been suggested that the representor must intend his representation to be acted upon (Croom-Johnson J in *Argy Trading Development Co* v. *Lapid Developments* [1977] 1 Lloyd's Rep 67, 76), but it is more likely that, as with offer and acceptance, this should be judged objectively.

40. *Woodhouse AC Israel Cocoa Ltd* v. *Nigerian Produce Marketing Ltd* [1972] AC 741. Lord Hailsham LC said that one should exclude far-fetched and strained interpretations while still insisting on sufficient precision and freedom from ambiguity to ensure that the representation will not (not may) be reasonably understood in the particular sense required (p 756). Lord Cross thought the question was whether the representee was justified in having no doubt that the words meant what he took them to mean (p 768).

41. *Combe* v. *Combe* [1951] 2 KB 215.

42. *Motor Oil Hellas (Corinth) Refineries* v. *Shipping Corporation of India* [1990] 1 Lloyd's Rep 391, 399. In *Central London Property Trust* v. *High Trees House* [1947] 1 KB 130, the promissory estoppel prevented a landlord suing for the full rent set out in the lease for the period of the war, but did not prevent it doing so after the war had ended.

speak.[43] This is because "inaction or silence, by contrast with positive conduct or statement, is colourless: it cannot influence a person to act ... unless it acquires a positive content such that that person is entitled to rely on it."[44] A person is under a duty to speak when a reasonable man would expect the person against whom the estoppel is being raised to act honestly and responsibly to bring the true facts to the attention of the other party.[45] The recent cases where it has been held that there was a duty to speak all concern situations where the person who failed to speak knew that the other party was under a misapprehension and tried to use that to his advantage,[46] and it seems likely that knowledge of the other party's error is a key requirement in the creation of a duty to speak.

7.1.1.3.2 ESTOPPEL BY CONVENTION

An estoppel by convention can arise where the parties to a transaction act[47] on an assumed state of the facts or law, the assumption being shared by both or made by one and acquiesced in by the other. The assumption must be communicated by one party to another, and the effect of an estoppel by convention is to preclude a party from denying the assumed facts or law if it would be unjust to allow him to go back on that assumption.[48]

7.1.1.3.3 ESTOPPEL BY REPRESENTATION

Estoppel by representation arises if one person (A) misleads another (B) about an existing state of facts, intending that B shall act on that representation. If B does act in that way in reliance on the representation, A will be estopped from asserting the true state of facts.[49]

43. For example, *The Stolt Loyalty* [1993] 2 Lloyd's Rep 281, 289 and *Allied Marine* v. *Vale do Rio Doce* [1985] 1 WLR 925, 937. This is sometimes referred to as estoppel by acquiescence or silence, but it is not an aspect of estoppel by convention (*The Indian Grace (No 2)* [1998] 1 Lloyd's Rep 1, 10).

44. *Moorgate Mercantile* v. *Twitchings* [1977] AC 890, 903 (Lord Wilberforce).

45. *Pacol* v. *Trade Lines* [1982] 1 Lloyd's Rep 456, 465 and *Tradax Export* v. *Dorada* [1982] 2 Lloyd's Rep 140, 157. A duty could also arise because the contract is one of the utmost good faith or there is a fiduciary relationship.

46. For example, *Spiro* v. *Lintern* [1973] 1 WLR 1002, *Pacol* v. *Trade Lines* [1982] 1 Lloyd's Rep 456, *Tradax Export* v. *Dorada* [1982] 2 Lloyd's Rep 140, *Allied Marine* v. *Vale do Rio Doce* [1985] 1 WLR 925, and *The Stolt Loyalty* [1993] 2 Lloyd's Rep 281.

47. Unless they do act on the assumption, no estoppel will arise: *Astilleros Canarios* v. *Cape Hatteras Shipping* [1982] 1 Lloyd's Rep 518, 527.

48. *The Indian Grace (No 2)* [1998] 1 Lloyd's Rep 1, 10. Before, for example, *Norwegian American Cruises* v. *Paul Mundy* [1988] 2 Lloyd's Rep 343, it was common to state the requirements of estoppel by convention in the language set out in *Spencer Bower & Turner on Estoppel by Representation* (3rd edn), p 157 (for example, *Amalgamated Investment & Property Co* v. *Texas Commerce International* [1982] 1 QB 84) but this is now better seen as an illustration rather than a definition (*Norwegian American Cruises* at pp 351–352 following *Hamel-Smyth* v. *Pycroft* (unreported, 5 February 1987)).

49. *Spencer Bower & Turner on Estoppel by Representation* (3rd edn), para 3, and, for example, *Purnell Secretarial Services* v. *Lease Management Services* (unreported, 24 March 1994).

7.1.1.3.4 MISLEADING CONFIRMATIONS

If one party sends a confirmation to another which is wrong, whether in a major way (e.g. the fixed and floating rate payers have been reversed) or in a more minor way (e.g. the payment dates have been wrongly stated), questions may arise whether the sender or the recipient is estopped from asserting the true position.

Dealing first with the recipient, if he does not spot the error but does not agree or otherwise to the confirmation, it is hard to see how he could be estopped from later asserting the true terms of the agreement. His silence does not constitute any representation as he is under no duty to speak and, until the confirmation is acted upon, there can be no estoppel by convention. If, however, the recipient knows the confirmation is wrong and fails to draw the mistake to the sender's attention in order to try to gain some advantage (e.g. termination on late payment), then he could come under a duty to speak and thus be estopped from asserting the truth, at least on a temporary basis. If the mistake goes further, and both parties act on it by, for example, making payments to each other,[50] then an estoppel by convention may prevent them subsequently asserting the true agreement.

Turning to the sender of a confirmation in the event that the recipient does not respond, it is hard to see a confirmation as a representation of fact which the sender intends the recipient to act on—it is intended as a confirmation of an existing agreement and, if anything is to be acted upon, it is that agreement. Nor are the requirements of promissory estoppel met because although there is an existing legal relationship between the parties, a confirmation is hardly a promise not to enforce strict legal rights. It is intended as confirmation of the existing legal position, rather than any attempt to vary that position. However, again if both parties act on the confirmation, the sender could be estopped by convention from subsequently asserting the true position.

If both parties actually sign a mistaken confirmation, or otherwise signify their agreement with it, the status of the confirmation is not entirely clear. Outside the terms of an ISDA or other master agreement, it is unlikely that the confirmation could be treated as forming a contract or amending the initial agreement because there will be neither consideration nor, generally, an intention to create legal relations—the legal relations have already been created, and the confirmation is merely intended to evidence those relations. Again, the only consequence is likely to be if the parties act on the terms in the confirmation, in which case there may be an estoppel by convention.

50. It seems unlikely that acting on the confirmation by, for example, hedging the risk on the transaction would constitute acting on the confirmation in this way. The sender will have no idea whether the recipient intends to hedge the transaction, and in any event any hedging is likely to be in reliance on the agreement rather than the confirmation. As both parties are equally in a position to know what the true position is, there also does not seem anything inequitable in either party asserting the true position before both have demonstrated their common belief in the error.

7.1.1.4 *The value of a confirmation*

Whether or not a confirmation is a document which creates a contract, none of this should be taken to discount or devalue the benefit of sending a confirmation or of obtaining the other party's signature on a confirmation. A confirmation will provide good evidence as to what the terms of the trade were, and it will only be in rare cases that a party can prove that the terms in the confirmation are not those which were actually agreed (for example, because tapes of the conversations are still available).

7.2 CONSTRUING AGREEMENTS

Before turning to the terms of ISDA's Master Agreement itself, it is necessary to consider the approach of the English courts to construction of agreements in general. The modern, but not in all respects uncontroversial, attitude was set out by Lord Hoffmann in *Investors Compensation Scheme* v. *West Bromwich Building Society*.[51] In that case, Lord Hoffmann said:

"I should preface my explanation by some of my reasons with some general remarks about the principles by which contractual documents are nowadays construed. I do not think that the fundamental change which has overtaken this branch of the law, particularly as a result of the speeches of Lord Wilberforce in *Prenn* v. *Simmonds* [1971] 1 WLR 1381 at 1384–1386 and *Reardon Smith Line Limited* v. *Hansen-Tangen, Hansen-Tangen* v. *Sanko Steamship Co* [1976] 1 WLR 989, is always sufficiently appreciated. The result has been, subject to one important exception, to assimilate the way in which such documents are interpreted by judges to the common-sense principles by which any serious utterance would be interpreted in ordinary life. Almost all the old intellectual baggage of 'legal' interpretation has been discarded. The principles may be summarised as follows:

(1) Interpretation is the ascertainment of the meaning which the document would convey to a reasonable person having all the background knowledge which would reasonably have been available to the parties in the situation in which they were at the time of the contract.

(2) The background was famously referred to by Lord Wilberforce as the 'matrix of fact', but this phrase is, if anything, an understated description of what the background may include. Subject to the requirement that it should have been reasonably available to the parties and to the exception mentioned next, it includes absolutely anything which would have affected the way in which the language of the document would have been understood by a reasonable man.

(3) The law excludes from the admissible background the previous negotiations of the parties and their declarations of subjective intent. They are admissible only in any action for rectification. The law makes this distinction for reasons of practical policy and, in this respect only, legal interpretation differs from the way in which we would interpret utterances in ordinary life. The boundaries of

51. [1998] 1 All ER 98. The quote below is from pp 114–115. The conduct of the parties after an agreement is made is not relevant to the construction of the agreement: *James Miller & Partners Ltd* v. *Whitworth Street Estates (Manchester) Ltd* [1970] AC 583.

this exception are to some extent unclear. But this is not the occasion on which to explore them.

(4) The meaning which a document (or any other utterance) would convey to a reasonable man is not the same thing as the meaning of its words. The meaning of words is a matter of dictionaries and grammars; the meaning of the document is what the parties using those words against the relevant background would reasonably have been understood to mean. The background may not merely enable the reasonable man to choose between the possible meanings of words which are ambiguous but even (as occasionally happens in ordinary life) to conclude that the parties must, for whatever reason, have used the wrong words or syntax . . .

(5) The 'rule' that words should be given their 'natural and ordinary meaning' reflects the common-sense proposition that we do not easily accept that people have made linguistic mistakes, particularly in formal documents. On the other hand, if one would nevertheless conclude from the background that something must have gone wrong with the language, the law does not require judges to attribute to the parties an intention which they plainly could not have had. Lord Diplock made this point more vigorously when he said in *Antaios Cia Naviera SA* v. *Salen Rederierna AB, The Antaios* [1985] AC 191 at 201: '. . . if a detailed semantic and syntactical analysis of words in a commercial contract is going to lead to a conclusion that flouts business common sense, it must be made to yield to business common sense.' "

Lord Hoffmann's approach to the construction of documents is not without its judicial critics. The criticism focuses in the main on the appropriateness of admitting "absolutely anything" by way of background to assist in the interpretation of documents. This has been criticised as it makes litigation even more expensive than might otherwise have been the case because parties will seek to bring in evidence of the supposed background in order to bolster their argument for a particular interpretation.[52] It has also been pointed out that the position of third parties (including assignees) has to be considered. Where the words of a contract have only one meaning, and that meaning is not self-evidently nonsensical, the words should be given that meaning; if "absolutely anything" can be taken into account as an aid to construction, the third party would not be able to take the words at face value for fear that the background necessitates a different interpretation. This would hardly be satisfactory.[53]

Lord Hoffmann's approach is also bound to generate and prolong uncertainty. Whilst he accepts that it will only be in rare cases that words will have other than their natural and ordinary meaning, that is unlikely to stop parties trying to establish such a meaning if the financial consequences of the natural meaning are sufficiently severe. Further, provisions in documents are often

52. See Staughton LJ in *Scottish Power plc* v. *Britoil (Exploration) Ltd* (unreported, 19 November 1997), Saville and Judge LJJ in *National Bank of Sharjah* v. *Dellborg* (unreported, 9 July 1997), and Lightman J's lecture to the Chancery Bar Association on 3 June 1998.

53. Saville LJ in *National Bank of Sharjah* v. *Dellborg* (unreported, 9 July 1997). Saville LJ took the view that where the words the parties have chosen have only one meaning, that that meaning is not self-evidently nonsensical, the law should take that to be their intended agreement and should not allow the surrounding circumstances to override what is clear and obvious.

ambiguous, whether it requires imagination to spot the ambiguity or because the words used lack clarity. If these ambiguities cannot be solved from the terms of the document itself, it is bound to make it harder to resolve the issues that arise.

These concerns are, however, unlikely to be relevant in most cases where a master agreement has been executed. As far as a confirmation or a schedule to a master agreement is concerned, the background may be of some assistance in resolving ambiguities. Where terms of a master agreement itself are involved, the background is of far less relevance. It could be that the circumstances show that the parties did not intend a provision of the master agreement to mean what it does in the numerous other master agreements that have been executed, but it is hard to see what those circumstances might be; the far more likely interpretation is that the words in one master agreement mean the same as in all other master agreements. As a result, in most cases, the key to the understanding of a master agreement will be a proper consideration of the words used. However, documents issued by ISDA, such as the *User's Guide to the 1992 ISDA Master Agreement,* on the meaning of the Agreement probably are admissible as an aid to construction since they represent background matters which the parties could reasonably have had in mind when they executed the master agreement.[54]

7.3 THE ISDA MASTER AGREEMENT

Since the first version was published in 1987, ISDA's Master Agreement has become the dominant set of terms governing derivatives transactions. Other contractual terms were in existence before that time, such as BBAIRS and FRABBA, but neither of these operated as a master agreement governing all relevant transactions, and both were limited to a particular type of transaction.[55] ISDA's Master Agreement can be used as standard terms for most transactions in which cash flows are exchanged. Having one set of terms governing a range of transactions is administratively convenient, it facilitates cross-product netting,[56] and the structure ensures that default on one transaction is a default on them all.[57] The current version of ISDA's Master Agreement, published in 1992, was extended to cover transactions which are physically settled as well as those

54. In *Investors Compensation Scheme* v. *West Bromwich Building Society* [1998] 1 All ER 98, Lord Hoffmann looked at an explanatory memorandum issued by the ICS as an aid to construction of the contract itself.

55. Both BBAIRS and FRABBA terms state that they shall apply to all relevant transactions on the London interbank market (BBAIRS) or shall be deemed to be incorporated in any contract (FRABBA). The BBA has no power to impose a market custom in this way, though the incorporation of some terms is undoubtedly good practice: see pp 37–38 concerning the requirements for market practice.

56. *Derivatives: Practices and Principles* (July 1993) by G30 Global Derivatives Study Group, recommends the use of a master agreement largely on the basis that it will provide for payment netting and close-out netting, using the full two-way payments approach (see pp 240–242 below).

57. This is not necessarily always an advantage under the terms of the Master Agreement. A cross-default clause would achieve the same aim but would give the non-defaulting party the option to close out other transactions rather than close out resulting automatically.

which are cash settled, but it does not include various terms which would normally be expected where physical assets are changing hands, most notably express warranties as to the title to those assets though these can be covered in the schedule.

The advantages of standard terms are obvious.[58] They reduce transaction costs by avoiding the need for a contract to be drawn up for each transaction. As a result, it is possible to conclude transactions more quickly and more cheaply than would otherwise be the case, promoting liquidity in the market. Standard terms also promote good market standards and should reduce legal risk in that the more commonly standard terms are used, the greater the discussion (including judicial consideration) of them and the greater the understanding of their meaning. The disadvantage is that standard terms are inevitably drawn up by committee and represent a compromise between different views which might fall short of the standards and consistency that a bilateral contract can achieve.[59] These deficiencies can be remedied in the schedule, but it may be harder in negotiation to achieve a departure from market standard terms than would otherwise be the case. This will, however, be a small price to pay in the great majority of cases when compared to the advantages of standard terms.

7.3.1 The architecture of ISDA documentation

The architecture[60] of ISDA documentation comprises the Master Agreement itself, a Schedule to that Agreement, and a confirmation for a particular transaction incorporating (with or without amendments) a set of ISDA definitions relevant to the transaction in question. Clause 1(b) of the Master Agreement provides that in the event of inconsistency between the documents, a confirmation prevails over all other documents for the relevant transaction documented in the confirmation, and that the schedule to a master agreement prevails over the master agreement itself.

There are, in fact, two forms of Master Agreement, a multicurrency version and a local currency version. The local currency version is essentially a cut

58. The proliferation of standard terms (from, for example, PSA/ISMA and EMTA as well as ISDA and the BBA) serves to show the demand for them and the advantages they can produce.

59. ISDA's Master Agreement is also drafted in mid-Atlantic legalese and, as such, is open to criticism at a time when the demand is increasingly, and rightly, for plain English (see, for example, *A Plain English Handbook: How to create clear SEC disclosure documents*, published by the SEC). A set of standard terms intended for use by end-users without, necessarily, the aid (or otherwise) of lawyers should perhaps be drafted in plainer English. (This problem is by no means confined to ISDA's documents.) Sir William Blackstone wrote (of statutory language) that "[w]hat is generally denominated legal language is in reality a mere technical language, calculated for eternal duration and easy to be apprehended both in present and future times; and on those accounts best suited to preserve those memorials which are intended for perpetual rules of action." Thomas Jefferson, however, railed against statutes "which from verbosity, their endless tautologies, their involutions of case within case, and parenthesis within parenthesis, and their multiplied efforts at certainty, by *saids* and *aforesaids*, by *ors* and *ands*, to make them more plain, are really rendered more perplexed and incomprehensible, not only to common readers, but to lawyers themselves".

60. This is the term used in ISDA's *User's Guide to the 1992 ISDA Master Agreement.*

down, and therefore simpler, version of the multicurrency master intended to govern transactions where there is no international element. In most cases, the multicurrency version is used, and this chapter will refer only to the multicurrency master agreement.

A master agreement is not a transaction in itself but is intended to govern any number of transactions falling within its scope.[61] Though it is preferable to execute a master agreement before entering into a transaction, it is common to enter into transactions and only subsequently to execute a master agreement. ISDA provides a number of forms of wording[62] to include in a confirmation if this is the case, some of which make the transaction subject to the bare terms of the master agreement, without any schedule. The wording requires that parties use their best or reasonable efforts to negotiate, execute and deliver a master agreement, but this is not a binding obligation because it is only an agreement to agree.[63] Nevertheless, it will usually be better to make a transaction subject to the terms of the master agreement, even if there is no schedule, than to wait until a master agreement is actually signed. The Master Agreement contains a number of clauses, notably events of default, which could prove of considerable importance if difficulties arise, and which might not be adequately covered as a matter of general law.[64]

The schedule to a master agreement is executed at the same time as the master agreement, and contains elections made by the parties under the various terms of the master agreement, together with any amendments or additions to the master agreement. It requires negotiation between the parties, but it is a negotiation which only needs to be carried out once, and most market professionals have their own standard form of the terms they wish to see included in a schedule.

A confirmation sets out the terms agreed between the parties for a particular transaction. As discussed above,[65] the Master Agreement is not entirely clear on the status of a confirmation but it seems likely (absent contrary intention) that it is not a contractual document as such but only confirmatory evidence of an existing transaction. Nevertheless, a confirmation does play a special role in ISDA's architecture, and ISDA has published a number of standard form

61. Quite when a transaction is governed by an ISDA Master Agreement is itself not an easy issue (see pp 190–192 below).

62. See, for example, ISDA's *User's Guide to the 1992 ISDA Master Agreement*, pp 38–39.

63. See, for example, *Walford* v. *Miles* [1992] 2 AC 128 and *Phillips* v. *Enron* (unreported, 12 October 1996).

64. The Master Agreement contains a number of options for the parties which are generally covered in the schedule to a master agreement. Most have provisions applicable in default of express agreement, but even where this is not so (e.g. governing law), this is unlikely to render the terms so uncertain as to be of no effect (e.g. for governing law, the parties can reasonably be treated as having selected the law which would govern the transaction as a matter of private international law). At worst, any terms which are too uncertain to be given effect would be ignored. ISDA's wording to incorporate its terms prior to execution of a master agreement probably does not have the effect of making all transactions entered into before this time one transaction and therefore rendering breach of one transaction breach of them all with contractual netting as a consequence. This can, however, easily be remedied by drafting.

65. See p 179 above.

confirmations setting out the issues requiring agreement for most common types of transaction.

A confirmation will invariably incorporate a set of definitions. The 1991 ISDA Definitions, with the 1998 Supplement, deal with basic concepts, such as currencies, dates, notional amounts, day count criteria and calculations, which enable confirmations to be shorter because they do not need to cover the same matters. There are also definitions relevant to particular transactions, for example, the 1998 FX and Currency Option Definitions.[66]

7.3.2 Transactions governed by a master agreement

If the parties have executed a master agreement, the first issue will usually be what transactions does it apply to. A master agreement on its own does nothing—it is only a set of standard terms which can govern a transaction entered into before or after those terms are agreed. ICOM is clear that it applies to all currency options entered into between the parties, whether or not also confirmed in writing, unless the parties agree otherwise in writing.[67] ISDA's Master Agreement has no defined scope in this way. It merely applies to "Transactions", that is, a transaction governed by the Agreement. As a result, even if a master agreement is executed between parties, a transaction must be expressed to be governed by its terms before the master agreement will have any application. If, however, the parties have executed a master agreement but fail to mention this during the telephone conversation in which the transaction was agreed or in the confirmation, it is still possible for the master agreement to be incorporated if (as is likely to be the case) there is a prior course of dealing using those terms. There must be a common understanding that the terms would apply, or one party must be entitled reasonably to conclude from the attitude of the other that the terms were to be incorporated.[68] Depending upon the circumstances, it could, however, be that the failure to mention the master agreement would be treated as a deliberate decision to exclude a transaction from its ambit.

Even if the parties enter into a transaction on the telephone and expressly agree that it will be subject to a master agreement, the position is not clear if they subsequently fail to execute a confirmation.[69] For example, section 2(a)(i) only obliges a party to make payments specified in each confirmation (though the oral agreement itself will inevitably also provide the same obligation whether or not a confirmation is entered into), section 5(a)(i) only makes it an event of default to

66. Published by ISDA, EMTA and The Foreign Exchange Committee.

67. Section 2.1 of ICOM (section 2.1 of IFEMA is to the same effect). The effect of requiring an agreement to the contrary to be in writing is questionable: see pp 204–205 below.

68. *British Crane Hire Corporation Ltd* v. *Ipswich Plant Hire Ltd* [1975] 1 QB 303.

69. Section 9(e)(ii) requires a confirmation to be entered into as soon as practicable, whether by execution in counterparts, exchange of telexes or otherwise. This is an obligation on both parties, not just one, but a course of conduct could establish that it was the responsibility of one party to prepare the first draft.

fail to make a payment due under "this Agreement", i.e. the master agreement and all confirmations,[70] and it is only the master agreement and all confirmations which form a single agreement.[71] It therefore appears that, for example, a failure to make payment on an unconfirmed oral agreement does not give rise to a breach of a master agreement and is not therefore a breach of any other confirmed transaction.

Nevertheless, even if an oral agreement is not confirmed, the master agreement is not wholly without effect. Section 3 provides that the representations in that section are deemed repeated by each party on the date on which a "Transaction" is entered into, i.e. when orally agreed. This poses no difficulty for the representation in section 3(a)(i) (duly organised corporation), but the representation in section 3(a)(ii) only relates to the power of the counterparty to execute the master agreement and confirmations, not to enter into a transaction, and section 3(a)(v) only confirms that the obligations under the master agreement and confirmations are legal, valid and binding on the counterparty. As a result, the effect of a master agreement on agreements which are not confirmed in accordance with the requirements of that agreement is very limited unless the schedule amends the master agreement.

The requirements for execution of a confirmation are set out in section 9(e)(ii) of the Master Agreement. This provides that they can be executed and delivered in counterparts[72] (including by fax), by exchange of telexes, by exchange of electronic messages or by other means agreed in the schedule. A confirmation must say that it is a confirmation. ISDA's standard forms for confirmations end by seeking confirmation from the recipient that the confirmation sets out the terms agreed by "executing the copy enclosed for that purpose and returning it to us or by sending us a letter or telex substantially similar to this letter, which letter or telex sets forth the material terms of the Transaction ...". This requirement that the reply only be "substantially" similar and set out the "material terms" could cause uncertainty. When is a letter "substantially" similar, and when is a term not "material"? If two confirmations differ, which is to prevail? The better course for an English law agreement is to seek confirmation of the accuracy of the terms set out.

This also begs the question of what is the position if one party sends a confirmation to the other who neither sends its own confirmation nor countersigns the one received. A confirmation is defined in the opening words of the Master Agreement as "the documents and other confirming evidence (each a 'Confirmation') exchanged between the parties". In the light of this, a confirmation sent by one party to the other but not countersigned is probably still a confirmation for the purposes of the master agreement. A confirmation

70. Section 1(c).
71. Section 1(c).
72. See p 205 below.

sent by one side to the other is still exchanged between the parties, and each such document is a confirmation.[73]

The drafting of the Master Agreement and the terms relating to confirmations are influenced by New York law requirements that certain contracts be evidenced in writing. Paragraph 5–701 of New York's General Law of Obligations ("GOL") provides that all agreements which are not to be performed within one year of being made are void (not merely unenforceable) unless there is some note or memorandum of the agreement in writing subscribed by the party against whom it is sought to enforce the agreement or his lawful agent. The note or memorandum must cover all essential terms of the agreement. This requirement potentially applies, for example, to interest rate swaps and other agreements where performance extends for a period over one year.

However, where foreign currency and other transactions which treat money as a commodity are concerned, the transaction may have to meet the requirements of the Uniform Commercial Code ("UCC"). Paragraph 2–201 of the UCC provides that contracts for the sale of goods for over US$500 are unenforceable unless there is some writing sufficient to indicate that a contract has been made and signed by the party against whom enforcement is sought or his agent or broker. The requirement for writing under the UCC is less rigorous than under the GOL, and there is an exception for "merchants", i.e. persons who deal in goods of the kind in question or who otherwise hold themselves out as having knowledge or skill peculiar to the practices or goods involved.[74] If a transaction is between merchants, it is sufficient if one sends a confirmation to the other within a reasonable time of the transaction being entered into, and the other fails to object within ten days of receipt.

7.3.3 Dating a master agreement

The Master Agreement states at the top that it is "dated as of ...". This is the date on which the parties intend it to take effect, but is not necessarily the date upon which it was agreed or executed. The signature section at the end of the Master Agreement requires the signatory to enter the date, which should be the date upon which he or she signed the agreement. There is no objection in English law to parties agreeing that terms and conditions should apply to transactions entered into before they were executed—this will amend the original agreements. English law has, however, traditionally regarded the backdating of documents very seriously, and a document should not therefore be misleading in

73. Section 9(c)(ii) does, however, say that a confirmation "shall be entered into as soon as practicable and may be executed and delivered in counterparts ... or be created by an exchange of telexes ...". This might suggest that either signature or exchange is required to create a confirmation, but it would be a strange result if the failure by one party to acknowledge an accurate confirmation could take it outside the scope of a master agreement.

74. Paragraph 2-104(1) of the UCC. The exception for merchants is in paragraph 2-201(2) of the UCC.

this regard. If a document is only dated "as of" a certain date, that does not mislead because it will be clear that that date is not necessarily the date of execution of the document. It is, nevertheless, good practice to date the signature of the agreement so that there can be no question of the document being misleading.[75]

If a document is backdated, it is potentially a criminal offence. Section 1 of the Forgery and Counterfeiting Act 1981 makes it an offence to make a false instrument with the intention of using it to induce someone to accept it as genuine, and by reason of so accepting it to do or not do some act to his own or any other person's prejudice. By section 9(1)(g) of the Act, an instrument is false if it purports to have been made or altered on a date at which it was not in fact made or altered. By sections 2 to 4 of the Act it is also an offence to make a copy of an instrument, to use an instrument, or to use a copy of an instrument, which in any of these cases is known or believed to be false with the intention of using it as set out in section 1.

7.3.4 Single agreement

One of the most significant features of having a master agreement and then a series of transactions subject to its terms is that all the transactions form a single agreement. This is of greatest significance in the event of a default by one of the parties. This is discussed further at various stages below, but in essence it means that a default under one transaction is a default under all transactions. This facilitates netting between transactions. Section 2.2 of both ICOM and IFEMA provides that all transactions subject to a master agreement "shall together constitute a single agreement between the Parties". ISDA's Master Agreement is less direct than this in that section 1(c) only provides that the parties enter into transactions "in reliance on the fact that this Master Agreement and all Confirmations form a single agreement ... and the parties would not otherwise enter into any Transactions". This does not say in so many words that all transactions subject to a master agreement are a single agreement, but that must be the effect.

7.3.5 Representations

The representations in section 3 of the Master Agreement are similar to those found in most financial agreements.[76] As with other financial agreements, the

75. ICOM and IFEMA also both have "as of" dates at the beginning of the terms, but do not display as prominently as the ISDA Master Agreement the date of signature. If a document is being drafted or arranged through lawyers, a common practice is for the lawyer to ask his or her client to execute, but not date, the document. The lawyers then date the document when they exchange it.

76. For example, representations of this sort are generally found in loan agreements, and ICOM (section 7) has similar, but not identical, representations (it does not have a representation as to the existence of the counterparties). The representations in BBAIRS (clause G1.1) are, however, in rather more summary form.

benefit of the representations is not necessarily that it gives a right to recover damages if the representation is inaccurate—in many cases there will be no right to recover damages; rather it is the hope that a responsible person on behalf of the counterparty will look into the issues raised by the representations and satisfy himself on the issues they set out. The representations are deemed repeated by each party on each date upon which a transaction subject to the master agreement is entered into. Since transactions are commonly entered into by traders in the course of telephone conversations, and it will seldom be part of their job to consider legal or legalistic issues, the hope that a responsible person will consider the issues may be fulfilled when a master agreement is signed, but it is less likely to be fulfilled at the time of each subsequent transaction.

7.3.5.1 *Status*

Section 3(a)(i) contains a representation that the parties exist under the laws of their incorporation or organisation.[77] If one of the parties does not exist, there is no agreement and therefore no representation to sue on. An agreement cannot be made by a non-existent entity, and if the agreement does not exist, nor does the representation. It would in any event be rare for a party to rely on a representation by the other party as to its existence; it would be normal for a party to confirm this for itself.

7.3.5.2 *Powers*

Section 3(a)(ii), headed "Powers", contains four representations. First, that the parties have power to execute the agreement. This relates to the power of the party to the agreement, rather than its agent who actually signs, and means that it has the corporate capacity to enter into the agreement. If it does not have the corporate capacity, and the agreement cannot be saved by other means, there will again be no agreement, and therefore no representation.[78] In some cases, corporate constitutions limit, for example, the amount the company can borrow, and this might include a representation that limits such as that have not been exceeded. This will, however, rarely be relevant in the case of derivatives.

Secondly, that the parties have power to deliver the agreement. Delivery is only relevant if the agreement is being entered into as a deed, in which case it comes into force on delivery, but the Master Agreement does not anticipate that this will be the case as it does not purport to be a deed. This representation therefore adds nothing to the representation that the parties have power to execute the agreement.

Thirdly, that the parties have power to perform their obligations under the

77. In English law, the usual description is of incorporation under the laws of England, but under some other laws (e.g. New York) the usual description is that a company is duly organised under its laws.

78. See Chapter 3 above.

agreement. This is probably the most significant of the representations in section 3(a)(ii), and in many respects encompasses all the others. Performance is the key feature of any agreement, and it is that that the parties both expect and rely on. This representation relates only to the corporate power to perform the agreement rather than the financial ability to do so.

Fourthly, that the parties have taken all necessary action to authorise the execution, delivery and performance of the agreement. This means that, for example, if a board or shareholders' resolution is necessary to give a company the power to enter into derivatives transactions, the company has passed those resolutions. It probably does not apply to third party consents that may be necessary as these are covered by section 3(a)(iv), and the section as a whole is concerned with corporate capacity.

If any of these representations is incorrect, the probable consequence is that the agreement is of no effect. If a party does not have power to enter into or perform an agreement, it will not have the power to represent that it does have that power. The representations are valuable, therefore, in focusing the parties' attention on the need to consider and deal with the issues they raise, but do not give any significant rights if the representations are wrong.

7.3.5.3 No violation or conflict

Section 3(a)(iii) also contains four distinct representations. First, that execution, delivery and performance of the agreement do not violate or conflict with any law applicable to the relevant party. This might cover, for example, the restrictions upon what insurance companies can do,[79] and, as such, each party is taking responsibility for the legal restrictions to which it is subject. If, however, the representation is incorrect, it will be a matter of construction of the relevant law as to whether it also prevents the giving of the representation in question. In many cases it will do so because otherwise it would provide an easy way around a restriction on a company's ability to enter into an agreement. In the case of the Financial Services Act 1986, if a counterparty needs to be authorised or exempted in order to enter into a particular derivatives transaction, this probably constitutes a representation that the counterparty has obtained that authorisation or exemption. If the other party suffers loss as a result of reliance on this representation, it may be able to recover damages for breach of this representation to compensate for it.[80]

Secondly, that execution, delivery and performance of the agreement do not violate or conflict with any provision of the parties' constitutional documents. This would probably sit easier in section 3(a)(ii) as it relates to corporate power, and in most, perhaps all, cases will not add anything to the representations in that section. If the agreement does violate the provisions of a company's

79. See pp 63ff above.
80. See also the statutory remedies given by the Financial Services Act 1986.

constitutional documents, it will in general make the agreement of no effect; and if it does not, it will generally be of limited concern to the other party.

Thirdly, that execution, delivery and performance of the agreement do not violate or conflict with any order or judgment of any court or other agency of government applicable to it or to any of its assets. English courts do not generally make prospective decisions as to the ability of a corporation to enter into transactions, but regulators might do so. For these purposes, "agency of government" should probably be given a wide interpretation, though the matter is not clear. For example, the Financial Services Authority has a wide sweep of regulatory functions given to it by legislation, but it is not part of the Government in the way that, for example, HM Treasury is. Nevertheless, it can be regarded as an agent (in a non-legalistic sense) of the Government in the performance of its functions as it does so under a governmental scheme for the regulation of the financial markets.

Fourthly, that execution, delivery and performance of the agreement do not violate or conflict with any contractual restriction binding on or affecting it or any of its assets. A contractual term saying, for example, that a company cannot enter into derivatives transactions will not, of itself, mean that a derivatives transaction entered into in breach of that provision is void,[81] but will place the relevant party in breach of contract, and may oblige it to pay damages if the other party suffers loss as a result.[82] This is unlikely to flow from the mere execution of a master agreement, but may follow from entering into a transaction governed by its terms.

A party which enters into an agreement with another which it knows to be in breach of a contractual obligation of the other party, could also be liable for damages in the tort of inducing breach of contract.[83] Knowledge, even if not precise, of the other contract is necessary—negligence is not enough—and there is no duty to enquire. If one party to a derivatives agreement knows that it will place its counterparty in breach of another contract, this section of the Master Agreement will not assist that party to escape liability. However, in cases where there is some doubt about the extent of knowledge, this section may be of some assistance in establishing an honest doubt, but on finding out about the other inconsistent contract, no further derivatives contracts should be entered into, as continuing dealing is likely to give rise to tortious liability even if the initial dealing did not do so.[84] In addition, if two parties do enter into a derivatives

81. See pp 202–203 below.

82. In practice, a term of this sort may be unusual. More common may be a term in a contract appointing an arranger of a transaction, possibly including derivatives, that the end-user will not seek to arrange the transaction through anyone else. Entering into an inconsistent arranger contract, or inducing the end-user to break the first contract, could lead to tortious liability.

83. See, for example, *Clerk & Lindsell on Torts* (14th edn), pp 1177–1221, for more details of this tort.

84. "... inconsistent dealing ... may, indeed, be commenced without knowledge by the third party of the contract thus broken; but if it is continued after the third party has notice of the contract, an actionable interference has been committed by him" (*DC Thompson & Co Ltd* v. *Deakin* [1952] Ch 646, 694).

transaction which they know to be in breach of the obligations of one of the parties, the transaction may be unenforceable as between those two parties.[85]

7.3.5.4 Consents

Section 3(a)(iv) of the Master Agreement provides that all governmental and other consents required with respect to the agreement have been obtained, are in full force and effect, and any conditions of the consents have been complied with. "Consent" is defined in section 14 in a very wide manner to include, for example, both authorisation and exemption. Nevertheless, the section only covers "consents that are required to have been obtained by it with respect to this Agreement", which suggests a degree of specificity with regard to the particular agreement rather than consents to carry on a derivatives business in general, such as authorisation or exemption under the Financial Services Act 1986.

Section 4(b) contains the counterpart to section 3(a)(iv). Section 4(b) requires each party to use "reasonable efforts" to maintain in full force and effect any consents necessary for the agreement. An obligation to use reasonable efforts is not very burdensome. An obligation to use best endeavours has been held to be an obligation "to do what they could reasonably in the circumstances. The standard of reasonableness is that of a reasonable and prudent board of directors acting properly in the interests of their company and applying their minds to their contractual obligations ..."[86] Reasonable endeavours, which is likely to be the same as reasonable efforts, means "appreciably less than best endeavours",[87] and does not therefore require the party with this obligation to take very onerous steps.

85. *British Homophone* v. *Kunz* (1935) 152 LT 589, 592 and *Chitty on Contract* (27th edn), pp 866–868.

86. *Terrell* v. *Mabie Todd & Co Ltd* [1952] 2 TLR 574. In *Sheffield District Railway Company* v. *Great Central Railway Company* (1911) 27 TLR 451, AT Lawrence J said that best endeavours "means what the words say; they do not mean second-best endeavours ... They do not mean that Great Central must so conduct its business as to offend its traders and drive them to competing routes. They do not mean that the limits of reason must be overstepped with regard to the cost of the service; but short of these qualifications the words mean that the Great Central Company must, broadly speaking, leave no stone unturned ..." In *Pathe Screen Entertainment* v. *Handmade Films* (unreported, 17 June 1991), Morland J thought that in the context with which he was concerned, it was not even necessary to leave no stone unturned. In *IBM* v. *Rockware Glass* [1980] FSR 335, Buckley LJ thought best endeavours meant taking "steps which a prudent, determined and reasonable owner, acting in his own interests and desiring to achieve that result would take". While Geoffrey Lane LJ thought it meant taking "all those reasonable steps which a prudent and determined man acting in his own interests and anxious to obtain planning permission would take". All definitions appear to incorporate an element of reasonableness.

87. *UBH (Mechanical Services) Ltd* v. *Standard Life Assurance* (*The Times*, 13 November 1986). In that case, Rougier J considered that "all reasonable endeavours" was mid-way between best endeavours and reasonable endeavours.

7.3.5.5 Obligations binding

Section 3(a)(v) provides a representation by each party that its obligations under this agreement (the master agreement and all confirmations) constitute its legal, valid and binding obligations, enforceable in accordance with their respective terms, subject to insolvency laws affecting creditors' rights generally and to equitable principles. This is the crux of any set of representations in that if the agreement is not binding, then the representations and all other terms are to no effect. What constitutes enforcement in accordance with the terms of the agreement is not necessarily an easy question. Where the obligation is to pay money, the courts will ultimately give a judgment for that sum of money,[88] and that judgment can be enforced by various means against the assets of the judgment debtor in order to recover the sum payable on the judgment. Where the obligation is delivery, the remedy will in most cases be damages rather than an order that the relevant commodity be delivered, but this is probably within the exception for general equitable principles as an order for specific performance of an agreement is an equitable remedy which will not be granted where, amongst other grounds, damages are an adequate remedy.

The exception for equitable principles also applies to the law relating to penalty clauses as the law relating to that derives from equity; so, for example, even if interest at the default rate is a penalty, the parties are not representing that it is payable.[89] The same cannot be said of the law relating to the currency in which court orders can be granted as the courts only took the power to give judgments other than in sterling over 90 years after the fusion of law and equity, and it is not therefore possible to say that this power is an equitable or legal power.[90]

The exception for insolvency procedures is of fundamental importance. For example, an administration order prevents enforcement steps being taken against the creditor,[91] and the aim of liquidation is to distribute the assets of an insolvent debtor to its creditors in accordance with the statutory scheme; a

88. Though see pp 222–223 as to interest, and pp 223–225 as to the currency of judgment.

89. The reference to equity may, however, be intended only to refer to discretionary remedies, like specific performance, rather than substantive, non-discretionary elements of equity.

90. It was originally the Supreme Court of Judicature Act 1873 which required the courts of England and Wales to apply both law and equity, abolishing the difference between the courts, and it is now in section 49 of the Supreme Court Act 1981. The reference in section 3(a)(v) to "regardless whether enforcement is sought in a proceeding in equity or at law" is therefore meaningless in an English context. In 1977 Lord Diplock, after quoting from a textbook on equity published in 1902 that law and equity run side by side in the same channel but do not mingle their waters, said that "by 1977 this metaphor has ... become both mischievous and deceptive. The innate conservatism of English lawyers may have made them slow to recognise that by the Supreme Court of Judicature Act 1873 the two systems of substantive and adjectival law formerly administered by the courts of law and Courts of Chancery ... were fused. As at the confluence of the Rhone and the Saône, it may be possible for a short distance to discern the source from which each part of the combined stream came, but there comes a point at which this ceases to be possible. If [the] fluvial metaphor is to be retained at all, the waters of the confluent streams of law and equity have surely mingled by now" (*United Scientific Holdings Ltd* v. *Burnley Borough Council* [1978] AC 904, 924–925).

91. Section 11 of the Insolvency Act 1986.

creditor is, therefore, generally prevented from obtaining judgment against the debtor and from enforcing any judgment it may have obtained before the insolvency proceedings commenced.

7.3.5.6 *Absence of events of default*

Section 3(b) provides representations that no event of default or potential event of default has occurred and is continuing, and that entering into or performing its obligations under the agreement will not cause one to occur. This is an absolute representation, not dependent upon the knowledge of the relevant party. Section 3(b) also contains a representation that, to the knowledge of the relevant party, no termination event has occurred. Termination events are defined in section 5(b)[92] but include, for example, illegality and the consequences of a merger. In the main they are events which the relevant party should be aware of, but as long as the party is in fact unaware of one, it will not constitute a breach of the representation with the consequences which flow from that; these consequences differ from those that would flow if there were an absolute representation in that breach of the representations is an event of default.

7.3.5.7 *Absence of litigation*

Section 3(c) contains a representation with three elements in order for it to be relevant: first, there must be proceedings pending or, to its knowledge, threatened against it or any of its affiliates[93]; secondly, those proceedings must be before any court, tribunal, government body, agency or official,[94] or any arbitrator; and, thirdly, the proceedings must be likely to affect the legality, validity or enforceability against it of the agreement, or its ability to perform its obligations.

The issue of when English proceedings become pending is not an easy one. The choice is between the date of issue of the proceedings and the date of service. The advantage of the latter is that the defendant will know at that point that there are proceedings against him whereas he might not know for up to six months if issue is the key date.[95] The reference to threatened proceedings being to the knowledge of the party indicates that knowledge is not a key element for the purpose of this representation, which might point to issue as being the key

92. See pp 248–250 below.

93. Affiliate is defined by reference to control or common control, and for these purposes control requires ownership of a majority of the voting power of the relevant entity. It is, prima facie, hard to see how legal action against an affiliate would affect the validity of an agreement entered into by a different company, even an affiliated one.

94. As a matter of grammar, "government" governs "body", "agency" and "official".

95. A claim form issued from the High Court in England must be served within four months if service is effected within England or Wales, or six months if it is effected outside, though these periods can be extended: CPR rule 7.5.

date. This is the traditional English approach,[96] but for the purposes of article 21 of the Brussels Convention, the courts have taken the view that they are only seised of proceedings when they are served.[97] Ultimately, it is a matter of construction of the Master Agreement, and it applies to proceedings both in England and elsewhere. There is no obvious answer either way, but issue of proceedings is the more likely.

The proceedings must also be pending or threatened before any court, tribunal, etc. This is clearly intended to be very wide, and could include disciplinary proceedings.

The proceedings must also be likely to affect the legality or enforceability against the party of its obligations under the agreement. The reference to "likely" to affect the transaction could imply a value judgement about the prospects of success of the action, and this will inevitably make it difficult for the other party to rely on this breach of this representation as an event of default because it will rarely have enough information to take a view on the likelihood of the action succeeding.[98]

Even if the party does have enough information to form a view as to the likely outcome of proceedings, the traditional view is that legal proceedings do not themselves affect a transaction; the courts simply declare what the law is and what it has always been.[99] If that is the correct interpretation, this part of this representation is of little impact. It might be, however, that it has to be interpreted as meaning that the proceedings concern, for example, the ability of the party to enter into derivatives transactions even if that does only result in a declaration.

The alternative limb is that the proceedings are likely to affect the ability of the party to perform its obligations. For these purposes, "ability" could include financial ability. If, therefore, the party faces a large claim which could imperil its future, that could fall within section 3(c).

7.3.5.8 Accuracy of specified information

Section 3(d) contains a limited representation that only applies if information has been furnished in writing and identified as being for the purposes of section 3(d) in the Schedule to the Master Agreement. Merely identifying it in a confirmation will not be enough, though the parties can enter into an agreement modifying the Schedule to include specified information.

96. See, for example, *Arab Monetary Fund* v. *Hashim (No 4)* [1992] 1 WLR 1176 where "pending" in RSC Ord 4, r 9(1) was interpreted to mean issue of a writ and not service.

97. *Dresser UK Limited* v. *Falcongate Freight Management* [1992] QB 502 and *The Sargasso* [1994] 3 All ER 180.

98. If the court has already given judgment, the matter could fall within section 3(a)(iii).

99. See, for example, *Kleinwort Benson* v. *Lincoln City Council* [1998] 4 All ER 513. In administrative law, a decision by an administrative body can in some circumstances have effect even though it is later quashed in judicial review proceedings (see, for example, Wade, *Administrative Law* (7th edn), pp 337–344).

7.3.5.9 *Branches*

Section 10(a) of the Master Agreement contains a representation that, if specified in the schedule to the Agreement, each party entering into a transaction through an office other than its head office represents that its obligations are the same as if it had entered into the transaction through its head office. If applicable, this means that one party is representing that the local law of the relevant branch does not detract from the ability of the party to enter into the agreement. If it does, then the other party can look to the head office to perform. The position is less clear if, say, foreign exchange controls are imposed on one branch after a transaction has been entered into. The representation made at the time the transaction was entered into remains correct. In these circumstances, if performance is illegal in the place it must necessarily take place, then the relevant obligation is unenforceable. A question will, however, arise as to whether the exchange control regulations affecting the branch create an illegality within section 5(b)(i).[100] This depends upon whether the regulations comprise applicable law, but it seems likely that they would do so.

7.3.5.10 *Warranty of authority*

If the representations set out in section 3 of the Master Agreement prove incorrect, they can in some circumstances give rise to a right to terminate a transaction; section 5(a)(iv) provides that it is an event of default if any of the representations are incorrect or misleading in any material respect, and this applies to the representations in sections 3(b) and (c). But as mentioned above, if the representations in section 3(a) are incorrect, the result will frequently be that there is no agreement and therefore no events of default or transaction to terminate. There might, however, be a claim against the signatory of the agreement for breach of warranty of authority. An agent (including the signatory of an agreement for a corporate counterparty) who acts for another is deemed to represent that he is duly authorised to do so.[101] This is an absolute representation in that it does not depend upon any fault on the part of the agent,[102] nevertheless there are important exceptions to the representation and, even if these can be overcome, in many cases it will not be worth bringing an action as the potential recoveries may not make it worthwhile.

There is only a deemed representation as to matters of fact, and not to matters of law because every man is supposed to know the law[103]; related to this is that there is no representation where the nature and extent of the agent's authority, or the material facts from which its nature and extent may be inferred, are fully

100. See pp 249–251 below on Illegality and Termination Events.

101. See *Bowstead & Reynolds on Agency* (16th edn), pp 592ff.

102. *Yonge* v. *Toynbee* [1910] KB 215.

103. *Beattie* v. *Lord Ebury* (1872) LR 7 Ch App 777 (affirmed by the House of Lords LR 7 HL 102), *Weekes* v. *Propert* (1873) LR 8 CP 427, 439, and *Eaglesfield* v. *Marquis of Londonderry* (1876) 4 Ch D 693, 709.

known to the other contracting party.[104] So, for example, the signatory on a swap transaction for a local authority gave no warranty of authority because the courts found that, as a matter of law, local authorities have no power to enter into swaps.[105] Similarly, if the power of a company to enter into derivatives transactions depends upon the construction of its memorandum of association, again there will probably be no breach of the warranty of authority as that is a matter of law. If, however, there is power, but the directors have not authorised the individual to enter into a transaction on behalf of the corporation, then there will be breach of the warranty of authority, provided all relevant matters are not known to both parties.

At a practical level, any claim on a warranty of authority will be against the individual who signs the agreement.[106] In most cases an individual will not be worth suing in respect of a derivatives transaction, at least unless he or she has insurance which covers the claim. If absence of authority is raised as a defence to a claim, joining the signatory may, however, in some circumstances have tactical advantages in concentrating minds on the merits of the defence even if it has little prospect of leading to recoveries.

7.3.6 Transfer

"Although it is true that the phrase 'assign this contract' is not strictly accurate, lawyers frequently use those words inaccurately to describe an assignment of the benefit of a contract since every lawyer knows that the burden of a contract cannot be assigned."[107] Section 7 of the Master Agreement prohibits any transfer of the agreement or an interest or obligation under it other than in limited circumstances.[108] As the quote indicates, the burden of a contract cannot be assigned without the agreement of all the parties, and therefore that element of section 7 is redundant. The benefit of a contract can be assigned in certain circumstances,[109] but a prohibition on assignment is effective to prevent a purported assignment having any effect.[110] The contract between assignor and

104. *Bowstead & Reynolds on Agency* (16th edn), pp 592–593.

105. *Hazell* v. *Hammersmith* [1992] 2 AC 1 (see pp 58–59 above).

106. It could be against another company if one company is acting as the agent of another. If want of authority is raised as a defence to an individual transaction, as opposed to the relationship as a whole, it will be the person who agreed on behalf of his principal that transaction who gives the warranties.

107. *Linden Gardens Trust Ltd* v. *Lenesta Sludge Disposals Ltd* [1994] 1 AC 85, 103 (Lord Browne-Wilkinson).

108. I.e. to avoid a termination event in accordance with section 6(b)(ii) (see pp 250–251 below), on a consolidation or amalgamation of substantially all its assets (section 7(a)) or if it is a transfer of an interest in an amount payable by a party in default (section 7(b)).

109. See *Chitty on Contracts* (27th edn), paras 19–024ff.

110. *Linden Gardens Trust Ltd* v. *Lenesta Sludge Disposals Ltd* [1994] 1 AC 85. A declaration of trust is probably similarly of no effect as between the counterparty and the purported beneficiary because the creation of a trust seeks to transfer the beneficial interest in the benefit of the contract to the beneficiary.

assignee which purports to make that assignment is probably valid, but it does not transfer any interest in the underlying contract.[111]

Section 7 of the Master Agreement provides that neither the agreement nor any interest or obligation in or under it may be transferred. This begs the question of whether a purported transfer by either party is a breach of the agreement entitling the other party to treat it as an event of default under section 5(a)(ii). Leaving aside questions arising from the construction of that section, in *Hendry* v. *Chartsearch*,[112] Millett LJ took the view that a purported assignment in breach of a prohibition of assignment was not a breach of contract as it did not affect the legal position of either assignor or assignee—it was simply of no effect whatsoever. Despite these comments, it should be possible to draft a contract to ensure that a purported assignment in breach of a prohibition is a breach of contract, but whether the Master Agreement does so is at the very least open to question.[113] In these circumstances, seeking to rely on an assignment as an event of default involves a risk.

Section 7 is effective to prevent any interest in the Master Agreement being passed to anyone else, but it is still possible to transfer the economic risk of a derivatives transaction to another party without actually transferring any interest in the benefit of the agreement itself. One party can enter into an agreement which provides that it will pay to a third party a sum equal to any sum it receives from the counterparty[114] without being in breach of section 7 because that section only prohibits transferring an interest in the agreement (whether by way of security or otherwise), which indicates that the section only applies to agreements which seek to create a legal or equitable interest in the agreement itself. Nevertheless, an agreement which seeks to achieve this economic effect without breach of section 7 could be in breach of any implied obligations of confidentiality which might attach to the master agreement.[115]

111. *Linden Gardens Trust Ltd* v. *Lenesta Sludge Disposals Ltd* [1994] 1 AC 85, 108. Section 7 of the Master Agreement provides that any purported transfer not in compliance with that section is void. This can only be interpreted as confirming the legal position that a transfer in breach of a contractual prohibition is void rather than saying anything about the contract between purported assignor and assignee.

112. Unreported, 23 July 1998.

113. Section 5(a)(ii) provides that a failure to comply with or perform any agreement or obligation is an event of default unless remedied within 30 days of notice being given. There is presumably an obligation not to seek to transfer any interest under the Agreement, but there is nothing which is capable of remedy as a purported transfer is of no effect.

114. It should be a sum equal to that received from the counterparty because an agreement to pass on the sum received from the counterparty runs the risk of creating an assignment of the right to receive that sum, which would be a breach of section 7.

115. See pp 35–38 above.

7.3.7 Amendments

One contract can normally be varied by another contract, whether under seal, in writing or oral.[116] Section 9(b) of the Master Agreement provides, however, that no amendment, modification or waiver to the agreement (including confirmations) is valid unless in writing.[117] Contractual clauses to this effect are common, but whether they work is open to real doubt.[118] The first question is likely to be the nature of any oral contract entered into in relation to an existing transaction. If it imposes an additional obligation, then it arguably is not an amendment or variation of the existing agreement, but this is likely only to be the case if it is truly independent. If it, for example, restricts a freedom that the existing contract gave, then it is still a modification to that contract because it prevents one party exercising the rights it would otherwise have had even if it does so by reference to another contract.

If the oral agreement does affect the terms of the existing agreement, then there are two rival arguments. First, as a matter of general law parties can, with very limited exceptions, enter into a contract orally, and that contract will be valid as long as it meets the requirements for a contract, notwithstanding any earlier agreement to the contrary. If the second contract is a valid contract, then it will have the effect of varying the first even if its form does not meet the requirements of the first. For example, the parties could agree that a contract was not capable of amendment, but that would not stop them from doing so in the future if they so wished.

Secondly, why should the parties not be free to agree a requirement as to form for any amendments? Parties can by agreement vary or remove the effect of much of the law of contract,[119] and there is no reason why the parties cannot remove the right they would otherwise have to amend a written contract orally. The law imposes certain requirements as to form in limited circumstances; why should the parties not be free to do the same? A clause of this sort could, it might be argued, show that there was no intention to create legal relations unless in writing, or no authority to vary a contract orally, but neither of these explanations is entirely convincing. The better argument might simply be that

116. The second, varying, contract must meet all the same requirements as to offer, acceptance, consideration and intention to create legal relations as any other contract. At common law, an agreement under seal could only be amended by another deed; equity, however, allowed deeds to be varied orally or in writing, and the equitable rule now prevails. This does not, however, apply to contracts which are required to be in writing, which can only be varied in writing.

117. A new transaction subject to the Master Agreement is probably not affected by section 9(b). Section 9(b) concerns amendment, modification or waiver in respect of this Agreement, which is defined in section 1(c) as including confirmations. In context, therefore, making a new transaction subject to a Master Agreement is exercising a right given by the agreement rather than amending it. The requirement for writing in section 9(b) differs from the requirement for confirmation in section 9(e)(ii).

118. See, for example, *Commercial Lawyer* (1997), Issue 19, p 28.

119. For example, the parties can by agreement remove the right which otherwise exists to pay in sterling a foreign currency obligation payable in the UK (see pp 222–223 below).

the courts should give effect to the will of the parties. There is good commercial reason—certainty—for requiring amendments to be in writing, and there is no basis in public policy to disregard the parties' wishes. The requirement is only as to form, is easily met, and does not offend any reasons which there might be for refusing to allow the parties to make an agreement incapable of subsequent variation.

There are no judicial decisions on clauses or this sort, and the courts could go either way on the issue. However, it is clearly preferable to have any amendment in writing to avoid argument on the point. A party which seeks to rely on an oral agreement amending the terms of an earlier transaction is likely to face a considerable evidential burden in showing the existence of the agreement, as well as an intention to create legal relations, faced with section 9(b).

Even if one party cannot show that there was an oral variation of an agreement, it might nevertheless in some limited circumstances be able to rely on a promissory estoppel if the requirements are met.[120] If an argument that the contract has been amended fails, however, it is likely to be hard to show the existence of an estoppel as it cannot be used as a means to avoid the requirements for contracts.

7.3.8 Counterparts

Section 9(e)(i) provides that "this Agreement" (i.e. the Master Agreement itself and confirmation, together with amendments, modifications and waivers) can be executed and delivered in counterparts. Technically, where one party, such as a lessor, executes one part of a deed making the grant of the interest in the real property, that part is the principal deed and the part executed by the lessor is the counterpart. The counterpart must, in the event of inconsistency, give way to the principal deed. Where two (or more) parties execute different copies of a deed, each is a duplicate and is as efficacious as all others.[121]

Where the master agreement and confirmations are concerned, neither will usually be executed as a deed, nor is either of the parties generally making any particular grant to the other. In these circumstances, the reference in section 9(e)(i) of the Master Agreement to counterparts should be read as indicating that it is not necessary for all parties to sign the same piece of paper, rather than as importing a technical[122] meaning to the term. The provision does, however, give greater flexibility in view of the concentration in the Master Agreement on written terms.[123]

120. See pp 182–183 above.
121. See *Halsbury's Laws of England*, vol 12, para 1304.
122. And probably forgotten (if ever known) by most lawyers.
123. See pp 190–192 above.

7.3.9 Notices

Most agreements provide for a means of serving notices which may be given under the terms of that agreement. In general, these either require that notice must be given in accordance with the requirements set out in the agreement, or provide that notice may be given in a particular way but it does not prevent notice being given in other ways. Section 12(a) of the Master Agreement opts for the latter approach, but does prevent certain notices being given in one particular way.

Section 12(a) provides that notice can be given to the other party to the address, or in accordance with the electronic messaging system, specified in the Schedule to the Agreement. It provides, however, that notices under sections 5 or 6, which relate to events of default, unquestionably the most significant notices which are likely to be given under the terms of the Master Agreement, cannot be given by fax (though they can be given by telex). This reluctance to accept fax carries through to section 12(a)(iii), which provides that a fax is only deemed effective when it is received by a responsible employee in legible form, the burden of proving this being on the sender. The requirement that a communication be seen by a responsible employee does not apply to any other form of communication, and, in practice, means that no notice of any importance can safely be given by fax, as that burden of proof will be very hard to discharge. Even the courts take a more sympathetic attitude to service by fax than that taken by the Master Agreement,[124] and the approach set out in the Master Agreement is probably now outdated as faxes have become more reliable.

7.3.10 Governing law

All contracts, at least those with any international element, should have a governing law clause. "[C]ontracts are incapable of existing in a legal vacuum. They are mere pieces of paper devoid of all legal effect unless they were made by reference to some system of private law which defines the obligations assumed by the parties to the contract by their use of particular forms of words."[125] If the parties fail to specify the governing law, it will be determined by reference to the private international law of the court in which the dispute is taking place.[126]

124. See, for example, CPR rules 6.2(1)(e) and 6.10. In *Anson* v. *Trump* [1998] 3 All ER 331, the Court of Appeal decided that service by fax was effected when a document was received by the recipient's fax equipment even if it was then held in the system's memory for some time before being printed out and read. This is consistent with the approach for letters where there is no requirement that a letter be opened or read for service to be effective.

125. *Amin Rashid* v. *Kuwait Insurance* [1984] AC 50, 65.

126. In the case of England, the relevant rules are set out in article 4 of the Rome Convention, introduced into English law by the Contracts (Applicable Law) Act 1990. Although the Rome Convention is an EU convention, it now represents English private international law on the topic and applies wherever the parties to the contract are domiciled and whatever governing law the Convention leads to. The Rome Convention does not, however, apply, amongst other matters, to arbitration agreements and agreements on the choice of courts (art 1(2)(d)) and whether an agent is able to bind a principal (art 1(2)(f)).

The advantage of express choice is not only that the parties can assess in advance the principles and approach to construction which govern the contract, but they avoid any dispute over the governing law—if a dispute does arise between the parties, an issue on the governing law of the agreement can delay the time at which the court will address the substantive issues between the parties, and can also make the litigation more expensive.

Section 13(a) of the Master Agreement provides that it is governed by the law specified in the Schedule. The standard form of Schedule offers a choice between English and New York law.[127] The law which governs an agreement applies to the interpretation of the agreement,[128] performance,[129] the consequences of breach,[130] and the various ways of extinguishing obligations.[131] In addition, the law which would govern a contract if there were one governs the question of the existence and validity of the contract,[132] but a contract must comply with any requirements of form (e.g. writing) of the law governing it or of the place where it was concluded if both parties were in the same country, or, if the parties are in different countries, the governing law or the requirements of the law of one of the countries where the parties are situated.[133] Nothing detracts from laws of the country where any dispute is taking place which are mandatory irrespective of governing law[134] or matters manifestly inconsistent with the public policy of that forum.[135]

The form of governing law clause in the Master Agreement only applies to the agreement itself. As a result, if a claim in tort (for example, negligent misrepresentation in the pre-contractual negotiations) were to be brought in relation to the agreement that claim would not necessarily be governed by the law governing the contract.[136] The general rule under the Private International

127. It adds that the choice of law is without reference to the choice of law doctrine. As far as English law is concerned, this addition is unnecessary as art 15 of the Rome Convention already excludes this.

128. Article 10(1)(a) of the Rome Convention. There is, therefore, no need to use the words traditionally used, in the Master Agreement and elsewhere, governed by and "construed in accordance with" English law—there probably never was any need to do so: *Vita Food Products* v. *Unus Shipping* [1939] AC 277.

129. Article 10(1)(b) of the Rome Convention.

130. Article 10(1)(c) of the Rome Convention. The provision is obscure in that it provides that it only applies within the limits conferred by procedural law, and the assessment of damages so far as it is governed by rules of law. See Dicey & Morris, *The Conflict of Laws* (12th edn), p 1263.

131. Article 10(1)(d) of the Rome Convention. Article 10(1)(e) of the Convention provides that the governing law also applies to the consequences of nullity of the contract, but this does not have the force of law in England: section 2(2) of the Contracts (Applicable Law) Act 1990.

132. Article 8(1) of the Rome Convention.

133. Article 9 of the Rome Convention.

134. Article 7(2) of the Rome Convention.

135. Article 16 of the Rome Convention. Dicey & Morris, *The Conflict of Laws* (12th edn), pp 1278–1280, suggests that the law relating to restraint of trade and champerty would be considered English public policy for these purposes but that the law relating to penalty clauses would not.

136. In *PT Adimatra Rayapratama* v. *Bankers Trust* (16 August 1995), the New York courts decided that the width of ISDA's jurisdiction clause and the governing law clause together meant that all claims arising from the relationship were governed by English law.

Law (Miscellaneous Provisions) Act 1995 is that the law applicable to a tort[137] is the law of the country in which the events constituting the tort occur; where the elements of the tort occur in different countries, it is the law of the country in which the most significant events occurred, but if it appears from a comparison of the significance of the factors connecting a tort with the country whose law would be applicable under the general rule and the significance of the factors connecting the tort with another country that it is substantially more appropriate for that other country to apply, the applicable law is the law of that other country.[138] If a governing law clause were, as a matter of construction, wide enough to cover claims in tort arising before or after the agreement was entered into, it is not clear whether it would be taken into account in determining the applicable law, but there seems no reason why it should not be as, at least, a factor in the court's assessment. Nor is it clear whether the parties can contract out of the statutory provision so that their choice becomes the factor in the court's decision.[139] Despite this uncertainty as to its effectiveness, extending the clause to cover torts may have advantages in that, if the chosen law would not otherwise be applicable, it does at least give an argument which would not otherwise be available; and if the chosen law would in any event govern the tort, the clause does no harm.

7.3.10.1 Governing law absent express choice by the parties

If the parties do not expressly choose the law which is to govern a derivatives contract, the governing law will be the law of the country with which the contract is most closely connected.[140] This is deemed to be the country where the party which is to effect the performance which is characteristic of the contract has, at the time the contract was entered into, its habitual residence or, in the case of a body corporate, its central administration (but if a contract is entered into in the course of that party's trade, and performance is to be effected through a place of business other than the principal place, the law of that other place applies).[141] These presumptions do not apply if characteristic performance cannot be determined, or if it appears that the contract is more closely connected with another country.[142]

These rules are not necessarily easy to apply in the case of derivatives. For example, if a swap or a foreign exchange contract is entered into between parties in different countries, it is hard to identify characteristic performance. Either, or

137. Except defamation, to which different rules apply.

138. Sections 11 and 12 of the Private International Law (Miscellaneous Provisions) Act 1995.

139. The parties can in effect agree that English law should govern a tort by not raising in court the issue of the applicable law. In those circumstances, the court will assume that whatever foreign law may be applicable is the same as English law.

140. Article 4(1) of the Rome Convention. It is the country with which the contract is most closely connected, not with which the parties are most closely connected.

141. Article 4(2) of the Rome Convention.

142. Article 4(3) of the Rome Convention. There are also some protections for consumers in article 5.

indeed both, parties could be obliged to make payment, and at the outset it is impossible to identify the payment of either party as characteristic of the contract. In this case, the choices for governing law are the locations of the parties, the currencies involved and the market upon which a deal was done. This last factor, if relevant, might be the most relevant in deciding the governing law.

In the case of an option, the choice for characteristic performance is between the party which paid the premium and has the right to exercise the option, or the party which is the subject of the option. Characteristic performance is likely to be that of the seller of the option, particularly if it is cash settled, though this is far from clear. If, however, neither constitutes characteristic performance, then it falls back to the country with which the contract has the closest connection.

7.3.11 Jurisdiction

The purpose of a jurisdiction clause is to set out where disputes in relation to an agreement should be determined. In the absence of a jurisdiction clause, there is a risk that a dispute will take place in a location which one of the parties regards as unfavourable. There is also a risk that there will be a procedural dispute over where the substantive dispute should be determined, which will both delay the resolution of the substantive dispute and make the whole procedure more expensive.

In choosing the forum in which disputes will be resolved, it is necessary to bear in mind that courts generally give judgments requiring one party to pay the other money. The fact of that judgment may be enough to persuade the party to pay—there may, for example, be regulatory or other reasons why it cannot allow a judgment against it to remain unsatisfied. If, however, the sum due on a judgment is not paid voluntarily, the judgment must be enforced against the assets of the judgment debtor in order to be turned into money. Where there is any risk that the other party will not meet a judgment debt voluntarily, the prime criterion in selecting the forum in which disputes will be resolved is whether a judgment given in that forum can be enforced against identifiable assets of the other party—a judgment is of no value if that is not possible. For these purposes, assets can be physical assets, shares in companies, bank deposits or anything else.

As far as global financial institutions are concerned, both enforcement and the location of assets are unlikely to be of significant concern; they are unlikely to be able to leave a judgment outstanding but, in any event, will probably have assets spread across the globe such that at least some are available for enforcement. For other institutions, there may be greater concern. If a party has assets in the jurisdiction chosen for the resolution of disputes, there will usually be no difficulty enforcing a judgment given in that jurisdiction against those assets. Judgments given in one country can, however, be enforced overseas in certain circumstances. It is easiest to enforce overseas if there is a treaty providing for the mutual enforcement of judgments.[143] The most powerful treaties in this respect are the Brussels and Lugano Conventions[144] (which are virtually identical), which provide for the enforcement of judgments given in one state in western Europe to be enforced in most others. Where, however, a court judgment given in an acceptable court is not enforceable where the other party has assets, an arbitration clause may be the only practical alternative.[145]

Financial agreements have traditionally given the courts of a named jurisdiction non-exclusive jurisdiction over disputes. The purpose of this is to give a degree of flexibility when a dispute actually arises. In most cases, however, that flexibility will enable either party to commence proceedings in a court which, under its rules, has jurisdiction. A "true" defendant (i.e. someone who is likely to owe money) can start proceedings[146] in a court he considers favourable to his cause in the hope that the other party will be obliged to fight those proceedings or that any other court where proceedings are started subsequently will stay its proceedings. Given this risk, where enforcement of a judgment is unlikely to be an issue or where that party has assets in western Europe, there is often little to be gained by a non-exclusive jurisdiction.[147] Further, as discussed below, as far as courts subject to the Brussels Convention are concerned, there is uncertainty as to the effect of seeking to give a court non-exclusive jurisdiction.

Section 13(b)(i) of ISDA's Master Agreement gives "jurisdiction" to the English courts if the agreement is governed by English law, and "non-exclusive jurisdiction" to the New York courts if the agreement is governed by New York law. The reason for the difference is not the desire for flexibility mentioned above but the problems caused in this regard by the Brussels Convention. The aim of the Brussels Convention is to provide for the free movement of judgments within the contracting states, and to achieve this it sets out jurisdictional rules

143. A treaty is, however, not the only way. Judgments can also be enforced by common law means, i.e. by the courts recognising that the judgment of a foreign court creates a debt, and enforcing that debt by separate action (see Dicey & Morris, *The Conflict of Laws* (12th edn), pp 461ff). There is no treaty between the UK and the USA, so the only way a judgment given by courts in the USA can be enforced in the UK is by this method.

144. These Conventions are identical for current purposes. For convenience, only the Brussels Convention will be referred to. The Brussels Convention applies to Belgium, Denmark, France, Germany, Greece, Ireland, Italy, Luxembourg, The Netherlands, Portugal, Spain and the UK. The Lugano Convention applies to Austria, Finland, Iceland, Sweden and Switzerland.

145. For example, a judgment given in the English courts is not in general enforceable within the states which were members of the Warsaw Pact, but an arbitration award might be as most of these states are parties to the New York Convention on the enforcement of arbitration awards. It is always, however, necessary to consider (both with regard to judgments and awards) whether the theoretical possibility of enforcement can be carried through in practice.

146. The proceedings could, for example, be for a negative declaration, i.e. a declaration that the party has no liability to the other.

147. It is possible to obtain interim relief in one jurisdiction in favour of substantive proceedings in another contracting state: art 24 of the Brussels Convention. In England, it is now possible to obtain interim relief (e.g. an injunction freezing assets) in support of proceedings in any other country, whether a contracting state or not: The Civil Jurisdiction and Judgments Act 1982 (Interim Relief) Order 1997 (1997 SI No 302), made under section 25(3) of the Civil Jurisdiction and Judgments Act 1982.

for the contracting states with a view to ensuring that only one court within the contracting states will be seised of a case. The judgment given by that court will be enforceable throughout the contracting states.

As far as jurisdiction clauses are concerned, article 17 of the Brussels Convention provides that:

"If the parties, one of whom is domiciled[148] in a Contracting State, have agreed that a court or the courts of a Contracting State are to have jurisdiction to settle any disputes which have arisen or may arise in connection with a particular legal relationship, that court or those courts shall have exclusive jurisdiction. Such an agreement conferring jurisdiction shall be either—

(a) in writing or evidenced in writing[149] . . .

Where such an agreement is concluded between parties none of whom is domiciled in a Contracting State, the courts of the other Contracting State shall have no jurisdiction over their disputes unless the court or courts chosen have declined jurisdiction.

. . .

If an agreement conferring jurisdiction was concluded for the benefit of only one of the parties, that party shall retain the right to bring proceedings in any other court which has jurisdiction by virtue of this Convention."

The Convention only regulates jurisdiction between the contracting states. If, therefore, a court outside the contracting states considers that it has jurisdiction, it can determine the case unaffected by the Convention. As between the contracting states, the Convention determines which court has jurisdiction, and a court which has jurisdiction must, in general, accept it.[150] If, however, neither of the parties to a contract is domiciled within any of the contracting states, the chosen court has a choice whether to accept jurisdiction, but no other contracting state can assume jurisdiction unless that court has first declined it. In England, the court has power in the international context to stay proceedings on grounds of *forum non conveniens* in the following circumstances: where proceedings are served within the jurisdiction of the English court, the defendant can show that England is not the natural or appropriate forum for the trial and that there is available another forum which is clearly more appropriate than England; and, where proceedings are served outside England, the plaintiff

148. Domicile is a matter for the domestic law of each state (articles 52 and 53 of the Brussels Convention). In England, it is set out in sections 41 to 46 of the Civil Jurisdiction and Judgments Act 1982. This provides that a company is domiciled in part of the UK if it was incorporated in the UK and has its registered office or some official address in the UK, or if its central management and control is exercised in the UK. Accordingly, the London branch of a US bank would not be treated as domiciled in the UK, but a subsidiary would be.

149. In *CSFP* v. *Société Générale d'Entreprises* (unreported, 4 July 1996), the Court of Appeal dismissed an argument that where a written contract incorporated by reference ISDA's Master Agreement, the jurisdiction clause in the Master Agreement did not fall within this requirement if one party did not actually have a copy of the Master Agreement.

150. The English courts do, however, take the view that they have the right to stay their proceedings on grounds of *forum non conveniens* in favour of a non-contracting state (*Re Harrods (Buenos Aires) Ltd* [1992] Ch 72) or where the defendant is not domiciled in a contracting state (*Sarrio* v. *KIA* [1997] 1 Lloyd's Rep 113). In addition, in *Turner* v. *Grovit* (unreported, 28 May 1999) the Court of Appeal granted an injunction to restrain parties pursuing an action in Spain launched in bad faith to oppress a plaintiff in England.

cannot show that England is clearly the appropriate forum.[151]

Where, however, proceedings are brought in England in breach of a jurisdiction clause, it requires a "strong cause" to be shown to persuade the court that it should not exercise its discretion to stay proceedings; similarly, if proceedings are brought in England in accordance with an exclusive jurisdiction clause, it will require a similarly strong cause to persuade the court to decline jurisdiction.[152]

As mentioned, the aim of the Brussels Convention is to provide for one court to have jurisdiction, and article 17 follows this pattern. A jurisdiction clause which gives non-exclusive jurisdiction does not fit easily into this approach—article 17 refers to the chosen court having exclusive jurisdiction. In these circumstances, a clause giving non-exclusive jurisdiction could be interpreted in one of three ways. First, it could be treated as wholly ineffective to confer jurisdiction on the chosen courts. This would, however, completely ignore the wishes of the parties.[153] Secondly, it could be treated as conferring exclusive jurisdiction on the chosen courts, excluding all others. This too would run counter to the parties' wishes. Thirdly, it could be treated as conferring jurisdiction on the chosen courts but also allowing any other court which has jurisdiction under the other provisions of the Convention to take jurisdiction. This is the interpretation given in *Kurz* v. *Stella Musical GmbH*.[154] *Kurz* is, however, only a first instance decision and is not without its critics.[155] There remains doubt about it, therefore, and for that reason the phrase non-exclusive is best omitted.

The effect, therefore, of section 13(b)(i) of the Master Agreement is to confer exclusive jurisdiction upon the English courts within the contracting states of the Brussels and Lugano Conventions, i.e. if proceedings within the scope of the jurisdiction clause are brought in the courts of any other contracting state, those courts should decline jurisdiction in favour of the English courts. If one of the parties wishes to retain flexibility where to bring proceedings, the final

151. *Spiliada Maritime Corp* v. *Cansulex Ltd* [1987] AC 460.

152. See, for example, *The El Amria* [1981] 2 Lloyd's Rep 119, 123, and *Continental Bank* v. *Aeakos* [1994] 1 WLR 588 (there are also some suggestions that the English courts will not even consider an application to stay proceedings if there is an exclusive jurisdiction clause in their favour: see Peel [1998] LMCLQ 182, 201). The court has even been prepared to grant injunctions preventing parties pursuing proceedings in other courts of contracting states if those proceedings were brought in breach of a jurisdiction clause. It is hard to reconcile this with the decision of the European Court of Justice in *Overseas Union Insurance* v. *New Hampshire Insurance* [1992] 1 QB 434, and it has been heavily criticised in *Baghlaf Al Safer Factory Co* v. *Pakistan National Shipping Corp* [1998] 2 Lloyd's Rep 229. The correct approach is probably for the court seised of a case in breach of a jurisdiction clause to decline jurisdiction, the English court being prevented by art 21 of the Brussels Convention from taking any steps pending that decision.

153. This approach is also out of keeping with the emphasis on the parties' will in *Meeth* v. *Glacetal* [1978] 3 ECR 2133, 2141.

154. [1992] Ch 196.

155. The criticism is mentioned, but not commented upon, in *Continental Bank* v. *Aeakos* [1994] 1 WLR 588, 594. Dicey & Morris, *The Conflict of Laws* (12th edn), p 431, is generally favourable to the decision, but Cheshire & North, *Private International Law* (12th edn), pp 316–317, is less so. The decision was followed in *Gamlestaden* v. *Casa de Suecia* [1994] 1 Lloyd's Rep 433.

paragraph quoted above from article 17 can be used. This is normally done by stating expressly that the clause is for the benefit of one only of the parties.[156]

The scope of the jurisdiction clause in section 13(b) is "proceedings relating to this Agreement". This clearly covers claims in contract (e.g. arising from non-payment). It probably also covers claims that the agreement is void because, for example, one party lacked the capacity to enter into it.[157] In addition, it is likely that the clause covers claims in tort arising from the negotiations leading to the contract, as the English courts at least have taken the view that there is a "presumption in favour of one-stop adjudication",[158] i.e. that all disputes arising from the same events should be determined in one place at one time rather than forcing the parties to determine, say, a negligent misrepresentation claim in one court and a contractual claim in another.

Section 13(b) of the Master Agreement goes on to provide that the parties waive any objection they may have to the chosen venue. This is probably of little practical effect. The clause confers exclusive jurisdiction on the English courts,[159] and even in those limited areas where the court has a discretion to decline jurisdiction[160] the courts will only decline jurisdiction if there is a strong cause shown for doing so. Nevertheless, the courts do have power to take and decline jurisdiction in breach of a jurisdiction clause,[161] and can presumably also act in breach of a clause of this sort too.

Section 13(b) also provides that nothing in the agreement precludes either party from bringing proceedings in any other jurisdiction outside, if the agreement is governed by English law (and, therefore, subject to the jurisdiction of the English courts), the contracting states of the Brussels Convention. This restriction within the contracting states is required as article 21 of the Convention is clear that where proceedings involving the same cause of action and between the same parties are brought before the courts of different contracting states, any court other than the first seised[162] must decline jurisdiction until the court first seised has decided whether it does have jurisdiction. But even outside the Brussels Convention, the English courts have

156. Stating that the clause is for the benefit of all the parties is of doubtful effect. It seems likely that for this paragraph from article 17 to be effective, at least one party must not have the benefit of the clause.

157. In *Benincasa* v. *Dentalkit* [1998] All ER (EC) 135, the European Court of Justice decided that a jurisdiction clause governed by the Brussels Convention was valid if it met the requirements of the Brussels Convention even if the rest of the contract was void. This follows the approach to arbitration clauses: see section 7 of the Arbitration Act 1996.

158. Hoffmann LJ in *Harbour Assurance Co (UK) Ltd* v. *Kansa General International Insurance Co Ltd* [1993] QB 701, 726. See also *Continental Bank* v. *Aeakos* [1994] 1 WLR 588, 593, *The Angelic Grace* [1995] 1 Lloyd's Rep 87, 89–91 and *Hough* v. *P&O* [1998] 3 WLR 851.

159. Even without the effect of the Brussels Convention, it would probably be treated as exclusive given the contrast with the New York courts (though the reason for the contrast is the Brussels Convention).

160. I.e. where none of the parties is domiciled in a contracting state or the circumstances mentioned in note 150 above.

161. See above.

162. See pp 199–200 above for when a court is seised of proceedings.

been reluctant to allow proceedings on the same cause of action in different jurisdictions, and therefore might well stay proceedings in England in favour of another court seised of the same issues or, if the plaintiff is the same in both jurisdictions, put him to election as to whether he wants to continue in England or that other jurisdiction. As a result, allowing suit outside the English courts in this way potentially gives rise to jurisdictional disputes as discussed above.

7.3.11.1 Process agents

Section 13(c) of the Master Agreement provides for each side to appoint a process agent.[163] Though the Master Agreement does not say so, a process agent should be in England if the English courts have jurisdiction. The purpose of appointing a process agent is not that it takes time to obtain leave from the court to serve process outside England—leave is not required to serve if the English court has jurisdiction under the Brussels Convention,[164] and even outside this it can be obtained quickly if necessary—the problem is more that the procedures required to serve overseas process in foreign states can be very slow. In some countries, foreign process can only be served through the mechanisms of the Hague Convention.[165] This requires the transmission of documents between the relevant government departments of the two states concerned before finally reaching the defendant. This can easily take many months to achieve, causing considerable delays in proceedings. Section 13(c) also provides that service can be effected in the manner provided for service of notices in section 12.[166] If, however, it is mandatory in a particular country to serve process through the Hague Convention, this will not help as performance of the contract will be illegal in the place where performance is required, and will not therefore be enforced by the English courts.[167]

163. The source of the power to appoint a process agent is CPR rule 6.15. The equivalent provision under the former court rules (RSC Ord 10, r 3(1)) did not, however, provide a comprehensive code—parties could agree means of service which fall outside its scope: *Kenneth Allison Ltd* v. *AE Limehouse & Co* [1992] 2 AC 105. There is no obvious reason to treat the CPR as having changed the position.

164. RSC Ord 11, r 1(2) (appendix 1 to the CPR).

165. The Convention on the Service Abroad of Judicial and Extra-judicial Documents in Civil or Commercial Matters signed at the Hague on 15 November 1965.

166. If this is outside England and jurisdiction is not given by the Brussels Convention, leave to serve out is still required.

167. *Ralli Bros* v. *Compania Naviera Sota y Aznar* [1920] 2 KB 287. In addition, RSC Ord 11, r 5(2) provides that nothing in the rules of the court authorises doing anything in a country in which service is to be effected which is contrary to the law of that country.

7.3.11.2 *Immunities*

Under English law, states[168] are immune from the jurisdiction of the English courts except if a state has submitted to the courts or in respect of a commercial transaction.[169] A jurisdiction clause like that in section 13(b) of the Master Agreement constitutes a submission to the jurisdiction of the courts, but the fact that a state can be brought before the courts may not be enough. In England, states are also immune from any enforcement procedures against their assets unless those assets are being used for commercial purposes or the state has consented to enforcement measures.[170] Section 13(d) of the Master Agreement provides this submission for the purposes of execution.

An ambassador to the UK has power on behalf of a state to submit to the jurisdiction of the English courts, as does an authorised signatory to a contract.[171] An ambassador also has power to agree that execution may be levied on the state's property,[172] but the legislation does not expressly provide that an authorised signatory has that same power. Nevertheless, the legislation cannot be interpreted as providing that only an ambassador can consent in this way; it is therefore likely to be simply a question of whether the signatory is duly authorised to waive a state's immunity over its assets.

On occasions, it is suggested that process which may need to be served on a state is served at the relevant embassy. Article 22 of the Vienna Convention on Diplomatic Relations[173] makes an embassy inviolate. This probably means that process cannot be served on the embassy even by post.[174] It is possible for this immunity to be waived, but it is probable under the terms of the Convention that only the ambassador can do this.[175] As a result, if service is to be effected on an embassy, a waiver of diplomatic immunity is required from the ambassador.

7.3.12 Payments

As mentioned above,[176] the primary obligation under the Master Agreement is to make each payment or delivery specified in each confirmation.[177] Payment must

168. This includes a sovereign, the government of a state and any department of the government, but not an entity (a "separate entity") which is distinct from the executive organs of the government and which is capable of suing or being sued: section 14 of the State Immunity Act 1978. A central bank enjoys the same immunity as a state even if it is a separate entity: section 14(4) of the State Immunity Act 1978.

169. Sections 2 and 3 of the State Immunity Act 1978.

170. Section 13 of the State Immunity Act 1978. The property of a central bank is not regarded as being used for commercial purposes: section 14(4) of the State Immunity Act 1978.

171. Section 2(7) of the State Immunity Act 1978.

172. Section 13(5) of the State Immunity Act 1978.

173. Introduced into English law by the Diplomatic Privileges Act 1964.

174. See Brownlie, *Principles of Public International Law* (4th edn), p 354.

175. Article 22 of the Vienna Convention provides that an embassy is inviolate "except with the consent of the head of mission".

176. See pp 194–195 above.

177. Section 2(a)(i) of the Master Agreement.

be on the due date for value on that date in the place of the account specified[178] in the relevant confirmation in freely transferable funds.[179]

This payment or delivery obligation is subject to the condition precedent[180] that no event of default or potential event of default has occurred. Events of default are discussed in greater detail below, but making a potential event of default a condition precedent to performance is important. Non-payment is not an event of default until notice of non-payment is given and payment is not made within three days of receipt of that notice.[181] Prima facie, therefore, if one party fails to make a payment but this period has not elapsed, the other party would still be obliged to make a payment which fell due on its part within this grace period. This is not so because a potential event of default is defined as "any event which, with the giving of notice or the lapse of time or both, would constitute an Event of Default".[182] As a result, a non-payment the grace period on which has not yet expired, or, indeed, one in respect of which no notice has been given, is a potential event of default and therefore payment by the non-defaulting party is not due because the condition precedent to payment of that second sum set out in clause 2(a)(i) has not been fulfilled.

This can, however, have consequences which are not necessarily fair. For example, if there is only one outstanding transaction subject to a master agreement and that transaction can only lead to payments one way (e.g. because it is a cap or an option which is to be cash settled), the effect of this is that if the party which would otherwise receive payment becomes insolvent, then the

178. Section 2(b) of the Master Agreement allows a party to change its account for receiving payment on at least five local business days' notice to the other party unless the other party gives "timely notice of a reasonable objection" to the change. Local business days for these purposes are business days in both the place where the new account is located and at the recipient's address for notice (see section 14). What is timely is not clear, but it is presumably less than five business days; if it were longer than this, a recipient could give notice of change five business days before a payment became due and the payment would then be due at that account only for the obligation to be retrospectively varied by a later notice of objection. What constitutes a reasonable objection is not clear, but if, for example, the account was changed to a jurisdiction which gave the payer a less favourable tax treatment, that might well constitute a reasonable ground for objection.

179. Section 2(a)(ii) of the Master Agreement. It also provides that payment must be in the manner customary for payments in the required currency. This presumably refers to the means of interbank transfer commonly used for a particular currency. Delivery is also to be made in the manner customary for the relevant obligation, unless otherwise specified.

180. The term "condition precedent" is not necessarily an easy one, but ultimately it is a matter of construction of the contract as to what it means in the particular context: *Total Gas Marketing Ltd* v. *Arco British Ltd* [1998] Lloyd's Rep 209. In this context it probably means that a payment is not due whilst an event of default or potential event of default has occurred and is continuing. If the default is cured (e.g. by late payment, though probably not including interest as the condition precedent is only as to payments specified in each confirmation), the payment becomes due as soon as reasonably practicable after the default has been cured (since interest is only payable by a party which defaults in performance (section 2(e)), no interest will be payable by the non-defaulting party even though the payment will be made after the date originally intended by the parties). It is only designation of an early termination date under section 6(a) which means that the payment by the non-defaulting party never becomes due.

181. Section 5(a)(i) of the Master Agreement.

182. Section 14 of the Master Agreement.

payment to that party never becomes due. The countervailing position is where one party is in serious financial difficulties and the overall position on the transactions is in favour of the other party. In these circumstances, if a payment on one transaction becomes due to the potentially insolvent party before anything falls due to the other party, the other party is in the difficult position of having to make payment in the knowledge that it may never actually get paid itself, of not making payment putting itself in default (with potential cross default issues on other transactions), or relying on an event of default it knows it might have difficulty proving.[183]

An analogous situation is where two payments are due on the same day, one (say) to an account in London, the other to an account in New York. In order to pay for value in London on the due date, the payment must be made before it is necessary to make the New York payment because of the time difference. A party could therefore find itself making a payment only to find that the other party defaults on the same day. The Master Agreement offers no solution to this potential problem, but it can be resolved by providing for payment to an escrow agent, payment to be released on receipt of both payments or returned to the payer in the event of an early termination event being designated.[184]

7.3.12.1 Payments and options

A related issue concerns the appropriateness of the condition precedent in section 2(a)(iii) of the Master Agreement if the transaction is an option with cash settlement so that, after the option premium has been paid,[185] there will only be payment by one party rather than the possibility of payments by both parties as, for example, under a swap. If the only party which could receive a payment is in default under another transaction governed by the same master agreement, that default prevents the payment on the option settlement sum becoming due. If the non-defaulting party does not designate an early termination date, the payment will never become due or be taken into account in any calculation of the sum due on termination. Whether this is fair is open to question; if the parties agree that it

183. See p 238 below. ICOM and IFEMA seek to solve this latter problem by allowing the parties to designate "Adequate Assurance", i.e. allowing one party to suspend its payment obligations during the pendency of a reasonable request for adequate assurances of the ability to perform its obligations. The same problem can arise if an illegality has occurred with regard to one of the parties (see pp 248–252 below).

184. See p 11 of ISDA's *User's Guide to the 1992 ISDA Master Agreements.* As a matter of English law an escrow agent is, subject to provision to the contrary, not usually a trustee of payments made to him but only a debtor (see, for example, *Manzanilla Ltd* v. *Corton Property Investments Ltd* (unreported, 13 November 1996). Use of an escrow agent therefore entails credit risk on the escrow agent unless express provision is made constituting him a trustee.

185. Section 3.2 of ICOM offers a range of options to the non-defaulting party in the event of non-payment of an option premium. These include accepting late payment, and giving two days' notice of non-payment and then treating the option as void or non-payment as an event of default. Non-payment of a premium must be treated like any other payment default under ISDA's Master Agreement.

is not, it can be solved by, for example, the confirmation for the option providing that after payment of the option premium, section 2(a)(iii) of the Master Agreement does not apply to the further payment due under the option.

Section 5(a)(i) of the Master Agreement gives a grace period for payments of three local business days after service of notice of non-payment. ICOM and IFEMA both have grace periods of two business days. ICOM also provides in section 5.3 for automatic exercise of an option if the option is in the money by more than 1 per cent. ISDA's Master Agreement does not provide for the automatic exercise of options, nor does it give a grace period for the giving of notice to exercise an option. The issue can, therefore, arise as to whether it is possible to give late notice of exercise of an option. In most, perhaps all, cases this will not be possible. Whilst time is not in general of the essence of a contract,[186] where an option is concerned a time will generally be treated as being of the essence of the contract as far as exercise of the option is concerned.

Two bases seem to be advanced for the conclusion that time is of the essence for the exercise of an option. First, the nature of the subject matter of the contract or the surrounding circumstances of an option show that the parties intended time to be of the essence. This has been applied to options for the sale of shares on the basis that the shares are highly speculative and volatile in nature, and an option is a clog on the freedom to dispose of property. As a result, it is essential for the grantor of the option to know with certainty when the option has ended and therefore when the property can be disposed of elsewhere.[187] Secondly, because an option is a unilateral offer which requires acceptance in the manner set out. The only question to be asked is whether the event (i.e. notice) giving rise to the obligation has occurred, to which the answer must either be yes or no.[188]

Both these explanations, however, come down to a question of construction as to whether the intention should be imputed to the parties that strict compliance with the time provision of an option is necessary for an exercise to be effective. Where an option results in a longer-term contract—for example, a swap—it is potentially easy to see that time is fundamental. For example, the grantor of the option might want to hedge its position on the underlying transaction, or it might already have hedged the position and therefore want to know if it needs to maintain the hedge. The cost of hedging or releasing a hedge is likely to be volatile. The existence or not of a longer-term contract could also have regulatory capital implications. This is less compelling where an option is to be cash settled. The option will only result in a cash payment, and it is less obvious that it is vital for the grantor of the option to know this on the date of

186. *United Scientific Holdings* v. *Burnley BC* [1978] AC 904. The issue is whether breach of each term of the contract entitles the innocent party to treat that breach as a repudiation rather than whether time is somehow of the essence of the whole contract: *British & Commonwealth Holdings* v. *Quadrex* [1989] 1 QB 842, 856.

187. For example, *Hare* v. *Nicoll* [1966] 2 QB 130.

188. For example, *United Dominions Trust* v. *Eagle Aircraft Services* [1968] 1 WLR 74 and *United Scientific Holdings* v. *Burnley BC* [1978] AC 904, 928–929 and 945.

agreed settlement or after. The date could be seen as vital for fixing the price but not for the formalistic step of notifying the grantor of the option that the payment is required. Nevertheless, the courts have in general required strict compliance with time provisions where options are concerned, and the only safe assumption is that an option must be exercised on time or the right to do so will be lost.

7.3.12.2 *The netting of payments*

Section 2(c) has a very limited netting provision for payments—it only applies to sums payable on the same date, in the same currencies and in respect of the same transaction. The parties are given the express ability to net across transactions, though again only if the payments are in the same currency on the same date. In practice this might not be of great value, and ISDA does also offer a wider set-off provision that the parties can adopt and which is applicable in the event of default by one of the parties.[189] Section 9(c) provides, however, that the rights under the Master Agreement are not exclusive of any rights provided by law. It might, therefore, just be arguable that even if netting of, say, two payments due on the same day in different currencies is not expressly permitted by the Master Agreement, it is nevertheless permitted through the application of equitable set-off. This is, however, unlikely. Equitable set-off can be excluded by the agreement of the parties,[190] and it is likely that the express inclusion of a limited right of set-off, coupled with the nature of a transaction in which the parties are delivering different currencies, would impliedly exclude any right of set-off.

In any event, for equitable set-off to apply, it is in general necessary for the two payments to be made in the same transaction, or at least inseparably connected with the transaction giving rise to the claim, and for one to impeach the demand made for the other. Where two payments arise out of the same transaction, this is likely to be the case, but where they arise from different transactions this is more difficult, and it may be that equitable set-off would not be available in those circumstances.[191]

7.3.12.3 *Changing the branch of payment*

Section 10(b) of the Master Agreement provides that neither party may change the office, which includes the head office, through which payments are made or received without the prior written consent of the other party. If parties could change the office through which payments were made it could change the tax treatment of payments or receipts, and it could also affect the extent to which

189. *User's Guide to the 1992 ISDA Master Agreements*, p 56.

190. *Coca-Cola* v. *Finsat* [1998] QB 43.

191. See generally Derham, *Set-Off* (2nd edn), pp 40–120 and Wood, *English and International Set-off*, pp 103–142. Equitable set-off provides a defence to a claim. There could also be legal set-off, but it is not a defence, is more limited in its scope, and only takes effect on a court giving judgment.

payments can be netted. There is no requirement that consent can only be withheld on reasonable grounds, and there seems no basis for implying a requirement of that sort in a carefully drafted contract.

7.3.12.4 Foreign payment moratoria

The law which governs an agreement applies to the performance of the agreement, the consequences of breach, and the various ways of extinguishing obligations.[192] As a result, if a foreign law provides that, for example, payment may not be made under a particular class of transactions, that law will not excuse performance of the contract as a matter of English law.[193] There are two principal exceptions to this rule. First, if performance necessarily involves an illegal act in a foreign country, it will not be enforceable as a matter of English law.[194] This does not apply if one party has to equip itself for performance by an illegal act in another country; the question is whether performance of the contract necessarily involves that act.[195] So, for example, if a derivatives counterparty incorporated in country A is obliged to make a payment to an account in New York, the fact that country A may by legislation have barred payment does not excuse performance. If, however, the payment is to be made to an account in country A, then performance will be illegal in the place where it necessarily takes place and so will be unenforceable as a matter of English law.[196]

The second exception is limited to currency "exchange contracts". Article VIII(2)(b) of the International Monetary Fund Agreement[197] (the Bretton Woods Agreement) provides that:

> "Exchange contracts which involve the currency of any member and which are contrary to the exchange control regulations of any member maintained or imposed consistently with this agreement shall be unenforceable in the territories of any member."

This begs the question of what is an "exchange contract" for these purposes. The interpretation of this by the English courts has been "rather tortuous".[198] The courts started with a wide definition of "any contracts which in any way

192. Article 10(1) of Rome Convention, introduced into English law by the Contracts (Applicable Law) Act 1990 (see pp 206ff above).

193. *National Bank of Greece* v. *Metliss* [1958] AC 509.

194. *Ralli Bros* v. *Cia Naviera Sota y Aznar* [1920] 2 KB 287. A contract is also invalid "if the real object and intention of the parties necessitates them joining in an endeavour to perform some act which is illegal by the law of such other country notwithstanding the fact that there may be, in a certain event, alternative modes or places of performance which permit the contract to be performed legally" (*Foster* v. *Driscoll* [1929] KB 470, 521)—this applies whether or not the contract is governed by English law (*Soleimany* v. *Soleimany* [1998] 3 WLR 811).

195. *Libyan Arab Bank* v. *Bankers Trust* [1989] QB 728, 744.

196. If foreign legislation making performance illegal was made after the contract was entered into, this supervening illegality will generally operate to frustrate the contract: *Chitty on Contracts* (27th edn), pp 1109–1110.

197. In force in English law by virtue of section 6(2) of the International Monetary Fund Act 1979, preserving the Bretton Woods Agreements Order 1946 even though the Act under which it was made, the Bretton Woods Agreements Act 1945, was repealed.

198. *Ispahani* v. *Bank Melli Iran* [1998] Lloyd's Rep Bank 133, 137.

affect the country's exchange resources"[199] before recanting this in favour of "contracts to exchange the currency of one country for another".[200] Even this limited definition is not free from ambiguities. If currencies are actually exchanged, then a transaction is clearly caught. If, however, a forward currency exchange contract is to be cash settled, as with non-deliverable forwards, then no exchange will actually take place—all that will happen is that a payment will be made in one currency by reference to movements in the exchange rate. It is, however, likely that transactions of this sort would fall within the definition of exchange contracts. The distinction drawn in *Wilson, Smithett & Cope Ltd* v. *Terruzzi*, the Court of Appeal case which adopted the narrower definition, was between contracts for the sale or purchase of merchandise or commodities and speculative contracts capable of damaging the currency stability and other interests of the country: "I hope the courts will be able to look at the substance of contracts and not at the form. If contracts are not legitimate contracts for the sale or purchase of merchandise or commodities, but are instead . . . 'monetary transactions in disguise' . . . as a means of manipulating currencies, they should be caught by section 2(b)."[201] In view of this approach, it is likely that contracts not involving delivery would still be treated as exchange contracts if the sum payable was calculated by reference to exchange rates.

There is also a question as to whether Article VIII, section 2(b) of the Bretton Woods Agreement should be applied to exchange contracts only at the time they are entered into or whether exchange control introduced after a contract has been entered into but before it has been performed will render the contract unenforceable by virtue of Article VIII, section 2(b). The better view is probably that it is performance which matters rather than the time a contract is entered into.[202] If the date of entry of an exchange contract were the key date, exchange control regulations introduced in an emergency in order to staunch an outflow of funds would enjoy very limited international legal support because the regulations would have limited effect until all existing contracts had been performed.

An exchange contract within the terms of the Bretton Woods Agreement is, however, not illegal, only unenforceable in the courts in the same way as a contract of guarantee is unenforceable if there is no note or memorandum in writing to evidence it.[203] A sum due on an exchange contract could therefore probably be used for set-off purposes even though the courts could not entertain

199. *Sharif* v. *Azad* [1967] 1 QB 605, 613–614.

200. *Wilson, Smithett & Cope* v. *Terruzzi* [1976] QB 683, approved by the House of Lords in *United City Merchants* v. *Bank of Canada* [1983] 1 AC 168, 188. Mann, *The Legal Aspect of Money* (5th edn), pp 377–386, and Gold, "'Exchange Contracts', Exchange Control and the IMF Agreement: some Animadversions on *Wilson, Smithett & Cope Ltd* v. *Terruzzi*" (1984) 33 ICLQ 777 both condemn the limited definition adopted by the courts and favour the original, wider, definition.

201. [1976] QB 683, 714 (Lord Denning MR).

202. See Gold, *The Fund Agreement in the Courts*, pp 60–66. Mann, *The Legal Aspect of Money* (5th edn), p 372, takes the opposite view.

203. *United City Merchants* v. *Bank of Canada* [1983] 1 AC 168, 189.

an action based on an exchange contract within the terms of the Bretton Woods Agreement.[204]

7.3.13 Payments in foreign currencies

The basic position in English law is that if a foreign currency is payable in England,[205] the payer has a choice of whether to pay that foreign currency or the sterling equivalent on the date of payment.[206] It is, however, possible for the parties to agree, expressly or impliedly, that there should be no right to pay in sterling (or, indeed, an obligation to pay only in sterling).[207] If currency is payable under an English law contract in a country other than England, the manner in which it can be made is, it seems, a matter for the law of the place of payment but whether, or to what extent, the payment discharges the debtor is a matter of English law[208]—so, for example, the rate of exchange is a matter for English law.

Section 2(a)(i) requires payments to be made as specified in each confirmation. A confirmation could expressly state that payment must be in a particular currency and not in any other, but absent a term of that sort the basic position may arguably be excluded in any event by section 8(a). The first sentence of section 8(a) requires each payment to be made in the currency specified for that payment. This appears to require the payment to be in that currency and, impliedly, in no other. The position is, however, complicated by the rest of section 8(a). It goes on to provide that to the extent permitted by applicable law, payment in the incorrect currency will not discharge the obligation in question

204. Wood, *English and International Set-off*, pp 741–744.

205. At one time it was argued that a claim for non-payment of a foreign currency could only be a claim in damages (see, for example, *Marrache* v. *Ashton* [1943] AC 311, 318), though the view that this, like a claim for sterling, was a debt claim was also taken (see, for example, *Grauman* v. *Treitel* [1940] 2 All ER 188). It now seems clear that a claim for a foreign currency sum is a claim in debt if a claim in the same circumstances for sterling would be a claim in debt: *Barclays Bank International Ltd* v. *Levin* [1977] 1 QB 270, 282 (though see, for example, Derham, *Set-Off* (2nd edn), pp 273–283, who argues that foreign exchange contracts treat foreign currencies as commodities not resulting in money obligations and, accordingly, only leading to claims in damages for non-performance).

206. *Libyan Arab Foreign Bank* v. *Bankers Trust Co* [1989] QB 728, 764–766 (rejecting the argument that the change in the law in *Miliangos* v. *George Frank (Textiles) Ltd* [1976] AC 443 allowing the English court to give judgment in foreign currencies changed this rule even though, in *Heisler* v. *Anglo-Dal* [1954] 1 WLR 1273, 1278, Somervell LJ had referred to the rule as related to the then rule that only sterling could be claimed in a writ). It is not clear what the basis of this rule is: in, for example, *Anderson* v. *Equitable Assurance Society of the United States* (1926) 134 LT 557, it was referred to as a matter of construction but in *Libyan Arab Foreign Bank* Staughton J appeared to treat it as a matter of law, perhaps implication as a matter of law.

207. *Libyan Arab Foreign Bank* v. *Bankers Trust Co* [1989] QB 728, 766.

208. Dicey & Morris, *The Conflict of Laws* (12th edn), pp 1579–1582 and article 10(2) of the Rome Convention on the Law Applicable to Contractual Obligations (Schedule 1 to the Contracts (Applicable Law) Act 1990).

except to the extent that tender results in the actual[209] receipt of the full amount in the correct currency by the payee,[210] acting in a reasonable manner and in good faith in converting the currency. This seems to imply that the payer can pay in a currency other than that specified, but the effect of that payment will depend upon its conversion into the correct currency. It does not expressly give the payee the right to reject a payment in the incorrect currency and, given the words providing that payment in the wrong currency will discharge the obligation if on conversion it yields a sufficient sum, it is unlikely that there is any such right. This probably reflects the reality that, if a payment is made in the incorrect currency, few will be inclined to send it back as, absent simple mistake, a payment in the wrong currency might indicate problems within the payer.[211]

If a payment is made in the wrong currency it is probably a breach of contract, but it is not a payment which the recipient is entitled to reject. Instead, the recipient must mitigate the position in the manner set out in the contract, namely by converting the currency into that in which the payment should have been made. If, on conversion, it yields a shortfall in the correct currency, there is a separate obligation on the payer to make good that shortfall in the correct currency; but if there is a surplus on conversion, there is an obligation on the payee to refund it promptly.[212]

7.3.13.1 Judgments in foreign currencies

The English court has the power to give judgments in currencies other than sterling.[213] Where a debt is concerned, a judgment will usually be given in the currency of payment but, if the payee has suffered a currency loss as a result of

209. Despite the use of the word "actual" which, on its own, would imply that the recipient was actually obliged to convert the sum received, section 8(d) makes it clear that actual conversion is not necessary. It provides that it is enough for a party to demonstrate that it would have suffered a loss had an actual conversion taken place. The calculation of loss can, therefore, be theoretical. "Actual" may indicate the need to show that it is possible to convert.

210. The Master Agreement actually provides that payment must result in receipt of the full amount of "all amounts payable in respect of this Agreement". Since "this Agreement" is the Master Agreement and all confirmations, this might imply that payment in the wrong currency brings forward the obligation to pay other sums which might be payable under the agreement even if not yet due. However, in context "payable" probably means due and payable, and probably only refers to the actual payment which has been made in the wrong currency.

211. IFEMA is generally to the same effect as ISDA's Master Agreement. Section 3.1 requires delivery of the amount of the relevant currency, but section 8.1 provides a currency indemnity in the event of payment in the wrong currency.

212. Section 8(a) could be regarded as a form of liquidated damages clause, the payee being obliged to mitigate its loss by conversion, actual or theoretical, and the payer being obliged to make good any loss resulting from that conversion. There can be little doubt that this would not be regarded as a penalty clause.

213. In *Miliangos* v. *George Frank (Textiles) Ltd* [1976] AC 443, the House of Lords overruled earlier authority and took the power to give judgments in foreign currencies on contracts governed by a foreign law where the money of account and payment were of that country or of another country, not the UK. The House of Lords left open other cases, but the courts quickly expanded this to cover contracts governed by English law (e.g. *Barclays Bank International Ltd* v. *Levin* [1977] 1 QB 270), and damages for breach of contract and tort (e.g. *The Despina R* [1979] AC 685). The test

late payment, additional damages can be recovered for that loss as long as it was reasonably in the contemplation of the parties at the time the contract was made.[214] The fact that judgment can be given in currencies other than sterling does not, however, necessarily avoid the need to convert the judgment into sterling. If enforcement measures are taken in England, the judgment must be converted into sterling at the date the court authorises enforcement of the judgment in terms of sterling,[215] i.e. authorises the seizure of assets belonging to the judgment debtor. Since there will inevitably be some delay before the enforcement actually takes place, this could lead to a currency loss or gain according to the movement of currencies in the intervening period.

Section 8(b) of the Master Agreement arguably seeks to address this possible gain or loss on enforcement by providing that if any judgment or order for payment of any sum due under the agreement is expressed in a currency other than the one in which payment was due, on recovery of that sum the recipient will convert it into the correct currency[216] and will either be entitled to a further payment sufficient to make up any shortfall or be obliged to refund any excess. As a matter of construction this probably does not apply to the situation where enforcement of a judgment is authorised, because it is only stated to apply where a judgment or order is given for an amount owing under the agreement. Where enforcement is authorised, any order will not be for the sum owing under the agreement but rather for a sum owing on the judgment, with which the claim on the agreement will have merged.[217]

If, however, section 8(b) of the Master Agreement does apply to a situation where enforcement of a judgment is authorised, there is uncertainty as to whether it would be effective. There are no authorities on the point but, if effective, it would allow the parties to contract out of the effect, in part at least,

for the currency of damages for breach of an English law contract is (1) whether the contract shows an agreed currency of account and payment such that the parties have accepted that for all transactions under the contract, it would be proper to give damages in that currency; (2) if not, compensation should be given in the currency which most truly expresses the loss (*The Despina R* [1979] AC 685, 700–701). Since the Master Agreement provides that payment should be made in a currency and any shortfall on conversion should be made in that same currency, this might well lead to damages for breach of contract being awarded in the currency in which payment should have been made (e.g. *Bunge* v. *Belcan* [1985] 3 All ER 378).

214. *President of India* v. *Lips Maritime Corp* [1988] AC 395. Section 9(d) of the Master Agreement provides that remedies are cumulative and not exclusive of any remedies provided at law.

215. *Miliangos* v. *George Frank (Textiles) Ltd* [1976] AC 443, 468–469. Though not expressly dealt with, the reference to "enforcement of the judgment in terms of sterling" appears to imply that if enforcement measures are taken against, for example, an account in the currency of the judgment, no question of conversion arises.

216. Section 8(b) of the Master Agreement provides that actual conversion is not required; the recipient only has to demonstrate what would have happened if conversion had been made. The conversion criteria in section 8(b) differ from those in section 8(a) as section 8(b) expressly includes in the exchange rate any premiums and costs of exchange, matters not mentioned in section 8(a).

217. Section 8(b)(iii) does apply the same provision where a judgment or order is made in respect of a judgment or order of another court for the payment of a sum owing in respect of the agreement. This, however, does not apply as the enforcement order will usually be made by the same court, but in any event it is probably intended to apply to the enforcement in one jurisdiction of a judgment given in another.

of a court order by obliging the judgment creditor to repay part of the sum to which he was entitled under the court order or by obliging the judgment debtor to pay sums over and above what he was obliged to pay by the court order. To seek to avoid the risk that these obligations would be treated as having merged with the judgment debt, section 8(c) of the Master Agreement states that they are separate indemnities. It may be, however, that they are incapable of being separate indemnities as they are too intimately connected with the sum claimed under the agreement. It could also be that an indemnity of this sort is contrary to public policy since it might create potentially interminable litigation, which would be the case if, say, sterling were to be on a permanent downward path. Similarly, it could be that clauses of this sort are simply contrary to public policy by allowing a judgment to be reopened even though there may not strictly be any *res judicata* or issue estoppel.[218] That said, however, where interest payable after judgment is concerned, the courts have been prepared to allow a judgment creditor to recover more than the statutory rate payable on a judgment as long as the obligation to pay that interest was an independent obligation which did not merge with the judgment.[219]

7.3.14 Interest payable on default

The interest structure under the Master Agreement is complex, and it is therefore useful to start with an overview of how it fits together before going on to the issues it raises. The structure is as follows:

1. If there is a payment default but no early termination date is designated[220] under section 6(a), interest is payable under section 2(e). This requires interest to be compounded daily and to be paid (before as well as after judgment) on demand at the default rate, i.e. the cost to the payee (without proof of actual cost and as certified by it) if it were to fund the relevant amount plus 1 per cent.
2. If an early termination date is designated under section 6(e), section 6(c)(ii) provides that no further payments will be required to be made under sections 2(a)(i) or 2(e). As a result, if interest has not actually been paid prior to designation of an early termination date, the obligation to make that payment disappears and is replaced by the

218. There is unlikely to be any issue estoppel or *res judicata* within the doctrine espoused in *Henderson* v. *Henderson* (1843) 3 Hare 100, 115 as that requires either that the court has decided a point or that it was one which could have been raised in the original litigation but was not raised (see, for example, *Talbot* v. *Berkshire County Council* [1994] QB 290, 296). Since it will not be known whether any sum is payable until after a judgment has been given and enforced, neither the court can decide it (except, perhaps, by granting or otherwise a declaration as to the enforceability of the provision) nor can it be raised in the action.

219. See pp 230–232 below. As mentioned below, the cases on interest payable after judgment are not satisfactory.

220. Or an early termination date occurs because the parties have specified automatic early termination in the Schedule to the Master Agreement.

obligation referred to in 3(b) below (if this were not so there would be double payment of interest).

3. If an early termination date is designated (which, under section 6(a) must be by not more than 20 days notice to the defaulting party), the non-defaulting party must make the calculations required by section 6(d). On the assumption that the parties do not designate another method in the schedule to the master agreement, the method used will be "Second Method and Market Quotation" under section 6(e). This requires the defaulting party to pay the non-defaulting party the sum of the settlement amount and the termination currency equivalent of the unpaid amounts, less the termination currency equivalent of unpaid amounts due to the defaulting party.
   (a) The settlement amount is the termination currency equivalent of the market quotations (or loss if market quotations cannot be determined) for each transaction which is terminated; and market quotations are the sums that would have the effect of preserving for the non-defaulting party the economic equivalent of any payment that would, but for the occurrence of the relevant early termination date, have been required after that date[221] (unpaid amounts, i.e. sums due but unpaid before the early termination date, are ignored for this purpose). The termination currency equivalent is the currency in which payment is required to be made, sums in other currencies being converted into it as at the relevant early termination date.
   (b) Unpaid amounts are defined as amounts that became payable prior to the early termination date (or would have become due but for section 2(a)(iii)[222]) including interest (both before and after judgment) at the applicable rate, compounded daily, from the date payment was required to the early termination date. The applicable rate is, in the case of sums due from the defaulting party, the default rate (see 1 above) and, in the case of the non-defaulting party, the non-default rate, i.e. the rate equal to the cost (without proof or evidence of actual cost) to the non-defaulting party (as certified by it) if it were to fund the relevant amount.

   If loss, rather than market quotation, is chosen, there is no express right to interest prior to the early termination date. Loss is, however, defined as the amount the innocent party reasonably determines in

221. The Master Agreement does not state expressly the date upon which market quotations must be obtained, but it seems clear that it is the early termination date (for example, it relates to payments after the early termination date and the currency conversion takes place as at the early termination date).

222. As a result, although payments by the non-defaulting party do not become due as a result of section 2(a)(iii), they are taken into account in calculating the settlement amount (provided that two-way payments are adopted).

good faith to be its total losses and costs as of the early termination date. If payment fell due before the early termination date, there is no reason why the losses determined cannot include interest on those payments.

4. Once the non-defaulting party has made the calculations required by section 6(d)(i), payment is due under section 6(d)(ii) two local business days after notice of the sum payable is received, together with interest at the applicable rate, compounded daily, from the early termination date to the date of payment.

In summary, therefore, if no early termination date is designated or occurs, interest is due under section 2(a)(iii); but if an early termination date is designated or occurs, that section ceases to be relevant and interest is due by virtue of the definition of unpaid amounts and section 6(d)(ii).

The provisions regarding interest raise three main legal issues: first, are the provisions enforceable or are they void as a penalty; secondly, can a contract determine the interest payable after a judgment as well as before it; and, thirdly, what is the effect of the certification provisions?[223]

7.3.14.1 *Interest and penalties*

A penalty clause is not void but it will not be enforced beyond the sum which represents the actual loss to the party seeking payment: there is therefore no advantage in suing on a penalty clause.[224] The classic statement as to when a contractual term is a penalty clause is by Lord Dunedin in *Dunlop Pneumatic Tyre Co* v. *New Garage and Motor Co*, where he said:

> "(1) Though the parties to a contract who use the words 'penalty' or 'liquidated damages' may prima facie be supposed to mean what they say, yet the expression used is not conclusive.[225] The court must find out whether the payment stipulated is in truth a penalty or liquidated damages ...
>
> (2) The essence of a penalty is a payment of money stipulated *in terrorem* of the offending party; the essence of liquidated damages is a genuine pre-estimate of damage.
>
> (3) The question whether a sum stipulated is a penalty or liquidated damages is a question of construction[226] to be decided upon the terms and inherent

223. The interest provisions in the Master Agreement are similar to those in BBAIRS in that BBAIRS too provides for interest to be certified by the payee as 1 per cent above the effective cost of funding to it of the relevant sum (clause G3).

224. *Jobson* v. *Johnson* [1989] 1 WLR 1026.

225. As a result, section 6(e)(iv) of the Master Agreement, which provides that the market quotation method of calculating loss is a reasonable pre-estimate of loss and not a penalty, is not conclusive, either for or against, the interest being a penalty.

226. As such, it is a matter of law rather than fact.

circumstances of each particular contract, judged as at the time of the making of the contract, not as of the time of breach[227] ...

(4) To assist this task of construction various tests have been suggested which, if applicable to the case under consideration, may prove helpful or even conclusive. Such are:

(a) It will be held to be a penalty if the sum stipulated for is extravagant and unconscionable in amount in comparison with the greatest loss which could conceivably be proved to have followed from the breach.

(b) It will be held to be a penalty if the breach consists only in not paying a sum of money, and the sum stipulated is a greater sum than the sum which ought to have been paid ...

(c) There is a presumption (but no more) that it is a penalty when 'a single lump sum is made payable by way of compensation, on the occurrence of one or more or all of several events, some of which may occasion serious and others but trifling damage.'

On the other hand:

(d) It is no obstacle to the sum stipulated being a genuine pre-estimate of damage, that the consequences of the breach are such as to make precise pre-estimation almost an impossibility. On the contrary, that is just the situation when it is probable that pre-estimated damage was the true bargain between the parties."[228]

As the power to strike down a penalty clause is a blatant interference with freedom of contract, it is designed for the sole purpose of relief against oppression, and has no place where there is no oppression.[229] The attitude to penalty clauses, at least between commercial counterparties, is, if anything, softening. For example, although whether a clause is a penalty clause has to be judged at the outset of a contract, fanciful examples of when it could operate in a penal manner are not taken into account:

"Whatever the degree of care exercised by the draftsman it will still be almost inevitable that an ingenious argument can be developed for saying that in a particular hypothetical situation a substantially higher sum will be recovered than would be recoverable if the plaintiff were required to prove his actual loss in that situation. Such a result would undermine the whole purpose to parties to a contract being able to agree beforehand what damages are to be recoverable in the event of a breach of contract. This would not be in the interest of either of the parties to the contract since it is to their advantage that they should be able to know with a reasonable degree of certainty the extent of their liability and risks ...

... the court should not adopt an approach to provisions as to liquidated damages which could ... defeat their purpose.

Except possibly in the case of situations where one of the parties to the contract is able

227. "The fact that the issue is to be determined objectively, judged at the date the contract was made, does not mean what actually happens subsequently is irrelevant. On the contrary, it can provide valuable evidence as to what could reasonably be expected to be the loss at the time the contract was made. Likewise, the fact that two parties who should be well capable of protecting their commercial interests agreed the allegedly penal provisions suggests that the formula for calculating liquidated damages is unlikely to be oppressive" (*Philips Hong Kong* v. *Attorney-General of Hong Kong* (1993) 61 BLR 41, 59–60).

228. [1915] AC 79, 86–88.

229. *Elsey* v. *JG Collins Insurance Agencies* (1978) 83 DLR (3d) 1, 15, approved by the Privy Council in *Philips Hong Kong* v. *Attorney-General of Hong Kong* (1993) 61 BLR 41, 58.

to dominate the other as to the choice of the terms of the contract, it will normally be insufficient to establish that a provision is objectively penal to identify situations where the application of the provision could result in a larger sum being recovered by the injured party than his actual loss ... as long as the sum payable in the event of non-compliance with the contract is not extravagant, having regard to the range of losses that it could reasonably be anticipated it would have to cover at the time the contract was made, it can still be a genuine pre-estimate of the loss that would be suffered and so a perfectly valid liquidated damages provision. The use in argument of unlikely illustrations should therefore not assist a party to defeat a provision as to liquidated damages."[230]

The approach of the Privy Council in this case was very much to limit the application of the law on penalty clauses in commercial situations, not least in order to provide the parties with certainty and to allow them to assess the risks they run from a particular transaction.

There can be no objection to interest as compensation for the late payment of money,[231] but the features of interest payments under the Master Agreement are: the interest is fixed by reference to the non-defaulting party's cost of funds[232] rather than an absolute rate (e.g. LIBOR); there is a margin of 1 per cent above this cost of funds; the rate payable by a non-defaulting party is lower in that it is fixed again by reference to that party's cost of funds but without the margin; and interest is compounded daily.[233] These features are, however, unlikely to make the interest provisions a penalty.

The closest case on the point is *Lordsvale Finance* v. *Bank of Zambia*[234] in which one party sought to recover default interest payable under the (fairly typical) provisions of a loan agreement. Before a default, interest on the loan was payable at LIBOR plus a margin; after default it was payable at the payee's cost of funds plus the margin plus 1 per cent, interest periods (and therefore compounding) to be fixed by the agent. Colman J took the view that the change of basis from LIBOR to cost of funds was to recompense the lender for being deprived of unpaid funds in future.[235] He considered that if the additional 1 per cent had been applied retrospectively it would have been a penalty, but he regarded a modest prospective increase in the interest rate as being no more than a reflection that a borrower in default is a less good credit risk than one who pays on time.[236]

230. *Philips Hong Kong* v. *Attorney-General of Hong Kong* (1993) 61 BLR 41, 54 and 58–59.

231. "... equity adopted the attitude in relation to penalty clauses that non-payment of money is adequately compensated by late payment with interest": *Jobson* v. *Johnson* [1989] 1 WLR 1026, 1041.

232. To emphasise that the interest is liquidated damages rather than actual loss, the definitions of the default rate and the non-default rate provide that they are a rate equal to the cost of funding, but without proof or evidence of any actual cost. The references to "a" rate, rather than the rate, and the absence of need for proof, show that they are theoretical rates rather than actual rates.

233. ICOM and IFEMA both provided for interest to be calculated by reference to overnight LIBOR and, to the extent permitted by law, to be compounded daily: sections 8.5 and 5.4 respectively.

234. [1996] QB 752.

235. [1996] QB 752, 761.

236. [1996] QB 752, 763.

There are clearly differences between the position under a loan agreement and under a derivatives transaction. For example, loan agreements traditionally work on the assumption that the lenders will borrow in the interbank markets the sums required for the loan; the lender's actual cost of funds is therefore relevant to the loss it suffers. Derivatives, at least most derivatives, do not necessarily work in the same way, and the actual loss might be the interest that could have been obtained on the funds rather than the cost of obtaining those funds from elsewhere.[237] The cost of funds approach applies, however, to all derivatives subject to the Master Agreement whether or not it is appropriate to the particular transaction. Similarly, on a loan the initial, pre-default, margin reflects the credit risk attached to the borrower, and increasing it on default is the obvious step. In a derivatives transaction, the credit risk is reflected in the terms offered, but putting a margin on the interest rate does not have the same symmetry.

Nevertheless, it is still hard to characterise an interest rate of 1 per cent above cost of funds as being to intimidate a party into complying with its contractual obligations. The interest rate the non-defaulting party has to pay is a reasonable estimate of the loss it suffers, even if it is not exact in each case. The 1 per cent increase of that rate reflects the credit risk on what has become in effect a forced loan and also the additional administration and other work involved in handling a derivatives transaction in default as opposed to one which is performing. Daily compounding also reflects the fact that the party in default can pay the sums due at any time, and therefore fixing a longer interest period is inappropriate.

7.3.14.2 Interest after judgment

Section 17 of the Judgments Act 1838 provides that:

> "Every judgment debt shall carry interest at the rate of [8%][238] from the time of entering up the judgment... until the same shall be satisfied, and such interest may be levied under a writ of execution on such judgment."

In addition, if a judgment is obtained upon a contractual debt, the contractual debt is merged in the judgment, and the only sum payable is the sum due on the judgment.[239] The issue is whether it is possible in effect to contract out of section 17 and of the consequences of the doctrine of merger. It appears that it is possible

237. This would be particularly so if the non-defaulting party was insolvent. The cost of funds to that party would in those circumstances be high but its loss would be the interest it could have earned because it would presumably not be looking to use the income in its business but rather to maintain its funds to pay creditors.

238. The rate of interest payable on judgments can be varied by the Lord Chancellor under section 44(1) of the Administration of Justice Act 1970. The rate applicable is the rate at the time the judgment was given, and does not change even if orders are made under that section. The rate only applies to judgments in sterling; under section 44A of the Administration of Justice Act 1970, inserted by section 1 of the Private International Law (Miscellaneous Provisions) Act 1995, the court has a discretion in respect of judgments in other currencies.

239. For example, *Ex p Fewings, In re Sneyd* (1883) 25 Ch D 338, 349–350, 353 and 355.

to do this, but whether it has been successfully achieved is a matter of construction of the relevant contract. There must be doubt as to whether the Master Agreement has achieved this aim.

The classic statement of the position in this area is by Fry LJ in *Ex p Fewings, In re Sneyd*, where he said that:

> "The . . . question is simply one of construction. When there is a covenant for the payment of a principal sum, and a judgment has been obtained upon the covenant for that sum, it is plain that the covenant is merged in the judgment, and, if there is a covenant to pay interest which is merely incidental to the covenant to pay the principal debt, that covenant is also merged in a judgment on the covenant to pay the principal debt. Of course a covenant to pay interest may be so expressed as not to merge in a judgment for the principal; for instance, if it was a covenant to pay interest so long as any part of the principal should remain due either on the covenant or on a judgment."[240]

The issue is, therefore, whether the obligation to pay interest in the Master Agreement is a separate and independent covenant, in which case it will not be merged in the judgment and a separate action can be started to recover additional interest after payment of the judgment debt, or whether it is merely incidental to the obligation to pay the principal, in which case it will not be possible to pursue interest after judgment on the principal.

Indications in the Master Agreement that the obligation to pay interest is a separate and independent obligation are confined to the references in sections 2(e) and 6(d)(ii) to interest being payable "before as well as after judgment".[241] Against this, the obligation to pay interest appears to be incidental to the principal obligation, and there is no equivalent for interest payments to section 8(c), which expressly provides that the obligation to pay additional sums if currency conversion leaves a shortfall is a separate and independent obligation. The best that can be said in these circumstances is that it is uncertain as to whether interest at the rate provided by the Master Agreement is recoverable after a judgment has been given, though on balance the reference to interest being due after judgment may be enough to create an independent obligation.

The law on this area is also unsatisfactory in that there remain unanswered questions. The cases concern attempts to recover contractual interest at a higher rate than the statutory rate, but in recent times the statutory rate has for long

240. (1883) 25 Ch D 338, 355. This approach was approved, for example, in *Economic Life Assurance Society* v. *Usborne* [1902] AC 147. In *London Borough of Ealing* v. *El Isaac* [1980] 2 All ER 549, 551 Templeman LJ expressed a degree of dissatisfaction with this approach on the curious ground that the merger doctrine "may be due to the fact that, in former ages, high interest rates marked the progress of the individual on the path to perdition; whereas in this day and age, high interest rates mark the road towards national prosperity."

241. The wording of these two sections is not identical, but it is hard to believe that any difference was intended: section 2(e) concerns interest only, and does not include an obligation to pay the principal sum (that is in section 2(a)(i)), whilst section 6(d)(ii) does contain the covenant to pay the principal together with interest.

periods been significantly above any contractual rate.[242] In these circumstances, it remains unclear whether the judgment debtor can take advantage of a lower contractual rate. There are suggestions that it is possible to contract out of statutory interest,[243] but these are not clear and do not address the point directly.

7.3.14.3 Certification

The provisions in the Master Agreement on interest provide that both the default rate and the non-default rate are a rate equal to the cost to the non-defaulting party of funding the relevant amount (plus 1 per cent in the case of the default rate), but without proof or evidence of any actual cost.[244] This latter element is merely a reflection of the fact that the interest payable is in the form of liquidated damages rather than any actual loss suffered by the non-defaulting party through actually having to fund the sums outstanding. The definitions go on, however, to provide that the rates are to be as certified by the non-defaulting party. As a matter of construction of the Master Agreement, this certification is unlikely to be conclusive; rather, it is a means of the non-defaulting party stating the rate he claims, but with additional solemnity over a notice making a claim. In a notice, the non-defaulting party might be tempted to put the highest rate it considers that it can reasonably defend, but the requirement of certification should induce greater consideration as to the actual rate, especially as the rate is something which may be hard for the defaulting party to check.[245] The non-defaulting party can, therefore, challenge the certification in the courts.[246]

If, however, the certification were to be construed as intended to be final and binding, the issue arises whether, as a matter of law, this is possible. In general it is not possible wholly to oust the jurisdiction of the courts,[247] but quite what the parties can do is not entirely clear. At one time it was thought that a "domestic

242. The statutory rate is simple interest, whereas the rate under the Master Agreement is compounded daily. Contractual interest will, therefore, eventually overtake statutory interest if the judgment debt is unpaid for a sufficient period.

243. For example, *Caudery* v. *Finnerty* (1892) 66 LT 684 in which judgment by consent was entered for a certain sum. The sum was to be paid by instalments, and execution was not to be issued as long as the instalments were kept up to date. After all instalments had been paid punctually, the judgment creditor sought to recover statutory interest. The court refused, brushing aside an argument that there was a statutory right to interest.

244. Excluding the other party from producing evidence could also be an exclusion clause falling within the scope of the Unfair Contract Terms Act 1977 according to Bridge LJ in *Howard Marine and Dredging Co Ltd* v. *A Ogden & Sons (Excavations) Ltd* [1978] 1 QB 574, 599. As to the Unfair Contract Terms Act 1977, see Chapter 8 below.

245. The wording contrasts with section 6(d)(i), which states that the records of a party obtaining quotations from third parties are to be conclusive evidence of the existence and accuracy of such quotation.

246. See the approach to construction at first instance in *The Glacier Bay* [1995] 1 Lloyd's Rep 560.

247. For example, *In re Wynn* [1952] 1 Ch 271 and *The Glacier Bay* [1996] 1 Lloyd's Rep 370, 377.

tribunal" could, by contract, be made the final arbiter of an issue of fact but not of law,[248] but it now appears that an expert can be appointed to determine issues between the parties and, as long as he answers the right question, his determination will be binding even if it is necessary for the expert to determine issues of law.[249]

This is, however, different from one of the parties being given the power to make a binding determination under the contract. In *The Glacier Bay*,[250] one of the parties was given the power to determine certain issues of fact. The Court of Appeal considered this "unusual", but did not strike it down. They emphasised the unusual nature of the agreement in question in that case—a company administering a compensation fund where the claimant would in most, perhaps all, cases be a member of the company and where the board of directors was there to hold the balance between the members. They accepted that determinations of the company with regard to matters of fact were to be final and binding for all purposes on matters of fact, "subject of course to any question of unfairness, bad faith or perversity".[251]

Since the rate of interest at which the non-defaulting party can borrow is a question of fact, it may, therefore, be that there is no fundamental obstacle to one party being given the right to decide finally an issue. The issue cannot, however, be said to be free from doubt, but it is clear that the courts are becoming more liberal in this area. For example, one argument raised in argument but not dealt with in the judgment is repugnancy.[252] If one party is obliged to pay interest at a rate determined in accordance with certain criteria, but the rate is to be finally determined by one of the parties, what is the position if that party determines a rate that is not in accordance with those criteria? The two provisions are inconsistent in that the right to pay (or receive) interest in accordance with the contract can be overridden by the party's determination other than in accordance with the selected criteria. (The position might be different if the rate of interest depended on the opinion of one of the parties; in that case the question for the courts is whether the party genuinely holds the relevant opinion.)

248. *Lee* v. *The Showmen's Guild of Great Britain* [1952] 2 QB 329, 342.

249. *Nikko Hotels (UK) Ltd* v. *MEPC* [1991] 2 EGLR 103 (but see the first instance decision in *The Glacier Bay* [1995] 1 Lloyd's Rep 560, 567).

250. [1996] 1 Lloyd's Rep 370.

251. [1996] 1 Lloyd's Rep 370, 379, followed in *Brown* v. *GIO Insurance Ltd* [1998] Lloyd's Rep IR 201.

252. This argument was addressed at first instance where Waller J said that "if a party has been granted contractual rights in one portion of the contract on fulfilment of certain conditions, the Court will not allow a term to stand which precludes the party from enforcing the right by action in the Court. Such a term would be repugnant giving the right by one hand and taking it away with the other and/or as an ouster of the jurisdiction of the courts and unenforceable for that reason" ([1995] 1 Lloyd's Rep 560, 566). In *Brown* v. *GIO Insurance Ltd* [1998] Lloyd's Rep IR 201, the Court of Appeal re-affirmed this approach, but indicated that as long as a party was not given the right to determine liability and the (implied) term discussed below was present, there was no objection to a party deciding an issue of fact or law.

But in any event, even if the Master Agreement does give one party the right to determine what the rate of interest is, that right will be restricted by implied terms. As mentioned above, in *The Glacier Bay*, the Court of Appeal thought the right of the company to make determinations was limited by obligations to act fairly, in good faith and without perversity.[253] Although in theory this is not the same as allowing the defaulting party to challenge the rate certified by the non-defaulting party, in practice it may not be so very different. If the defaulting party can demonstrate that the rate certified by the non-defaulting party is not the rate at which it could actually have obtained funds, or at least that it differs by more than an insignificant margin, it may be hard for the non-defaulting party to withstand an allegation that it has acted unfairly, in bad faith or perversely.[254] Merely being wrong is, however, not enough to make a decision unreasonable or unfair.

7.3.15 Events of default

The events of default in any financial agreement are possibly the most important part of that agreement. They determine whether and when a party is entitled to bring the contract to an end, a matter which can be vital. If, for example, a transaction is hedged or is a hedge, uncertainty as to whether the transaction will be performed potentially exposes the party to market risk which it was seeking to avoid, and makes it difficult to know whether to find replacement arrangements for fear of taking on an additional position if the transaction is in fact performed. The function of events of default is to give the parties certainty or the ability to create certainty by serving appropriate notices.

ISDA's Master Agreement has eight categories of events of default which will be discussed before turning to the means of calling an event of default and the consequences of doing so. The Master Agreement requires a series of notices in order to operate its provisions. In many circumstances the parties will be well aware of the facts set out in a notice before it is given. This does not, however, excuse a party from giving that notice. The giving of notice is, in the main, a

253. [1996] 1 Lloyd's Rep 370, 378–379; see also *Brown* v. *GIO Insurance Ltd* [1998] Lloyd's Rep IR 201. This is similar to the approach of the courts to certification powers in building contracts where there will usually be an obligation to act "honestly, fairly and reasonably" (e.g. *Balfour Beatty* v. *Docklands Light Railway*, unreported, 3 April 1996). The reference to fairness is probably the counterpart to Denning LJ's comment in *Lee* v. *The Showmen's Guild of Great Britain* [1952] 2 QB 329, 342 that a "domestic tribunal" must observe the principles of natural justice.

254. *Brown* v. *GIO Insurance Ltd* [1998] Lloyd's Rep IR 201. Chadwick LJ in particular treated the issue in the same way as expert determination (see pp 289–291 below): if the party answers the right question in the wrong way, the decision is still binding. It may also be arguable that, in circumstances where the Unfair Contract Terms Act 1977 applies (as to which, see Chapter 8), a clause allowing one party to certify any matter is an exclusion clause as it excludes or restricts rules of evidence or procedure, and a clause that does this is an exclusion clause for the purposes of the Act: section 13(1)(c).

precondition to the right to terminate the agreement in accordance with its terms, and it has a clear commercial purpose in providing certainty to the parties as to what each party intends so that each can take an informed decision as to what course of action to pursue.[255]

7.3.15.1 *Failure to pay or make delivery*

The failure to pay or make delivery when due under section 2(a)(i) or 2(e) is a breach of contract but is not an event of default without more. The innocent can sue for the sum due but it cannot without further steps rely on a non-payment as an event of default.[256] To create an event of default as a result of a non-payment or non-delivery, section 5(a)(i) requires that a notice[257] must be served[258] stating that there has been a failure to pay or deliver, and that failure must be remedied within three local business days. If there is a late payment, interest will also be due on demand,[259] and that too can form the basis of a notice requiring remedy within three days, failing which it will be an event of default.

If one party makes delivery, but the other refuses to accept delivery or to make payment, it is not entirely clear whether that refusal constitutes a failure to pay within section 5(a)(i) or a breach of the agreement within section 5(a)(ii) (see below). The difference is that a failure to pay only requires three days' notice to constitute an event of default, but other breaches require 30 days. It seems likely, however, that this would constitute a failure to pay within section 5(a)(i) even if the refusal to accept delivery also constituted another breach falling within section 5(a)(ii).

7.3.15.2 *Other defaults*

If one party fails to comply with or to perform any obligations under the terms of the agreement other than certain tax matters and giving notice of an event of

255. *Nuova Safim* v. *Sakura* [1998] Lloyd's Rep Bank 142, 157, and *Senate Electrical Wholesalers Ltd* v. *Alcatel Submarine Networks Ltd* (unreported, 22 June 1998). There are some cases which suggest that "the law never compels a person to do that which is useless and unnecessary" (*Barrett Bros (Taxis) Ltd* v. *Davies Lickiss* [1966] 1 WLR 1334, 1339), such as *The Mozart* [1985] 1 Lloyd's Rep 239 and *Vallo Giovani* v. *Gebro van Weelde* [1985] 1 Lloyd's Rep 563. In *Senate Electrical Wholesalers* it was treated as a matter of construction as to whether or not it is futile to require strict compliance and the commercial purpose to be served by notice. As was recognised in *Nuova Safim* with regard to ISDA's Master Agreement (though in that case the 1987 version), there is a clear commercial purpose in, indeed a need for, strict compliance where derivatives are concerned.

256. Section 9(d) of the Master Agreement provides that the rights under the Agreement are not exclusive of rights provided by the law. This is discussed further at pp 247–248 below.

257. A notice must be construed objectively as a reasonable recipient would have understood it in the context of the surrounding circumstances: *Mannai Investment Co Ltd* v. *Eagle Star Life Assurance* [1997] AC 749, 767–768; *Nuova Safim* v. *The Sakura Bank Ltd* [1998] Lloyd's Rep Bank 142, 157. In practice, it is prudent to make reference to section 5(a)(i) of the Master Agreement and the fact that, unless remedied within three local business days, it will constitute an event of default.

258. Service must be in accordance with section 12(a) which, unless varied by the Schedule, prohibits service by fax: see pp 205–206 above.

259. See p 225 above.

default, section 5(a)(ii) requires an even longer notice period, 30 days, before it becomes an event of default.

7.3.15.3 Credit support

A failure on the part of a credit support provider to comply with its obligations is an event of default under section 5(a)(iii), subject to any grace period, as is the expiration of a credit support document other than in accordance with its terms. Section 5(a)(iii)(3) also provides that any disaffirmation, repudiation or rejection of the credit support documentation is also an event of default under the Master Agreement. This does depend upon the credit support document coming into existence as a binding obligation; if it does not, it is hard to see how stating that fact, even if contrary to the position of the beneficiary of the supposed credit support, can be an event of default as there never was a credit support document for the provider to disaffirm.

7.3.15.4 Misrepresentation

Under section 5(a)(iv), if a representation, other than certain tax representations, proves incorrect or misleading in any material respect when given or repeated, that constitutes an event of default. Although "representation" is not defined, the reference to representations being repeated is presumably a reference to the representations under section 3. This event of default is unlikely to apply, for example, to an oral representation made prior to, or even after, a transaction was entered into. Further, the requirement that the representation be misleading in a material respect is a possible cause of uncertainty; what is and what is not material is something upon which parties can reasonably differ.

7.3.15.5 Specific transactions

Section 5(a)(v) of the Master Agreement provides that if a party or a credit support provider defaults on a specified transaction and, after the grace period, the transaction is accelerated or terminated, that is an event of default. For these purposes, a specified transaction is a derivatives transaction between the parties to the agreement or a credit support provider—it does not include transactions such as repos, loans or other transactions common on the financial markets which would not normally be considered to be derivatives. These transactions must be governed by terms other than the Master Agreement. This clause therefore has the effect of bringing together, potentially, all derivatives between the same parties whatever terms govern them by allowing a default on any transaction to lead to the termination of transactions governed by the Master Agreement. ICOM and LICOM have similar provisions in their events of default; as a result, an event of default under a transaction governed by the Master Agreement will enable the innocent party to terminate transactions governed by those terms too.

7.3.15.6 *Cross default*

If specified in the Schedule, section 5(a)(vi) makes a failure to pay indebtedness of over a specified threshold amount an event of default. For these purposes, indebtedness only relates to borrowed money (whether as borrower or guarantor), rather than any other form of indebtedness. Unless the other party is, for example, a member of a syndicate which has suffered the default, it is likely to be hard to prove that there has been a default on this form of indebtedness, and reliance on this is therefore likely to entail significant risks.

The drafting of section 5(a)(vi) is also not very clear. It has two parts: the first refers to default on indebtedness which results or could result in that indebtedness being accelerated; the second relates to indebtedness not paid on its due date. If, for example, one party has a threshold amount of $10 million and it defaults on a payment of $5 million which would entitle the lender to accelerate a loan of $20 million, but that acceleration has not actually happened, it is not clear whether this constitutes an event of default. If section 5(a)(iv) means that the default must exceed the threshold amount, then it is not an event of default, but if, as seems more likely, the threshold amount refers to the total which could be accelerated, then it is an event of default. This could, however, create an event of default even if the default were only the failure to pay $1.

Further, if a loan of $6 million is accelerated because of a default and that same party also defaults on a loan with a single repayment of $6 million, it is not clear whether these would be aggregated—if so, there would be an event of default—or whether they must be treated separately. Prima facie, accelerated indebtedness which is not paid comes within the second of the two limbs of section 5(a)(vi) and the two sums would therefore be aggregated in order to create an event of default. It may be, however, that the reference in the first limb of section 5(a)(vi) to accelerated indebtedness which has become due would be treated as excluding accelerated indebtedness from the second limb. This would be unfortunate, and the better interpretation is that the two limbs are not mutually exclusive. As a result, accelerated indebtedness, and indeed, other kinds of indebtedness, can fall within either of the limbs of section 5(a)(iv).

7.3.15.7 *Bankruptcy*

Insolvency does not in general automatically terminate a contract.[260] The ability to do so without delay is therefore important. Section 5(a)(vii) sets out a whole range of insolvency and insolvency-related[261] events of default, some of which

260. For example, *Re Sneezum* (1876) 3 Ch D 463, 473–474, *Ex p Chalmers* (1873) LR 8 Ch App 289 and *Universal Cargo Carriers Corporation* v. *Citati* [1957] 2 QB 401, 442–443. A declaration of insolvency (as opposed to the fact of it) may, however, constitute a repudiation of contract which the innocent party can accept (e.g. *Citati* at p 443 and *Baker* v. *Lloyds Bank* [1920] 2 KB 322, 326).

261. These are generally drafted by reference to Anglo-Saxon legal concepts, but section 5(a)(vii)(8) refers to analogous events in other countries.

require proof of a particular act by the counterparty (e.g. a general assignment in favour of creditors) or an official act (e.g. a resolution being passed for its winding up) whilst others are harder to prove. For example, section 5(a)(vii)(2) makes it an event of default if the counterparty becomes insolvent, is unable to pay its debts, or fails or admits in writing its inability generally to pay its debts as they fall due. In this context, becoming insolvent probably implies a balance sheet test—i.e. its liabilities exceed its assets[262]—but what an inability to pay debts means, particularly when contrasted with a failure or admission in writing of its inability to pay its debts generally as they fall due, is more obscure. In any event, proving this or proving that a counterparty is unable to pay its debts as they fall due is likely to be very hard without some kind of admission.[263]

Section 5(a)(vii) refers to a winding-up petition being presented which results either in a winding-up order or in not being dismissed, discharged, stayed or restrained within 30 days. The normal course with regard to a groundless winding-up petition is first to seek an injunction to restrain its advertisement,[264] which does not come within the steps which avoid an event of default occurring, and then to seek its dismissal. It could be that the subject of the winding-up petition will not even know of the petition for approaching 30 days, and, even if it does, it may be difficult to have the petition discharged within 30 days. ICOM and IFEMA are, in any event, more aggressive in this area. They distinguish between insolvency proceedings commenced by regulators, which constitute events of default without more, and those commenced by others, which constitute events of default unless dismissed within five days of institution.

7.3.15.8 Merger without assumption

Whilst the insolvency related events of default are drafted with Anglo-Saxon legal concepts in mind, section 5(a)(viii) is more concerned with other approaches to corporate existence. In England, the main way to take over a company is to acquire its shares, but that only involves a change of ownership rather than any change in legal entity. In other jurisdictions, a formal merger of legal entities to form a new one is sometimes possible, or for the assets and liabilities of one entity to be passed to another and for the first to cease to be.

262. Even this is not without difficulty as accounting practices vary throughout the world (e.g. the extent to which unrealised losses must be included in a balance sheet). The approach to insolvency should not depend upon the accounting standards of one of parties to the transaction but on the construction of the agreement, which suggests that a common sense approach to insolvency should be taken.

263. Section 122 of the Insolvency Act 1986 allows a company to be wound up if, amongst other grounds, it is unable to pay its debts. Section 123 provides that a company is deemed unable to pay its debts if it fails to comply with a statutory demand for a period of three weeks, it is proved to the satisfaction of the court that it is unable to pay its debts as they fall due, or it is proved to the satisfaction of the court that the value of the company's assets is less than the amount of its liabilities, taking into account contingent and prospective liabilities.

264. Winding-up petitions must be advertised in the *London Gazette* not less than seven days before the hearing of the petition: rule 4.11 of the Insolvency Rules 1986.

Section 5(a)(viii) makes it an event of default if this happens but the surviving entity does not assume the liabilities under the agreement.

Section 5(a)(iii) makes it an event of default if the party or a credit support provider merges or transfers substantially all its assets to another entity and that entity fails to assume the party's liability. In an Anglo-Saxon context, the section could, however, apply if a company transfers all or substantially all its assets to another company, and that other company does not assume the obligations of the transferee at the time of the transfer. How the transferee assumes liability in these circumstances is not entirely clear as the transferor will remain the party to the contract, but the transferee could make an open offer to be liable or perhaps execute a deed poll taking on the liabilities of the transferor.

7.3.15.9 The consequences of an event of default

If the parties have specified automatic early termination in the schedule to the master agreement, an early termination event will occur automatically upon the occurrence of certain of the insolvency-related events of default.[265] The advantage of this is that it happens instantly and without the delays that the requirement to serve a notice can cause.[266] The disadvantage is that an event of default might occur without either party being aware of it, and without the innocent party having the opportunity to decide whether it wants to, or it is in its interests to, terminate all transactions subject to the master agreement. The effect of designating automatic early termination can also be to terminate transactions retrospectively. If the relevant event is presentation of a winding-up petition, it only becomes an event of default under section 5(a)(vii)(4) if a winding-up order is made or if the petition is not dismissed within 30 days. If this does happen, however, the early termination date if automatic early termination is specified is the date of presentation of the petition.

It also seems to require the sum due on termination to be calculated after the early termination date but probably by reference to the early termination date.[267] Since the innocent party will not be able to backdate any removal or adjustment of hedging or other related transactions, this potentially exposes it to movement in the markets between the occurrence of the early termination date and its having the opportunity to take steps in response to the default.

If automatic early termination has not been specified but an event of default

265. Section 6(a) of the Master Agreement.

266. Automatic early termination may also be necessary in the case of counterparties incorporated in certain foreign states (e.g. Germany) in order to ensure the enforceability in that state of the close out provisions in the event of that party's bankruptcy.

267. This is not entirely clear. See pp 240–243 below for more details on the calculation of the sums due, but the definition of market quotation requires the innocent party to obtain quotations "as soon as reasonably practicable after the relevant Early Termination Date"; this seems to refer to the obtaining of quotations, not the date by reference to which the quotations are calculated, but is not clear (for example, it could be said that there cannot be a quotation for a date earlier than the present because the quoter will not be prepared to deal at that price, but a quote could be obtained for an earlier date with an added cash payment to take account of movements between the reference

has occurred and is continuing, the innocent party is entitled under section 6(a) to designate an early termination date by not more than 20 days' notice to the counterparty.[268] It is the designation of an early termination event which is the key step; once it is designated the consequences follow even if the event of default is remedied before the early termination event itself, and no further payments are required under the agreement other than in accordance with the calculations required to be made on termination.[269]

Whether an early termination event occurs automatically or is specifically designated, the effect is to terminate all transactions subject to the master agreement. The innocent party cannot choose to terminate only those transactions it considers in its interests to terminate, leaving outstanding those it wishes; all transactions are terminated. If it is clear that there is a default, this might not be a problem. If, however, there is any uncertainty over it, terminating all transactions might involve taking a risk. If one party purports to rely on a breach by the other in order to terminate all transactions but the breach has not in fact occurred, that party may itself be in repudiatory breach of contract itself since, by claiming to terminate, it is stating that it will not perform its future obligations. If so, the other party can accept that repudiatory breach and, as a result, be discharged from its future performance. This may result in the party which originally purported to terminate losing the market value of the relevant transactions.[270]

7.3.15.10 The sum due on an event of default

Under section 6(d)(i), on or as soon as reasonably practicable after an early termination event, each party is to make the calculations, if any, required by it in accordance with section 6(e). In practice, however, it is likely to be only the party which has designated the early termination date which has any incentive to do this,[271] and there is no real penalty for failing to do so. The parties must send each other a statement showing in reasonable detail the calculations, including the quotations obtained, and give details of the account to which sums payable to it should be paid. Records of quotations obtained are said to be conclusive evidence of the existence and accuracy of a quotation.[272] Payment is due on the

date and the actual date). The loss method requires a party to determine its loss as of the early termination date or, if that is not reasonably practicable, as of the earliest date thereafter as is reasonably practicable. The issue of practicability appears to relate to the ability to assess loss as of that date rather than to the fact of backdating—the reference to "as of" clearly shows that backdating is required.

268. It may also be necessary to serve a notice to create an event of default (e.g. under sections 5(a)(i) and (ii)).

269. Section 6(c)(i) and (ii) of the Master Agreement.

270. See pp 247–248 below on other remedies.

271. If, however, the defaulting party considers that the result of the calculations will be a sum due to it, it may do the calculations.

272. The effectiveness of clauses making evidence conclusive is discussed at pp 232–234 above.

date notice of the sum due is effective.[273]

The purpose of the calculations required by section 6(e) is to provide a single sum payable by one party to the other. The sum is payable in the termination currency selected by the parties in the schedule, failing which it is US dollars,[274] and all sums in other currencies are to be converted into the termination currency at the early termination date. There are two "methods" of calculation and two means of arriving at the sum due.

The two means of calculating the sum due are market quotation and loss. Market calculation depends primarily on the definition of the settlement amount, to which is added the difference between the unpaid amounts of each party (i.e. all sums which fell due or which would, but for its designation, have fallen due before the early termination date). The settlement amount is the sum of the market quotations for all terminated transactions, i.e. the sum which the innocent party would have to pay or be paid in order to enter into a replacement transaction for each of those terminated. The quotations are to be obtained from four leading dealers in the relevant market,[275] and the quotations should to the extent reasonably practicable be as of the early termination date. Although quotations should if possible be obtained from four dealers, the Master Agreement contemplates that only three might be obtained.[276] Three is sufficient, but if only two or less can be obtained for any particular transaction, it will be deemed that market quotations cannot be determined and the loss approach must be applied.[277] If four quotations are obtained, the highest and lowest are discarded, and the average taken of the two remaining, and if three quotations are obtained, the highest and lowest are similarly discarded leaving the middle one to stand.

If loss applies, the sum due is not necessarily determined by reference to market quotations, though it may be. Loss is the amount which the innocent party reasonably determines in good faith to be the total of its losses and costs (but not legal fees and out of pocket expenses referred to section 11), taking into account gains, from the terminated transactions. This includes loss of bargain, i.e. in effect the market value of the transaction, or the cost of terminating or re-establishing a hedge. Loss is to be calculated as of the early termination date or, if that is not reasonably practicable, the earliest date thereafter as is reasonably practicable. Loss is often used where there is a thin market in a

273. Section 6(d)(ii) of the Master Agreement. Interest on payments has been discussed at pp 225–234 above.

274. The default currency, US dollars, is only specified in the Schedule. As a result, if the parties do not execute a schedule, strictly there is nothing to provide the default currency. Nevertheless, the schedule can be treated as incorporated by implication for this purpose.

275. The definition of reference market-makers states that they should be of the highest credit standing, and also that they should, to the extent practicable, have offices "in the same city". It is not clear whether the dealers should all have offices in the same city, no matter where that city is, or whether they should have offices in the same city as the innocent or defaulting party. It seems likely that it is in the same city as the defaulting party.

276. This follows from the definition of market quotation.

277. See the definitions of settlement amount and market quotation.

particular instrument with the result that it is likely to be difficult to obtain any market quotations,[278] but in other situations it is likely to be easier to show a loss determined by a straightforward method than to prove actual loss from a transaction.

The difference between the two "methods" is that in the first method, payments can only be made by the defaulting party and not to the defaulting party, whereas in the second payments can be made either way depending upon the market value of the transactions terminated. It is clearly more advantageous to the innocent party to opt for the first method because any default by the other party will enable it to escape potentially onerous obligations, but the G30 recommend that full two-way payments be used, i.e. the second method, because this "discourages default and enhances cross-product and cross-affiliate set-off".[279] Two-way payments are also seen by some as fairer, particularly if the defaulting party has bought transactions like caps or cash-settled options where the only payment that could ever be made is to the defaulting party.[280]

7.3.15.11 Is the settlement amount affected by the credit status of the parties?

Two related issues arise where market quotation is used to determine the amount recoverable on termination. The first is whether the credit status of the defaulting party at the time of the default affects the sum due, and the second is whether the credit status of the innocent party affects the sum due.

As to the first, the definition of market quotation requires quotations to enter into a transaction which would preserve the "economic equivalent of any payment or delivery ... that would ... but for the occurrence of the relevant Early Termination Date have been required after that date". If, say, a defaulting party is hopelessly insolvent, it might be argued that the economic equivalent of payments due from that party is nil or close to nil. This, however, cannot be the effect of the definition of market quotation. The reference is to the economic equivalent of payments that would have been required, not of payments which would in practice have been made but for the occurrence of the early termination date. The assessment of economic equivalence therefore assumes those payments are made, and does not discount them because of the defaulting party's inability to pay.

As to the second, a market quotation is for the amount which would be paid by or to the innocent party in consideration of an agreement between that party and the quoter (taking into account any credit support documents) to preserve the economic equivalent of the terminated transaction. If the innocent party was

278. The definition of settlement amounts and market quotation does, however, allow reversion to loss if at least three market quotations are not available.

279. *Derivatives; Practices and Principles* by the G30 Global Derivatives Study Group (p 16).

280. There is no objection in principle to payment being made to a defaulting party if the contract clearly requires that: *Lancaster* v. *J F Turner & Co* [1924] 2 KB 222.

perceived to be in rude financial health when the transaction was entered into but by the time of its counterparty's default was perceived to be on the brink of insolvency or beyond, are those reduced financial circumstances to be taken into account in the quotation? If the transaction could require two-way payments over a period of time, the financial status of one party could affect significantly the quotation offered. This again seems very unlikely. The quote is for the economic equivalent of the payments which would have been made but for the early termination date. The emphasis is, therefore, on the economic equivalent of payments, not on the ability of the parties to make them. The calculation therefore assumes that the parties will make the payments.

7.3.15.12 Is the right to terminate all transactions for one breach enforceable?

Parties to a contract are generally entitled to agree whatever terms they wish, subject to limited general law restrictions. Parties can, therefore, agree that on the happening of a particular event, one will pay the other a sum of money and/or that the contract should terminate. One of the general law restrictions is the law relating to penalty clauses.[281] This does, however, only apply where the event which triggers a payment is a breach of contract; if it is an event other than breach, the law on penalty clauses has no application.[282] It is questionable whether any of the events in section 5(a) of the Master Agreement which give rise to the right to terminate all outstanding transactions is a breach of contract. For example, the Master Agreement does not expressly say that the parties must not become insolvent—it merely gives a right to terminate all transactions if one party does become insolvent. If there is no implied term prohibiting insolvency, the law relating to penalties has no application, and the parties are free to agree whatever they want.

This same argument is even applicable to termination for non-payment. The obligation to make payments is in section 2(a)(i) of the Master Agreement. Failure to make payment is a breach of contract giving rise to a claim for the relevant sum. The right to terminate does not, however, arise from that failure. Before there is a right to terminate, a notice must be served under section 5(a)(i) and three local business days must elapse without payment being made. Section 5(a)(i) does not oblige the defaulting party to make payment on service of a notice under that section—the obligation to make payment already exists under section 2(a)(i)—it merely provides that if payment is not made, the innocent party has the right to terminate all transactions. This argument undoubtedly has a degree of artificiality, but the courts have long recognised that the law relating

281. See pp 227–229 above on the law relating to penalty clauses.

282. *Export Credit Guarantee Department* v. *Universal Oil Products Co* [1983] 1 WLR 399 and *Jervis* v. *Harris* [1996] Ch 195, 206.

to penalties is not necessarily satisfactory,[283] still less is it coherent. In these circumstances, this argument has a prospect of success.[284]

The application of this argument to termination for non-payment of sums due is, however, less obvious than that relating to termination as a result of insolvency. If it were not to be accepted, it could lead to different results according to the particular part of section 5(a) upon which termination is based. In view of the fact that all the events of default are treated in exactly the same manner (and, indeed, that they are described as defaults), there is a temptation to treat them all the same. This is not, however, necessarily the right approach, and it may be that different results do flow according to the grounds for termination.[285]

If, however, events of default do constitute breaches of the master agreement, then, absent a repudiatory breach of contract, on termination of a contract the innocent party is only entitled to recover the sums due at the time of termination and not damages representing the value of the contract for its remaining term (loss of bargain); any provision for the payment of other sums is void as a penalty. This principle is, however, of little practical relevance because parties are free to determine in a contract what constitutes a repudiatory breach, and a clause doing this is not subject to the law on penalties. If the parties decide that a certain breach is a repudiation, regardless of whether it would be treated as such at common law, then the innocent party is entitled to recover not only what is due at the date of termination but also damages for the loss of future performance.[286]

The issue this raises is, therefore, whether the Master Agreement does make the events of default repudiatory breaches such that the innocent party can recover damages for future performance. There can be little doubt that it is intended to do so, though a clear statement would put the matter beyond doubt.[287] If so, there can be little doubt that the provisions allowing termination on an event of default do not offend the law relating to penalty clauses and, subject to the next section, on termination the innocent party can recover

283. For example, *Lombard North Central plc* v. *Butterworth* [1987] 1 QB 527, 546.

284. It is not dissimilar from the view expressed by Millett LJ in *Jervis* v. *Harris* [1996] Ch 195. In that case, a lease required the tenant to repair the property. It also gave the landlord the right to enter the premises and carry out necessary works itself and recover the costs of doing so from the tenant. The Court of Appeal held that tenant's obligation to pay the landlord's costs did not arise from the anterior breach of the repairing covenant but from the landlord incurring expenditure. It was not, therefore, subject to the law on penalties.

285. See Lewison, *The Interpretation of Contracts* (2nd edn), pp 423–425.

286. See, in relation to this paragraph, *Lombard North Central plc* v. *Butterworth* [1987] 1 QB 527, particularly 535–536 and 540–541.

287. Or, for example, time could be made of the essence for non-payment within three local business days of receipt of notice under section 5(a)(i); a clause making time of the essence does make late payment a repudiatory breach even though, as a matter of general law, that is not necessarily the case (*Lombard North Central plc* v. *Butterworth* [1987] 1 QB 527, 545–546). In a loan transaction, a clause providing for the repayment of the capital on breach, no matter how trivial, is not a penalty, but it would be if it also provided for the payment of interest for the whole term of the loan: *The Angelic Star* [1988] 1 Lloyd's Rep 122.

damages in respect of the loss of future performance and not just sums due at the time of termination.

7.3.15.13 Are means of calculating the sums due on termination enforceable?

If the means of calculating the sums due on termination of all transactions is invalid, it will be because of the law relating to penalties.[288] From the legal point of view, there is no real doubt that the two calculation means, market quotation and loss, are both enforceable. Market quotation is a form of liquidated damages clause, as section 6(e)(iv) acknowledges. Since it calculates the cost of replacing the transaction lost on termination, it is a means of arriving at a genuine pre-estimate of the actual loss and, as such, is a liquidated damages clause rather than a penalty clause. Loss does not simply allow the innocent party to recover whatever loss it can prove it has suffered and which would be recoverable in law, but it is close to it. It too is a form of liquidated damages clause, and there is no reason to question its validity.

Greater doubt surrounds the first method, i.e. the method which provides that on termination payments may be required from the defaulting party but never to that party even if the transactions terminated were, overall, in the money as far as the defaulting party was concerned. The nature of termination for repudiatory breach is that it relieves the parties from performance of future obligations, replacing them with an obligation on the defaulting party to pay damages.[289] There is, therefore, no fundamental objection to depriving one party of the potential benefits of the future performance of a contract.[290] The termination of a contract does not, however, deprive the parties of the benefit of rights which have already been unconditionally acquired, i.e. situations where there is no other condition (positive or negative) to be fulfilled before there is a right to be paid the sum of money.[291] Prima facie, therefore, if at the time of termination one party owes another a sum of money, then that sum remains due even if the parties are discharged from future obligations. The right to withhold in the event of any breach, no matter how trivial, payments which are unconditionally due is a penalty.[292]

The application of these principles to the Master Agreement is not, however, straightforward. The issue only arises with regard to sums due before notice

288. This assumes, contrary to the argument above, that termination does occur for breach of contract. If not, the law on penalties has no application.

289. See, for example, *Moschi* v. *Lep Air Services* [1973] AC 331, 349–351 and *Photo Productions* v. *Securicor* [1980] AC 827, 849–850.

290. The fact that one party may be subject to insolvency procedures does not affect this.

291. *Colonial Bank* v. *European Grain and Shipping Ltd* [1983] AC 1056, 1090–1098 and *Hurst* v. *Bryk* [1998] 2 WLR 269, 288.

292. *Gilbert-Ash (Northern) Ltd* v. *Modern Engineering (Bristol) Ltd* [1974] AC 689, 698, 703, 711 and 723. In *The Vainqueur José* [1979] 1 Lloyd's Rep 557, 578, Mocatta J simply said, without explanation, that the principle cited by the House of Lords in *Gilbert-Ash* had no application to insurance law.

specifying an early termination event is served. Sums falling due between that notice and the early termination date do not become unconditionally due, or due at all, because of section 2(a)(iii). The questions these principles raise are: first, whether it is ever possible for another sum to be unconditionally due to the party in default; and, secondly, whether it makes any difference that the event of default is the liquidation of the defaulting party.

With regard to the first point, if one payment is overdue, there is no obligation to make any other payment, because section 2(a)(iii) makes any payment conditional on there being no event of default or potential event of default.[293] If, therefore, the only defaults are payment defaults, the situation cannot arise. It is, however, possible for one party to owe a sum to another unconditionally and for that party then, for example, to become subject to an event of default, such as insolvency or cross default. In those circumstances, if an early termination date occurs or is designated on the basis of the insolvency or cross default, the first method and section 6(c)(ii) could result in the defaulting party forfeiting the right to be paid the sum otherwise due.[294] Merely not being paid that sum is insufficient to create a penalty—if it is taken into account, as the Master Agreement requires, in calculating the sum due to the innocent party, then the defaulting party receives full value for it by way of a reduction in the sums otherwise due to the innocent party. If, however, the calculations lead to a balance in favour of the defaulting party then, arguably, it has not received full, perhaps any, value for the sum due to it before the designation of the early termination date. Provisions which produce this result are, therefore, potentially penal.

Even this is not straightforward. Suppose, for example, that there are two transactions subject to a master agreement. On the first, party A owes party B £100, being the last payment due on that transaction. Party B then becomes insolvent and A designates an early termination date. The market value of the second transaction is £50 in A's favour. The calculations required by the master agreement lead to a balance in B's favour of £50. In so far as the master agreement prevents B from claiming this balance, it is unenforceable.

Suppose, however, that there are four transactions subject to a master agreement. These are the same two described above together with a third with a market value in A's favour of £100 and a fourth with a market value in B's favour also of £100. Again the balance is £50 in favour of B. If, however, the sum due to B on the first transaction is set off against the value of the third transaction, no question of forfeiting B's unconditional claim to that £100 can arise—it gets full value through the set-off. The remaining two sums represent future performance, and B therefore has no claim in respect of them even though the balance is £50 in its favour. If, however, the third and fourth transactions are

293. See p 216 above.

294. Equity's power to relieve from forfeiture is not relevant in these circumstances because it is only available for contracts concerning the transfer of proprietary or possessory rights: *Scandinavian Tanker AB* v. *Flota Petrolera Ecuatoriana* [1983] 2 AC 694.

set off against each other, then the balance and claim is the same as in the first example. The correct approach, however, is more likely to be that because section 1(c) of the Master Agreement makes all transactions one single agreement, there is only one figure due by way of damages for loss of future performance, the division into distinct transactions only being for the purposes of ease of calculation. In this example, this leads to £50 being due to A. B is then able to set off against this sum the £100 unconditionally due to it, leaving a £50 balance in B's favour, and any provision which prevents B from recovering this is unenforceable. Further, whether a clause is a penalty clause has to be judged by reference to the time at which the contract was entered into, rather than by the circumstances at the time of breach.[295]

With regard to the second point (insolvency), where the effect of a contract is that an asset actually owned by a company at the commencement of its liquidation would be dealt with otherwise than in accordance with the statutory scheme, then to that extent the contract as a matter of public policy is avoided.[296] The statutory scheme in general requires the assets of a company in liquidation to be collected and distributed for the benefit of creditors. The question is, therefore, whether a debt due to the company at the commencement of its liquidation, and which it could then have taken legal action to recover, is an asset actually owned by the company at that time. It seems likely that it is. If this were not so, the terms of every debt could provide that a sum otherwise absolutely due should cease to be due on insolvency or that any debts owed by the insolvent could be doubled in order to ensure that they more than extinguished any liability owed to the insolvent party.[297]

In conclusion, therefore, if a sum is actually due to the defaulting party before the designation or occurrence of an early termination event, and full value is not given to the defaulting party for that sum by way of set-off, the defaulting party is likely still to be able to claim that sum notwithstanding the choice of the first method. The risk is even greater if the sum is due at the commencement of the liquidation of the defaulting party. This is, however, likely to be a very rare occurrence, for the most part of academic interest rather than a matter of practical concern.

7.3.16 Other remedies

Section 9(d) of ISDA's Master Agreement provides that the remedies set out in the Master Agreement are not exclusive of any rights, powers, remedies and privileges provided by law. If one party is in default, therefore, the other party can look to general law remedies if any are available. In most cases, these will

295. See pp 227–229 above.

296. Peter Gibson J in *Carreras Rothmans Ltd* v. *Freeman Matthews Treasure Ltd* [1985] 1 Ch 207, 226 setting out the principle to be extracted from the House of Lords case of *British Eagle International Air Lines Ltd* v. *Compagnie Nationale Air France* [1975] 1 WLR 758.

297. *Ex p Mackay* (1873) 8 Ch App 643, 647.

add nothing or no advantage to the remedies expressly provided by the Master Agreement. A party could, however, choose not to close out all transactions subject to its master agreement and instead simply sue for a sum due—this might be advantageous if, for example, closing out at that time would clearly lead to a net sum due to the defaulting party—and if the default is on the last payment outstanding it is in effect the only remedy.

In some circumstances, however, a party might want to avoid the necessity of serving notices or to rely on circumstances outside the terms of the events of default to terminate transactions.[298] For example, if one party through its acts or conduct intimates an intention to abandon and altogether refuse performance of a contract, that can be accepted as a repudiatory breach discharging the innocent party from future performance and entitling it to claim damages.[299] This requires a clear refusal to perform contractual obligations.[300] The test is, however, how the reasonable person would interpret the words or actions in question.[301] If a party wishes to rely on the impossibility of the other party performing its obligations, it must prove that it is actually impossible, not just that a reasonable person would conclude this to be so.[302]

Where there are a number of transactions subject to a master agreement (and therefore forming one contract), it will be questionable whether a refusal to perform one transaction will constitute a repudiatory breach of them all. A repudiatory breach must deprive the non-defaulting party of substantially the whole of the benefit the contract was intended to bestow on it. If it does not, the non-defaulting party will be left with its remedies under the master agreement or the right to take action in respect of the particular breach in question. Where that breach is a failure to pay, there is a clear right to sue for the sum due, but in other circumstances the remedies may be less clear cut. For example, if the breach is a refusal in advance to take delivery, it may still be necessary for the non-defaulting party to attempt to make delivery, even if that means that it has to obtain the relevant securities in order to do so, which might only add to the costs involved.[303]

7.3.17 Termination events

Termination events play a similar role to events of default, but apply in more limited circumstances. Section 5(b) provides that a termination event occurs

298. See *Chitty on Contracts* (27th edn), pp 1149ff.
299. *Freeth* v. *Burr* (1874) LR 9 CP 208, 213–214.
300. *Woodar* v. *Wimpey* [1980] 1 WLR 277, 280.
301. *Universal Cargo Carriers* v. *Citati* [1957] QB 401, 436.
302. *Hochster* v. *De la Tour* (1853) 2 E&B 678. In that case, it was said that if someone agrees to execute a lease over premises or to sell certain goods, but before the due date executes a lease in favour of another party or sells the goods to someone else, that still will not constitute impossibility because before the due date a surrender of the goods might be obtained or the goods might be repurchased.
303. See, for example, *Benjamin on Sale of Goods* (16th edn), pp 429ff.

when it becomes illegal for one party to perform its obligations or if a party merges with another and the surviving entity is materially weaker than the original party.[304]

Illegality occurs if any change in any applicable law or in the interpretation by a court of the law makes it unlawful for that party to perform its obligations.[305] For these purposes, law is defined as any "treaty, law, rule or regulation". Law is applicable to one of the parties if, presumably, it is part of the law of the place of incorporation of the party, the law of the place where the branch through which the deal was done is situated, or the governing law of the transaction.[306] Further, there must be a change in the law after the transaction was entered into. For these purposes, legislation or the equivalent is clearly capable of changing the law, but section 5(b)(i) also refers to a change in the interpretation of the law by a court, tribunal or regulatory authority with competent jurisdiction. This raises a number of issues. Courts in England do not, in theory at least, make law, rather they declare what it has always been.[307] Nevertheless, to make any sense of this section the courts must be recognised as making law (as is the reality of the situation), but it begs the question of what will constitute a change. If the House of Lords overrules one of its own decisions or an earlier decision of the Court of Appeal, that would clearly be a change in the law brought about by a judicial decision; but if the Court of Appeal overrules a first instance decision, which is not binding on any other courts, the position is less clear. It is still less clear if one court distinguishes the decision of another thus limiting what had been thought to be its effect or if the courts disapprove a comment in a leading textbook which had been generally accepted to state the law accurately.

"Credit Event Upon Merger" occurs if one party merges with, or transfers all or substantially all of its assets to, another company and the creditworthiness of that company is materially weaker than the original party was. This refers to mergers of a kind not generally possible in England where one company's assets and liabilities are transferred to another company, and the original company dissolved—it does not apply to the traditional English form of takeover, which amounts only to a change in the ownership of the shares in a company and which does not directly affect the creditworthiness of an individual company.[308] It is, however, possible for an English company to transfer all or substantially all its assets to another company; if the transferee fails to assume liability for the

304. This ignores the tax events which could constitute termination events.

305. Section 5(b)(i) of the Master Agreement.

306. It could be argued that applicable law only means the law governing the agreement, or perhaps a law recognised by that law as of relevance, but this is probably too restricted an interpretation. Section 5(b)(i) refers to "any applicable law" which clearly anticipates that there can be more than one applicable law.

307. See, for example, *R* v. *Governor of HM Prison Brockhill ex p Evans* [1998] 4 All ER 993 and *Kleinwort Benson* v. *Lincoln City Council* [1998] 4 All ER 513. A consequence of the theory that courts only declare the law is that their decisions have retrospective effect.

308. Though it may affect the perception of creditworthiness, and indeed the reality in terms of the likelihood of support, if a company is sold by a prosperous to a less prosperous group, the company itself and its assets remain unchanged by the share sale.

transferor's obligations, it will be an event of default under section 5(a)(viii), but if the transferee does assume liability but is materially weaker, it will be a termination event.

7.3.17.1 *The consequences of a termination event*

The occurrence of a termination event on its own is of no effect. It only entitles the "Affected Party" to give a notice following which certain steps must be taken. In the case of illegality, the affected party has an incentive to give notice, but there may be little to persuade an affected party on a merger to give notice as it would require it to assert that it is a materially weaker credit risk than the former party, which may not be an assertion that it finds attractive to make, at least unless the only alternative is breach. Generally, it will be the other party which wishes to bring about the termination of transactions because of the other party's weakened status, but it is not entitled to do so as only the affected party can serve notice of the occurrence of a termination event.

Section 6(b)(i) provides that notice of the occurrence of a termination event must be given promptly. The right to rely on the provisions in section 6(c) is dependent upon giving notice promptly; if it is not given promptly, the right to do so is lost because in a hedging transaction the other party needs to know where it stands quickly so that it can take whatever action is necessary to protect its interests.[309] Notice is still necessary even if the other party knows of the occurrence of the relevant event.[310] If notice is given, the giver must also provide the recipient with such other information about the termination event as that party may reasonably require. Giving notice of illegality does not suspend or otherwise excuse the obligation to make payments due in the period before an early termination event is designated (see below).[311]

If notice is given of an illegality, section 6(b)(ii) requires the party affected, as a condition to its later right to terminate, to use all reasonable efforts to transfer its rights and obligations to another of its offices or an affiliate. If this is not done

309. *Nuova Safim SpA* v. *The Sakura Bank Ltd* [1998] Lloyd's Rep Bank 142, 156.

310. *Nuova Safim SpA* v. *The Sakura Bank Ltd* [1998] Lloyd's Rep Bank 142, 156. In this case, Thomas J was slightly ambiguous, rejecting the argument that notice was not required because the other party knew of the event because "even though they plainly knew of the [events], they did not know that they made performance of obligations illegal or that NS would so contend." This last part is probably the key element—since only the affected party can rely on a termination event, the other party is entitled to know promptly what attitude it takes (see also *Senate Electrical Wholesalers Ltd* v. *Alcatel Submarine Networks Ltd*, unreported, 22 June 1998).

311. If payment is due from the party affected by the illegality, that party can rely on section 5(c) to avoid any non-payment leading to an event of default (see below), but if the payment is due from the other party, the position is more difficult. Prima facie, that payment has to be made even if the payer knows that the result of designation of an early termination date because of the illegality will be a net sum due to it which, because of the illegality, will not in practice be paid. On designation, however, the payment appears to cease to be due as a result of section 9(c)(ii) and is taken into account as an unpaid amount in the calculations of the sums payable on termination.

within 20 days, it must give notice of its failure within that period.[312] After this, the other party may, but is not obliged to, effect such a transfer within 30 days of the notice being given. If transfer is not made within that 30 days, either party may by not more than 20 days' notice to the other designate an early termination date. If both parties are affected by the illegality,[313] they are obliged to use reasonable efforts to reach agreement within 30 days to avoid the termination event, following which either can designate an early termination date. If a credit event upon merger occurs, the party whose creditworthiness has not diminished is, without any further notice periods, entitled to designate an early termination date. In all cases, an early termination event can only be designated if the termination event is still continuing.

If an early termination date is designated, the consequences are much as if it had been designated following an event of default,[314] except that only transactions affected by the relevant termination event, rather than all transactions subject to the master agreement, are terminated. The sum payable on termination is due to the party in whose favour it is, regardless of which one is affected by the termination event (i.e. second method in section 6(e) applies). If both parties are affected, each determines a settlement amount or loss, and the sum payable is half the difference between those two sums plus half the difference between any unpaid amounts.

7.3.17.2 The relationship between events of default and termination events

If a party to a derivatives transaction fails to make a payment when due, it will constitute a breach of section 2(a)(i) of the Master Agreement, and, with service of appropriate notices, could lead to an event of default under sections 5(a)(i) and 6(a). If that non-payment is because, say, of a payment moratorium in the country of that party such that it would be illegal to pay, there will also be an illegality within section 5(b)(i) which, with service of appropriate notices, could lead to a termination event under section 6(b). Which is to take priority? Section 5(c) provides that if an event or circumstance which would otherwise give rise to an event of default also constitutes an illegality, it will be treated as an illegality and not as an event of default. This does, however, depend upon the event being treated as an illegality in accordance with the provisions of section 6(b) of the Master Agreement.[315] As a result, notice must be served under section 6(b) before section 5(c) has any application.

This raises the question of when notice under section 6(b) must be served in

312. It is questionable whether giving notice a day late would deprive the affected party of the rights it would have had if notice was given on time.

313. For example, because they are in the same country or because it affects the governing law of the agreement.

314. See pp 239ff above (the interest rate payable is marginally less on termination following a termination event than following an event of default). No question of there being any penalty can apply because there is no breach of the agreement.

315. *Nuova Safim SpA* v. *The Sakura Bank Ltd* [1998] Lloyd's Rep Bank 142, 159.

order to forestall an event of default. As mentioned above, notice is expressly required to be served promptly, and "it would be a wholly uncommercial approach to the swap agreement to permit a party to rely on Illegality as a Termination Event and invoking the termination procedure in section 6(b) many months after it became aware of the event constituting the Illegality."[316] Subject to this overriding requirement, however, when in relation to the notices required to produce an event of default is notice under section 6(b) required for section 5(c) to take effect? The options would appear to be that notice under section 6(b) must come before a notice leading to an event of default (e.g. notice under section 5(a)(i)), before the designation of an early termination date, before the early termination date itself, or within a reasonable period after the early termination date.

It may be arguable that as long as the notice of an illegality is prompt, section 5(c) is applicable regardless of the stage procedures leading to an early termination date based on an event of default have reached. This is, however, unrealistic both commercially and legally. Termination of transactions may require a party to close out a hedge or put in place another transaction to replace the one which has been terminated. The cost of this is, essentially, the sum recoverable by designation of an early termination date, but this will vary from day to day. It is unrealistic to allow someone who knows that the reason it has not paid is because of an illegality to watch the procedures for termination taking place but only to draw attention to the illegality after they have finished. Similarly, what is prompt as a matter of law may depend upon the circumstances. If no payments are imminent, it may be that less urgency is required than if a payment has taken place because of an illegality. In these circumstances, a notice under section 6(b) must be given at the latest before an early termination date based on an event of default and, depending upon the timescale and circumstances, possibly well before that date.

Where an event of default and a termination event are unconnected, with the result that section 5(c) has no application, the Master Agreement gives no guidance as to which takes priority. In those circumstances, it may well simply depend upon which party serves notices leading to the first early termination event.

7.3.18 Credit support

ISDA's Master Agreement makes frequent reference to a credit support provider—for example, the insolvency of a credit support provider is an event of default under section 5(a)(vii) of the Master Agreement. A credit support provider is defined as the party identified as such in the Schedule, and will usually be a guarantor of the obligations of the party to the agreement, but does not have to be. For example, if a transaction is with a subsidiary of another

316. *Nuova Safim SpA* v. *The Sakura Bank Ltd* [1998] Lloyd's Rep Bank 142, 156.

company, but that company will not give a guarantee, identifying it as a credit support provider will, for example, allow the other party to treat a default on a derivatives transaction by the parent as an event of default with regard to the subsidiary.[317]

The Master Agreement also makes reference to credit support documents, again defined as the documents identified as such in the Schedule. ISDA has published two credit support documents subject to English law, a Credit Support Deed and a Credit Support Annex.[318] Both allow one party to call for, in effect, margin from the other if the mark to market value of the transaction falls below a specified level. In the case of the Deed, the margin, which can be cash or securities, is to be segregated from the counterparty's other assets and is security in the traditional sense.[319] This prevents the secured party making any use of the assets before it is required to return them or enforces the security, and may entail consideration of registration[320] and other local law requirements both at the place of incorporation of the other party and at the place where the securities are situated. Certain procedures for the sale of the assets may also be required on enforcement of the security.

In the case of the Annex, however, property in the margin passes to the other party so that it can, for example, sell the margin if it comprises securities or use it for repo transactions subject to the obligation to return equivalent securities if the market moves in favour of the party putting up the security.[321] The provision of margin constitutes a transaction under the Master Agreement with the result that, on designation or occurrence of an early termination date, the value of the margin is treated as an unpaid amount to be brought into the calculation of the sum due to the parties.[322] This is potentially cheaper and easier than enforcing a security interest (though with increased risk for the party putting up the security

317. Section 5(a)(v) of the ISDA Master Agreement.

318. See Hval, "Credit Support Agreements: an analysis of ISDA's latest standardised documentation governed by English law" [1996] BJIBFL 378.

319. Paragraph 2(b) of the Credit Support Deed provides, for example, that the party putting up the margin mortgages, charges and pledges it to the other party, and paragraph 6(b) provides that it remains the property of the party putting it up.

320. As far as an English company is concerned, registration may not be required because the Deed creates a fixed charge over the security rather than a floating charge, though this could depend upon the nature of the securities involved. Sections 395 and 396 of the Companies Act 1985 are also tortuous in the extreme (for example, section 396(1)(c) requires registration of a charge which, if created by an individual, would require registration as a bill of sale; the legislation regarding bills of sale is old fashioned and hard to follow). The Deed does not create a floating charge (if it did, registration would be required) because the chargor cannot carry on business in the ordinary way with the assets charged: *Re Yorkshire Woolcombers Association Ltd* [1903] 2 Ch 284.

321. Paragraph 6(d) of the Credit Support Deed expressly bars the use of margin put up under that document, whereas section 5(a) of the Annex provides that title passes to the receiving party free of any incumbrances.

322. If, however, Loss is chosen, for the purposes of section 6(e) of the Master Agreement, unpaid amounts are not formally brought into account in the calculation. Nevertheless, as Loss requires the determination in good faith of the non-defaulting party's total losses and costs, and the credit support constitutes another transaction subject to the Master Agreement, its value must be taken into account in calculating the losses suffered.

in the event of the secured party's insolvency), but does run the risk of recharacterisation, i.e. that notwithstanding the parties' expressed desire that there should be an outright transfer of the assets, it would be treated as only creating a security interest.[323]

323. As a matter of English law, this seems, however, highly unlikely. "The duty of the Court is to examine every part of the agreement, every stipulation which it contains, and to consider their mutual bearing upon each other; but it is entirely beyond the function of the Court to discard the plain meaning of any term in the agreement unless there can be found within its four corners other language and other stipulations which necessarily deprive such term of its primary significance" (*McEntire* v. *Crossley* [1895] AC 457, 467; see also *Welsh Development Agency* v. *Export Finance* [1992] BCLC 148). In this instance, the plain meaning of the terms of the Annex is that no security interest is created. Upon the insolvency of the secured party or the party putting up the security, the only occasion when it is likely to matter, the insolvency laws applicable to that party may be relevant as may be the laws of the place where the security is situated.

CHAPTER 8

EXCLUDING AND LIMITING LIABILITY

8.1 INTRODUCTION

When addressing the issue of liability, it can be tempting to seek to exclude everything. That is, however, unrealistic—if an exclusion clause is sufficiently wide in ambit it will deprive one party's promises of all contractual force, leaving the "contract" as a mere declaration of intent.[1] The basic obligations—payment or delivery—must, in practice, remain, but the question is what other obligations, responsibilities, or liabilities are to be, and can be, excluded. Unless there is a clear idea of what is to be excluded, it will inevitably be difficult to draft provisions to achieve the desired result, assuming that to be possible within the judicial, statutory and regulatory framework.

In deals between market professionals, excluding or limiting liability is probably not a significant issue as liabilities will seldom extend beyond the primary contractual obligations to make payments or deliveries. When dealing with others, however, the issue is likely to be of greater significance, both to make it clear what role is being undertaken[2] and to seek to control the risks involved. This inevitably brings a tension between what is considered commercially acceptable and what is desirable from the risk management point of view.[3]

1. *Suisse Atlantique Société d'Armement Maritime SA* v. *NV Rotterdamsche Kolen Centrale* [1967] AC 361, 432.

2. Exclusion clauses can be seen in some circumstances as defining one party's obligations rather than excluding liability they may otherwise have had. As far as pre-contractual duties are concerned, this is feasible but less so as far as contractual duties under derivatives contracts are concerned.

3. For example, when addressing the question of why one party had not expressly mentioned negligence in an indemnity clause, Steyn LJ said in *EE Caledonia* v. *Orbit Valve* [1994] 1 WLR 1515, 1523: "Why do draftsmen not take note of clear and consistent line of judicial decisions [requiring express mention of negligence]? For my part, I have no doubt that the draftsman on the underground to whom such a question was addressed would say 'one does not wish to frighten off one or other of the parties.' Omissions of express reference to negligence tend to be deliberate."

8.1.1 Construction of exclusion clauses

Once a decision has been made as to what is to be excluded, it is also necessary to seek to address in the drafting the problems created by the judicial "hostility"[4] towards exclusion clauses. Particularly since the passing of the Unfair Contract Terms Act 1977, the courts have paid lip service to the view that, at least in commercial situations where the parties are not of unequal bargaining power, it is for the parties to apportion the risks between them, and the courts should not interfere with strained interpretations of exclusion clauses to achieve what the judges perceive to be the desired result,[5] but the extent to which this is actually carried into practice remains questionable. The courts do not simply apply to exclusion clauses the normal rules applicable to the construction of contracts,[6] but apply instead a special set of guidelines relevant only to exclusion clauses.

Principally, the courts require that an exclusion clause be clear and unambiguous, and the greater the departure from the judicial view as to what the obligations of the parties ought to be, the greater the degree of clarity required.[7] The basis of this is the presumed intention of the parties based on the supposed inherent improbability that one party intends to release another from liabilities otherwise falling on him.[8] If one party puts forward terms including a clause relieving that party from liability, it will also be construed strictly against him.[9]

The judicial hostility to exclusion clauses leads to risk. There is inevitably a danger that an exclusion clause will, whatever the circumstances, be subject to imaginative interpretations in an attempt to escape its consequences. It is difficult to predict the extent to which the courts will do this because different

4. *Ailsa Craig Fishing Co* v. *Malvern Fishing* [1983] 1 WLR 964, 966. See also Lord Denning MR's account, "in his uniquely colourful and graphic style", of this hostility in the Court of Appeal in *George Mitchell (Chesterhall) Ltd* v. *Finney Lock Seeds Ltd* [1983] QB 284, 296–301. There is less hostility towards clauses which cap liability than towards those which exclude it: *Ailsa Craig Fishing Co* v. *Malvern Fishing* [1983] 1 WLR 964, 966 and 970 and *George Mitchell (Chesterhall) Ltd* v. *Finney Lock Seeds Ltd* [1983] 2 AC 803, 813–814.

5. For example, *Photo Production Ltd* v. *Securicor Transport Ltd* [1980] AC 827, 843 and 851.

6. See pp 185–187 above.

7. *Suisse Atlantique Société d'Armement Maritime SA* v. *NV Rotterdamsche Kolen Centrale* [1967] AC 361, 432 and *Photo Productions Ltd* v. *Securicor Transport Ltd* [1980] AC 827, 850–851. In *Deepak Fertilisers* v. *ICI Chemicals & Polymers Ltd* [1999] 1 Lloyd's Rep 387, 393, the Court of Appeal described Lord Diplock's view in *Photo Productions* (at pp 850–851) as "the authoritative statement".

8. *Ailsa Craig Fishing Co* v. *Malvern Fishing* [1983] 1 WLR 964, 970. Construction depends, however, on the intention of both parties obtained objectively from the words used and the relevant surrounding circumstances.

9. I.e. the *contra proferentem* principle (see, for example, *Suisse Atlantique Société d'Armement Maritime SA* v. *NV Rotterdamsche Kolen Centrale* [1967] AC 361, 427). "[The *contra proferentem*] rule is, however, an aid of last resort. It would be wrong to use it to create ambiguity where none realistically exists, and then to resolve the question by reference to it" (Steyn J in *Singer Co (UK) Ltd* v. *Tees and Hartlepool Port Authority* [1988] 2 Lloyd's Rep 164, 169).

judges take different approaches.[10] The only safe approach is clarity, even excessive clarity, but that runs into the problem of commercial acceptability. The problem is not merely that one party does not wish to express clearly its desire to limit its liability but that both parties may be reluctant to put on paper what they will acknowledge orally. The starkness of the written word can lead to a blurring of what the parties intend to achieve, and that can lead to risk for the party subsequently seeking to rely on a clause.

8.1.2 Regulatory control of exclusion clauses

In addition to the judicial approach to exclusion clauses, there are regulatory requirements. For example, SFA rule 5.24 provides that:

> "(1) A firm must not, in any written communication or agreement, seek to exclude or restrict any duty or liability to a customer under the [Financial Services Act 1986], or under the regulatory system.
>
> (2) Similarly, unless it is reasonable to do so in the circumstances, a firm must not, in any written communication or agreement, seek to exclude or restrict—
>
> (a) any other duty to act with skill, care and diligence which is owed to a private customer in connection with the provision to him of investment services in the course of regulated business; or
>
> (b) any liability owed to a private customer in connection with regulated business for failure to exercise the degree of skill, care and diligence which may reasonably be expected of it in the provision of that business.
>
> (3) A firm must not seek unreasonably to rely on any provision seeking to exclude or restrict any such duty or liability."

This only applies to SFA controlled business—not, for example, to exempted business within section 43 of the Financial Services Act 1986. SFA rule 5.24(1) is of limited application because, for example, duties of care in pre-contractual negotiations do not arise under the regulatory system, and therefore are not covered by the rule. The regulatory system generally grants few substantive rights to customers or counterparties (with the exception of private customers, and they are covered more fully by rule 5.24(2)) breach of which could lead to their suffering a loss. Nevertheless, if an attempt is made to exclude an obligation arising under the regulatory system, that attempt will give the other party, whether or not a private customer, a cause of action under section 62 of the Financial Services Act 1986.[11]

Rule 5.24(2) concerns only private customers,[12] and prevents the exclusion or limitation of contractual and general law duties of skill, care and diligence, as well as similar regulatory obligations, unless it would be reasonable to do so. To some extent this mirrors the provisions of the Unfair Contract Terms Act 1977,

10. For example, the approaches of the judges of the Court of Appeal who heard *EE Caledonia* v. *Orbit Valve* [1994] 1 WLR 1515 differed significantly from the approach to similar issues of the judges in *Breaveglen Ltd* v. *Sleeman Ltd* (unreported, 9 May 1997).

11. See p 160 above.

12. See p 159 above.

though that only applies to contractual and general duties to take reasonable care, and a duty of "skill, care and diligence" could, perhaps, arguably be wider. SFA rule 5.24(3) goes beyond the statutory provisions, however. The Unfair Contract Terms Act 1977 requires the reasonableness of a clause excluding liability for a duty to take reasonable care to be judged only at one point in time (for example, if it is contractual, when the contract was made[13]). Rule 5.24(3) adds an extra test, namely that it should also be reasonable to rely on the clause, a test which presumably has to be satisfied when a party chooses to rely on the clause. Since the rule refers to "such duties", it only applies to those duties to private customers referred to in rule 5.24(2).[14] Private investors have a right of action under section 62 of the Financial Services Act 1986 if they suffer loss as a result of breach of an SRO's rules by an authorised person.

8.2 PRE-CONTRACTUAL OBLIGATIONS AND LIABILITIES

8.2.1 Common law controls

As discussed in Chapter 4, the primary control on pre-contractual negotiations is the law relating to misrepresentation. For there to be any liability, it requires a misrepresentation by one party and reliance on it by the other; in addition, as far as negligent misrepresentation is concerned, it requires an assumption of responsibility by one party to the other, an assumption which will usually be present in the process of contractual negotiations.

A clause seeking to address pre-contractual misrepresentation must, therefore, deal with these issues. As a result, it is common to provide that each party has made its own decision to enter into the transaction and has not relied on any representations made by the other.[15] If each party has agreed[16] that in entering into the agreement, it has not relied on the other, there can be no liability, but it is prudent to go on in any clause and expressly draw this conclusion because of the requirement that someone seeking to rely on a clause of this nature should not be "mealy-mouthed" about its effect.[17]

13. See p 261 below.

14. Rule 5.24(3) cannot refer to the duties referred to in rule 5.24(1) because those duties cannot be excluded at all and therefore reliance, reasonable or otherwise, on a clause excluding those liabilities does not arise.

15. ISDA published a clause along these lines in 1996, and section 10 of ICOM and section 7 of IFEMA follow the same pattern. Clauses like this are usually allied with clauses such as section 9(a) (entire agreement) of ISDA's Master Agreement (see p 179 above).

16. Some clauses do not agree that this is the case but one party merely acknowledges that it is so. An acknowledgement might operate only as a representation and, as a result, can only take effect as an estoppel; indeed, an agreement might only operate by way of estoppel too (*Lowe* v. *Lombank Ltd* [1960] 1 WLR 196). It might be hard to prove the requirements of estoppel (see pp 181–183 above).

17. *Thomas Witter Ltd* v. *TPB Industries Ltd* [1996] 2 All ER 573, 596 (a case involving the sale of a business). In *Thomas Witter* (at p 597), Jacob J doubted whether a clause which did not expressly say that the result was that there was no liability, would prevent a party from showing that it had in fact relied on a representation, though he accepted that it could have difficulty in proving its

Once a clause does draw the conclusion that one party has no remedies against the other for any pre-contractual misrepresentations, it becomes necessary to state expressly that the clause covers negligence. This is because of the principle laid down in *Canada Steamship Lines Ltd* v. *The King* in which Lord Morton of Henryton said:

> "(1) If the clause contains language which expressly exempts the person in whose favour it is made (hereinafter called the 'proferens') from the consequences of the negligence of his own servants, effect must be given to that provision ...
> (2) If there is no express reference to negligence, the court must consider whether the words used are wide enough, in their ordinary meaning, to cover negligence on the part of the servants of the proferens ...
> (3) If the words used are wide enough for the above purpose, the court must then consider whether 'the head of damage may be based on some ground other than that of negligence' ... The other 'ground' must not be so fanciful or remote that the proferens cannot be supposed to have desired protection against it; but subject to this qualification ... the existence of a possible head of damage other than that of negligence is fatal to the proferens even if the words used are prima facie wide enough to cover negligence ..."[18]

The status of this approach is open to question. It has been said that it rests on the inherent improbability of the parties agreeing to exempt one of them from negligence.[19] It has also been said that it is not a matter of law and that the ultimate question concerns the intention of the parties, this approach being merely a guideline to ascertain their presumed intention.[20] The courts have also applied Lord Morton's approach rigidly.[21] In these circumstances, there is a clear risk that courts will apply Lord Morton's tests, and it is therefore prudent to try to meet its requirements.

Lord Morton's first step allows the courts to recognise a clause which expressly exempts from negligence, which requires either the word negligence to

case. The clause in that case was an "acknowledgement" that one party was not induced to enter into the transaction by any representations, other than those set out in the contract; the position could arguably be different if there were an agreement on this basis. Jacob J suggested (at p 595) that a clause should read: "The vendor agrees that he will have no remedy in respect of any untrue statement made to him upon which he relied in entering this contract and that his only remedies can be for breach of contract."

18. [1952] AC 192, 208.

19. For example, *Smith* v. *South Wales Switchgear Co Ltd* [1978] 1 WLR 165, 168.

20. For example, *Smith* v. *South Wales Switchgear Co Ltd* [1978] 1 WLR 165, 178, *Monarch Airlines Ltd* v. *London Luton Airport Ltd* [1998] 1 Lloyd's Rep 403, 408 and *Breaveglen Ltd* v. *Sleeman Ltd* (unreported, 9 May 1997). In *Monarch Airlines,* Clarke J doubted whether the *Canada Steamship* approach applied if the clause was in the form that one party was "only liable if" or "not liable unless", and in *Breaveglen* Leggatt LJ said that "Lord Morton's tests guide the approach to be adopted in ascertaining the presumed intention of the parties, if not otherwise apparent from the contract. But that is not necessary where appropriate steps have been taken to allocate risk. Where a sensible construction leads to the conclusion that the proferens is indemnified against his own negligence, neither the House of Lords nor this court [the Court of Appeal] following them have shown any inhibition in accepting that result without seeking to resile from it by recourse to Lord Morton's tests."

21. For example, Lord Fraser of Tullybelton in *Smith* v. *South Wales Switchgear Co Ltd* [1978] 1 WLR 165 and *EE Caledonia* v. *Orbit Valve* [1994] 1 WLR 1515.

be used or a synonym for it—it is not enough simply to use general terms which would be wide enough to cover negligence.[22] An exclusion clause should, therefore, draw the conclusion that one party has no remedies against the other for any pre-contractual misrepresentations, whether or not those misrepresentations were negligent. A failure to do this runs the risk of pushing the matter into Lord Morton's second and third tests, the latter of which requires the assessment of whether there are any claims other than in negligence to which the clause could apply. As it is possible to rescind a contract for a misrepresentation which is not negligent,[23] there is a real risk that a clause which does not mention negligence expressly would be treated as applying only to innocent misrepresentation.[24]

8.2.2 Statutory controls

Even if negligence is mentioned expressly in an exclusion clause, the clause must still meet the two closely related statutory controls on excluding liability for misrepresentation. Section 3 of the Misrepresentation Act 1967[25] provides that a contract term which excludes or restricts the liability of one party,[26] or the remedies available to the other, arising from a pre-contractual misrepresentation is of no effect unless it meets the requirement of reasonableness in section 11(1) of the Unfair Contract Terms Act 1977 ("UCTA"). In addition, section 2(2) of UCTA provides that one party cannot exclude or restrict his liability for negligence[27] except in so far as the term doing so meets the requirement of reasonableness set out in section 11(1).

The requirements which any clause must meet as to reasonableness are the same which ever of the two Acts applies, but the scope of the Acts is not the same in three respects. First, UCTA only applies to business liability, that is liability for breach of obligations or duties arising from things done or to be done in the course of a business.[28] Section 3 of the Misrepresentation Act 1967 is not so limited. Secondly, UCTA applies to liability in the tort of negligence, whether that liability is of a party to the contract or a third party. Section 3 of the Misrepresentation Act 1967 applies to any liability of a party to the contract in

22. *Smith* v. *South Wales Switchgear Co Ltd* [1978] 1 WLR 165, 173 and *Shell Chemicals UK Ltd* v. *P & O Roadtanks Ltd* [1995] 1 Lloyd's Rep 297, 301.

23. See Chapter 4 above.

24. *Toomey* v. *Eagle Star Insurance Co Ltd (No 2)* [1995] 2 Lloyd's Rep 88.

25. Substituted for the original section by section 8(1) of the Unfair Contract Terms Act 1977.

26. In considering under UCTA or the Misrepresentation Act 1967 whether a clause does exclude or restrict liability, the approach is to consider first whether there would be liability but for the term relied on as excluding it: *Phillips Products Ltd* v. *Hyland* [1987] 2 All ER 620, 625. As a result, the argument that an exclusion clause does not exclude liability but defines the obligations of the parties is hard to run.

27. Negligence is defined in section 1(1) of the Unfair Contract Terms Act 1977 as including any common law duty to take reasonable care or exercise reasonable skill as well as a contractual obligation to take reasonable care or exercise reasonable skill in the performance of a contract.

28. Section 1(3) of the Unfair Contract Terms Act 1977.

respect of a misrepresentation before the contract was made. Section 3 can, therefore, apply to a right to rescind for misrepresentation, whether innocent or not, and liability in damages under the Act as well as liability in the tort of negligent misrepresentation as long as it is liability of a party to the contract. Thirdly, section 27 of UCTA provides that section 2 does not apply to a contractual term if English law is the governing law of the contract only by the choice of the parties and, apart from that choice, the law of a country outside the United Kingdom would apply. This raises the issue of what would the governing law have been but for choice of the parties, which is discussed above.[29]

8.2.2.1 The requirement of reasonableness

If a contract term falls within the scope of section 2(2) of UCTA or section 3 of the Misrepresentation Act 1967, it is of no effect except in so far as the term meets the requirement of reasonableness set out in section 11(1) of UCTA. The requirement of reasonableness is that a contract term should have been a fair and reasonable one to be included in the contract having regard to the circumstances which were, or ought reasonably to have been, known to or in the contemplation of the parties when the contract was made.[30] The onus is on the person claiming that a term satisfies the requirement of reasonableness to show that it does.[31] UCTA contains in Schedule 2 a list of matters to which regard should be had in assessing the reasonableness of a term where the contract is one under which goods pass,[32] but those matters are usually regarded as being of general application to the requirement of reasonableness.[33] There is, however, no exhaustive list of factors that must be taken into account.[34]

If the effectiveness of a clause does depend upon it being shown to be reasonable, this inevitably involves significant uncertainty. Ultimately, it will depend upon a decision by a judge, and his decision is bound to depend heavily upon his general outlook, his experience, and his views on the transaction in question, with the appellate courts reluctant to interfere. The outcome will, in many cases, be very hard to predict, not least because even the courts have accepted that there will sometimes be room for legitimate differences of judicial

29. See pp 208–209 above.

30. If the provision is not a contractual one but only a notice, as could be the case with section 2(2) of UCTA, the test is whether it is fair and reasonable to allow reliance on the notice having regard to all the circumstances obtaining when the liability arose or, but for the notice, would have arisen: section 11(3) of UCTA.

31. Section 11(5) of UCTA and section 3 of the Misrepresentation Act 1967.

32. Sections 6, 7 and 11(2) of UCTA.

33. For example *Stewart Gill Ltd* v. *Horatio Meyer & Co Ltd* [1992] 1 QB 600, 608 and *Overland Shoes Ltd* v. *Schenkers Ltd* [1998] 1 Lloyd's Rep 498, 505.

34. *Smith* v. *Eric S Bush* [1990] 1 AC 831, 858.

opinion.[35] It will also depend heavily on the facts—it is quite possible for a clause to be reasonable in one case but unreasonable in another.[36] Nevertheless, although there will often be uncertainty as to the effectiveness of a disclaimer to which the statutes apply, if a claim is made to which the disclaimer might apply, the uncertainty will at least provide an argument which may result in a better settlement than might have been available had no disclaimer been present.

The factors that might be taken into account in assessing whether a clause is fair and reasonable include the following (though no one factor is likely to be decisive, it being necessary to take into account all the circumstances[37]):

(1) The bargaining positions of the parties relative to each other, taking into account alternative means by which the customer's requirements could be met.[38] If the market is competitive, and the customer (if there is a party which can be described as such) could, or perhaps has, approached other possible counterparties to assess the terms upon which they would do business, then the bargaining position is likely to be treated as equal. The mere fact that one party can be seen as big and the other small does not necessarily give the big party a better bargaining position if the market is competitive.

(2) Whether the customer received an inducement to agree to the term, or in accepting it had the opportunity of entering into a similar contract with other persons but without having to accept a similar term.[39] This is not easy to understand, but again, perhaps, turns on the competitiveness of the market. If a party wants to enter into a derivatives transaction, it is likely to be offered a package, which might include a disclaimer. If it does test the market and accepts the best package including the disclaimer, it can presumably be said to have received an inducement to accept the term as part of the overall package. But if everyone offers a package including a comparable disclaimer, then that might not be relevant but the fact that everyone does offer to deal

35. Though the decision by the first instance judge is not an exercise of discretion, "a decision ... will have this in common with the exercise of a discretion, that, having regard to the various matters to which the [relevant statutes] direct attention, the court must entertain a whole range of considerations, put them in the scales on one side or the other, and decide at the end of the day on which side the balance comes down. There will sometimes be room for legitimate difference of judicial opinion as to what the answer should be, where it will be impossible to say that one view is demonstrably wrong and the other demonstrably right. It must follow ... that, when asked to review such a decision on appeal, the appellate court should treat the original decision with the utmost respect and refrain from interference with it unless satisfied that it proceeded upon some erroneous principle or was plainly and obviously wrong" (Lord Bridge in *George Mitchell (Chesterhall) Ltd* v. *Finney Lock Seeds Ltd* [1983] 2 AC 803, 816).

36. *Phillips Products Ltd* v. *Hyland* [1987] 2 All ER 620, 628.

37. *Singer Co (UK) Ltd* v. *Tees and Hartlepool Port Authority* [1988] 2 Lloyd's Rep 164, 170.

38. Paragraph (a) of Schedule 2 to UCTA (see also, for example, *Smith* v. *Eric S Bush* [1990] 1 AC 831, 858).

39. Paragraph (b) of Schedule 2 to UCTA.

on similar terms could be seen as evidence that the terms are reasonable.[40]

(3) Whether the customer knew or ought reasonably to have known of the existence and extent of the term (having regard, among other things, to the custom of the trade and any previous course of dealing between the parties).[41] This will rarely be relevant in the case of derivatives as it is directed more to small print on the back of order forms than to negotiated transactions.[42]

(4) Where the term excludes or restricts liability if some condition is not complied with, whether it was reasonable at the time of the contract to expect that compliance with that condition would be practicable.[43] This might cover a requirement that a party notify the other of any claim within a specific period of becoming aware of the possible claim failing which the other is to have no liability.

(5) Whether the goods were manufactured, processed or adapted to the special order of the customer.[44] If a particular derivative is designed to meet a customer's specific needs, this may just have some relevance but in most cases it will not.

(6) The difficulty of the task being undertaken, the more difficult the task the more reasonable it is to exclude liability.[45] This may have relevance to derivatives as it is, for example, very difficult to predict movements in interest and currency rates, though many try to do so.[46]

(7) The practical consequences of the decision on the reasonableness of a term, including the availability of insurance against the loss in

40. The courts have shown particular sympathy to market standard terms which can be said to have been negotiated by representatives from both sides of an industry. For example, in *Walker* v. *Boyle* [1982] 1 WLR 495 Dillon J decided that a term in the National Conditions of Sale (used in real property transactions) was unreasonable taking into account that it was not the product of negotiations. In *Singer Co (UK) Ltd* v. *Tees and Hartlepool Port Authority* [1988] 2 Lloyd's Rep 164 and *Overland Shoes Ltd* v. *Schenkers Ltd* [1998] 1 Lloyd's Rep 498, it was decided that terms were reasonable in part because they had been negotiated by both sides of industry.

41. Paragraph (c) of Schedule 2 to UCTA.

42. In *Stag Line Ltd* v. *Tyne Ship Repairers Group Ltd* [1984] 2 Lloyd's Rep 211, 222, Staughton J said, only half in jest, that he was "tempted to hold that all the conditions are unfair and unreasonable for two reasons: first, they are in such small print that one can barely read them; secondly, the draughtsmanship is so convoluted and prolix that one almost needs an LL.B to understand them."

43. Paragraph (d) of Schedule 2 to UCTA.

44. Paragraph (e) of Schedule 2 to UCTA.

45. *Smith* v. *Eric S Bush* [1990] 1 AC 831, 858.

46. The difficulty in doing so also goes to the extent to which a forecast is reasonable, in so far as reasonableness is relevant.

question.[47] Discussion of the availability of insurance is usually in the context, for example, of damage to goods or advice on physical items. As far as derivatives are concerned, a transaction may in effect provide the customer with insurance if it is seeking to hedge an underlying position. Insurance may be available for the same risk (e.g. credit insurance), but this goes more to the competitiveness of the market than to the question of who should bear a particular risk. The availability of insurance to a financial institution for, say, negligent advice may, however, be relevant. In this context, the courts have shown more sympathy for clauses excluding the right of set-off because they do not prevent a claim being brought but only have cash flow consequences for the parties.[48]

(8) The availability of legal advice to the parties and their sophistication.[49] This may go to the issue of whether the parties understood the consequences of the contract they were entering into, but if the inequality of bargaining power is such that, even though one party does understand, it still has no choice but to accept, it may not be relevant.

(9) The extent to which a term could affect both parties rather than just one.[50] If a clause could reasonably apply to both parties, then it is more likely to be reasonable than if it can apply only to one.

8.2.2.2 *The consequences of unreasonableness*

A contractual term within section 2(2) of UCTA or section 3 of the Misrepresentation Act 1967 is of no effect except in so far as it is reasonable. The issue is to be judged at the time the contract is made and without regard to the particular use one party wishes later to make of it.[51] It is, therefore, enough for a party to show that in some circumstances, even if not the circumstances that have actually arisen, the term would be unfair and unreasonable for the whole of the term to be of no effect—the court will not put a blue pencil through the most

47. For example, *Smith* v. *Eric S Bush* [1990] 1 AC 831, 858–859, *Singer Co (UK) Ltd* v. *Tees and Hartlepool Port Authority* [1988] 2 Lloyd's Rep 164, 169–170 ("... a purpose of an exception clause in this type of case is to transfer the insurance burden from the subcontractor to the owner of the goods"), and *Flamar Interocean Ltd* v. *Denmac Ltd* [1990] 1 Lloyd's Rep 434 ("In the absence of circumstances where one of the parties alleges that the existence or extent of insurance cover was actually discussed in antecedent negotiations ... [w]hat will be inferred or assumed in appropriate cases ... is merely that the parties contracted on the basis of the insurance that was available [rather than the parties' actual insurance arrangements].").

48. *Stewart Gill Ltd* v. *Horatio Meyer & Co Ltd* [1992] 1 QB 600 decided that no set-off clauses were exclusion clauses within the meaning of UCTA and that the clause in that case was unreasonable. Later cases (e.g. *WRM Group Ltd* v. *Wood* (unreported, 21 November 1997) and *Overland Shoes Ltd* v. *Schenkers Ltd* [1998] 1 Lloyd's Rep 498) are more sympathetic to no set-off clauses.

49. For example, *McCullagh* v. *Lane Fox* [1996] PNLR 205 (Hobhouse LJ).

50. *Shearson Lehman Hutton Inc* v. *McLaine Watson & Co Ltd* [1989] 2 Lloyd's Rep 570, 612.

51. *Stewart Gill Ltd* v. *Horatio Meyer & Co Ltd* [1992] 1 QB 600, 607.

offensive parts and say what is left is reasonable[52] or decide what would be a reasonable exclusion and apply the clause to that extent.

In *Thomas Witter Ltd* v. *TBP Industries Ltd*, the clause in question in that case applied as a matter of construction to fraudulent, negligent and innocent misrepresentation. Jacob J decided that it was unreasonable to seek to exclude liability for fraudulent misrepresentation. He therefore concluded that the clause was of no effect at all even if it would have been reasonable to exclude liability for negligent or innocent misrepresentation.[53] As a result of this decision, it is prudent to exclude fraud expressly from the scope of any clause seeking to disclaim liability. A failure to do this runs the risk that the clause as a whole will almost automatically be regarded as unreasonable, even though it would have been reasonable to exclude liability in the circumstances which have actually arisen.[54]

If a whole term is of no effect because it is unreasonable, this begs the question of what is a term for these purposes. This is not easy. In *Thomas Witter*, it was one contractual clause, clause 17.2, which clearly represented a whole concept and could not sensibly be split up.[55] In *R W Green* v. *Cade Bros Farms*, Griffiths J held that one sentence of a single contractual term (requiring notification of a claim within three days of delivery) was unreasonable and therefore of no effect, but another sentence (limiting the amount that could be claimed) was reasonable.[56] In these circumstances, it makes sense to seek to divide up the constituent parts of a disclaimer into different clauses, at least different sentences within a clause, in order to try to prevent a decision that one part of clause is unreasonable from infecting other parts of a clause which might, on their own, be reasonable.

8.3 CONTRACTUAL OBLIGATIONS

The primary obligation in a derivatives contract will generally be to make a payment. As discussed above,[57] that obligation cannot realistically be excluded if the contract is to remain legally binding and not be reduced to a statement of intent. As far as ISDA's Master Agreement is concerned, it is arguable that both

52. *Stewart Gill Ltd* v. *Horatio Meyer & Co Ltd* [1992] 1 QB 600, 609.

53. [1996] 2 All ER 573, 597–598.

54. It is, in any event, probably impossible as a matter of public policy to exclude liability for fraudulent misrepresentation (deceit) (*Pearson* v. *Mayor of Dublin* [1907] AC 351) though it may be that liability for the fraud of employees can be excluded (*Pearson* at p 354). The right to set off sums due against damages claimed for an allegedly fraudulent misrepresentation can be excluded as this does not prevent a party from pursuing a claim in deceit: *WRM Group Ltd* v. *Wood* (unreported, 21 November 1997).

55. See [1996] 2 All ER 573, 595.

56. [1978] 1 Lloyd's Rep 602. In *Stewart Gill Ltd* v. *Horatio Meyer & Co Ltd* [1992] 1 QB 600, it appears that the Court of Appeal decided that clause 13(1)(b) of a contract was of no effect, but they did not comment on the other parts of clause 13.

57. See p 255 above.

the loss and market quotation methods of calculating the sum due on termination following an event of default represent the entire damages recoverable notwithstanding that section 9(d) states that the rights under the Agreement are not exclusive of any rights, powers, remedies and privileges provided by law.[58] Nevertheless, if this is not so, the next issue is what other damages might a counterparty be able to recover for breach of a derivatives agreement.

8.3.1 Consequential loss

The damages recoverable for breach of contract fall into two categories: first, damages which may fairly and reasonably be considered as arising naturally, i.e. according to the usual course of things, from the breach of contract itself, or which may reasonably be supposed to have been in the contemplation of both parties; and, secondly, damages flowing from special circumstances under which the contract was made which were communicated by one party to the other.[59]

As far as the first category is concerned, if the innocent party accepts breach as constituting a repudiation entitling it to end the contract, the loss arising from breach is likely to be the market value of the contract at the time of the breach, i.e. the measure of loss provided by ISDA's Master Agreement. A derivatives contract in general represents a series of payments, and the loss is therefore the anticipated value of those payments. The second category is more difficult in the case of a derivatives contract. If, say, one party buys a cap because rising interest rates could drive it out of business and it informs the counterparty of this, a failure to pay sums due on the cap could foreseeably lead to the insolvency, or at least to damages in excess of the value of the contract.[60] The position with regard to an advisory mandate is less complicated, and the second category could cover damages flowing from the specific purpose for which the advisee wanted the advice rather than just the general consequences of negligent advice.

It now seems clear that this second category will be excluded by a contractual term disclaiming liability for consequential losses.[61] A problem, however, is that it is possible to have liability for negligence simultaneously in both contract and

58. See pp 247–248 above. In *Suisse Atlantique Société d'Armement Maritime SA* v. *NV Rotterdamsche Kolen Centrale* [1967] AC 361 a demurrrage clause was construed as limiting the sums recoverable to those set out.

59. *Hadley* v. *Baxendale* (1854) 9 Exch 341, 354–355 (see also *Victoria Laundry* v. *Newman Industries* [1949] 2 KB 528 and *The Heron II* [1969] 1 AC 530).

60. It has been said that a failure to pay money can never result in damages beyond the sum of money involved (e.g. *Fletcher* v. *Tayleur* (1855) 17 CB 21, 29 and *Alsabah Maritime Service Co* v. *Philippine International Shipping Corp* [1984] 1 Lloyd's Rep 291), but the contrary has also been asserted (e.g. *Trans Trust SPRL* v. *Danubian Trading Co* [1952] 2 QB 297 and *Wadsworth* v. *Lydall* [1981] 1 WLR 598). The true position, according to *McGregor on Damages* (16th edn), p 734, is that there is no rule to this effect, and the approach to damages must be governed by the approach of *Hadley* v. *Baxendale* (1854) 9 Exch 341.

61. *British Sugar plc* v. *NEI Power Projects Ltd* (1997) 87 BLR 42.

tort, and a party can elect to sue in one or both depending upon the advantages to it of each cause of action.[62] This may well be the case with an advisory mandate, at least unless it makes it clear that the only remedies are to be under the terms of the contract and not in tort. The scope of damages in the tort of negligence is based, like that in contract, on reasonable foreseeability, but the test is easier to meet in contract than it is in tort, i.e. a lower degree of foreseeability is required.[63] Quite what effect an exclusion of consequential losses will have on a claim in tort is not clear, but, at least where there is simultaneous liability in contract and tort, it would presumably exclude all those damages recoverable in tort which, if the matter were governed by contract, would be excluded.

8.3.2 Damages caps

Another common way to limit damages is to put a financial limit on the damages recoverable. In the case of a derivatives contract, this may involve picking a figure out of the air, but where advice is being given for a fee, it could be the amount of the fee or the insurance cover carried for potential liability in the question.

8.3.3 Time limits

It is also common in some spheres to require a claim to be brought within a specific time period significantly shorter than the usual limitation period in contract and tort of six years from the accrual of the cause of action.

8.3.4 No set-off clauses

No set-off clauses do not limit liability but provide that one party must pay in full on time even though it has a claim against the payee which it can, as a matter of law, set off against the principal claim. These clauses are normal in financial agreements, and prevent one party putting up what can be seen as an excuse not to pay enabling that party to improve its bargaining position by delay. Instead, a no set-off clause obliges the party to pay now and argue later.[64]

8.3.5 Statutory controls

8.3.5.1 UCTA

The statutory controls on contractual liability are less far reaching than those applicable to misrepresentation. The controls, in section 3 of UCTA, only apply

62. *Henderson* v. *Merrett* [1995] 2 AC 145.
63. *The Heron II* [1969] AC 350, 385–386.
64. See p 264 above.

where one party deals as a consumer or on the other's written standard terms. For these purposes, someone deals as a consumer if he neither makes the contract in the course of a business nor holds himself out as doing so and the other party does make the agreement in the course of a business.[65] Merely because a counterparty is a company does not automatically mean that it is not a consumer, but for most practical purposes it will have that result.[66]

What constitutes standard terms is not an easy question. It is clear that UCTA was drafted with small print on the back of invoices and order forms in mind, but the wording has been given a wider interpretation than that. In *St Albans City and District Council* v. *International Computers Ltd*,[67] there was negotiation over the exclusion clause itself which appeared in general conditions attached to a contract but, in order to enter into the contract quickly, the plaintiffs dropped their objection to the clause. This was still held to be a contract on standard terms as the contract was still made on those terms even though there was negotiation to seek to vary them.[68]

This case, however, concerned standard printed terms attached to a tender. Where a standard word processed form is used which is adapted to each individual transaction, though perhaps with minimal changes because the policy of the institution requires the inclusion of certain clauses, the position is not clear. In *Flamar Interocean Ltd* v. *Denmac Ltd*, Potter J decided that the contract before him was not on standard terms. He commented that "it is plain [the form of agreement] was negotiated between the parties, in that the standard form of management agreement which the defendant possessed at the time (and I leave aside the question of whether such standard form of agreement would in any event amount to 'standard terms of business' in the sense contemplated by UCTA) was subject to a number of alterations to fit the circumstances of the plaintiffs' case before its terms were finalised by the parties."[69] At first instance in the *St Albans* case this was distinguished on the basis that not "all the terms have

65. Section 12(1) of UCTA (in addition, on a sale by auction or competitive tender the buyer is deemed not to be a consumer: section 12(2)). UCTA is in any event only concerned with "business liability": section 1(3).

66. In *R & B Customs Brokers Co Ltd* v. *United Dominions Trust Ltd* [1988] 1 WLR 321, a company bought a car for its owner, and was held to be a consumer for the purposes of UCTA. Dillon LJ accepted (pp 330–331) that one-off adventure in the nature of trade could be carried out in the course of a business, but also that some activities, as in that case, were only incidental to the business of the company and would require a degree of regularity before being entered into in the course of business. If a company enters into a derivatives transaction as a speculative money making transaction, it is likely of itself to constitute a business, and if it does so to hedge an underlying exposure then it is part of the business to which that exposure relates. (See also *Stevenson* v. *Rogers* [1999] 2 WLR 1064.)

67. [1996] 4 All ER 481, particularly 490–491 (see also the first instance decision: unreported, 3 October 1994).

68. In this case, the relevant clause capped liability at £100,000. This produces the irony that had the defendants conceded an increase to, say, £105,000 (or, indeed, decreased the cap to £95,000), they would have been better placed to argue that the contract was not on their standard terms with the result that the clause could not therefore have been declared ineffective under UCTA.

69. [1990] 1 Lloyd's Rep 434, 438.

to be fixed in advance by the supplier. In many contracts there may be negotiations as to, for example, quality or price but none as to the crucial exempting terms."[70] The judicial attitude was most clearly stated in *The Chester Grosvenor Hotel Company Ltd* v. *Alfred McAlpine Management Ltd* as follows:

"... where a party invariably contracts in the same written terms without material variation, those terms will become its 'standard for contract' or 'written standard terms of business'. However, it does not follow that because terms are not employed invariably, or without material variation, they cannot be standard terms ... the question is one of fact and degree. What are alleged to be standard terms may be used so infrequently by comparison with other terms that they cannot realistically be regarded as standard, or on any particular occasion may be so mutilated that they must be regarded as having lost their essential identity. What is required for terms to be standard is that they should be regarded by the party which advances them as its standard terms and that it should habitually contract on those terms. If it contracts also in other terms, it must be determined in any given case, and as a matter of fact, whether this has occurred so frequently that the terms in question cannot be regarded as standard, and if on any occasion a party has substantially modified its prepared terms, it is a question of fact whether those terms have been so altered that they must be regarded as not having been employed on that occasion."[71]

Where this leaves the position in any particular case is bound to be uncertain. It is sensible and prudent business practice to have a standard form of contract for a particular type of business—it will rarely be realistic or economic to draft all contracts from scratch—but using standard terms which include a disclaimer runs the risk of exposing that disclaimer to the requirement of reasonableness. Negotiation is on its own not enough to take a contract out of the grip of UCTA. At one extreme, *St Albans* might be taken to indicate that if a derivatives party has a standard set of terms, including an exclusion clause, which it puts to the other side, they remain standard terms for the purposes of UCTA as long as the actual exclusion clause itself remains the same. That seems, however, improbable, and the issue is more likely to be whether the terms as a whole remain standard rather than whether one particular clause is untouched as a result of negotiation. This leaves the position that a disclaimer could in theory be altered in negotiation with very few other terms changed, but the disclaimer still subject to the requirement of reasonableness.[72]

If a deal is done on one party's written standard terms, then section 3(2) of UCTA provides:

70. Scott Baker J, *St Albans City and District Council* v. *International Computers Ltd*, unreported, 3 October 1994.

71. (1991) 56 BLR 115, 133. In that case the terms were held to be standard; McAlpines had entered into 19 contracts of which nine were said to have been on the same terms alleged to have been standard.

72. There is no reason why ISDA's Master Agreement and clauses prepared by them cannot be one party's standard terms if they adopt those terms and use them as standard. It is less clear if it could be shown that the other party also used the same terms as its standard but happened not to provide the first draft in the case in question. In any event, if both parties use the same standard terms, it will be hard for one to argue that one clause is unreasonable.

"As against [a consumer or someone dealing on the other's standard written terms of business], the other cannot by reference to any contract term—

(a) when himself in breach of contract, exclude or restrict any liability of his in respect of the breach; or
(b) claim to be entitled—
    (i) to render a contractual performance substantially different from that which was reasonably expected of him, or
    (ii) in respect of the whole or any part of his contractual obligations, to render no performance at all,

except in so far as (in any of the cases mentioned above in this subsection) the contract term satisfies the requirement of reasonableness."

As far as derivatives contracts themselves are concerned, this may not be of great relevance. The fundamental obligation is to make payment, and that will rarely if ever be excluded in the event of breach. Where the contractual obligation is, in the main, an obligation to make a payment in certain circumstances, it is also hard to conceive of there being any performance which would be substantially different other than non-payment, which would fall within section 3(2)(a).[73] It is possible that section 3(2)(b)(ii) could, for example, apply to a clause setting out events of default which entitled the innocent party to terminate the contract and therefore not to perform its obligations at all.[74]

Section 3(2)(a) could be relevant to an advisory obligation. If, for example, there is an obligation to take reasonable care, then any attempt to restrict the damages which might be payable in the event of breach would be subject to the requirement of reasonableness.

The requirement of reasonableness itself has been discussed above in relation to pre-contractual liabilities.[75] That discussion is equally relevant to contractual liability.

8.3.5.2 The Unfair Terms in Consumer Contracts Regulations

The Unfair Terms in Consumer Contracts Regulations[76] apply only to contracts entered into with natural persons acting for purposes which are outside their business and if the other party is a seller of goods acting for purposes relating to his business or is a supplier of goods or services acting for the purposes of his business. It may be questionable whether entering into a derivatives contract is

73. "To be substantial the discrepancy must . . . be significant in a practical sense": Lord Bingham CJ in *The Zockoll Group Ltd* v. *Mercury Communications Ltd* (unreported, 3 March 1998). In the same case, the Court of Appeal decided that what was reasonably expected of a party cannot be decided by construction of the contract. They decided, however, that where one party appreciated the risk involved, that would be fatal to a claim based on section 3(2)(b)(i) of UCTA.

74. *Chitty on Contracts* (27th edn), p 676 takes the view that this is unlikely and, in any event, that if it did a term entitling termination would be reasonable.

75. See pp 261–264 above.

76. SI 1994 No 3159.

supplying a service,[77] but it seems likely that it would be treated as the supply of financial services where a consumer is concerned.

If the Regulations are relevant, they apply to contract terms which have not been individually negotiated, i.e. a term which has been drafted in advance and of which the consumer has not been able to influence the substance.[78] A contract term of this sort is not binding on a consumer if it is unfair, i.e. that, contrary to the requirement of good faith, it causes a significant imbalance in the parties' rights and obligations under the contract to the detriment of the consumer.[79] The assessment of this is to be made taking into account the nature of the services and referring, as at the time of the conclusion of the contract, to all circumstances attending the contract and to all the other terms of the contract.[80] In assessing good faith, regard is to be had to the strength of the bargaining position of the parties, whether the consumer had an inducement to agree to the term, whether the services were supplied to the special order of the consumer, and the extent to which the supplier has dealt fairly and equitably with the consumer.[81]

Schedule 3 to the Regulations contains an "indicative and illustrative" list of terms which may be regarded as unfair. These include terms which inappropriately exclude or limit the legal rights of the consumer in the event of total or partial non-performance or inadequate performance by the supplier.[82]

8.4 PROTECTING THIRD PARTIES

Assuming that an exclusion clause is wide enough to protect against a particular liability and meets any statutory requirements, the party subject to the clause will seek a way around that clause. One common way is to look for a third party to sue. If the only available claim is on the contract, there will be no one else to sue,[83] but it may be that someone else is liable for breach of tortious or other non-contractual responsibilities arising from what has been done under the contract. This has arisen commonly in shipping cases, where stevedores can be liable to cargo owners in tort or in the law relating to bailment. Bailment is unlikely to be relevant to derivatives,[84] but the tort of negligence could be

77. In addition, for example, a forward commodity contract which provides a delivery obligation could be a contract for the sale of goods.

78. Regulations 3(1) and (3). The fact that a specific term has been individually negotiated does not prevent the Regulations applying to the rest of the contract if an overall assessment indicates that it is a preformulated standard contract: regulation 3(4). The onus is on the person who claims that a term was individually negotiated to show that it was: regulation 3(5).

79. Regulations 4(1) and 5(1).

80. Regulation 4(2).

81. Regulation 4(3) and Schedule 2 to the Regulations.

82. Paragraph 1(b) to Schedule 3 to the Regulations.

83. In rare cases, the tort of inducing breach of contract may be available.

84. It could be relevant if, unusually, the contract requires one party to hold a bearer instrument on behalf of the other.

relevant if the contract includes an obligation to take reasonable care, and the failure to take reasonable care can be put down to the acts of an individual, a subsidiary or a subcontractor. The opportunities to claim that an agent owes a direct duty of care are limited,[85] but it is not impossible. In these circumstances, the issue becomes how to prevent a contractual party circumventing a contractual limitation clause by suing a non-party.[86]

8.4.1 "Himalaya" clauses

The courts have recognised the commercial need for a means to provide an exemption from liability for third parties,[87] but it remains theoretically difficult for this to be done.[88] Whether it will be done in any particular case comes down to the court's view of the merits of a particular case, and this inevitably leads to uncertainty. A standard clause in bills of lading, a "Himalaya" clause,[89] provides that every "servant, agent and subcontractor shall have the benefit of all exceptions, limitations, provision, conditions and liberties herein benefiting the carrier as if such provisions were expressly made for their benefit, and, in entering into this contract, the carrier, to the extent of these provisions, does so not only on his behalf, but also as agent and trustee for such servants, agents and subcontractors."[90] The courts have allowed stevedores to take advantage of Himalaya clauses on the basis that:

> "... the bill of lading brought into existence a bargain initially unilateral but capable of becoming mutual, between the shipper and the [stevedores], made through the carrier as agent. This became a full contract when the [stevedores] performed services of discharging the goods. The performance of these services for the benefit of the shipper was the consideration for the agreement by the shipper that the [stevedores] should have the benefit of the exemptions and limitations contained in the bill of lading."[91]

The theoretical purity of this approach is doubtful, but the courts have in the

85. See pp 101–102 above.

86. The Law Commission's paper, *Contracts for the Benefit of Third Parties* (Law Com 242) recommended statutory reform to correct the position. In 1999, the Government introduced legislation into Parliament to implement the Law Commission's recommendations.

87. *The Mahkutai* [1996] AC 650, 663. This attitude contrasts with the general hostility to exclusion clauses, but stems largely from shipping cases where limitations on liability are of long standing, well understood by the courts, and the issue is in reality only as to which party's insurer should pay.

88. In *Scruttons Ltd* v. *Midland Silicones Ltd* [1962] AC 446, the House of Lords rejected a theory of vicarious immunity derived from *Elder, Dempster & Co Ltd* v. *Paterson, Zochonis & Co Ltd* [1924] AC 522, and reasserted the traditional view that strangers to a contract cannot benefit from it.

89. So called after the vessel involved in *Adler* v. *Dickson* [1955] 1 QB 158.

90. See *The Mahkutai* [1996] AC 650, 662. In this case, the Privy Council decided that an exclusive jurisdiction clause did not fall within the wording "all exceptions, limitations, provision, conditions and liberties herein benefiting the carrier".

91. *The Eurymedon* [1975] AC 154, 167–168. The act said to benefit from the exclusion clause must be referable to performance of the contract in which the clause is contained: *Raymond Burke Motors Ltd* v. *The Mersey Docks & Harbour Co* [1986] 1 Lloyd's Rep 155.

main ignored this where stevedores are concerned,[92] and it has been suggested that caution is required in extending these principles to a wider field.[93] Whilst there are sound policy reasons to extend the benefit of clauses of this sort to those who are not parties to the contract, whether this will in fact be done in the context of derivatives is inevitably uncertain.

8.4.2 Promises not to sue

A route to protect third parties which is, perhaps, somewhat less uncertain than the use of an adaptation of a Himalaya clause is to provide expressly in the contract that a counterparty will not sue any agents, employees or subcontractors of the other party but, if it does sue in breach of this covenant and is not restrained from doing so, it will pay the other party a sum equal to any sum which the agent, employee or subcontractor is ordered to pay the counterparty. A clause of this sort does not allow the agent to invoke the protection of an exclusion clause directly, but it does allow the contracting party to seek an injunction to prevent the counterparty suing an agent or to claim sums equal to those the counterparty might recover, thereby rendering any litigation futile.

In *Deepak Fertilisers* v. *ICI Chemicals & Polymers Ltd*,[94] the Court of Appeal said that the circumstances in which the courts would restrain proceedings in these circumstances were:

> "1. Equitable fraud (something which is unconscionably unfair) is the basis upon which the courts will restrain or stay the proceedings on the application of a stranger to the proceedings. The power to do so is discretionary.
> 2. Something more than a promise not to sue is required. The applicant must show that he has some interest of his own to protect. This has been expressed in various ways viz: 'Some other good reason', 'the real possibility of prejudice' and 'some legal or equitable right to protect such as an obligation to indemnify the defendant'.
> 3. Whether the applicant has shown that he has such an interest depends upon the facts of each case. Where for example there is an issue as to whether the applicant will be required to indemnify the defendant if proceedings continue the court must consider the likelihood of a claim for an indemnity being made

92. See, for example, *The New York Star* [1981] 1 WLR 138, 143–144 and *The Mahkutai* [1996] AC 650, 663–665.

93. *Southern Water Authority* v. *Carey* [1985] 2 All ER 1077, 1084. Against this, in *The Law of Contracts*, 9th edn, p 571, Treitel is clear that the benefits given to stevedores should be extended to others. In *Southern Water* (at p 1083), the judge was also dismissive of the argument that a contractor could take the benefit of an exclusion clause as trustee for agents. *Chitty on Contracts* (27th edn), p 663 nevertheless comments that "it is possible that such a trust would be upheld (the contracting party acting as bare trustee) provided that the identity of the beneficiaries of the trust is sufficiently certain."

94. [1999] 1 Lloyd's Rep 387, 401.

> and its merits if it is said to be obviously unsustainable, but no prolonged investigation of the issues or potential issues is called for."[95]

Though discretionary, in most cases the courts will restrain proceedings taken in breach of contract. Further, if the contract provides an obligation on the party suing in breach of agreement to pay a sum equal to anything it is awarded against the third party, it will make any action circular and therefore useless, which may provide an additional reason to grant an injunction.[96]

An agreement of this sort is not subject to the statutory controls in UCTA.[97]

95. In *European Asian Bank AG* v. *Punjab and Sind Bank* [1982] 2 Lloyd's Rep 356, 361, Stephenson LJ said that to obtain an injunction restraining proceedings, a party "must show that he will be defrauded if the proceedings are allowed to go on, either (1) because the plaintiff has made a promise, express or implied from their relationship or otherwise, not to bring such proceedings; or (2) because of some other good reason such as that success in the proceedings would impair some legal or equitable right of the stranger seeking the stay ... (1) The fraud on the plaintiff's part is equitable fraud ... '[which] may be said to include properly all acts, omissions and concealments which involve a breach of legal or equitable duty, trust or confidence justly reposed, and are injurious to another ... Fraud in all cases implies a wilful act on the part of anyone whereby another is sought to be deprived by illegal or inequitable means of what he is entitled to, either at law or in equity.' (2) Such fraudulent conduct may be treated as a breach of an implied promise not to take the proceedings to be restrained."

96. *The Elbe Maru* [1978] 1 Lloyd's Rep 206, 210.

97. *Neptune Orient Lines Ltd* v. *JVC (UK) Ltd* [1983] 2 Lloyd's Rep 438.

CHAPTER 9

INSOLVENT COUNTERPARTIES

9.1 THREATENED INSOLVENCY

If a counterparty has become formally insolvent, then the position will generally be relatively clear—that counterparty will not be able to perform its obligations and the other party will at some stage be able to close out its transactions and thereby crystallise its exposure. If it merely looks as if a counterparty is or will become insolvent but no formal steps have yet been taken or admissions been made, the position is more difficult, especially if the solvent party is due to make a payment. It could contend that the counterparty is insolvent and therefore that an event of default had occurred under section 5(a)(vii) of ISDA's Master Agreement, or other similar provisions, but it then bears the burden of proving this if it is challenged. It will seldom have sufficient information to know whether or not the counterparty is in fact insolvent, and is therefore taking a risk. If it is wrong, then it is quite possible that it is in repudiatory breach of the transaction, or, if there is a master agreement, of all transactions subject to the master agreement; if so, the counterparty is entitled to accept that repudiation which will bring the contract to an end and discharge it from future performance.

Similarly, the solvent party could argue that it is impossible by reason of the insolvency for the other party to perform its obligations and, as a result, the solvent party is discharged from its obligations. This entails significant risks as well. To rely successfully on impossibility, it is necessary to be able to prove as a matter of fact that it will be impossible for the other party to perform its obligations at the due time; mere suspicion, even on reasonable grounds, is not enough. For example, if someone is obliged to deliver a particular security but before the due date disposes of it to a third party, that will not be sufficient to establish impossibility because it may repurchase the securities before the due date.[1]

If the counterparty has actually done something to indicate its insolvency or to show that it will not perform, then the other party might feel more comfortable in relying on insolvency as an event of default, or it might be able to rely on the

1. *Hochster* v. *De la Tour* (1853) 2 E&B 678, 688.

counterparty's conduct as constituting an anticipatory breach of contract. For this, it is necessary for one party through its words or conduct to intimate an intention to abandon and altogether refuse to perform its contractual obligations; the other party can accept that anticipatory breach and will, as a result, be discharged from future performance and can claim damages.[2] This requires a clear refusal to perform contractual obligations,[3] but the test is not absolute but only how a reasonable person would have interpreted the words or actions in question.[4]

Absent any indication of this sort from the counterparty, the solvent party is in a difficult position. No course of action is without risks, but it is a question of weighing up the hazards of any particular step. The position is particularly acute if there are a number of transactions subject to a master agreement, and the next payment is due from the solvent party to the possibly insolvent party. The solvent party has a choice; it can pay but, if the other party really is insolvent, it will lose that payment; or it can decline to pay but, if the other party is not in fact insolvent or is rescued, it risks being in breach of contract itself as a result of which the other party may be entitled to terminate all derivatives transactions between the two.[5]

ICOM and IFEMA seek to meet this dilemma by section 11.14.[6] This provides that if a party has "reasonable grounds for insecurity" and the other fails to give "adequate assurances of its ability to perform any of its obligations" within two business days of a written request, then there is an event of default. This is undoubtedly of assistance, but still begs questions: for example, what constitutes reasonable grounds for insecurity and what are adequate assurances? Nevertheless, it is likely to be easier to be satisfied that there are reasonable grounds for insecurity than that it is possible to prove insolvency if it is challenged.

9.2 ADMINISTRATION

9.2.1 Introduction

Administration was introduced by the Insolvency Act 1986 to meet a perceived weakness in the insolvency procedures available before that Act. If a company had granted a creditor a floating charge, a receiver could be appointed with power, under a properly drawn charge, to run the business with a view to its sale as a going concern. If no floating charge had been granted, the only practicable

2. *Freeth* v. *Burr* (1874) LR 9 CP 208, 213–214.
3. *Woodar* v. *Wimpey* [1980] 1 WLR 277, 280.
4. *Universal Cargo Carriers* v. *Citati* [1957] QB 401, 436.
5. There could also be cross default consequences on other transactions, though if other parties seek to rely on a cross default they too are likely to be taking a risk of being able to prove that there is in fact a default.
6. This requires selection by the parties in the Schedule.

remedy was often liquidation, but a liquidator has no power to continue the business of a company. Liquidation would therefore result in the company being closed down and its assets sold in a piecemeal fashion. Sale as a going concern normally realises more than sale of the individual assets, and therefore an inability to carry on business because there was no floating charge was often detrimental to creditors. The administration procedure was intended to meet this problem.[7]

9.2.2 The requirements for administration

An application for an administration order can be made by the company, its directors or one or more creditors.[8] The court can make the order if it is satisfied that the company[9] is or is likely to be unable to pay its debts[10] and considers that the making of the order would be likely to achieve one of the purposes set out in section 8(3) of the Insolvency Act 1986.[11] These purposes are: the survival of the company, or the whole or any part of its undertaking, as a going concern; the approval of a voluntary arrangement[12]; the sanctioning under section 425 of the Companies Act 1985 of a compromise between the company and its creditors[13]; or a more advantageous realisation of the company's assets than would be effected on a winding up. An administration order cannot in practice be made if it is opposed by anyone entitled to appoint an administrative receiver.[14]

7. See, for example, *Bristol Airport Ltd* v. *Powdrill* [1990] 1 Ch 744, 756.

8. Section 9(1) of the Insolvency Act 1986. In addition, section 74 of the Financial Services Act 1986 allows an SRO and the Secretary of State in certain circumstances to apply for an administration order. In practice, creditors will rarely have enough information to make an application.

9. Section 8(4) of the Insolvency Act 1986 provides that administration orders cannot be made in relation to a company which has gone into liquidation—by then it is too late—nor an insurance company within the meaning of the Insurance Companies Act 1982 (see p 63 above—a separate regime applies to insurance companies) or an authorised institution or former authorised institution within the meaning of the Banking Act 1987. The Banks (Administration Proceedings) Order 1989, SI 1989 No 1276, has, however, allowed administration orders to be made against authorised and former authorised institutions.

10. For these purposes, the definition of unable to pay its debts is in section 123 of the Insolvency Act 1986. This includes an inability to pay debts as they fall due, and the value of a company's assets exceeding its liabilities, taking into account its contingent and prospective liabilities.

11. Section 8(1) of the Insolvency Act 1986. The purpose(s) for which the administration order is made must be specified in the order.

12. Voluntary arrangements are covered by Part I of the Insolvency Act 1986, which provides for an arrangement between the company and its creditors approved by three-quarters in number of the creditors to bind all creditors who had notice of and were entitled to vote at the meeting.

13. Section 425 of the Companies Act 1985 provides that a compromise or arrangement between a company and its creditors binds all creditors if it is approved by three-quarters in value and sanctioned by the court.

14. Anyone entitled to appoint an administrative receiver must be given notice of the application (section 9(2) of the Insolvency Act 1986), the court cannot appoint an administrator if there is an administrative receiver save in very limited circumstances (section 9(3)), and an application for an administration order does not prevent the appointment of an administrative receiver (section 10(2)(b)). Anyone entitled to appoint an administrative receiver is, therefore, able to trump an application for an administration order by appointing an administrative receiver.

If an administration order is made, the effect is that for the period that it is in force, the affairs, business and property of the company are managed by the administrator(s) appointed by the court.[15] In carrying out his functions, the administrator acts as the agent of the company.[16] Administration is intended to be only an interim and temporary regime, giving the company a breathing space whilst the administrator seeks to achieve the purposes for which he has been appointed.[17] The administrator must within three months of appointment, or longer if the court extends the time, lay before a meeting of the company's creditors, called on not less than 14 days' notice, his proposals for achieving the purposes for which the administration order was made.[18] At this meeting, the creditors may approve, with or without modifications,[19] the administrator's proposals, following which the administrator must report the outcome of the meeting to the court.

If the creditors' meeting rejects the proposals, the court may make such order as it sees fit, including discharging the administration order.[20] If the proposals are approved, the meeting can also appoint a creditors' committee with power to summon the administrator before it to provide information it may reasonably request about the carrying out of the administrator's functions,[21] to assist the administrator in the discharge of his functions[22] and to fix the administrator's remuneration.[23]

Voting at a meeting of creditors depends upon giving the administrator details

15. Section 8(2) of the Insolvency Act 1986. An administrator must be a licensed insolvency practitioner: sections 388 and 389 of the Act.

16. Section 14(5) of the Insolvency Act 1986. A third party dealing with an administrator in good faith is not concerned to enquire whether the administrator is acting within his powers: section 14(6) of the Act.

17. *Re Atlantic Computer Systems plc* [1992] 1 All ER 476, 489.

18. Section 23(1) of the Insolvency Act 1986. The proposals must be sent to all creditors as well as filed with the Registrar of Companies. Creditors representing one tenth in value of the company's creditors can also requisition a meeting (section 17(3) of the Insolvency Act 1986) though they must, initially at least, pay the costs of doing so (rule 2.21(3) of the Insolvency Rules 1986).

19. The administrator must consent to any modification: section 24(2) of the Insolvency Act 1986.

20. Section 24 of the Insolvency Act 1986.

21. Section 26 of the Insolvency Act 1986. A creditors' committee has between three and five members, which can include bodies corporate, who are creditors of the company (rule 2.32 of the Insolvency Rules 1986). Membership of the committee does not prevent a person from dealing with the company while the administration order is in force provided that any transactions are in good faith and for value (rule 2.46(1) of the Insolvency Rules 1986).

22. Rule 2.34(1) of the Insolvency Rules 1986.

23. Rule 2.47(3) of the Insolvency Rules 1986. There are also provisions for the administrator to take the matter to a full creditors' meeting and to the court, and also for creditors to go to the court (rules 2.47–50). As to remuneration, see the Report of Mr Justice Ferris' Working Party on *The remuneration of office-holders and certain related matters* published in 1998.

in writing of the debt due from the company and lodging a proxy form.[24] It is up to the chairman of the meeting, invariably the administrator,[25] to decide whether to admit a creditor's claim for the purposes of an entitlement to vote, subject to any appeal to the court.[26] If, however, the chairman is in doubt about whether a claim should be admitted, he should mark it as objected and allow the creditor to vote, subject to that vote being subsequently declared invalid if the objection is sustained, and the court making such order with regard to the vote.[27] Voting is calculated according to the amount of a creditor's debt at the date of the administration order, less any sums paid after that date,[28] but a creditor is not entitled to vote in respect of a debt for an unliquidated sum or any debt whose value is not ascertained except where the chairman agrees to put a minimum value on the debt for the purposes of voting.[29] In the case of derivatives, sums overdue at the time of the administration order are capable of being voted, even if they arise from the closing out of a contract, but where there are no sums actually due but the mark to market value of the contract would leave a sum due from the company in administration, prima facie there is no right to vote unless the chairman is prepared to put a minimum value on the claim.[30]

9.2.3 The effect of an administration order on derivatives transactions

The effect of both an application for an administration order and an order itself is that:

(1) no resolution may be passed or order made for the winding up of the company;
(2) no steps may be taken to enforce any security over the company's property, or to repossess goods in the company's possession under any hire purchase, conditional sale, chattel leasing or retention of title

24. Rule 2.22(1) of the Insolvency Rules 1986. The chairman of the meeting may admit a creditor to vote notwithstanding a failure to submit the required forms if he is satisfied that it was due to circumstances beyond the creditor's control (rule 2.22(2)). A creditor can also split its vote: *Re Polly Peck International plc* [1991] BCC 503.
25. Rule 2.20 of the Insolvency Rules 1986.
26. Rule 2.23(1) and (2) of the Insolvency Rules 1986. In the case of a meeting summoned by the administrator to consider his proposals, an appeal must be made within 28 days of the administrator reporting on the meeting to the court: rule 2.23(5) of the Insolvency Rules 1986.
27. Rules 2.23(3) and (4) of the Insolvency Rules 1986.
28. Rule 2.22(4) of the Insolvency Rules 1986.
29. Rule 2.22(5) of the Insolvency Rules 1986.
30. In this connection, rule 2.27 of the Insolvency Rules 1986 provides that creditors under hire purchase, conditional sale and chattel leasing agreements can only vote for the sum due and payable as at the date of the administration order, ignoring any sum attributable to the exercise of any right which has become exercisable solely by virtue of the administration order: rule 2.27 of the Insolvency Rules 1986. Secured creditors can also only vote for the balance due after deducting an estimated value of the security (rule 2.24), and negotiable instruments are also treated in some respects as security (rule 2.25).

agreement except with the consent of the court or, if there is one, the administrator; and

(3) no other proceedings and no execution or other legal process may be commenced or continued, and no distress may be levied, against the company or its property except with the consent of the court or, if there is one, the administrator.[31]

The effect of an administration order is not to alter legal rights but merely to place a moratorium on the enforcement of creditors' rights to the extent provided by the Insolvency Act 1986.[32] As far as derivatives are concerned, the Act prevents any legal proceedings, but does not prevent the exercise of contractual rights.[33] An administration order does not itself have any effect on a contract, but a counterparty has a choice whether to exercise such rights as it may have to close out transactions, for example under sections 5(a)(vii)(2) or (6) of ISDA's Master Agreement, or to allow the transactions to continue. Closing out will produce certainty as to the credit exposure, and will entitle the solvent party to vote on any proposals put forward by the administrator. Closing out might, however, lose the benefit of any third party taking over the positions of the company in administration if that is likely and, for example, the purposes of the administration include the survival of the company or part of its undertaking as a going concern. If the transaction with the company in administration hedges another transaction, then closing out will also leave market exposure which the solvent party did not intend; there is, however, a serious risk that the market exposure will exist in any event because, if a company has gone into administration, it is likely that it will not perform its obligations.

Sections 10(1) and 11(3) of the Insolvency Act 1986 do not prevent a party

31. Sections 10(1) and 11(3) of the Insolvency Act 1986. Section 161(4) of the Companies Act 1989 provides that these sections of the Insolvency Act do not apply to restrict any default proceedings taken by any recognised exchange or clearing house, i.e. proceedings under rules which provide for the taking of action in the event of a person appearing unable, or likely to become unable, to meet its obligations with regard to a "market contract" (section 188(1)). A market contract is a contract entered into (a) by a member or designated non-member (i.e. a person against whom default proceedings can be taken) of an exchange with a person other than the exchange which are either contracts made on the exchange or contracts in the making of which the member or designated non-member was subject to the rules of the exchange, and (b) contracts with the exchange: section 155(2). Section 175 of the Companies Act 1989 exempts "market charges" from the effect of the last of these restrictions, i.e. charges in favour of a recognised investment exchange or clearing house, though the effect of this exemption is limited by the Financial Markets and Insolvency Regulations 1991 (SI 1991 No 880). The Financial Markets and Insolvency Regulations 1998 extended this protection to OTC transactions cleared through an exchange or clearing house whether or not entered into on the exchange.

32. *Barclays Mercantile Business Finance Ltd* v. *Sibec Developments Ltd* [1992] 1 WLR 1253, 1257.

33. *Re Olympia & York Canary Wharf Ltd* [1993] BCC 154, *McMullen & Sons Ltd* v. *Cerrone* [1994] BCC 25 and (impliedly) *Bristol Airport plc* v. *Powdrill* [1990] 1 Ch 744, 766. In *Exchange Travel Agency Ltd* v. *Triton Property Trust plc* [1991] BCC 341, 345, Harman J probably took the opposite view, which is not unarguable. "Property" is defined in the Insolvency Act 1986 to include contractual rights (section 436), and the question is therefore whether exercising contractual rights is "other legal process" within sections 10(1)(c) and 11(3)(d) of the Insolvency Act 1986 (for these

from exercising a right of equitable set-off[34] as it does not entail security, legal proceedings or other legal process.[35] Nor is it likely that contractual set-off is prevented as long as it is just an exercise of contractual rights. However, *Re BCCI (No 8)* establishes that it is conceptually possible to create a charge over a debt in favour of the debtor to secure obligations of the depositor.[36] If, therefore, a charge is created, then relying on that charge is likely to constitute enforcement and, as a result, is prohibited by the Insolvency Act 1986. A well drawn charge will, however, also contain an express contractual right of set-off, and this right is not the same as a charge. There seems no reason why recourse cannot be had to this contractual right rather than to the charge. If so, that right is not subject to the restrictions arising on administration.[37]

9.3 ADMINISTRATIVE RECEIVERSHIP

The name "administrative receivership" was introduced by the Insolvency Act 1986, though administrative receivership, without being described as such, had existed for many years before that Act. An administrative receiver is:

> "(a) a receiver or manager of the whole (or substantially the whole) of a company's property appointed by or on behalf of the holders of any debentures of the company secured by a charge which, as created, was a floating charge, or by such a charge and one or more other securities; or

purposes, "other proceedings" are "legal proceedings or quasi-legal proceedings such as arbitration": *Bristol Airport plc* v. *Powdrill* [1990] 1 Ch 744, 765). The aim of administration is to allow a company to continue to trade, and the termination of contracts is likely to impede this. Nevertheless, restricting the exercise of contractual rights would be very hard to manage and would create huge uncertainty (e.g., if a contract terminates automatically on administration, would that be the exercise of contractual rights?).

34. I.e. set-off arising, in general, from the same transaction (see p 219 above).

35. See, for example, Fletcher, Higham & Trower, *The Law and Practice of Corporate Administration*, pp 27–28 and Derham, *Set-off* (2nd edn), pp 152–153.

36. [1997] 4 All ER 568, 575–578.

37. In *Re BCCI (No 8)* [1997] 4 All ER 568, Lord Hoffmann emphasised that a charge gave a proprietary interest in the property charged (p 576), that a secured creditor is not obliged to resort to his security (p 572) and, after referring to the view expressed in the Court of Appeal that a charge in these circumstances was a conceptual impossibility, went on "The Court of Appeal said that a bank could obtain effective security in other ways. If the deposit was made by a principal debtor, it could rely upon contractual rights of set-off... If the deposit was made by a third party, it could enter into contractual arrangements such as the limitation of the right to withdraw the deposit in this case, thereby making the deposit a 'flawed asset'. All this is true. It may well be that the security provided in these ways will in most cases be as good as that provided by a proprietary right. But that seems to me no reason to prevent banks and their customers from creating charges if, for reasons of their own, they want to do so" (p 577). Lord Hoffmann's use of the word "security" is a reference to the effect of the contractual arrangement rather than an assertion that a contractual right of set-off is security in the legal sense, whether for the purposes of section 11(3)(c) of the Insolvency Act 1986 or otherwise. Section 248 of the Insolvency Act 1986 defines "security" as "any mortgage, charge, lien or other security", and in *Bristol Airport plc* v. *Powdrill* [1990] 1 Ch 744, 760, Sir Nicolas Browne-Wilkinson V-C said that "other security" should be given its natural meaning. A contractual right of set-off does not fall within the natural meaning of security.

(b) a person who would be such a receiver or manager but for the appointment of some other person as the receiver of part of the company's property."[38]

Essentially, the appointment of an administrative receiver is a remedy for a secured creditor with a floating charge over the company's assets.[39] The task of an administrative receiver is to realise the company's assets and pay the proceeds to his appointor to discharge the secured debt. An administrative receiver will invariably have power to carry on the business of the company,[40] and may seek to sell the business of the company as going concern. In carrying out his functions, an administrative receiver acts as an agent of the company until it goes into liquidation[41] when he acts either as the agent of his appointor or, more usually, as principal.[42] Even though he ceases to be agent of the company, he can still exercise all the powers given to him, including suing in the name of the company to recover sums due to it.

As far as an unsecured creditor of a company is concerned, the appointment of an administrative receiver does not prevent it from closing out any positions if entitled to do so under the terms of the relevant contract. Nor does the appointment of an administrative receiver prevent legal or other action against the company, though it will in most cases render it futile. The appointment of an administrative receiver crystallises a floating charge over the assets of a company which turns the charge into a fixed charge. The assets are available to the secured creditor to meet its debt, and only if there is a surplus will they be available to unsecured creditors.[43] In most instances, however, the company will go into liquidation following administrative receivership.

An administrative receiver is personally liable for any contract entered into by him in the carrying out of his functions, and has an indemnity out of the assets of the company for liabilities incurred under those contracts.[44] An administrative receiver can, if it suits his purposes, perform a derivatives contract entered into by the company, but in doing so he incurs no personal liability even if he then

38. Section 29(2) of the Insolvency Act 1986. A properly drawn charge (or charges) will charge by way of fixed charge all property capable of being so charged, the remainder being subject to a floating charge. The reason is that assets subject to a floating charge must be used first to pay preferential creditors whereas assets subject to a fixed charge are not subject to this prior right: section 175(2)(b) of the Insolvency Act 1986.

39. Other receivers carry out the same function but with regard to specific assets of the company rather than the assets and undertakings of the company generally.

40. Section 42(1) of the Insolvency Act 1986, together with paragraph 14 of Schedule 1, gives an administrative receiver power to do so unless inconsistent with the provisions of the charge under which he was appointed.

41. Section 44(1)(a) of the Insolvency Act 1986.

42. See Lightman & Moss, *The Law of Receivers of Companies* (2nd edn), pp 185–186.

43. An administrative receiver is obliged within three months, or such longer period as the court may allow, of his appointment to send creditors a report setting out, amongst other matters, the amount likely to be available for the payment of unsecured creditors: section 48(1) of the Insolvency Act 1986.

44. Section 44(1)(b) and (c) of the Insolvency Act 1986.

ceases performance in breach of the company's obligations—the counterparty remains an unsecured creditor of the company ranking behind the secured creditors.[45]

9.4 INSOLVENT LIQUIDATION

If a counterparty goes into insolvent liquidation,[46] then in most cases unsecured creditors will receive a dividend representing only a small part of the sums due to them, the dividend being paid a significant period after the sums became due. The function of a liquidator is to collect the company's assets and to use those assets to pay, so far as can be done, the company's debts in accordance with the statutory scheme. After secured debts and the expenses of the liquidation, preferential creditors are paid[47] following which the debts due to unsecured creditors rank equally. For these purposes, "debts" are defined in rule 13.12 of the Insolvency Rules 1986 as:

> "(a) any debt or liability to which the company is subject at the date on which it goes into liquidation; [and]
> (b) any debt or liability to which the company may become subject after that date by reason of any obligation incurred before that date ..."

As a result, a creditor on a derivatives transaction has a choice: it can close out the transaction, assuming it has power to do so; or it can do nothing. If the transaction is closed out under the terms of a master agreement because of the insolvency, then a sum will become due under the provisions of the master agreement. In a liquidation, claims by creditors are measured, in theory at least, by reference to what was due at the commencement of the liquidation.[48] A compulsory winding up is deemed to commence at the date of the presentation of the winding-up petition[49] and a voluntary winding up when the creditors' resolution is passed.[50] The sum due on close out will become due after the commencement of the liquidation, but a proof can still be lodged for that sum,[51] though it should be discounted back to the commencement of the liquidation at

45. See Lightman & Moss, *The Law of Receivers of Companies* (2nd edn), pp 139–140.
46. This can be either a creditors' voluntary liquidation where the creditors vote at a meeting to wind up the company or a compulsory winding up where the court orders the company to be wound up.
47. Section 175 of the Insolvency Act 1986. Preferential creditors include various taxes and certain sums due to employees.
48. *Stein* v. *Blake* [1996] 1 AC 243, 252.
49. Section 129 of the Insolvency Act 1986.
50. Section 86 of the Insolvency Act 1986.
51. See, for example, *Re Asphaltic Wood Pavement Company* (1885) 30 Ch D 216.

a rate of 5 per cent per annum.[52] In addition, if the sum due on close out included interest, that interest is only provable for the period up to the commencement of the liquidation,[53] and if the sum is due other than in sterling, it is converted to sterling at the date of the commencement of the liquidation.[54]

If a transaction is closed out, the issue is simply one of calculating the sum due to the creditor as at the commencement of the liquidation. Liquidation does not of itself deprive the solvent party of its contractual rights[55] or automatically terminate a contract.[56] If the contract is closed out, the issue is what is due under the contract in accordance with its terms. If, however, the contract is not closed out, the liquidator has a choice. The liquidator can elect to do nothing. If so, then the solvent party's claim in the liquidation will fall to be estimated in accordance with the Insolvency Rules 1986. Rule 4.86 provides that the liquidator must estimate the value of any debt which, by reason of being subject to any insolvency, does not bear a certain value (he can also revise an earlier estimate), and the amount of the estimate is provable in the liquidation. If the contingency, for example a credit event under a credit default swap, has occurred between the commencement of the liquidation and the date relevant for payments to creditors, then the amount due on the occurrence of the contingency will be treated as having been due at the commencement of the liquidation.[57]

A claim will be subject to the principle of set-off in rule 4.90 of the Insolvency Rules 1986. This provides that where, before a company went into liquidation, there had been mutual credits, mutual debts[58] or other mutual dealings, an account must be taken of what is due[59] from each party to the other and those sums set off against each other. This operates automatically to extinguish the gross claims and replace them with a claim for the net balance only.[60] As a result, the claims[61] by the insolvent company against the other party are set off against the claims against the solvent party to produce one net sum which is treated as being due at the commencement of the liquidation.

Rather than doing nothing, the liquidator could give notice to disclaim a contract which he considers onerous,[62] though in practice this is rarely likely to

52. Rules 4.94 and 11.13 of the Insolvency Rules 1986.
53. Rule 4.93 of the Insolvency Rules 1986.
54. Rule 4.91 of the Insolvency Rules 1986.
55. Though it does prevent action to enforce rights, and automatic set-off under Insolvency Rule 4.90 (and *Stein* v. *Blake* [1996] 1 AC 243) can affect rights.
56. See p 237 above.
57. *Stein* v. *Blake* [1996] 1 AC 243, 252.
58. "Debt" is defined very widely in rule 13.12: see p 283 above.
59. "... when [rule 4.90] speaks of taking an account of what is 'due' from each party, it does not mean that the sums in question must be due and payable, whether at the [liquidation] date or even the date when the calculation falls to be made. The claims may have been contingent at the time of the calculation, but they are nevertheless included in the account" (*Stein* v. *Blake* [1996] 1 AC 243, 252).
60. *Stein* v. *Blake* [1996] 1 AC 243.
61. They must be pecuniary, i.e. money, claims: *Re BCCI (No 8)* [1997] 4 All ER 568, 578–579.
62. Section 178(2) of the Insolvency Act 1986. A liquidator cannot disclaim a market contract (see p 280 above): section 164(1) of the Companies Act 1989.

be done. The effect of disclaimer is to determine, as from the date of the disclaimer, the obligations of the company, but it does not affect the obligations of the solvent party.[63] However, anyone sustaining loss or damage in consequence of the disclaimer is a creditor of the company to the extent of that loss or damage, and may prove for it.[64]

9.5 FOREIGN LIQUIDATIONS

If a counterparty goes into liquidation in the country of its incorporation, then the English courts will in general recognise the rights given to the foreign liquidator under local law to act on behalf of the company.[65] Recognition does not necessarily entail acceptance of all the incidents of foreign insolvency law, however, and a creditor may have two principal options. First, if the insolvent party has assets in England, it may seek to persuade the court to freeze those assets through a freezing injunction,[66] to grant it judgment, and then to allow it to enforce its claims directly against those assets. Secondly, it may seek to wind up the foreign company in England if that is favourable.

As to the first of these options, the English courts have of late[67] shown themselves inclined to take a global approach to insolvency event though there is, as yet at least, no international insolvency treaty.[68] As a result, where there is a foreign insolvency, they have been inclined to refuse to allow individual creditors to detain assets and then enforce any judgment against those individual

63. Section 178(4) of the Insolvency Act 1986.

64. Section 178(6) of the Insolvency Act 1986.

65. See Smart, *Cross-Border Insolvency* (2nd edn), pp 166–167.

66. Regarding freezing (Mareva) injunctions, see Gee, *Mareva Injunctions and Anton Piller Relief* (4th edn). In summary, in order to obtain a Mareva injunction it is necessary to show that (1) there is a good arguable case on the merits; (2) there is a real risk that the defendant will deal with its assets, whether by removal from the jurisdiction or by disposal within the jurisdiction, with the result that they are not available when judgment against it is given; and (3) it is just and convenient to grant a Mareva injunction. The courts can grant a Mareva injunction either if the substantive proceedings are in England or in support of substantive proceedings overseas. A Mareva injunction will usually only be granted with regard to assets in England and Wales, but the courts can, in rare cases usually involving fraud, grant a Mareva injunction over assets outside England and Wales (though even when this is done, it is often necessary to obtain a similar order, or recognition of the English order, in relevant overseas jurisdictions). A Mareva injunction does not give any priority over assets; it merely acts as an order to the defendant not to deal with his assets. If the defendant does breach the injunction, he is in contempt of court. If a third party assists him to do this, knowing of the injunction, he too can be in contempt of court. Mareva injunctions will only very rarely be granted against banks.

67. Primarily in the light of the collapse of the Maxwell and BCCI groups.

68. For example, *Barclays Bank plc* v. *Homan* [1992] BCC 757, *Banque Indosuez SA* v. *Ferromet Resources Inc* [1993] BCLC 112 and Lord Hoffmann's 1996 Denning Lecture, quoted in Smart, *Cross-Border Insolvency* (2nd edn), p 232 (but cf the earlier case of *Felixstowe Dock and Railway Co* v. *United States Lines Inc* [1989] QB 360). See also Smart [1999] *Insolvency Lawyer* 1. There is a European Convention on Insolvency Proceedings, but it is not (yet) in force in England. The international nature of the court's approach could, in practice, depend upon a perception of the jurisdiction in which the principal liquidation is taking place.

assets. If assets cannot be detained for execution, there becomes little point in proceedings in England.

The alternative approach is for there to be an "ancillary" liquidation in England. The English court has jurisdiction to wind up foreign companies if the company (a) has been dissolved, has ceased to carry on business or is carrying on business only for the purposes of winding up its affairs, (b) is unable to pay its debts, or (c) it is just and equitable that it should be wound up.[69] The court has a discretion whether to wind up a foreign company but will generally do so if: there is a sufficient connection with England which may, but does not necessarily have to, consist of assets within the jurisdiction; there is a reasonable possibility of benefit for those applying for the winding-up order; one or more persons interested in the distribution of the company's assets must be subject to the jurisdiction of the English court.[70] In most cases, assets within the jurisdiction of the English court will be the key reason for presenting a winding-up petition.

"Ancillary" winding up is not a status formally recognised by the insolvency legislation.[71] In principle, an English liquidator has, as a matter of English law, authority to recover assets anywhere in the world.[72] In an ancillary winding up, the liquidator will generally confine himself to assets in England and then pass those assets to the liquidator in the place of incorporation for distribution to creditors. English insolvency law is, however, mandatory, and the court has no power to disapply it. As a result, in *Re BCCI (No 10)*,[73] the set-off rules were much more restricted in the place of incorporation, Luxembourg, than in England. Before funds were passed to the Luxembourg liquidators, Sir Richard Scott V-C required the English liquidators to retain sufficient sums so that creditors would not lose the benefit of English set-off provision.

69. Section 221(5) of the Insolvency Act 1986. An overseas company is an unregistered company for these purposes: section 225 of the Insolvency Act 1986.

70. *Re Real Estate Development Co* [1991] BCLC 210, 217, summarising what Knox J considered the law to be. The last requirement laid down by Knox J is somewhat obscure (see Smart, *Cross-Border Insolvency* (2nd edn), pp 105–107). See also Smart [1999] *Insolvency Lawyer* 1.

71. As to ancillary winding up, see generally *Re BCCI (No 10)* [1997] Ch 213.

72. Whether the courts of other countries would recognise the rights of an English liquidator to recover assets within their jurisdiction is another question altogether.

73. [1997] Ch 213.

CHAPTER 10

CONTENTIOUS DERIVATIVES

10.1 RESOLVING DISPUTES

Disputes are inevitable in derivatives as in every other commercial field. Disputes can take many years to resolve, can take on a life of their own, and can prove very expensive, both in lawyers' fees and the management time required to run a dispute. A dispute might, for example, be over the market price on a particular day, what the terms of the contract are, the meaning of those terms, whether there is a contract, or what representations were made before the contract, and it might turn on a point of law or a point of fact, but it is invariably better if the dispute can be resolved quickly and without rancour, as long as the price of doing so is reasonable. If the price demanded is not reasonable, then negotiation can turn into commercial blackmail. Establishing at an early stage what is reasonable is not necessarily easy, but any form of consensual resolution requires both parties to want to resolve the dispute. If that willingness is not there, the dispute will rarely be resolved without cost and delay.

There are various ways of resolving disputes. This chapter will touch briefly upon negotiation, expert determination and arbitration and litigation. Of these, expert determination and arbitration require the agreement of the parties to the dispute, something which can be difficult after the dispute has arisen. These are often, therefore, best dealt with in the transaction documentation. Similarly, there can be disputes over where litigation should take place, something that is also best resolved in a contract, though ultimately courts have compulsory jurisdiction and can therefore give a determination whether or not the parties have consented. A dispute over where a dispute should take place does, however, take time and cost money, and does not address the underlying issues. Further, if a dispute is determined by a court which cannot give a judgment which is enforceable against the assets of the other party, the time and money spent upon the dispute could be wasted.[1]

1. See pp 209ff above.

10.1.1 Negotiation

Overwhelmingly the most common way to resolve a dispute is through negotiation even if more formal procedures have also been taken. Negotiation might be through commercial channels, through lawyers, or through both, the choice depending upon the tactics of the situation. Negotiation can, however, only lead to a resolution if the parties reach agreement upon the terms on which the dispute should be resolved. Negotiation does not impose a solution on the parties.

If the parties want to resolve a dispute but have been unable to do so directly themselves, an increasingly common means to reach a negotiated solution, and one now encouraged by the courts, is alternative dispute resolution ("ADR"). ADR is a range of techniques, usually involving a third party who seeks to bring the parties together. The most common form of ADR is mediation, "a process in which a neutral mediator ... will help the parties in dispute to try to work out their own principles and terms for the resolution of the issues between them. Mediators do not arbitrate and have no authority to make or impose decisions regarding the parties' issues."[2] Typically, a mediation will involve the parties summarising their positions on paper in advance, and then making opening statements at the mediation itself. The parties will then divide into separate rooms with the mediator going between them to explore the issues, and to seek common ground and possible solutions. The role of the mediator includes defusing hostility, clarifying issues, suggesting and transmitting offers and counter-offers, testing the reality of a party's position, and allowing a party to have its say.

Mediation is by far the most common form of ADR, but ADR can also include mini-trials and neutral evaluation. Mini-trial[3] is a "without prejudice formalised settlement procedure in which advocates present their client's best case and reasons for settlement within strict time limits to a panel composed of one executive decision-maker representing each party. It is followed immediately by direct negotiation [between the decision-makers]. The parties are often assisted by a neutral retained to assist the panel to assess the representations. The procedures will vary according to ground rules agreed by the parties. If a neutral is retained, he may be requested to preside and maintain the rules and agreed timetable, to assist with negotiations and, if so agreed, to give an opinion on the likely outcome of litigation."[4]

Neutral evaluation is the use of a neutral to give his or her opinion on the

2. The Law Society's Specimen Code of Practice for Mediators, *Guide to the Professional Conduct of Solicitors* (7th edn), p 375. The term conciliation is also used, some saying that the difference is that a conciliator expresses his own (non-binding) views as to the merits of a dispute, others taking the reverse position. Whether called a mediator or a conciliator, the third party commonly does not express views on the merits of a dispute unless it is agreed that he or she should do so.

3. Also called executive hearings, executive tribunals, and formalised settlement conferences.

4. Mackie, Miles and Marsh, *Commercial Dispute Resolution, an ADR Practice Guide*, p 7.

potential outcome of a dispute or some aspect of it. The opinion has no binding effect, and is intended to give the parties a realistic assessment of the issues between them to help them to reach a resolution themselves. Because the neutral has to be given facts upon which to express an opinion, it is of limited use where there is any significant factual dispute.

The advantages of ADR are commonly stated to be: if it succeeds it is far cheaper than litigation, and if it fails not much is wasted; it does not depend upon the availability of court time but can proceed as fast as the parties want it to; it can be useful in maintaining business relationships by providing a mechanism to resolve disputes early and without animosity; courts can in general only provide for the payment of a sum of money whereas through ADR the parties can provide more flexible solutions; and, it is confidential.

The disadvantages of ADR are often stated to be: it cannot provide court assistance (e.g. a Mareva (freezing) injunction); it does not bring pressure to bear upon a recalcitrant party and can be used to waste time if one party has no genuine interest in settlement; it cannot set a precedent and therefore give a message to others in the same position; it is private and therefore attracts no publicity even if that might be of value; if one party has overwhelming economic power, seeking to negotiate with them or, for the other side, indulging in negotiation, may prove futile or frustrating; and if there is no real dispute and a court might, for example, grant summary judgment, it can merely delay the resolution of the dispute.

If the parties to a dispute genuinely want to resolve it without the cost and delay of legal proceedings, ADR can be of value if there are real differences between the parties. Where, however, one party suspects that the other is simply not paying because it cannot or because it does not wish to do so, then ADR is of more limited value; if direct negotiation has not succeeded, the pressures of formalised proceedings may be more appropriate. Nevertheless, if it seems at the outset that ADR may be appropriate, it is possible to include provision for it in a contract, though the enforceability of ADR clauses is open to question.[5]

10.1.2 Expert determination

"Expert determination is a means by which the parties to a contract jointly instruct a third party to decide an issue."[6] The expert is not a judge or arbitrator and is not therefore bound to decide on the evidence put before him having duly

5. The argument against ADR clauses is that they are only agreements to agree or to negotiate and are therefore unenforceable (*Walford* v. *Miles* [1992] 2 AC 128, 138). Clauses can, however, be drafted as an agreement to take part in ADR procedures as a condition precedent to the right to take legal proceedings, a view taken by some Australian courts (see, for example, Mackie, Miles & Marsh, *Commercial Dispute Resolution*, pp 177ff).

6. Kendall, *Expert Determination* (2nd edn), p 1.

heard the arguments of both parties.[7] The contract may provide for the parties to make submissions to the expert or to provide him with information if he requests it, but in general an expert is appointed because he is an expert in the relevant area with the intention that he should decide the issue before him on the basis of his expertise. Experts, who are rarely lawyers,[8] are commonly used where there is a technical dispute, such as the valuation of shares. ISDA's standard form confirmation for credit default swaps includes a provision allowing a party dissatisfied with a determination by the other party on whether the fall in the value of the underlying instrument is material to require the issue to be determined by an expert.[9] Other pricing and valuation issues could be resolved by an expert.

The advantages of expert determination are: an expert can give a determination far more quickly than most other forms of dispute resolution because he is not bound by the need to go through formal procedures; expert determination can be cheap because, although an expert will have to be paid, the costs are likely to be significantly less than those of more formalised procedures involving lawyers; expert determination is confidential; an expert's determination will usually be said to be final, and the courts will only overturn an expert's determination in limited circumstances[10]; and expert determination is generally less acrimonious than litigation or arbitration can be and can therefore help to preserve commercial relationships.

The disadvantages of expert determination are: it does not produce a result which is directly enforceable—it is necessary to take court proceedings as a result of the expert's determination to convert that determination into a judgment which can be enforced against assets; the expert's qualities might be open to question with the result that the outcome can be unpredictable; if an expert does make an eccentric determination, it is difficult to correct it; and there can be a lack of rigour in the determination.

If there is an expert determination clause in an agreement which is mandatory, then the court will generally stay any proceedings started in breach of that clause.[11] If the expert does then make a determination, the effect has been summarised as follows:

7. Because he is not a judge or arbitrator, an expert does not enjoy the immunity from suit that they do: *Arenson* v. *Casson* [1977] AC 405. As a result, before accepting appointment, an expert will want to exclude all liability for his decision, other than for fraud.

8. Though an expert may be able to take legal advice if appropriate: *Nikko* v. *MEPC* [1991] 2 EGLR 103 (approved by the Court of Appeal in *The Glacier Bay* [1996] 1 Lloyd's Rep 370, 377–378).

9. See the confirmation published in 1997. The confirmation requires the aggrieved party to elect for expert determination within one business day of the other party having reached its decision which is, perhaps, somewhat hasty. The confirmation does not, however, appear to require the use of an expert but merely offers it as an option to the aggrieved party.

10. See below.

11. *Channel Tunnel* v. *Balfour Beatty* [1993] AC 334, 352–353. In *Cott* v. *Barber* [1997] 3 All ER 540 the court did decline to stay proceedings in favour of expert determination because there were no rules governing the determination and the expert had no experience.

"(1) Questions as to the role of the Expert, the ambit of his remit (or jurisdiction) and the character of his remit (whether exclusive or concurrent with a like jurisdiction vested in the Court) are to be determined as a matter of construction of the Agreement;

(2) If the Agreement confers upon the Expert the exclusive remit to determine a question (subject to (3) and (4) below) the jurisdiction of the court to determine that question is excluded because (as a matter of substantive law) for the purposes of ascertaining the rights and duties of the parties under the Agreement the determination of the Expert alone is relevant and any determination by the Court is irrelevant. It is irrelevant whether the Court would have reached a different conclusion or whether the Court considers that the Expert's decision is wrong, for the parties have in either event agreed to abide by the decision of the Expert;

(3) If the Expert in making his determination goes outside his remit, e.g. by determining a different question from that remitted to him or in his determination fails to comply with any conditions which the Agreement requires him to comply with in making his determination, the Court may intervene and set his decision aside. Such determination by the Expert as a matter of construction of the Agreement is not a determination which the parties agreed should affect the rights and duties of the parties, and the Court will say so;

(4) Likewise the Court may set aside a decision of the Expert where (as in this case) the Agreement so provides if his determination discloses a manifest error;

(5) The Court has jurisdiction ahead of a determination by the Expert to determine a question as to the limits of his remit or the conditions which the Expert must comply with in making his determination, but (as a rule of procedural convenience) will (save in exceptional circumstances) decline to do so. This is because the question is ordinarily merely hypothetical, only proving live if, after seeing the decision of the Expert, one party considers that the Expert got it wrong. To apply to the Court in anticipation of his decision (and before it is clear that he has got it wrong) is likely to prove wasteful of time and costs—the saving of which may be presumed to have been the, or at least one of the, objectives of the parties in agreeing to the determination by the Expert."[12]

In summary, therefore, as long as the expert does what he is instructed by the contract to do, his decision will be very hard to challenge.

12. *British Shipbuilders* v. *VSEL* [1997] 1 Lloyd's Rep 106, 109. See also *Jones* v. *Sherwood Computer Services* [1992] 1 WLR 277.

10.1.3 Arbitration and courts

Even where a contract provides for, say, expert determination, it is still necessary for it to go on to provide whether a dispute is to be resolved in a court or through arbitration. The first and foremost issue in choosing between courts and arbitration is enforceability. If a court judgment or an arbitration award is not enforceable against the assets of the other party, then there may be little that can be done to compel the other party to comply with an arbitration award or court judgment. It may comply for regulatory or commercial reasons, but neither enable the party in whose favour a decision has been made to compel compliance.

For these purposes, enforcement means the ability to convert an award or judgment into legal process in a location where the defaulting party has assets which will allow those assets to be seized and sold to meet the sum due on the judgment or arbitral award. Assets may be shares, bank accounts, debts or anything else, and do not have to be in the home country of the other party, but it is in general necessary to be able to identify assets before enforcement measures can be taken against them. How a judgment or award can be enforced is a matter of local law and practice in each country.[13] An English court judgment or an arbitration award made in England can generally be enforced in England without difficulty if assets can be identified. Foreign judgments and awards can be enforced in England in two ways: first, under a treaty and, secondly, at common law.

England has treaties regarding court judgments with, for example, Australia and Canada, as well as many other Commonwealth countries,[14] but the most far-reaching treaties are the Brussels and Lugano Conventions. These, which are substantially the same, allow judgments given in any member state of the EU or EFTA to be enforced in any other member state. As far as arbitration awards are concerned, the New York Convention of 1958 allows arbitration awards given in one state to be enforced, subject to limited exceptions, in any other state which is a party to the Convention. A large number of countries are parties to the New York Convention, including, for example, some members of the former Warsaw Pact in which court judgments are in practice unenforceable.

Common law enforcement of a foreign judgment or arbitration award operates by treating the judgment of a foreign court or tribunal as creating a debt upon which court action can be taken in England leading to an English judgment. It is not, therefore, direct enforcement, but can lead to much the same end if the courts will grant summary judgment without any detailed reinvestigation of the underlying merits. The only way to enforce, for example, a

13. It is always necessary to consider the practicality of enforcement as well as the legality. Legally enforcement might be possible, but can it be achieved in practice and, if so, within a reasonable timeframe at a reasonable cost?

14. Enforceability is generally effected under the Administration of Justice Act 1920, but in the case of a small number of other states, such as Israel, it is under the Foreign Judgments (Reciprocal Enforcement) Act 1933.

New York or Hong Kong judgment in England is by this means, though it is not necessarily straightforward.[15] In summary, a judgment will be enforced if it derives from a final and conclusive judgment for a definite sum of money, which is not in respect of a fine, penalty[16] or tax, and, first, the foreign court had jurisdiction over the defendant (this will be the case if there is a relevant jurisdiction clause), secondly, the proceedings were not opposed to natural justice, thirdly, the judgment was not obtained by fraud,[17] fourthly, the judgment does not conflict with another judgment which is enforceable in England, and, fifthly, enforcement would not be contrary to public policy.[18]

As mentioned above, if both an arbitration award and a court judgment can be enforced against the other party's assets, then there is a choice of which to opt for in a contract; but if only one is enforceable where the other party has assets, there is in practice no choice (other than not to do the business in the first place). Where there is a choice, the advantages of arbitration are commonly stated to be as follows. First, arbitration proceedings are confidential[19] whereas court proceedings are, in general, public. Secondly, arbitration can be more flexible. For example, the parties can lay down their own timetable and procedures (for example, an arbitration on papers only and with no oral hearings or disclosure of documents). This can make it a quick procedure, and one cheaper than traditional litigation. Realistically, though, in most cases the parties will need to agree this at the time they make the contract as agreement on, for example, fast procedures may not be possible once a dispute has arisen. Thirdly, courts are often regarded, with or without justification, as being biased in favour of the local party. Arbitration can take place in a neutral venue before arbitrators with no obvious ties to the parties. Fourthly, in courts the judge is always a lawyer, but an arbitrator does not have to be a lawyer. If the issue is a technical one, it may be better to have an arbitrator with a background in the relevant area. Fifthly, an arbitration award will normally be final and therefore does not suffer the various appeals that can follow court proceedings.[20]

15. See Dicey & Morris, *The Conflict of Laws* (12th edn), pp 461–519.

16. Including a judgment for multiple damages: section 5(2)(a) of the Protection of Trading Interests Act 1980.

17. This is potentially a wide exception as it covers cases where the foreign court has considered but rejected evidence of fraud (see, for example, *Owens Bank* v. *Bracco* [1992] 2 AC 443, *Owens Bank* v. *Etoile Commerciale* [1995] 1 WLR 44 and *Interdesco* v. *Nullifire* [1992] 1 Lloyd's Rep 180).

18. In addition, there are certain powers given to the Secretary of State under section 9 of the Foreign Judgments (Reciprocal Enforcement) Act 1933 to prohibit enforcement generally (which have never been used) and sections 1, 3 and 5(2)(b) of the Protection of Trading Interests Act 1980 to prohibit enforcement of judgments stemming from certain foreign laws which he has specified as affecting international trade or restrictive trade practices. Orders have been made with regard to some US and Australian laws.

19. *Ali Shipping* v. *Shipyard Trogdir* [1998] 2 All ER 136.

20. For example, right of appeal to the courts on a point of law can be excluded and this is done in, for example, the rules of the ICC (article 28(6)) and of the LCIA (article 26.9) which both contain a waiver of rights of appeal. The parties cannot exclude the right to challenge an award on the basis that the arbitrators exceeded their jurisdiction or that there was some serious irregularity in the proceedings which caused the substantial injustice: sections 67, 68 and 4 of the Arbitration Act 1996.

The disadvantages of arbitration are commonly considered to be as follows. First, it depends upon a prior agreement between the parties, and, as a result, third parties cannot be joined against their will. If, therefore, a derivatives trader has back to back transactions and the same issue arises on both but there is an arbitration clause in only one of the two contracts, it cannot join the other party to the arbitration nor, in most cases, ignore the arbitration clause and deal with the whole matter in court. It could, therefore, have to deal with the same issue both in the courts and in an arbitration. This will multiply the costs involved as well as run the risk of conflicting decisions. Even if there are arbitration clauses in both contracts, the arbitrations cannot be consolidated without the consent of all the parties, which may be hard to obtain once a dispute has arisen. Multi-party arbitration clauses are possible, but they will generally require to be set up at the outset which, in the context of derivatives, will in most cases be impracticable. Secondly, arbitration can sometimes be more costly than litigation. Court fees are relatively low, but the parties have to pay the arbitrators, which, particularly if there are three, can prove expensive. The parties also have to pay for the venue of the arbitration. Thirdly, arbitration can be slower than litigation, particularly if there are three arbitrators and the parties have not laid down fast track procedures. It can take a long time to establish a time or times when three busy arbitrators can all attend for hearings and deliberate on their decision. Fourthly, the qualities of the arbitrators can be an unknown quantity. If there are three arbitrators, one appointed by each party and the third, the chairman, chosen by the two arbitrators, there can be a concern (whether justified or not) that the arbitrator chosen by the other party has an undue affinity with the other's case and concern as to how strong the chairman will be. Allied to this, there can also be concern that the arbitrators will be more concerned to split the difference, to ensure that both parties feel they have got something out of the process, than to give a robust decision on the merits. Fifthly, there can be procedural uncertainty if the parties have not laid down in advance the procedures to be followed. There is scope for the parties to argue about the procedures, which can lead to delay, and also uncertainty as to what they will ultimately be.[21] Arbitrators in England probably have power to grant summary judgment,[22] but they may be less willing to do so than courts. Sixthly, the difficulties of bringing an appeal make it often impossible to correct any errors in arbitration awards.

There are some well-established and successful arbitration schemes, particularly in, for example, the shipping and commodities fields, but not as yet in the

21. Section 34(2) of the Arbitration Act 1996 lists some procedural and evidential matters the arbitrators must decide, including what documents should be disclosed, whether the strict rules of evidence should apply and whether the tribunal should take the initiative in finding facts and the law.

22. The better view is that this follows from sections 33 and 34 of the Arbitration Act 1996, especially now the courts can no longer grant summary judgment in a case governed by an arbitration clause: *Halki Shipping* v. *Sopex Oils* [1998] 1 Lloyd's Rep 465 (before the Arbitration Act 1996 the courts used to grant summary judgment despite an arbitration clause on the basis that if it was appropriate to give summary judgment, there was no dispute to which the clause could apply).

financial area. To be effective within the derivatives industry there would need to be a market system for resolving disputes which incorporated arbitration, but there is no sign of this emerging or, indeed, of any great demand for it. In these circumstances, where there is a genuine choice between arbitration and court proceedings, court proceedings are probably preferable. This is particularly so where there is any risk that third parties might be brought into the dispute (as, for example, on back to back transactions or transactions which turn on the same facts), but even outside that area court proceedings will often be quicker and cheaper than arbitration unless the parties have agreed on fast track procedures in advance. Court proceedings can also bring greater seriousness, robustness and certainty.

If arbitration is chosen, then certain issues need to be addressed, including the following. First, the venue of the arbitration. This decides which courts have supervisory jurisdiction over the arbitration and what, if any, mandatory rules must be complied with in the course of the arbitration. Secondly, the number of arbitrators. It is tempting to have three, one appointed by each party and the third chosen by the appointees. This has the advantage of apparent fairness; and if there are three arbitrators any eccentricity on the part of one might be of less importance. Three arbitrators does, however, build delay into any arbitration, as well as adding to the cost. For example, under the UNCITRAL rules, the respondent has 30 days from the appointment of the first arbitrator to appoint its arbitrator, and the two arbitrators then have a further 30 days to agree on the presiding arbitrator.[23] This builds in 60 or more days of delay.[24] Further, convening a hearing of three arbitrators is likely to take longer than if only one is involved. Thirdly, the language of the arbitration. If none is specified, it might be necessary for everything to be translated into more than one language, which will add to the delay and cost. Fourthly, whether to use an arbitral institution or a stand-alone arbitration. An arbitral institution has the advantage of providing administrative services, including fixing arbitrators' fees and supervising the arbitration process, but in return will charge fees. If it charges fees calculated by reference to the amount involved in the dispute, this can prove expensive if there is a large sum at stake.[25]

10.2 HANDLING DISPUTES

If a dispute does arise, the vital thing is not to do anything which might prejudice bringing that dispute to a successful resolution. What is a successful resolution

23. Article 7 of the UNCITRAL Arbitration Rules. UNCITRAL is the United Nations Commission on International Trade Law whose arbitration rules were recommended by Resolution 31/98 of the General Assembly of the United Nations adopted on 15 December 1976.

24. The rules of the LCIA and the ICC are not quite so slow in this regard.

25. The ICC charges on a percentage basis whereas the LCIA charges on the basis of the time spent on the matter.

and how to handle it will depend heavily on the facts of the dispute—if a party is the claimant and considers that it has a strong case against a financially embarrassed defendant, the approach to the dispute is likely to be very different than if there is genuine uncertainty as to the likely outcome. Alongside the actual dispute with the other party, there may also be regulatory issues which need to be taken into account. If complaints of wrongdoing are made against a financial institution, the regulator may also want to investigate the issue to see whether there has been any breach of applicable regulations.

The principal practical step in the handling of a dispute is to avoid bringing into existence any documents which might show the firm's behaviour in an adverse light. Any documents of this sort may have to be disclosed to the other party in the course of litigation and also to the regulator. Both are likely to make great play of adverse internal comment, either to create embarrassment or to affect the outcome of the issue. One way to avoid this problem is simply not to record anything in a document,[26] but that will seldom be practicable. The other way is to seek to ensure that everything that is committed to paper is covered by legal professional privilege. The effect of legal professional privilege is that a litigant cannot be compelled to disclose it, though it can be waived or the right to rely on it removed by statute or contract.[27]

Legal professional privilege has two forms: litigation privilege and legal advice privilege.[28] The former is potentially more wide ranging, but requires litigation to be reasonably in prospect. The latter does not require litigation, but does require the intervention of lawyers.

10.2.1 Litigation privilege

For litigation privilege to apply, the dominant purpose for which a document is brought into existence, whether at the instigation of a lawyer or the party itself, must be to enable legal advice to be sought or given with regard to litigation, or to seek or provide information or evidence to be used in or in connection with litigation.[29] The purpose in question is not necessarily the author of the

26. Whether the document is on paper, e-mail, other electronic messaging service, tape or anything else that can be replayed after the event.

27. The court cannot compel disclosure of privileged material: *R* v. *Derby Magistrates Court ex p B* [1996] 1 AC 487, 508–509, 511–512. The relationship between an SRO and its members is contractual, but the SFA expressly preserves privilege in rule 7–8(4); IMRO is less clear on the point, but the effect of rule 2.7 and para 41 of the Consultation Conclusions dated 24 July 1994 is to preserve privilege.

28. For a more detailed treatment of privilege, see Passmore, *Privilege*.

29. *Anderson* v. *Bank of British Columbia* (1876) 2 Ch D 644, 649, *Waugh* v. *British Railways Board* [1980] AC 521, and *Buttes Gas* v. *Hammer (No 3)* [1981] 1 QB 223. In *Secretary of State for Industry* v. *Baker* [1998] 2 WLR 667, Sir Richard Scott V-C argued that privilege should only apply to documents reflecting legal advice and not other documents in aid of litigation. He did, however, recognise that this was not the conventional view, and that there was authority binding on him to the contrary (see also Passmore (1997) 147 NLJ 1665).

document but rather the person who "procured its genesis".[30] Litigation need not be in existence, but it does need to be reasonably in prospect, and it is enough if documents are brought into existence to assist in making a decision whether or not to litigate.[31]

The best way to establish that the dominant purpose of a document is litigation is to record it in the document or in documents requesting that the document in question be prepared. This would not prevent a finding that litigation was not the true purpose, but it will help. If there is no clear paper trail establishing the purpose, then it will be arguable that the purpose of a document was not litigation but, for example, to establish what had happened; if something has apparently not gone according to plan, an institution has an interest in finding out what has happened, but that is not a privileged purpose. In addition, it will usually be sensible if any documents created once it is clear that litigation is a possibility are addressed to lawyers. Not only could that lay the basis for an argument that legal advice privilege applies but it could also bolster an argument based on litigation privilege because lawyers traditionally conduct litigation.

The problems with documents extend beyond those actually brought into existence after a dispute has arisen. They also apply to documents obtained from third parties, whether a parent, another company in the same group, or a third party. The law in this area is not consistent, but appears to be as follows: if a party or its lawyer obtains an unprivileged original document for the purposes of litigation, it is not privileged[32]; if a party had an unprivileged original which it lost but then obtains a copy from the third party, that copy is not privileged[33]; if a party obtains from a third party for the purposes of litigation copies of unprivileged documents, these documents are probably privileged[34]; and, if a lawyer copies a selection of unprivileged documents held by a third party, and the lawyer has exercised skill and judgement in the selection or the selection betrays the trend of his advice, the copies are privileged.[35] In these circumstances, the safer course will generally be to inspect documents held by third

30. *Guinness Peat* v. *Fitzroy Robinson* [1987] 1 WLR 1027, 1037. So, for example, if a bank asks its accountants to prepare a report on troubled loans, the purpose in question is the bank's, not the accountants': *Price Waterhouse* v. *BCCI* [1992] BCLC 583, 591.

31. *Re Highgrade Traders* [1984] BCLC 151, 172–174.

32. *Ventouris* v. *Mountain* [1991] 1 WLR 607 and *Vernon* v. *Bosley (No 2)* [1997] 1 All ER 614, 628.

33. *Dubai Bank* v. *Galadari* [1990] 1 Ch 98.

34. *The Palermo* (1883) 9 PD 6 and *Watson* v. *Cammell Laird* [1959] 1 WLR 702. These are binding Court of Appeal decisions, but the courts are now fairly hostile to them: see, for example, *Buttes Gas* v. *Hammer (No 3)* [1981] 1 QB 223, 244, *Dubai Bank* v. *Galadari* [1990] 1 Ch 98, *Ventouris* v. *Mountain* [1991] 1 WLR 607 and *Robert Hitchings Ltd* v. *International Computers Ltd* (unreported, 10 December 1996).

35. *Lyell* v. *Kennedy (No 3)* (1884) 27 Ch D 1, *Dubai Bank* v. *Galadari* [1990] 1 Ch 98, 107 and *Ventouris* v. *Mountain* [1991] 1 WLR 607, 615, 621 (in this case, Bingham LJ commented that "I can see no reason in principle why a pre-existing document obtained by a solicitor for the purposes of litigation should be privileged from production and inspection, save perhaps in the *Lyell* v. *Kennedy (No 3)* situation which, in an age of indiscriminate photocopying, cannot occur too often").

parties rather than merely to demand the originals or copies. In that way, only those which are helpful need be obtained, and any risks arising from possession of unhelpful documents, and of any change in the law, can be avoided.

10.2.2 Legal advice privilege

The test for legal advice privilege was laid down by Taylor LJ in *Balabel* v. *Air India*[36]:

> "... the test is whether the communication or other document was made confidentially for the purposes of legal advice. Those purposes have to be construed broadly. Privilege obviously attached to a document conveying legal advice from a solicitor to a client and to a specific request from the client for such advice. But it does not follow that all other communications between them lack privilege. In most solicitor and client relationships, especially where a transaction involves protracted dealings, advice may be required or appropriate on matters great or small at various stages. There is a continuum of communication and meetings between the solicitor and the client ... Where information is passed by the solicitor or client to the other as part of the continuum aimed at keeping both informed so that advice may be sought and given as required, privilege will attach ... Moreover, legal advice is not confined to telling the client the law; it must include advice as to what should prudently and sensibly be done in the relevant legal context."

The key is that there should be a relationship of client and lawyer, the dominant[37] purpose of which is the obtaining and giving of legal advice. The lawyer can be an inhouse lawyer[38]or a foreign lawyer.[39]

Documents generated by the lawyer's client for the purpose of obtaining legal advice are privileged,[40] but documents generated by third parties (except if acting as the agent of the client) to put before lawyers for the purpose of obtaining legal advice are not.[41] So, for example, a report by an external accountant is not privileged, but a report by an internal accountant or compliance officer probably is privileged as long as the dominant purpose is seeking legal advice. This is not, however, an entirely logical situation, and therefore it is safer if the only things put down on paper are specifically addressed to the lawyers with an express or implied request for legal advice.

If privileged legal advice is received, internal documents or parts of documents reproducing or otherwise revealing the advice are also privileged, whatever the purpose or motive (short of fraud) for which the document comes into existence.[42] There is, however, some residual doubt about the extent of this privilege, and therefore it is prudent to restrict documentary dissemination of legal advice.[43]

36. [1988] 1 Ch 317, 330. See also *NRG* v. *Bacon & Woodrow* [1995] 1 All ER 976, 982–983.
37. *Hellenic Mutual* v. *Harrison, The "Sagheera"* [1997] 1 Lloyd's Rep 160, 167–168.
38. *Alfred Crompton* v. *Customs and Excise Commissioners (No 2)* [1974] AC 405, 430–431.
39. See, e.g., *IBM* v. *Phoenix International* [1995] 1 All ER 413, 427–429.
40. For example, *The Southwark and Vauxhall Water Co* v. *Quick* (1878) 3 QBD 315.
41. *Re Highgrade Traders Ltd* [1984] BCLC 151, 164–165.
42. *Bank of Nova Scotia* v. *Hellenic Mutual, The "Good Luck"* [1992] 2 Lloyd's Rep 540.
43. See Style & Hollander, *Documentary Evidence* (6th edn), p 178.

10.2.3 Common interest privilege

Common interest privilege can apply to both litigation and legal advice privilege,[44] though the boundaries are far from clear. The privilege applies where parties have the same interest in litigation or advice, and share documents or information which would, in the hands of one alone, be privileged. It was initially suggested that this was only possible between parties sharing a common solicitor,[45] later in circumstances that they were capable of instructing the same solicitor,[46] and later still that it was sufficient that the third party had a relationship with the party and the transaction which, in relation to the advice or other communications, brings that third party within the ambit of confidence which would prevail between a legal adviser and his client.[47] Quite where the boundaries lie is not clear, but it appears that the boundaries are widening.[48]

Common interest privilege has been held to apply to insurers and insured, reinsurer and reinsured, and agent and principal.[49] It has been held not to apply to banker and borrower.[50] There can be little doubt that it would apply between subsidiary and parent, but there are difficulties with the extent of permissible conflict between the two parties sharing information. The position here is unclear,[51] but the prudent course is to be cautious in disclosure in those circumstances.

It is increasingly common, at least where companies with no direct connection are concerned, to follow the US practice and enter into an agreement if two parties have the same interest in litigation in order to record the common interest and the obligations of the parties to protect privilege in any information which might be shared.

10.2.4 Loss of privilege

Confidentiality lies at the heart of privilege. As a result, if legal advice is made public, the privilege is lost. This does not, however, apply to disclosure to any third party—it does not apply to those who can claim common interest privilege (see above), or agents, but quite where the boundary lies is not clear. It may be arguable that a limited disclosure, particularly if it expressly seeks to preserve

44. *Svenska* v. *Sun Alliance* [1995] 2 Lloyd's Rep 84, 87–88.
45. *Buttes Gas* v. *Hammer (No 3)* [1981] 1 QB 223, 251, 267.
46. *The Good Luck* [1992] 2 Lloyd's Rep 540, 542.
47. *Formica* v. *ECGD* [1995] 1 Lloyd's Rep 692, 699 and *Svenska* v. *Sun Alliance* [1995] 2 Lloyd's Rep 84, 87.
48. *The Sagheera* [1997] 1 Lloyd's Rep 160, 167.
49. Respectively, *Guinness Peat* v. *Fitzroy Robinson* [1987] 1 WLR 1027, 1038–1039; *Formica* v. *ECGD* [1995] 1 Lloyd's Rep 692, 697–700, and *Svenska* v. *Sun Alliance* [1995] 2 Lloyd's Rep 84; *The World Era (No 2)* [1993] 1 Lloyd's Rep 363, 366.
50. *The Good Luck* [1992] 2 Lloyd's Rep 540.
51. See, for example, *The World Era (No 2)* [1993] 1 Lloyd's Rep 363, where Phillips J took a wide view, and *Lee* v. *SW Thames RHA* [1985] 1 WLR 845, where the Court of Appeal took a narrow view.

privilege, will not waive privilege against anyone else.[52] There is, however, a real risk that showing a document to someone outside the ring of common interest could result in the loss of privilege.

For example, in *Credit Lyonnais* v. *Kaufmann*,[53] lawyers and accountants were commissioned by Credit Lyonnais to prepare reports on regulatory compliance for the TSA (the SFA's predecessor). The reports were actually addressed to the TSA. When Mr Kaufmann, who sued Credit Lyonnais over the same matters, sought discovery of the reports, Arden J ordered Credit Lyonnais to disclose them to Mr Kaufmann. The arguments raised against discovery were based on public interest immunity, and no argument based on legal professional privilege was raised, presumably because the reports were addressed to the TSA and because they were not confidential. The result might well have been the same even if the reports had been addressed to Credit Lyonnais.

There is even a risk in referring to legal advice in discussions with the other party as this could constitute a waiver of privilege in that advice.[54]

10.2.5 Without prejudice communications

A principle allied to privilege is that governing "without prejudice" discussions and correspondence. Without prejudice discussions cannot be referred to in court without the consent of both parties and, therefore, concessions made in the course of those discussions cannot prejudice a case. The policy behind this is that parties should be encouraged to settle disputes, and this would not be the case if any concessions made could be referred to in court.[55] The principle applies to all negotiations genuinely aimed at settlement whether or not the phrase "without prejudice" is used.[56] Conversely, even if the phrase "without

52. *City of Gotha* v. *Sotheby's* (*The Times*, 3 July 1997). In *British Coal Corporation* v. *Dennis Rye Limited* [1988] 1 WLR 1113, the Court of Appeal held that disclosure of documents subject to litigation to the police who then made disclosure to the defendant in a criminal prosecution did not waive privilege as against the same defendant in civil proceedings. "The plaintiff made the documents available for a limited purpose only, namely to assist in the conduct first of a criminal investigation and then of a criminal trial. This action of the plaintiff, looked at objectively as it must be, cannot be construed as a waiver of any rights available to them in the present civil action for the purpose of which the privilege exists" (Neill LJ at 1121). This concerned litigation privilege, and the Court of Appeal also referred to a duty to assist the criminal prosecution (1121). The case is, therefore, easily distinguishable. *Cross and Tapper on Evidence* (8th edn), p 475, comment that a conversation between a client and solicitor in the presence of a third party does not necessarily waive privilege "although it will no doubt usually be held to have this effect", and they cite New Zealand authority in support of this view. Style and Hollander, *Documentary Evidence* (6th edn), p 224, say that it is possible for a document to cease to be confidential as between some parties but not others.

53. Unreported, 20 December 1994.

54. There is even a risk in referring to legal advice in discussions with the other party as this could constitute a waiver of privilege in that advice: see Matthews and Malek, *Discovery*, pp 230–231. Matthews and Malek recognise that the position is not clear cut.

55. *Cutts* v. *Head* [1984] Ch 290, 306.

56. *Rush & Tompkins Ltd* v. *GLC* [1989] 1 AC 1280, 1299–1300. It is possible to make an open offer, but it is incumbent on the person doing so to make this clear, especially if it is in the course of without prejudice negotiations: *Cheddar Valley Engineering Ltd* v. *Chaddlewood Homes Ltd* [1992] 1 WLR 820 and *Dixons Stores Group Ltd* v. *Thames Television plc* [1993] 1 All ER 349.

prejudice" is used, it will not protect communications from disclosure in court if they are not genuinely aimed at settlement as, for example, when they only assert one party's rights.[57] If a settlement is reached in the course of without prejudice correspondence, then the correspondence necessary to establish that there is an agreement may be referred to in court if there is any dispute over the terms of the settlement.[58]

57. *Buckinghamshire CC* v. *Moran* [1989] 2 All ER 225 and *Standrin* v. *Yenton Minster Homes Ltd* (*The Times*, 22 July 1991).

58. *Tomlin* v. *Standard Telephones & Cables Ltd* [1969] 3 All ER 201.

APPENDIX

(Multicurrency—Cross Border)

ISDA®

International Swaps & Derivatives Association, Inc.

MASTER AGREEMENT

dated as of ....

.... and ....
have entered and/or anticipate entering into one or more transactions (each a "Transaction") that are or will be governed by this Master Agreement, which includes the schedule (the "Schedule"), and the documents and other confirming evidence (each a "Confirmation") exchanged between the parties confirming those Transactions.

Accordingly, the parties agree as follows:—

1. INTERPRETATION

(a) Definitions

The terms defined in Section 14 and in the Schedule will have the meanings therein specified for the purpose of this Master Agreement.

(b) Inconsistency

In the event of any inconsistency between the provisions of the Schedule and the other provisions of this Master Agreement, the Schedule will prevail. In the event of any inconsistency between the provisions of any Confirmation and this Master Agreement (including the Schedule), such Confirmation will prevail for the purpose of the relevant Transaction.

(c) Single Agreement

All Transactions are entered into in reliance on the fact that this Master Agreement and all Confirmations form a single agreement between the parties (collectively referred to as this "Agreement"), and the parties would not otherwise enter into any Transactions.

2. OBLIGATIONS

(a) General Conditions

(i) Each party will make each payment or delivery specified in each Confirmation to be made by it, subject to the other provisions of this Agreement.

(ii) Payments under this Agreement will be made on the due date for value on that date in the place of the account specified in the relevant Confirmation or otherwise pursuant to this Agreement, in freely transferable funds and in the manner customary for payments in the required currency. Where settlement is by delivery (that is, other than by payment), such delivery will be made for receipt on the due date in the manner customary for the relevant obligation unless otherwise specified in the relevant Confirmation or elsewhere in this Agreement.

(iii) Each obligation of each party under Section 2(a)(i) is subject to (1) the condition precedent that no Event of Default or Potential Event of Default with respect to the other party has occurred and is continuing, (2) the condition precedent that no Early Termination Date in respect of the relevant Transaction has occurred or been effectively designated and (3) each other applicable condition precedent specified in this Agreement.

(b) Change of Account

Either party may change its account for receiving a payment or delivery by giving notice to the other party at least five Local Business Days prior to the scheduled date for the payment or delivery to which such change applies unless such other party gives timely notice of a reasonable objection to such change.

(c) Netting

If on any date amounts would otherwise be payable:—

(i) in the same currency; and
(ii) in respect of the same Transaction,

by each party to the other, then, on such date, each party's obligation to make payment of any such amount will be automatically satisfied and discharged and, if the aggregate amount that would otherwise have been payable by one party exceeds the aggregate amount that would otherwise have been payable by the other party, replaced by an obligation upon the party by whom the larger aggregate amount would have been payable to pay to the other party the excess of the larger aggregate amount over the smaller aggregate amount.

The parties may elect in respect of two or more Transactions that a net amount will be determined in respect of all amounts payable on the same date in the same currency in respect of such Transactions, regardless of whether such amounts are payable in respect of the same Transaction. The election may be made in the Schedule or a Confirmation by specifying that subparagraph (ii) above will not apply to the Transactions identified as being subject to the election, together with the starting date (in which case subparagraph (ii) above will not, or will cease to, apply to such Transactions from such date). This election may be made separately for different groups of Transactions and will apply separately to each pairing of Offices through which the parties make and receive payments or deliveries.

(d) Deduction or Withholding for Tax

(i) Gross-Up

All payments under this Agreement will be made without any deduction or withholding for or on account of any Tax unless such deduction or withholding is required by any applicable law, as modified by the practice of any relevant governmental revenue authority, then in effect. If a party is so required to deduct or withhold, then that party ("X") will:—

(1) promptly notify the other party ("Y") of such requirement;
(2) pay to the relevant authorities the full amount required to be deducted or withheld (including the full amount required to be deducted or withheld from any additional amount paid by X to Y under this Section 2(d)) promptly upon the earlier of determining that such deduction or withholding is required or receiving notice that such amount has been assessed against Y;
(3) promptly forward to Y an official receipt (or a certified copy), or other documentation reasonably acceptable to Y, evidencing such payment to such authorities; and
(4) if such Tax is an Indemnifiable Tax, pay to Y, in addition to the payment to which Y is otherwise entitled under this Agreement, such additional amount as is necessary to ensure that the net amount actually received by Y (free and clear of Indemnifiable Taxes, whether assessed against X or Y) will equal the full amount Y would have received had no such deduction or withholding been required. However, X will not be required to pay any additional amount to Y to the extent that it would not be required to be paid but for:—
    (A) the failure by Y to comply with or perform any agreement contained in Section 4(a)(i), 4(a)(iii) or 4(d); or
    (B) the failure of a representation made by Y pursuant to Section 3(f) to be accurate and true unless such failure would not have occurred but for (I) any action taken by a taxing authority, or brought in a court of competent jurisdiction, on or after the date on which a Transaction is entered into (regardless of whether such action is taken or brought with respect to a party to this Agreement) or (II) a Change in Tax Law.

(ii) Liability

If:—

(1) X is required by any applicable law, as modified by the practice of any relevant governmental revenue authority, to make any deduction or withholding in respect of which X would not be required to pay an additional amount to Y under Section 2(d)(i)(4);
(2) X does not so deduct or withhold; and
(3) a liability resulting from such Tax is assessed directly against X,

then, except to the extent Y has satisfied or then satisfies the liability resulting from such Tax, Y will promptly pay to X the amount of such liability (including any related liability for interest, but including any related liability for penalties only if Y has failed to comply with or perform any agreement contained in Section 4(a)(i), 4(a)(iii) or 4(d)).

(e) Default Interest; Other Amounts

Prior to the occurrence or effective designation of an Early Termination Date in respect of the relevant Transaction, a party that defaults in the performance of any payment obligation will, to the extent permitted by law and subject to Section 6(c), be required to pay interest (before as well as after judgment) on the overdue amount to the other party on demand in the same currency as such overdue amount, for the period from (and including) the original due date for payment to (but excluding) the date of actual payment, at the Default Rate. Such interest will be calculated on the basis of daily compounding and the actual number of days elapsed. If, prior to the occurrence or effective designation of an Early Termination Date in respect of the relevant Transaction, a party defaults in the performance of any obligation required to be settled by delivery, it will compensate the other party on demand if and to the extent provided for in the relevant Confirmation or elsewhere in this Agreement.

3. REPRESENTATIONS

Each party represents to the other party (which representations will be deemed to be repeated by each party on each date on which a Transaction is entered into and, in the case of the representations in Section 3(f), at all times until the termination of this Agreement) that:—

(a) Basic Representations

(i) Status

It is duly organised and validly existing under the laws of the jurisdiction of its organisation or incorporation and, if relevant under such laws, in good standing;

(ii) Powers

It has the power to execute this Agreement and any other documentation relating to this Agreement to which it is a party, to deliver this Agreement and any other documentation relating to this Agreement that it is required by this Agreement to deliver and to perform its obligations under this Agreement and any obligations it has under any Credit Support Document to which it is a party and has taken all necessary action to authorise such execution, delivery and performance;

(iii) No Violation or Conflict

Such execution, delivery and performance do not violate or conflict with any law applicable to it, any provision of its constitutional documents, any order or judgment of any court or other agency of government applicable to it or any of its assets or any contractual restriction binding on or affecting it or any of its assets;

(iv) Consents

All governmental and other consents that are required to have been obtained by it with respect to this Agreement or any Credit Support Document to which it is a party have been obtained and are in full force and effect and all conditions of any such consents have been complied with; and

(v) Obligations Binding

Its obligations under this Agreement and any Credit Support Document to which it is a party constitute its legal, valid and binding obligations, enforceable in accordance with their respective terms (subject to applicable bankruptcy, reorganisation, insolvency, moratorium or similar laws affecting creditors' rights generally and subject, as to enforceability, to equitable principles of general application (regardless of whether enforcement is sought in a proceeding in equity or at law)).

(b) Absence of Certain Events

No Event of Default or Potential Event of Default or, to its knowledge, Termination Event with respect to it has occurred and is continuing and no such event or circumstance would occur as a result of its entering into or performing its obligations under this Agreement or any Credit Support Document to which it is a party.

(c) Absence of Litigation

There is not pending or, to its knowledge, threatened against it or any of its Affiliates any action, suit or proceeding at law or in equity or before any court, tribunal, governmental body, agency or official or any arbitrator that is likely to affect the legality, validity or enforceability against it of this Agreement or any Credit Support Document to which it is a party or its ability to perform its obligations under this Agreement or such Credit Support Document.

(d) Accuracy of Specified Information

All applicable information that is furnished in writing by or on behalf of it to the other party and is identified for the purpose of this Section 3(d) in the Schedule is, as of the date of the information, true, accurate and complete in every material respect.

(e) Payer Tax Representation

Each representation specified in the Schedule as being made by it for the purpose of this Section 3(e) is accurate and true.

(f) Payee Tax Representations

Each representation specified in the Schedule as being made by it for the purpose of this Section 3(f) is accurate and true.

4. AGREEMENTS

Each party agrees with the other that, so long as either party has or may have any obligation under this Agreement or under any Credit Support Document to which it is a party:—

(a) Furnish Specified Information

It will deliver to the other party or, in certain cases under subparagraph (iii) below, to such government or taxing authority as the other party reasonably directs:—

(i) any forms, documents or certificates relating to taxation specified in the Schedule or any Confirmation;

(ii) any other documents specified in the Schedule or any Confirmation; and

(iii) upon reasonable demand by such other party, any form or document that may be required or reasonably requested in writing in order to allow such other party or its Credit Support Provider to make a payment under this Agreement or any applicable Credit Support Document without any deduction or withholding for or on account of any Tax or with such deduction or withholding at a reduced rate (so long as the completion, execution or submission of such form or document would not materially prejudice the legal or commercial position of the party in receipt of such demand), with any such form or document to be accurate and completed in a manner reasonably satisfactory to such other party and to be executed and to be delivered with any reasonably required certification,

in each case by the date specified in the Schedule or such Confirmation or, if none is specified, as soon as reasonably practicable.

(b) Maintain Authorisations

It will use all reasonable efforts to maintain in full force and effect all consents of any governmental or other authority that are required to be obtained by it with respect to this Agreement or any Credit Support Document to which it is a party and will use all reasonable efforts to obtain any that may become necessary in the future.

(c) Comply with Laws

It will comply in all material respects with all applicable laws and orders to which it may be subject if failure so to comply would materially impair its ability to perform its obligations under this Agreement or any Credit Support Document to which it is a party.

(d) Tax Agreement

It will give notice of any failure of a representation made by it under Section 3(f) to be accurate and true promptly upon learning of such failure.

(e) Payment of Stamp Tax

Subject to Section 11, it will pay any Stamp Tax levied or imposed upon it or in respect of its execution or performance of this Agreement by a jurisdiction in which it is incorporated, organised, managed and controlled, or considered to have its seat, or in which a branch or office through which it is acting for the purpose of this Agreement is located ("Stamp Tax Jurisdiction") and will indemnify the other party against any Stamp Tax levied or imposed upon the other party or in respect of the other party's execution or performance of this Agreement by any such Stamp Tax Jurisdiction which is not also a Stamp Tax Juridiction with respect to the other party.

5. EVENTS OF DEFAULT AND TERMINATION EVENTS

(a) Events of Default

The occurrence at any time with respect to a party or, if applicable, any Credit Support Provider of such party or any Specified Entity of such party of any of the following events constitutes an event of default (an "Event of Default") with respect to such party:—

(i) Failure to Pay or Deliver

Failure by the party to make, when due, any payment under this Agreement or delivery under Section 2(a)(i) or 2(e) required to be made by it if such failure is not remedied on or before the third Local Business Day after notice of such failure is given to the party;

(ii) Breach of Agreement

Failure by the party to comply with or perform any agreement or obligation (other than an obligation to make any payment under this Agreement or delivery under Section 2(a)(i) or 2(e) or to give notice of a Termination Event or any agreement or obligation under Section 4(a)(i), 4(a)(iii) or 4(d)) to be complied with or performed by the party in accordance with this Agreement if such failure is not remedied on or before the thirtieth day after notice of such failure is given to the party;

(iii) Credit Support Default

(1) Failure by the party or any Credit Support Provider of such party to comply with or perform any agreement or obligation to be complied with or performed by it in accordance with any Credit Support Document if such failure is continuing after any applicable grace period has elapsed;
(2) the expiration or termination of such Credit Support Document or the failing or ceasing of such Credit Support Document to be in full force and effect for the purpose of this Agreement (in either case other than in accordance with its terms) prior to the satisfaction of all obligations of such party under each Transaction to which such Credit Support Document relates without the written consent of the other party; or
(3) the party or such Credit Support Provider disaffirms, disclaims, repudiates or rejects, in whole or in part, or challenges the validity of, such Credit Support Document;

(iv) Misrepresentation

A representation (other than a representation under Section 3(e) or (f)) made or repeated or deemed to have been made or repeated by the party or any Credit Support Provider of such party in this Agreement or any Credit Support Document proves to have been incorrect or misleading in any material respect when made or repeated or deemed to have been made or repeated;

(v) Default under Specified Transaction

The party, any Credit Support Provider of such party or any applicable Specified Entity of such party (1) defaults under a Specified Transaction and, after giving effect to any applicable notice requirement or grace period, there occurs a liquidation of, an acceleration of obligations under, or an early termination of, that Specified Transaction, (2) defaults, after giving effect to any applicable notice requirement or grace period, in making any payment or delivery due on the last payment, delivery or exchange date of, or any payment on early termination of, a Specified Transaction (or such default continues for at least three Local Business Days if there is no applicable notice requirement or grace period) or (3) disaffirms, disclaims, repudiates or rejects, in whole or in part, a Specified Transaction (or such action is taken by any person or entity appointed or empowered to operate it or act on its behalf);

(vi) Cross Default

If "Cross Default" is specified in the Schedule as applying to the party, the occurrence or existence of (1) a default, event of default or other similar condition or event (however described) in respect of such party, any Credit Support Provider of such party or any applicable Specified Entity of such party under one or more agreements or instruments relating to Specified Indebtedness of any of them (individually or collectively) in an aggregate amount of not less than the applicable Threshold Amount (as specified in the Schedule) which has resulted in such Specified Indebtedness becoming, or becoming capable at such time of being declared, due and payable under such agreements or instruments, before it would otherwise have been due and payable or (2) a default by such party, such Credit Support Provider or such Specified Entity (individually or collectively) in making one or more payments on the due date thereof in an aggregate amount of not less than the applicable Threshold Amount under such agreements or instruments (after giving effect to any applicable notice requirement or grace period);

(vii) Bankruptcy

The party, any Credit Support Provider of such party or any applicable Specified Entity of such party:—

(1) is dissolved (other than pursuant to a consolidation, amalgamation or merger); (2) becomes insolvent or is unable to pay its debts or fails or admits in writing its inability generally to pay its debts as they become due; (3) makes a general assignment, arrangement or composition with or for the benefit of its creditors; (4) institutes or has instituted against it a proceeding seeking a judgment of insolvency or bankruptcy or any other relief under any bankruptcy or insolvency law or other similar law affecting creditors' rights, or a petition is presented for its winding-up or liquidation, and, in the case of any such proceeding or petition instituted or presented against it, such proceeding or petition (A) results in a judgment of insolvency or bankruptcy or the entry of an order for relief or the making of an order for its winding-up or liquidation or (B) is not dismissed, discharged, stayed or restrained in each case within 30 days of the institution or presentation thereof; (5) has a resolution passed for its winding-up, official management or liquidation (other than pursuant to a consolidation, amalgamation or merger); (6) seeks or becomes subject to the appointment of an administrator, provisional liquidator, conservator, receiver, trustee, custodian or other similar official for it or for all or substantially all its assets; (7) has a secured party take possession of all or substantially all its assets or has a distress, execution, attachment, sequestration or other legal process levied, enforced or sued on or against all or substantially all its assets and such secured party maintains possession, or any such process is not dismissed, discharged, stayed or restrained, in each case within 30 days thereafter; (8) causes or is subject to any event with respect to it which, under the applicable laws of any jurisdiction, has an analogous effect to any of the events specified in clauses (1) to (7) (inclusive); or (9) takes any action in furtherance of, or indicating its consent to, approval of, or acquiescence in, any of the foregoing acts; or

(viii) Merger Without Assumption

The party or any Credit Support Provider of such party consolidates or amalgamates with, or merges with or into, or transfers all or substantially all its assets to, another entity and, at the time of such consolidation, amalgamation, merger or transfer:—

(1) the resulting, surviving or transferee entity fails to assume all the obligations of

such party or such Credit Support Provider under this Agreement or any Credit Support Document to which it or its predecessor was a party by operation of law or pursuant to an agreement reasonably satisfactory to the other party to this Agreement; or

(2) the benefits of any Credit Support Document fail to extend (without the consent of the other party) to the performance by such resulting, surviving or transferee entity of its obligations under this Agreement.

(b) Termination Events

The occurrence at any time with respect to a party or, if applicable, any Credit Support Provider of such party or any Specified Entity of such party of any event specified below constitutes an Illegality if the event is specified in (i) below, a Tax Event if the event is specified in (ii) below or a Tax Event Upon Merger if the event is specified in (iii) below, and, if specified to be applicable, a Credit Event Upon Merger if the event is specified pursuant to (iv) below or an Additional Termination Event if the event is specified pursuant to (v) below:—

(i) Illegality

Due to the adoption of, or any change in, any applicable law after the date on which a Transaction is entered into, or due to the promulgation of, or any change in, the interpretation by any court, tribunal or regulatory authority with competent jurisdiction of any applicable law after such date, it becomes unlawful (other than as a result of a breach by the party of Section 4(b)) for such party (which will be the Affected Party):—

(1) to perform any absolute or contingent obligation to make a payment or delivery or to receive a payment or delivery in respect of such Transaction or to comply with any other material provision of this Agreement relating to such Transaction; or

(2) to perform, or for any Credit Support Provider of such party to perform, any contingent or other obligation which the party (or such Credit Support Provider) has under any Credit Support Document relating to such Transaction;

(ii) Tax Event

Due to (x) any action taken by a taxing authority, or brought in a court of competent jurisdiction, on or after the date on which a Transaction is entered into (regardless of whether such action is taken or brought with respect to a party to this Agreement) or (y) a Change in Tax Law, the party (which will be the Affected Party) will, or there is a substantial likelihood that it will, on the next succeeding Schedule Payment Date (1) be required to pay to the other party an additional amount in respect of an Indemnifiable Tax under Section 2(d)(i)(4) (except in respect of interest under Section 2(e), 6(d)(ii) or 6(e)) or (2) receive a payment from which an amount is required to be deducted or withheld for or on account of a Tax (except in respect of interest under Section 2(e), 6(d)(ii) or 6(e)) and no additional amount is required to be paid in respect of such Tax under Section 2(d)(i)(4) (other than by reason of Section 2(d)(i)(4)(A) or (B));

(iii) Tax Event Upon Merger

The party (the "Burdened Party") on the next succeeding Scheduled Payment Date will either (1) be required to pay an additional amount in respect of an Indemnifiable Tax under Section 2(d)(i)(4) (except in respect of interest under Section 2(e), 6(d)(ii) or 6(e)) or (2) receive a payment from which an amount has been deducted or withheld for or on account of any Indemnifiable Tax in respect of which the other party is not required to pay an additional amount (other than by reason of Section 2(d)(i)(4)(A) or (B)), in either case as a result of a party consolidating or amalgamating with, or merging with or into, or transferring all or substantially all its assets to, another entity (which will be the Affected Party) where such action does not constitute an event described in Section 5(a)(viii);

(iv) Credit Event Upon Merger

If "Credit Event Upon Merger" is specified in the Schedule as applying to the party, such part ("X"), any Credit Support Provider of X or any applicable Specified Entity of X consolidates or amalgamates with, or merges with or into, or transfers all or substantially all its assets to, another entity and such action does not constitute an event described in Section 5(a)(viii) but the creditworthiness of the resulting, surviving or transferee entity is materially weaker than that of X, such Credit Support Provider or such Specified Entity, as the case may be, immediately prior to such action (and, in such event, X or its successor or transferee, as appropriate, will be the Affected Party); or

(v) Additional Termination Event

If any "Additional Termination Event" is specified in the Schedule or any Confirmation as applying, the occurrence of such event (and, in such event, the Affected Party or Affected Parties shall be as specified for such Additional Termination Event in the Schedule or such Confirmation).

(c) Event of Default and Illegality

If an event or circumstance which would otherwise constitute or give rise to an Event of Default also constitutes an Illegality, it will be treated as an Illegality and will not constitute an Event of Default.

6. EARLY TERMINATION

(a) Right to Terminate Following Event of Default

If at any time an Event of Default with respect to a party (the "Defaulting Party") has occurred and is then continuing, the other party (the "Non-defaulting Party") may, by not more than 20 days notice to the Defaulting Party specifying the relevant Event of Default, designate a day not earlier than the day such notice is effective as an Early Termination Date in respect of all outstanding Transactions. If, however, "Automatic Early Termination" is specified in the Schedule as applying to a party, then an Early Termination Date in respect of all outstanding Transactions will occur immediately upon the occurrence with respect to such party of an Event of Default specified in Section 5(a)(vii)(1), (3), (5), (6) or, to the extent analogous thereto, (8), and as of the time immediately preceding the institution of the relevant proceeding or the presentation of the relevant petition upon the occurrence with respect to such party of an Event of Default specified in Section 5(a)(vii)(4) or, to the extent analogous thereto, (8).

(b) Right to Terminate Following Termination Event

(i) Notice

If a Termination Event occurs, an Affected Party will, promptly upon becoming aware of it, notify the other party, specifying the nature of that Termination Event and each Affected Transaction and will also give such other information about that Termination Event as the other party may reasonably require.

(ii) Transfer to Avoid Termination Event

If either an Illegality under Section 5(b)(i)(1) or a Tax Event occurs and there is only one Affected Party, or if a Tax Event Upon Merger occurs and the Burdened Party is the Affected Party, the Affected Party will, as a condition to its right to designate an Early Termination Date under Section 6(b)(iv), use all reasonable efforts (which will not require such party to incur a loss, excluding immaterial, incidental expenses) to transfer within 20 days after it gives notice under Section 6(b)(i) all its rights and obligations under this Agreement in respect of the Affected Transactions to another of its Offices or Affiliates so that such Termination Event ceases to exist.

If the Affected Party is not able to make such a transfer it will give notice to the other party to that effect within such 20 day period, whereupon the other party may effect such a transfer within 30 days after the notice is given under Section 6(b)(i).

Any such transfer by a party under this Section 6(b)(ii) will be subject to and conditional upon the prior written consent of the other party, which consent will not be withheld if such other party's policies in effect at such time would permit it to enter into transactions with the transferee on the terms proposed.

(iii) Two Affected Parties

If an Illegality under Section 5(b)(i)(1) or a Tax Event occurs and there are two Affected Parties, each party will use all reasonable efforts to reach agreement within 30 days after notice thereof is given under Section 6(b)(i) on action to avoid that Termination Event.

(iv) Right to Terminate

If:—

(1) a transfer under Section 6(b)(ii) or an agreement under Section 6(b)(iii), as the case may be, has not been effected with respect to all Affected Transactions within 30 days after an Affected Party gives notice under Section 6(b)(i); or

(2) an Illegality under Section 5(b)(i)(2), a Credit Event Upon Merger or an Additional Termination Event occurs, or a Tax Event Upon Merger occurs and the Burdened Party is not the Affected Party,

either party in the case of an Illegality, the Burdened Party in the case of a Tax Event Upon Merger, any Affected Party in the case of a Tax Event or an Additional Termination Event if there is more than one Affected Party, or the party which is not the Affected Party in the case of a Credit Event Upon Merger or an Additional Termination Event if there is only one Affected Party may, by not more than 20 days notice to the other party and provided that the relevant Termination Event is then continuing, designate a day not earlier than the day such notice is effective as an Early Termination Date in respect of all Affected Transactions.

(c) Effect of Designation

(i) If notice designating an Early Termination Date is given under Section 6(a) or (b), the Early Termination Date will occur on the date so designated, whether or not the relevant Event of Default or Termination Event is then continuing.

(ii) Upon the occurrence or effective designation of an Early Termination Date, no further payments or deliveries under Section 2(a)(i) or 2(e) in respect of the Terminated Transactions will be required to be made, but without prejudice to the other provisions of this Agreement. The amount, if any, payable in respect of an Early Termination Date shall be determined pursuant to Section 6(e).

(d) Calculations

(i) Statement

On or as soon as reasonably practicable following the occurrence of an Early Termination Date, each party will make the calculations on its part, if any, contemplated by Section 6(e) and will provide to the other party a statement (1) showing, in reasonable detail, such calculations (including all relevant quotations and specifying any amount payable under Section 6(e)) and (2) giving details of the relevant account to which any amount payable to it is to be paid. In the absence of written confirmation from the source of a quotation obtained in determining a Market Quotation, the records of the party obtaining such quotation will be conclusive evidence of the existence and accuracy of such quotation.

(ii) Payment Date

An amount calculated as being due in respect of an Early Termination Date under Section 6(e) will be payable on the day that notice of the amount payable is effective (in the case of an Early Termination Date which is designated or occurs as a result of an Event of Default) and on the day which is two Local Business Days after the day on which notice of the amount payable is effective (in the case of an Early Termination Date which is designated as a result of a Termination Event). Such amount will be paid together with (to the extent permitted under applicable law) interest thereon (before as well as after judgment) in the Termination Currency, from (and including) the relevant Early Termination Date to (but excluding) the date such amount is paid, at the Applicable Rate. Such interest will be calculated on the basis of daily compounding and the actual number of days elapsed.

(e) Payments on Early Termination

If an Early Termination Date occurs, the following provisions shall apply based on the parties' election in the Schedule of a payment measure, either "Market Quotation" or "Loss", and a payment method, either the "First Method" or the "Second Method". If the parties fail to designate a payment measure or payment method in the Schedule, it will be deemed that "Market Quotation" or the "Second Method", as the case may be, shall apply. The amount, if any, payable in respect of an Early Termination Date and determined pursuant to this Section will be subject to any Set-off.

(i) Events of Default

If the Early Termination Date results from an Event of Default:—

(1) *First Method and Market Quotation.* If the First Method and Market

Quotation apply, the Defaulting Party will pay to the Non-defaulting Party the excess, if a positive number, of (A) the sum of the Settlement Amount (determined by the Non-defaulting Party) in respect of the Terminated Transactions and the Termination Currency Equivalent of the Unpaid Amounts owing to the Non-defaulting Party over (B) the Termination Currency Equivalent to the Unpaid Amounts owing to the Defaulting Party.

(2) *First Method and Loss.* If the First Method and Loss apply, the Defaulting Party will pay to the Non-defaulting Party, if a positive number, the Non-defaulting Party's Loss in respect of this Agreement.

(3) *Second Method and Market Quotation.* If the Second Method and Market Quotation apply, an amount will be payable equal to (A) the sum of the Settlement Amount (determined by the Non-defaulting Party) in respect of the Terminated Transactions and the Termination Currency Equivalent of the Unpaid Amounts owing to the Non-defaulting Party less (B) the Termination Currency Equivalent of the Unpaid Amounts owing to the Defaulting Party. If that amount is a positive number, the Defaulting Party will pay it to the Non-defaulting Party; if it is a negative number, the Non-defaulting Party will pay the absolute value of that amount to the Defaulting Party.

(4) *Second Method and Loss.* If the Second Method and Loss apply, an amount will be payable equal to the Non-defaulting Party's Loss in respect of this Agreement. If that amount is a positive number, the Defaulting Party will pay it to the Non-defaulting Party; if it is a negative number, the Non-defaulting Party will pay the absolute value of that amount to the Defaulting Party.

(ii) Termination Events

If the Early Termination Date results from a Termination Event:—

(1) *One Affected Party.* If there is one Affected Party, the amount payable will be determined in accordance with Section 6(e)(i)(3), if Market Quotation applies, or Section 6(e)(i)(4), if Loss applies, except that, in either case, references to the Defaulting Party and to the Non-defaulting Party will be deemed to be references to the Affected Party and the party which is not the Affected Party, respectively, and, if Loss applies and fewer than all the Transactions are being terminated, Loss shall be calculated in respect of all Terminated Transactions.

(2) *Two Affected Parties.* If there are two Affected Parties:—

(A) if Market Quotation applies, each party will determine a Settlement Amount in respect of the Terminated Transactions, and an amount will be payable equal to (I) the sum of (a) one-half of the difference between the Settlement Amount of the party with the higher Settlement Amount ("X") and the Settlement Amount of the party with the lower Settlement Amount ("Y") and (b) the Termination Currency Equivalent of the Unpaid Amounts owing to X less (II) the Termination Currency Equivalent of the Unpaid Amounts owing to Y; and

(B) if Loss applies, each party will determine its Loss in respect of this Agreement (or, if fewer than all the Transactions are being terminated, in respect of all Terminated Transactions) and an amount will be payable equal to one-half of the difference between the Loss of the party with the higher Loss ("X") and the Loss of the party with the lower Loss ("Y").

If the amount payable is a positive number, Y will pay it to X; if it is a negative number, X will pay the absolute value of that amount to Y.

(iii) Adjustment for Bankruptcy

In circumstances where an Early Termination Date occurs because "Automatic Early Termination" applies in respect of a party, the amount determined under this Section 6(e) will be subject to such adjustments as are appropriate and permitted by law to reflect any payments or deliveries made by one party to the other under this Agreement (and retained by such other party) during the period from the relevant Early Termination Date to the date for payment determined under Section 6(d)(ii).

(iv) Pre-Estimate

The parties agree that if Market Quotation applies an amount recoverable under this Section 6(e) is a reasonable pre-estimate of loss and not a penalty. Such amount is payable for the loss of bargain and the loss of protection against future risks and except as otherwise provided in this Agreement neither party will be entitled to recover any additional damages as a consequence of such losses.

7. TRANSFER

Subject to Section 6(b)(ii), neither this Agreement nor any interest or obligation in or under this Agreement may be transferred (whether by way of security or otherwise) by either party without the prior written consent of the other party, except that:—

(a) a party may make such a transfer of this Agreement pursuant to a consolidation or amalgamation with, or merger with or into, or transfer of all or substantially all its assets to, another entity (but without prejudice to any other right or remedy under this Agreement); and

(b) a party may make such a transfer of all or any part of its interest in any amount payable to it from a Defaulting Party under Section 6(e).

Any purported transfer that is not in compliance with this Section will be void.

8. CONTRACTUAL CURRENCY

(a) Payment in the Contractual Currency

Each payment under this Agreement will be made in the relevant currency specified in this Agreement for that payment (the "Contractual Currency"). To the extent permitted by applicable law, any obligation to make payments under this Agreement in the Contractual Currency will not be discharged or satisfied by any tender in any currency other than the Contractual Currency, except to the extent such tender results in the actual receipt by the party to which payment is owed, acting in a reasonable manner and in good faith in converting the currency so tendered into the Contractual Currency, of the full amount in the Contractual Currency of all amounts payable in respect of this Agreement. If for any reason the amount in the Contractual Currency so received falls short of the amount in the Contractual Currency payable in respect of this Agreement, the party required to make the payment will, to the extent permitted by applicable law, immediately pay such additional amount in the Contractual Currency as may be necessary to compensate for the shortfall. If for any reason the amount in the Contractual Currency so received exceeds the amount in the Contractual Currency payable in respect of this Agreement, the party receiving the payment will refund promptly the amount of such excess.

(b) Judgments

To the extent permitted by applicable law, if any judgment or order expressed in a currency other than the Contractual Currency is rendered (i) for the payment of any amount owing in respect of this Agreement, (ii) for the payment of any amount relating to any early termination in respect of this Agreement or (iii) in respect of a judgment or order of another court for the payment of any amount described in (i) or (ii) above, the party seeking recovery, after recovery in full of the aggregate amount to which such party is entitled pursuant to the judgment or order, will be entitled to receive immediately from the other party the amount of any shortfall of the Contractual Currency received by such party as a consequence of sums paid in such other currency and will refund promptly to the other party any excess of the Contractual Currency received by such party as a consequence of sums paid in such other currency if such shortfall or such excess arises or results from any variation between the rate of exchange at which the Contractual Currency is converted into the currency of the judgment or order for the purposes of such judgment or order and the rate of exchange at which such party is able, acting in a reasonable manner and in good faith in converting the currency received into the Contractual Currency, to purchase the Contractual Currency with the amount of the currency of the judgment or order actually received by such party. The term "rate of exchange" includes, without limitation, any premiums and costs of exchange payable in connection with the purchase of or conversions into the Contractual Currency.

(c) Separate Indemnities

To the extent permitted by applicable law, these indemnities constitute separate and independent obligations from the other obligations in this Agreement, will be enforceable as separate and independent causes of action, will apply notwithstanding any indulgence granted by the party to which any payment is owed and will not be affected by judgment being obtained or claim or proof being made for any other sums payable in respect of this Agreement.

(d) Evidence of Loss

For the purpose of this Section 8, it will be sufficient for a party to demonstrate that it would have suffered a loss had an actual exchange or purchase been made.

9. MISCELLANEOUS

(a) Entire Agreement

This Agreement constitutes the entire agreement and understanding of the parties with respect to its subject matter and supersedes all oral communication and prior writings with respect thereto.

(b) Amendments

No amendment, modification or waiver in respect of this Agreement will be effective unless in writing (including a writing evidenced by a facsimile transmission) and executed by each of the parties or confirmed by an exchange of telexes or electronic messages on an electronic messaging system.

(c) Survival of Obligations

Without prejudice to Sections 2(a)(iii) and 6(c)(ii), the obligations of the parties under this Agreement will survive the termination of any Transaction.

(d) Remedies Cumulative

Except as provided in this Agreement, the rights, powers, remedies and privileges provided in this Agreement are cumulative and not exclusive of any rights, powers, remedies and privileges provided by law.

(e) Counterparts and Confirmations

(i) This Agreement (and each amendment, modification and waiver in respect of it) may be executed and delivered in counterparts (including by facsimile transmission), each of which will be deemed an original.

(ii) The parties intend that they are legally bound by the terms of each Transaction from the moment they agree to those terms (whether orally or otherwise). A Confirmation shall be entered into as soon as practicable and may be executed and delivered in counterparts (including by facsimile transmission) or be created by an exchange of telexes or by an exchange of electronic messages on an electronic messaging system, which in each case will be sufficient for all purposes to evidence a binding supplement to this Agreement. The parties will specify therein or through another effective means that any such counterpart, telex or electronic message constitutes a Confirmation.

(f) No Waiver of Rights

A failure or delay in exercising any right, power or privilege in respect of this Agreement will not be presumed to operate as a waiver, and a single or partial exercise of any right, power or privilege will not be presumed to preclude any subsequent or further exercise, of that right, power or privilege or the exercise of any other right, power or privilege.

(g) Headings

The headings used in this Agreement are for convenience of reference only and are not to affect the construction of or to be taken into consideration in interpreting this Agreement.

10. OFFICES; MULTIBRANCH PARTIES

(a) If Section 10(a) is specified in the Schedule as applying, each party that enters into a Transaction through an Office other than its head or home office represents to the other party that, notwithstanding the place of booking office or jurisdiction of incorporation or organisation of such party, the obligations of such party are the same as if it had entered into the Transaction through its head or home office. This representation will be deemed to be repeated by such party on each date on which a Transaction is entered into.

(b) Neither party may change the Office through which it makes and receives payments or deliveries for the purpose of a Transaction without the prior written consent of the other party.
(c) If a party is specified as a Multibranch Party in the Schedule, such Multibranch Party may make and receive payments or deliveries under any Transaction through any Office listed in the Schedule, and the Office through which it makes and receives payments or deliveries with respect to a Transaction will be specified in the relevant Confirmation.

11. EXPENSES

A Defaulting Party will, on demand, indemnify and hold harmless the other party for and against all reasonable out-of-pocket expenses, including legal fees and Stamp Tax, incurred by such other party by reason of the enforcement and protection of its rights under this Agreement or any Credit Support Document to which the Defaulting Party is a party or by reason of the early termination of any Transaction, including, but not limited to, costs of collection.

12. NOTICES

(a) Effectiveness

Any notice or other communication in respect of this Agreement may be given in any manner set forth below (except that a notice or other communication under Section 5 or 6 may not be given by facsimile transmission or electronic messaging system) to the address or number or in accordance with the electronic messaging system details provided (see the Schedule) and will be deemed effective as indicated:—

(i) if in writing and delivered in person or by courier, on the date it is delivered;
(ii) if sent by telex, on the date the recipient's answerback is received;
(iii) if sent by facsimile transmission, on the date that transmission is received by a responsible employee of the recipient in legible form (it being agreed that the burden of proving receipt will be on the sender and will not be met by a transmission report generated by the sender's facsimile machine);
(iv) if sent by certified or registered mail (airmail, if overseas) or the equivalent (return receipt requested), on the date that mail is delivered or its delivery is attempted; or
(v) if sent by electronic messaging system, on the date that electronic message is received,

unless the date of that delivery (or attempted delivery) or that receipt, as applicable, is not a Local Business Day or that communication is delivered (or attempted) or received, as applicable, after the close of business on a Local Business Day, in which case that communication shall be deemed given and effective on the first following day that is a Local Business Day.

(b) Change of Addresses

Either party may by notice to the other change the address, telex or facsimile number or electronic messaging system details at which notices or other communications are to be given to it.

13. GOVERNING LAW AND JURISDICTION

(a) Governing Law

This Agreement will be governed by and construed in accordance with the law specified in the Schedule.

(b) Jurisdiction

With respect to any suit, action or proceedings relating to this Agreement ("Proceedings"), each party irrevocably:—

(i) submits to the jurisdiction of the English courts, if this Agreement is expressed to be governed by English law, or to the non-exclusive jurisdiction of the courts of the State of New York and the United States District Court located in the Borough of Manhattan in New York City, if this Agreement is expressed to be governed by the laws of the State of New York; and

(ii) waives any objection which it may have at any time to the laying of venue of any Proceedings brought in any such court, waives any claim that such Proceedings have been brought in an inconvenient forum and further waives the right to object, with respect to such Proceedings, that such court does not have any jurisdiction over such party.

Nothing in this Agreement precludes either party from bringing Proceedings in any other jurisdiction (outside, if this Agreement is expressed to be governed by English law, the Contracting States, as defined in Section 1(3) of the Civil Jurisdiction and Judgments Act 1982 or any modification, extension or re-enactment thereof for the time being in force) nor will the bringing of Proceedings in any one or more jurisdictions preclude the bringing of Proceedings in any other jurisdiction.

(c) Service of Process

Each party irrevocably appoints the Process Agent (if any) specified opposite its name in the Schedule to receive, for it and on its behalf, service of process in any Proceedings. If for any reason any party's Process Agent is unable to act as such, such party will promptly notify the other party and within 30 days appoint a substitute process agent acceptable to the other party. The parties irrevocably consent to service of process given in the manner provided for notices in Section 12. Nothing in this Agreement will affect the right of either party to serve process in any other manner permitted by law.

(d) Waiver of Immunities

Each party irrevocably waives, to the fullest extent permitted by applicable law, with respect to itself and its revenues and assets (irrespective of their use or intended use), all immunity on the grounds of sovereignty or other similar grounds from (i) suit, (ii) jurisdiction of any court, (iii) relief by way of injunction, order for specific performance or for recovery of property, (iv) attachment of its assets (whether before or after judgment) and (v) execution or enforcement of any judgment to which it or its revenues or assets might otherwise be entitled in any Proceedings in the courts of any jurisdiction and irrevocably agrees, to the extent permitted by applicable law, that it will not claim any such immunity in any Proceedings.

14. DEFINITIONS

As used in this Agreement:—

"Additional Termination Event" has the meaning specified in Section 5(b).

"Affected Party" has the meaning specified in Section 5(b).

"Affected Transactions" means (a) with respect to any Termination Event consisting of an Illegality, Tax Event or Tax Event Upon Merger, all Transactions affected by the occurrence of such Termination Event and (b) with respect to any other Termination Event, all Transactions.

"Affiliate" means, subject to the Schedule, in relation to any person, any entity controlled, directly or indirectly, by the person, any entity that controls, directly or indirectly, the person or any entity directly or indirectly under common control with the person. For this purpose, "control" of any entity or person means ownership of a majority of the voting power of the entity or person.

"Applicable Rate" means:—

(a) in respect of obligations payable or deliverable (or which would have been but for Section 2(a)(iii)) by a Defaulting Party, the Default Rate;
(b) in respect of an obligation to pay an amount under Section 6(e) of either party from and after the date (determined in accordance with Section 6(d)(ii)) on which that amount is payable, the Default Rate;
(c) in respect of all other obligations payable or deliverable (or which would have been but for Section 2(a)(iii)) by a Non-defaulting Party, the Non-default Rate; and
(d) in all other cases, the Termination Rate.

"Burdened Party" has the meaning specified in Section 5(b).

"Change in Tax Law" means the enactment, promulgation, execution or ratification of, or any change in or amendment to, any law (or in the application or official interpretation of any law) that occurs on or after the date on which the relevant Transaction is entered into.

"consent" includes a consent, approval, action, authorisation, exemption, notice, filing, registration or exchange control consent.

"Credit Event Upon Merger" has the meaning specified in Section 5(b).

"Credit Support Document" means any agreement or instrument that is specified as such in this Agreement.

"Credit Support Provider" has the meaning specified in the Schedule.

"Default Rate" means a rate per annum equal to the cost (without proof or evidence of any actual cost) to the relevant payee (as certified by it) if it were to fund or of funding the relevant amount plus 1% per annum.

"**Defaulting Party**" has the meaning specified in Section 6(a).

"**Early Termination Date**" means the date determined in accordance with Section 6(a) or 6(b)(iv).

"**Event of Default**" has the meaning specified in Section 5(a) and, if applicable, in the Schedule.

"**Illegality**" has the meaning specified in Section 5(b).

"**Indemnifiable Tax**" means any Tax other than a Tax that would not be imposed in respect of a payment under this Agreement but for a present or former connection between the jurisdiction of the government or taxation authority imposing such Tax and the recipient of such payment or a person related to such recipient (including, without limitation, a connection arising from such recipient or related person being or having been a citizen or resident of such jurisdiction, or being or having been organised, present or engaged in a trade or business in such jurisdiction, or having or having had a permanent establishment or fixed place of business in such jurisdiction, but excluding a connection arising solely from such recipient or related person having executed, delivered, performed its obligations or received a payment under, or enforced, this Agreement or a Credit Support Document).

"**law**" includes any treaty, law, rule or regulation (as modified, in the case of tax matters, by the practice of any relevant governmental revenue authority) and "**lawful**" and "**unlawful**" will be construed accordingly.

"**Local Business Day**" means, subject to the Schedule, a day on which commercial banks are open for business (including dealings in foreign exchange and foreign currency deposits) (a) in relation to any obligation under Section 2(a)(i), in the place(s) specified in the relevant Confirmation or, if not so specified, as otherwise agreed by the parties in writing or determined pursuant to provisions contained, or incorporated by reference, in this Agreement, (b) in relation to any other payment, in the place where the relevant account is located and, if different, in the principal financial centre, if any, of the currency of such payment, (c) in relation to any notice or other communication, including notice contemplated under Section 5(a)(i), in the city specified in the address for notice provided by the recipient and, in the case of a notice contemplated by Section 2(b), in the place where the relevant new account is to be located and (d) in relation to Section 5(a)(v)(2), in the relevant locations for performance with respect to such Specified Transaction.

"**Loss**" means, with respect to this Agreement or one or more Terminated Transactions, as the case may be, and a party, the Termination Currency Equivalent of an amount that party reasonably determines in good faith to be its total losses and costs (or gain, in which case expressed as a negative number) in connection with this Agreement or that Terminated Transaction or group of Terminated Transactions, as the case may be, including any loss of bargain, cost of funding or, at the election of such party but without duplication, loss or cost incurred as a result of its terminating, liquidating, obtaining or reestablishing any hedge or related trading position (or any gain resulting from any of them). Loss includes losses and costs (or gains) in respect of any payment or delivery required to have been made (assuming satisfaction of each applicable condition precedent) on or before the relevant Early Termination Date and not made, except, so as to avoid duplication, if Section 6(e)(i)(1) or (3) or 6(e)(ii)(2)(A) applies. Loss does not include a party's legal fees and out-of-pocket expenses referred to under Section 11. A party will determine its Loss as of the relevant Early Termination Date, or, if that is not reasonably practicable, as of the earliest date thereafter as is reasonably practicable. A party may (but need not) determine its Loss by reference to quotations of relevant rates or prices from one or more leading dealers in the relevant markets.

"Market Quotation" means, with respect to one or more Terminated Transactions and a party making the determination, an amount determined on the basis of quotations from Reference Market-makers. Each quotation will be for an amount, if any, that would be paid to such party (expressed as a negative number) or by such party (expressed as a positive number) in consideration of an agreement between such party (taking into account any existing Credit Support Document with respect to the obligations of such party) and the quoting Reference Market-maker to enter into a transaction (the "Replacement Transaction") that would have the effect of preserving for such party the economic equivalent of any payment or delivery (whether the underlying obligation was absolute or contingent and assuming the satisfaction of each applicable condition precedent) by the parties under Section 2(a)(i) in respect of such Terminated Transaction or group of Terminated Transactions that would, but for the occurrence of the relevant Early Termination Date, have been required after that date. For this purpose, Unpaid Amounts in respect of the Terminated Transaction or group of Terminated Transactions are to be excluded but, without limitation, any payment or delivery that would, but for the relevant Early Termination Date, have been required (assuming satisfaction of each applicable condition precedent) after that Early Termination Date is to be included. The Replacement Transaction would be subject to such documentation as such party and the Reference Market-maker may, in good faith, agree. The party making the determination (or its agent) will request each Reference Market-maker to provide its quotation to the extent reasonably practicable as of the same day and time (without regard to different time zones) on or as soon as reasonably practicable after the relevant Early Termination Date. The day and time as of which those quotations are to be obtained will be selected in good faith by the party obliged to make a determination under Section 6(e), and, if each party is so obliged, after consultation with the other. If more than three quotations are provided, the Market Quotation will be the arithmetic mean of the quotations, without regard to the quotations having the highest and lowest values. If exactly three such quotations are provided, the Market Quotation will be the quotation remaining after disregarding the highest and lowest quotations. For this purpose, if more than one quotation has the same highest value or lowest value, then one of such quotations shall be disregarded. If fewer than three quotations are provided, it will be deemed that the Market Quotation in respect of such Terminated Transaction or group of Terminated Transactions cannot be determined.

"Non-default Rate" means a rate per annum equal to the cost (without proof or evidence of any actual cost) to the Non-defaulting Party (as certified by it) if it were to fund the relevant amount.

"Non-defaulting Party" has the meaning specified in Section 6(a).

"Office" means a branch or office of a party, which may be such party's head or home office.

"Potential Event of Default" means any event which, with the giving of notice or the lapse of time or both, would constitute an Event of Default.

"Reference Market-makers" means four leading dealers in the relevant market selected by the party determining a Market Quotation in good faith (a) from among dealers of the highest credit standing which satisfy all the criteria that such party applies generally at the time in deciding whether to offer or to make an extension of credit and (b) to the extent practicable, from among such dealers having an office in the same city.

"Relevant Jurisdiction" means, with respect to a party, the jurisdictions (a) in which the party is incorporated, organised, managed and controlled or considered to have its seat, (b) where an Office through which the party is acting for purposes of this Agreement is located, (c) in which the party executes this Agreement and (d) in relation to any payment, from or through which such payment is made.

"Scheduled Payment Date" means a date on which a payment or delivery is to be made under Section 2(a)(i) with respect to a Transaction.

"Set-off" means set-off, offset, combination of accounts, right of retention or withholding or similar right of requirement to which the payer of an amount under Section 6 is entitled or subject (whether arising under this Agreement, another contract, applicable law or otherwise) that is exercised by, or imposed on, such payer.

"Settlement Amount" means, with respect to a party and any Early Termination Date, the sum of:—

(a) the Termination Currency Equivalent of the Market Quotations (whether positive or negative) for each Terminated Transaction or group of Terminated Transactions for which a Market Quotation is determined; and

(b) such party's Loss (whether positive or negative and without reference to any Unpaid Amounts) for each Terminated Transaction or group of Terminated Transactions for which a Market Quotation cannot be determined or would not (in the reasonable belief of the party making the determination) produce a commercially reasonable result.

"Specified Entity" has the meaning specified in the Schedule.

"Specified Indebtedness" means, subject to the Schedule, any obligation (whether present or future, contingent or otherwise, as principal or surety or otherwise) in respect of borrowed money.

"Specified Transaction" means, subject to the Schedule, (a) any transaction (including an agreement with respect thereto) now existing or hereafter entered into between one party to this Agreement (or any Credit Support Provider of such party or any applicable Specified Entity of such party) and the other party to this Agreement (or any Credit Support Provider of such other party or any applicable Specified Entity of such other party) which is a rate swap transaction, basis swap, forward rate transaction, commodity swap, commodity option, equity or equity index swap, equity or equity index option, bond option, interest rate option, foreign exchange transaction, cap transaction, floor transaction, collar transaction, currency swap transaction, cross-currency rate swap transaction, currency option or any other similar transaction (including any option with respect to any of these transactions), (b) any combination of these transactions and (c) any other transaction identified as a Specified Transaction in this Agreement or the relevant confirmation.

"Stamp Tax" means any stamp, registration, documentation or similar tax.

"Tax" means any present or future taxs, levy, impost, duty, charge, assessment or fee of any nature (including interest, penalties and additions thereto) that is imposed by any government or other taxing authority in respect of any payment under this Agreement other than a stamp, registration, documentation or similar tax.

"Tax Event" has the meaning specified in Section 5(b).

"Tax Event Upon Merger" has the meaning specified in Section 5(b).

"Terminated Transactions" means with respect to any Early Termination Date (a) if resulting from a Termination Event, all Affected Transactions and (b) if resulting from an Event of Default, all Transactions (in either case) in effect immediately before the effectiveness of the notice designating that Early Termination Date (or, if "Automatic Early Termination" applies, immediately before that Early Termination Date).

"Termination Currency" has the meaning specified in the Schedule.

"Termination Currency Equivalent" means, in respect of any amount denominated in the Termination Currency, such Termination Currency amount and, in respect of any amount denominated in a currency other than the Termination Currency (the "Other Currency"), the amount in the Termination Currency determined by the party making the relevant determination as being required to purchase such amount of such Other Currency as at the relevant Early Termination Date, or, if the relevant Market Quotation or Loss (as the case may be), is determined as of a later date, that later date, with the Termination Currency at the rate equal to the spot exchange rate of the foreign exchange agent (selected as provided below) for the purchase of such Other Currency with the Termination Currency at or about 11:00 a.m. (in the city in which such foreign exchange agent is located) on such date as would be customary for the determination of such a rate for the purchase of such Other Currency for value on the relevant Early Termination Date or that later date. The foreign exchange agent will, if only one party is obliged to make a determination under Section 6(e), be selected in good faith by that party and otherwise will be agreed by the parties.

"Termination Event" means an Illegality, a Tax Event or a Tax Event Upon Merger or, if specified to be applicable, a Credit Event Upon Merger or an Additional Termination Event.

"Termination Rate" means a rate per annum equal to the arithmetic mean of the cost (without proof or evidence of any actual cost) to each party (as certified by such party) if it were to fund or of funding such amounts.

"Unpaid Amounts" owing to any party means, with respect to an Early Termination Date, the aggregate of (a) in respect of all Terminated Transactions, the amounts that became payable (or that would have become payable but for Section 2(a)(iii)) to such party under Section 2(a)(i) on or prior to such Early Termination Date and which remain unpaid as at such Early Termination Date and (b) in respect of each Terminated Transaction, for each obligation under Section 2(a)(i) which was (or would have been but for Section 2(a)(iii)) required to be settled by delivery to such party on or prior to such Early Termination Date and which has not been so settled as at such Early Termination Date, an amount equal to the fair market value of that which was (or would have been) required to be delivered as of the originally scheduled date for delivery, in each case together with (to the extent permitted under applicable law) interest, in the currency of such amounts, from (and including) the date such amounts or obligations were or would have been required to have been paid or performed to (but excluding) such Early Termination Date, at the Applicable Rate. Such amounts of interest will be calculated on the basis of daily compounding and the actual number of days elapsed. The fair market value of any obligation referred to in clause (b) above shall be reasonably determined by the party obliged to make the determination under Section 6(e) or, if each party is so obliged, it shall be the average of the Termination Currency Equivalents of the fair market values reasonably determined by both parties.

IN WITNESS WHEREOF the parties have executed this document on the respective dates specified below with effect from the date specified on the first page of this document.

....	....
(Name of Party)	(Name of Party)
By:	By: ....
Name:	Name:
Title:	Title:
Date:	Date:

ISDA®

International Swaps & Derivatives Association, Inc.

SCHEDULE TO THE MASTER AGREEMENT

(Multicurrency—Cross Border)

dated as of ....

between .... and ....
("Party A") ("Party B")

Part 1. Termination Provisions

(a) **"Specified Entity"** means in relation to Party A for the purpose of:—

Section 5(a)(v), ...

Section 5(a)(vi), ...

Section 5(a)(vii), ...

Section 5(b)(iv), ...

and in relation to Party B for the purpose of:—

Section 5(a)(v), ...

Section 5(a)(vi), ...

Section 5(a)(vii), ...

Section 5(b)(iv), ...

(b) **"Specified Transaction"** will have the meaning specified in Section 14 of this Agreement unless another meaning is specified here ....

....

....

(c) The **"Cross Default"** provisions of Section 5(a)(vi) will/will not* apply to Party A
will/will not* apply to Party B

If such provisions apply:—

* Delete as applicable.

"Specified Indebtedness" will have the meaning specified in Section 14 of this Agreement unless another meaning is specified here ....

....

"Threshold Amount" means ....

....

(d) The **"Credit Event Upon Merger"** provisions of Section 5(b)(iv)
will/will not* apply to Party A
will/will not* apply to Party B

(e) The **"Automatic Early Termination"** provision of Section 6(a)
will/will not* apply to Party A
will/will not* apply to Party B

(f) **Payments on Early Termination.** For the purpose of Section 6(e) of this Agreement:—

(i) Market Quotation/Loss* will apply.

(ii) The First Method/The Second Method* will apply.

(g) **"Termination Currency"** means ...., if such currency is specified and freely available, and otherwise United States Dollars.

(h) **Additional Termination Event** will/will not apply*. The following shall constitute an Additional Termination Event:— ....

....

....

....

....

....

For the purpose of the foregoing Termination Event, the Affected Party or Affected Parties shall be:— ....

....

Part 2. Tax Representations

(a) Payer Representations

For the purpose of Section 3(e) of this Agreement, Party A will/will not* make the following representation and Party B will/will not* make the following representation:—

It is not required by any applicable law, as modified by the practice of any relevant governmental revenue authority, of any Relevant Jurisdiction to make any deduction or withholding for or on account of any Tax from any payment (other than interest under Section 2(e), 6(d)(ii) or 6(e) of this Agreement) to be made by it to

* Delete as applicable.

the other party under this Agreement. In making this representation, it may rely on (i) the accuracy of any representations made by the other party pursuant to Section 3(f) of this Agreement, (ii) the satisfaction of the agreement contained in Section 4(a)(i) or 4(a)(iii) of this Agreement and the accuracy and effectiveness of any document provided by the other party pursuant to Section 4(a)(i) or 4(a)(iii) of this Agreement and (iii) the satisfaction of the agreement of the other party contained in Section 4(d) of this Agreement, *provided* that it shall not be a breach of this representation where reliance is placed on clause (ii) and the other party does not deliver a form or document under Section 4(a)(iii) by reason of material prejudice to its legal or commercial position.

(b) Payee Representations

For the purpose of Section 3(f) of this Agreement, Party A and Party B make the representations specified below, if any:

(i) The following representation will/will not* apply to Party A and will/will not* apply to Party B:—

It is fully eligible for the benefits of the "Business Profits" or "Industrial and Commercial Profits" provision, as the case may be, the "Interest" provision or the "Other Income" provision (if any) of the Specified Treaty with respect to any payment described in such provisions and received or to be received by it in connection with this Agreement and no such payment is attributable to a trade or business carried on by it through a permanent establishment in the Specified Jurisdiction.

If such representation applies, then:—

"Specified Treaty" means with respect to Party A ....

"Specified Jurisdiction" means with respect to Party A ....

"Specified Treaty" means with respect to Party B ....

"Specified Jurisdiction" means with respect to Party B ....

(ii) The following representation will/will not* apply to Party A and will/will not* apply to Party B:—

Each payment received or to be received by it in connection with this Agreement will be effectively connected with its conduct of a trade or business in the Specified Jurisdiction.

If such representation applies, then:—

"Specified Jurisdiction" means with respect to Party A ....

"Specified Jurisdiction" means with respect to Party B...

(iii) The following representation will/will not* apply to Party A and will/will not* apply to Party B:—

(A) It is entering into each Transaction in the ordinary course of its trade as, and is, either (1) a recognised U.K. bank or (2) a recognised U.K. swaps dealer (in either case (1) or (2), for the purposes of the United Kingdom Inland Revenue extra statutory concession C17 on interest and currency swaps dated March 14, 1989), and (B) it will bring into account payments made and received in respect of each Transaction

* Delete as applicable.

in computing its income for United Kingdom tax purposes.

(iv) Other Payee Representations:— ....

....

....

....

N.B. The above representations may need modification if either party is a Multibranch Party.

Part 3. Agreement to Deliver Documents

For the purpose of Sections 4(a)(i) and (ii) of this Agreement, each party agrees to deliver the following documents, as applicable:—

(a) Tax forms, documents or certificates to be delivered are:—

Party required to deliver document	Form/Document/ Certificate	Date by which to be delivered
....	....	....
....	....	....
....	....	....
....	....	....
....	....	....

(b) Other documents to be delivered are:—

Party required to deliver document	Form/Document/ Certificate	Date by which to be delivered	Covered by Section 3(d) Representation
....	....	....	Yes/No*
....	....	....	Yes/No*
....	....	....	Yes/No*
....	....	....	Yes/No*
....	....	....	Yes/No*

Part 4. Miscellaneous

(a) **Address for Notices.** For the purpose of Section 12(a) of this Agreement:—

Address for notices or communications to Party A:—

Address: ....

* Delete as applicable.

Attention: ....

Telex No.: .... Answerback: ....

Facsimile No.: .... Telephone No.: ....

Electronic Messaging System Details: ....

Address for notices or communications to Party B:—

Address: ....

Attention: ....

Telex No.: .... Answerback: ....

Facsimile No.: .... Telephone No.: ....

Electronic Messaging System Details: ....

(b) **Process Agent.** For the purpose of Section 13(c) of this Agreement:—

Party A appoints as its Process Agent ....

Party B appoints as its Process Agent ....

(c) **Offices.** The provisions of Section 10(a) will/will not* apply to this Agreement.

(d) **Multibranch Party.** For the purpose of Section 10(c) of this Agreement:—

Party A is/is not* a Multibranch Party and, if so, may act through the following Offices:—

....

....

Party B is/is not* a Multibranch Party and, if so, may act through the following Offices:—

....

....

(e) **Calculation Agent.** The Calculation Agent is ...., unless otherwise specified in a Confirmation in relation to the relevant Transaction.

(f) **Credit Support Document.** Details of any Credit Support Document:— ....

....

....

....

(g) **Credit Support Provider.** Credit Support Provider means in relation to Party A, ...

....

....

* Delete as applicable.

Credit Support Provider means in relation to Party B, ...

....

....

(h) **Governing Law.** This Agreement will be governed by and construed in accordance with English law/the laws of the State of New York (without reference to choice of law doctrine)*.

(i) **Netting of Payments.** Subparagraph (ii) of Section 2(c) of this Agreement will not apply to the following Transactions or groups of Transactions (in each case starting from the date of this Agreement/in each case starting from ....*)

....

....

....

(j) **"Affiliate"** will have the meaning specified in Section 14 of this Agreement unless another meaning is specified here ....

....

Part 5. Other Provisions

* Delete as applicable.

INDEX